Language and Thought in Early Greek Philosophy

Language and Thought in Early Greek Philosophy

edited by Kevin Robb

Series Editor: Eugene Freeman
Editor of The Monist: John Hospers
Managing Editor: Sherwood J. B. Sugden

The Hegeler Institute

Monist Library of Philosophy
La Salle, Illinois
1983

First Edition

ISBN: 0-914417-01-0

The Hegeler Institute
publishers of *The Monist*, an International Quarterly Journal
of General Philosophical Inquiry
and of the Monist Library of Philosophy
Box 600, La Salle, Illinois 61301

Printed in the United States of America.

TABLE OF CONTENTS

INTRODUCTION

When Eric Havelock published *Preface to Plato* in 1963—twenty years ago as this volume is made ready for print—he felt it necessary to argue at some length for the late introduction of the alphabet into Greece, for the essentially oral character of the Archaic age, for changes in modes of Greek composition and thought which were a direct result of changes in modes of communication as Greece advanced from the oral to the written word, and finally for the crucial role of Plato as the thinker in whose text the full results of literacy, conceptual and linguistic, were first fully displayed. If this sweeping thesis, at least in some of its parts, seems less bold and frankly less shocking today than it did twenty years ago—and a survey of the reviews which greeted *Preface to Plato* would provide a measure of contemporary shock—the reason is that now so many aspects of Havelock's argument have been accepted by a majority of Hellenists and historians of Greek thought. Some aspects, of course, remain in dispute, and some, like the question of the relationship of thought to language, may permanently elude philosophical consensus.

Two theses of *Preface to Plato* are no longer in dispute save in matters of detail. The first is the dating of the Greek alphabet. The second is the causal role (however weighted) of the progress in Hellas from total orality to popular literacy—the first such transition the world was to know—in the development of Greek culture, its literature, philosophy, and social institutions. For establishing the latter thesis Greek scholarship will forever be in debt to Eric Havelock, its first outstanding proponent.

The issue of the late arrival of the Phoenician script into Hellas is no longer a live one, although until recently the date favored by most scholars, following the leading Semiticists, ranged from the eleventh to the early ninth centuries. Rhys Carpenter had in 1933 argued for a date in the last quarter of the eighth century (a date further supported in 1938) but his views initially won little acceptance. A measure of the change in scholarly climate is to be found in a statement from a well known Semiticist, P. Lyle McCarter, in a monograph published under the auspices of the Harvard Semitic Museum, *The Antiquity of the Greek Alphabet and the Early Phoenician Scripts*. McCarter writes that what has become the "orthodoxy among Semiticists today" was reflected in the earlier (by thirteen years) 1962 article on the alphabet by Thomas O. Lambdin in the *Interpreter's Dictionary of the Bible*.

At the time Lambdin published his views it was the uncomfortable heterodoxy.

> The earliest Greek inscriptions are generally dated to the late eighth or early seventh century, and there is no concrete reason for supposing that the alphabet had any lengthy prehistory among the Greeks.

McCarter notes that among both Semiticists and Hellenists the debate has presently settled down to concerning which quarter of the eighth century saw the alphabet enter Hellas, a consensus which would have saved Havelock much ink and labor in the notes of *Preface to Plato* had it been the orthodoxy in Greek scholarship in 1963.

In his general thesis concerning cultures as they move from orality to literacy, and especially as it applies to Greek culture, Havelock has insisted that questions often ignored by historians of culture and thought must be more precisely addressed: At what point was a script available in a society? How adequate was it to record oral forms? How sophisticated were the modes of oral preservation exploited by the society into which that script would mark a decisive intrusion destined to alter every aspect of social and intellectual life? How rapidly, if ever, did it create a body of habitual readers?

In the Greek case, Havelock was the first scholar to perceive the relationship between the late introduction of the alphabet as defended by Carpenter and the work of Milman Parry demonstrating that evidence existed in the surviving Greek texts which forced the conclusion that the *Iliad* and the *Odyssey* were compositions of a sort which, independently, oral poetry was known to be. Havelock brought these two discoveries together in order to argue for the important conclusion that Greece was an exclusively oral culture as late as the end of the eighth century and that its poetry, mainly but not exclusively epic, was its manner of preliterate cultural storage, the way in which all that a sophisticated society had found true and worth preserving in words was retained and passed down through the generations. Homer and Hesiod—not to mention a Pindar or the tragedians—once again became what they had been to Xenophanes and Heraclitus and Plato and indeed to all Greeks: the great teachers of Greece, the preservers of its most precious truths, the record of the greatness of ancestors, the guide and source of instruction of a sort a man needs to get through his life, personal, practical and civic. In telling that story as well as it will ever be told, Eric Havelock has provided all who love Greece with a moment of *mimēsis* in which, however distantly, they can relive the poetry of Greece and feel they are members of what Xenophanes called the family of Hellenic song.

Havelock's thesis put the contention between philosopher and poet which is the heart of the argument of the *Republic* into perspective, but what of Plato's predecessors, the Presocratics? If they had won the intellectual battlefield for philosophy and science in an earlier century then Plato would be a bizarre Hellenic Don Quixote doing eloquent battle with ghosts and imaginary opponents. It is to the Presocratics that Havelock turns—or returns, for his published writings reveal that they have never been far from his mind—in the leading paper of this volume, his most sustained and thorough treatment of the subject to date. It is a major addition to what has become one of the most important, controversial, debated, and stimulating theses in Greek philosophical scholarship. I predict that, at the very least, it will have an effect similar to the one which *Preface to Plato* has had on all its careful readers: even if in the end one must dissent, one's reflections on early Greek literature and philosophy will never be quite the same again.

The opportunity of publishing so important (and long awaited) a work in the *Monist* intrigued John Hospers, the newly-appointed editor of the journal, but all regular issues and their topics had been announced for years in advance. Professor Hospers took the matter directly to the Hegeler Foundation. It was decided to publish the work as a volume in the distinguished Monist Library of Philosophy series. The book would go to press in 1983, the same year which would see Harvard University Press bring out a new printing of *Preface to Plato* and Princeton University Press bring out a collection of Havelock's papers: *The Literate Revolution in Greece and Its Cultural Consequences*. Professor Hospers asked me if I would contact a group of scholars who were acknowledged as being foremost in the field to inquire if they could, in less than a year, contribute to a volume on early Greek philosophy. Professor Hospers also suggested the names of several philosophers known to him. My invitation to contributors was that they either respond directly to Part One of Havelock's leading paper, by way of supplement or dissent, or contribute an original paper on a topic related to some aspect of the leading paper. I deliberately invited as contributors professional colleagues of Eric Havelock's own generation, former students who have become noted scholars, and some philosophers and scholars who knew Havelock's work and who had indicated (in their published works or in conversation) the wish to question and quarrel a bit with this or that philosophical implication of his broad and challenging thesis. I had in mind a comment of Joseph Russo concerning Parry which would apply analogously to every major work Eric Havelock has written: "Milman Parry's monumental contribution to Homeric Studies taught us to read the *Iliad and Odyssey* in a new light. It also raised some difficult questions."

Those who have been his colleagues and students know that Professor Havelock relishes nothing so much as good debate on a topic of intellectual history, and I and others who have so often profited and learned from such debate felt it would be appropriate that this volume which honors his work, published in a series which carries the name of an old and distinguished journal in which so many great philosophers have published their challenges to established opinion, should furnish some moments of one.

Several debts are here acknowledged. In the planning stage of this volume John Hospers held many of the pieces together when they might have fallen apart, and in the editing stage the experienced hand and informed judgement of Wallace Nethery shaped disparately written manuscripts into a consistent form with which an American printer could work. At various stages indispensable support was afforded by friends and colleagues, notably Wallis Annenberg, Norman Fertig, Cynthia Mothersole, Bernard Stalter, and not least Sherwood J. B. Sugden, the Managing Editor of *The Monist*. A colleague and former student, Professor Joanne Beil of the Department of Philosophy at the University of South Florida, has kindly provided from her wide and thoughtful research a select bibliography on the topic of literacy and orality as it relates to cultures and philosophy. Finally, the contributors to this volume have by their learning and the vigor of their argument secured for it a permanent place in all future such bibliographies, for which the editor is grateful.

—K. R.

THE LINGUISTIC TASK OF THE PRESOCRATICS
PART ONE:
IONIAN SCIENCE IN SEARCH OF
AN ABSTRACT VOCABULARY*

1. From the Ear to the Eye

During the last twenty years I have gradually put together a thesis concerning the character of classic Greek culture which has been welcomed by some and which others perhaps understandably have found offensive. Before coming directly to my present subject, the language used by the Presocratic philosophers, it is necessary to recall in summary form what this thesis is.

I propose first that the original society which invented this culture—not the Mycenaean one, which is irrelevant, but that Greece which came into existence during the epoch described by art historians as the geometric and orientalizing era—was in its formative and creative stages wholly nonliterate. Persistent attempts to place the introduction of alphabetic writing in the early eighth century are inspired not by any evidence for its existence at that time but by a prejudice that literacy was a prerequisite for the Greek civilized achievement in those periods. It is evident that this achievement had already crystallized itself under four aspects: the development of an astonishingly sophisticated but unwritten language, the resources of which are exploited in the Homeric poems; the rise and perfection of a sophisticated art of pottery manufacture and decoration; the production in perishable materials of architectural forms designed for public use which became the model for later and more permanent monuments built of stone; and the invention of a social and governmental structure, namely, the city state, which as a model of municipal administration persisted through the vicissitudes of a thousand years, and in which the Greeks took a conscious pride. These were all invented by a people none of whom could either read or write.

If this is a fact, an important corollary would seem to follow from it. Put simply, the character of early Greek literacy cannot be completely understood without reference to the nonliteracy which had so closely preceded it. The law, literature, and institutions of the archaic and high classical period, unlike those of later periods, are likely to retain forms and habits which echo even at a distance the forms and habits of a culture of oral communication.

This is all the more likely to be the case when one considers the impact of alphabetic writing upon a society hitherto innocent of its use. Under modern conditions, when, for example, a European colonial administration has imposed itself upon a nonliterate society, as in Africa, the elite among the sub-

---

* Part one of this paper was originally presented to an audience at the Collège de France on March 14, 1980.

ject people acquire literacy rapidly. This is because, first, the conquerors bring
with them a well-tested technique for teaching letters, incorporated in a
school system designed for this purpose; second, they bring with them an
endless supply of documented speech both printed and handwritten requiring
to be read, in all variety of forms of law, commerce, literature, and religion.
Finally, the existence of this material supplies a powerful, popular motive for
becoming literate as quickly as possible in order to be able to read it.

When the alphabetic invention made its appearance in Greece, none of
these conditions obtained. They had to be acquired by degrees. The schooling
of Greek children and adolescents under oral conditions had consisted of
what the Greeks continued to call *mousikē*, a drill in performance upon
musical instruments, in singing and elocution, in memorization of poetry, and
in deportment and manners. Into such a curriculum the teaching of letters
took the form of an intrusion. Testimonies which bear upon the early history
of Greek education are rare and indirect, but they point to the conclusion that
in Athens the teaching of letters at the primary level which produces the
habitual reader did not become standard practice before the last third of the
fifth century B.C.

The literature of Greece known to us, beginning with epic and early lyric,
was written down. For we know it as we read it, and we owe this ability to
those, whoever they were, who first wrote, before the originals were later
copied by others. But did the Greeks of the period "know" this body of work
as "literature" in the same way we do, by the use of the eye? Or did they for
the most part know it only as they heard it and retained oral recall of it? The
proposition I would offer is that Greek authors generally up to about the
beginning of the fifth century, and Athenian authors down to as late as the
Periclean age, composed their works under a form of audience control,
managing their language so as to meet the needs of listeners rather than
readers. This had precise effects upon the style and substance of what they
said. For the moment I postpone consideration of what these effects were.
But the general law governing such composition is clear. Language must be
so managed as to provide maximum appeal to the ear and evoke maximum
response from the ear. The rules of composition are acoustic, not visual, and
rely on the operation of an echo principle, not a visual patterning of
paragraphs and themes.

Homeric scholarship since Milman Parry has found it convenient to
classify Homer as an exclusively oral, that is, acoustic author. I am not quite
convinced that this is so; or rather, as I have indicated elsewhere, it is possible
that the *Iliad* and *Odyssey* as we now have them may owe something to the
eye; that they represent an act of arrangement and amalgamation carried out
after separate portions of the epics had been alphabetized; and that this may
have occurred in Athens in the age of Pisistratus, as a later tradition asserted.

This proposition, however, is not an essential part of my thesis. What I have come to feel as certain is that already in the two poems that pass under the name of Hesiod we begin to detect the influence of the eye of the reader intruding upon that of the ear of the oral composer. I have indeed elsewhere gone so far as to argue that we detect in the *Works and Days* a reader's acquaintance with a written text of Homer or portions of Homer.

Be that as it may, I would offer the general conclusion that what we call Greek literature from Hesiod down through the classical period is composed in a condition of increasing tension between the demands of the ear and the new possibilities afforded by the eye, that its composers managed language on the one hand so as to appeal to and evoke response from the nonliterate; and on the other were exploring fresh modes and rules of composition which would prove acceptable and pleasurable to the literate.

The writer as we have come to know him ever since Hellenistic times still obeys acoustic rules, at least if he is a writer of literature, though perhaps less so otherwise. His language must retain some acoustic melody if it is to have full effect upon his reader. But just because he writes for readers, he has to please the eye as much as the ear, and this produces arrangements of words and sentences which do not have the genius of genuinely oral speech. We are all obscurely aware that the so-called literature of the Greek archaic and high classical periods is somehow different from any of the later literature of Europe. It intrigues us and puzzles us, but do we ever feel we completely understand it? Is it possible that the secret of its peculiar power, exercised at a distance from ourselves, lies precisely in a paradox inherent in its construction: namely, that it is an oral literature composed under conditions which are becoming increasingly literate, a phenomenon which later and fully literate cultures find it difficult to comprehend?

2. Presocratic Orality

This introduction brings me to my subject, the Presocratics, whose authorship falls within the archaic and high classical periods. If the thesis previously expounded is correct, they too are poised between literacy and nonliteracy. Their style of composition is a form of mediation between ear and eye. They expect an audience of listeners, yet look forward to a reception at the hands of readers. They betray symptoms of this situation in some of the things they actually say. Professedly they are didactic; their purpose, as they often say or imply, is not to please in the manner of other Greek authors, but to instruct. The presence of this purpose makes them more consciously aware that there is a relationship between themselves and their "public," which must be exploited by constant admonition, and the forms taken by this admonition often indicate the role of an oral author which they feel called upon to play.

Thus Xenophanes, the first who can still be read in the words he actually used, makes it his business to propose rules for the proper conduct of a symposium(B1). Why choose such a subject for himself, unless it is to the symposium that he himself looks to provide the occasion for the publication of his own compositions, a view supported by the fact that he also thinks it his business to advise on the content of what is sung or recited on such an occasion? Here surely is an oral composer who expects in the first instance to be listened to rather than read. He thinks that what he has to say is important, and requires attention and reward from the city-state greater than what is customarily awarded to successful athletes. What he possesses, so he argues in this context, is a *sophia* (B2, 12, and 14), a skill of words, which belongs to the bard and the poet. Elsewhere he refers to communication conducted with a friend whose Hellenic fame will last "as long as the family of Hellenic bards endures"(B6). As for himself, his own meditations "have for sixty-seven years been buffeted up and down the land of Hellas"(B8), evidently a reference to his career as a reciter, whose method of publication relied on itinerant contact with audiences who could hear him personally rather than read words in written circulation.

The claim to speak with authority and the desire to convince receive intensified expression in the sayings of Heraclitus. This makes him audience-conscious to an unusual degree, and the audience which he castigates and to which he appeals is always one that listens, even when it does not understand, but never reads what he may have written(B1, 19, 34, 50). Even of himself he says, speaking of his own relationship with such other authors as he knows, "Of all those whose statements I have heard . . ."(B108), as though these authorities had been recited to him rather than read by him. Parmenides' poem is cast in the form of an oral statement addressed to him by a goddess, which he is admonished to listen to(B2.1). He must avoid employing "an unseeing eye and an echoing ear and tongue"(B7. 4—5). He is forbidden "to speak or to think" what is untrue, for untruth is "not speakable"(B8.8). Empedocles claims to be his own prophet, with a message which men "cannot look upon or listen to or grasp with their senses"(B2.7—8). His own "tongue and mouth" (B3.1—2) speak a spring of purified speech, which he appeals to the Muse to sustain "so far as ephemeral men may be allowed to hear it" (B3.4). His poem is cast in the form of a hortatory address to a friend (or disciple) who is exhorted to "listen to the non-deceptive course of my statement"(B17.26). "You have heard a mythos the source of which is divine" (B23.11). "Listen to these (matters); my mythos is not off the mark" (B62.3). Even Melissus, composing a dialectical prose in what seems at first sight to be the style of a writer, can refer to human knowledge of the world as a matter of "seeing and hearing,"(B8[2]), never as something acquired through acquaintance with reading.

The mention of Melissus' prose brings us to consider the compositional styles adopted by the Presocratics. Three of them are not only poets but, as we have seen, speak as though they were oral poets who expected to be heard rather than read. An equally oral method of publication is presupposed by the linguistic style of Heraclitus. The one hundred and twenty-nine statements assigned to him as authentic are properly speaking not "fragments" excerpted and quoted from a continuous prose work, but self-contained sayings designed for memorization and containing elements of rhythm to further this end. The Presocratic poets avail themselves of the resources of the Homeric hexameter, the elegiac pentameter, and even the iambus to communicate their meditations. When the prose of Zeno, Melissus, Anaxagoras, and Diogenes is scrutinized closely, it can be seen to be built up out of a succession of sentences in which the shape of the aphorism is detectable. That is to say, the earliest philosophical prose is contrived out of the original genius of the self-contained maxim, now remodeled to produce a continuous argument. The basis of its style, I therefore suggest, is still derived from oral forms of communication.

The prose writers, however, betray a dawning awareness that before them lies a document which they are inscribing, and to which they can refer the audience whom they are addressing. The first evidence of this change may appear in Melissus when he says, "This [previous] statement is the chief token that one alone exists; yes, and the following are tokens too. . ."(B8[1]). His language is curiously poised between the modes of acoustic and documented speech. The "tokens" belong to the former, and the syntactical connection "yes, and" is Homeric. But the retrospective act by which he reviews what has just been stated may suggest that he is looking at what he has written. More explicitly, Anaxagoras refers back to what he has said as though it might be something objectified: "So much then for what has been said by me concerning the separation, namely that . . ."(B4); and again "an allotment of everything exists in everything, as has been said by me in the previous (statements)"(B12). Finally, Diogenes makes explicit reference to his philosophy as taking documented form—the first such reference in what is extant of the Presocratics: "As will have been demonstrated convincingly in this written composition (*sun-graphē*)"(B4). The introduction to his work similarly reflects a writer's consciousness: "I opine that it is incumbent upon one who begins any statement to present his beginning unambiguously, and his exposition simply and emphatically"(B1).

Previous philosophers, on the other hand, when they wish to review their doctrines or promise additions to them, do so in terms which suggest that they are still thinking of them as a flow or stream or path taken by orally pronounced speech. Thus Xenophanes:

Now moreover I will ascend another statement and point out the path.(B7)

The same metaphor, of speech as a path or road, is reiterated by Parmenides; but this time it is a circular one, so that he can say:

> It is all one to me from where I may begin. For thereto I shall come again in turn.(B5)

When he wishes to signal that he is finishing chapter one and is opening chapter two, he does so as follows:

> In this for you I cease [my] reliable statement and sense (*noēma*) in the matter of truth. Next after this mortal opinion must you learn as you listen to the deceitful order of my verses.(B8.50–52)

Empedocles, recapitulating for the benefit of his disciple, does so as follows:

> Come now, behold this that witnesses to former converse if perchance in previous [statements] there resided something defective in configuration.(B21.1–2)

What he is going to say is treated as oral testimony given to support previous oral statements, as they might be uttered in an oral lawsuit. "Configuration" (morphē) in epic usage refers to the "shaping" of the winged word by the bard, not the visual shape of script. Only "behold" suggests the eye of the reader, but the verb is an epic reminiscence of the "look" one person gives another. In another formula of recapitulation he says:

> But now shall I myself turn about and come to a passageway of verses.
> [even] that which before I stated, channeling statement out of statement.(B35.1–2)

Like Parmenides, this philosopher pursues a circular path of verse which, retrospectively viewed, becomes a stream of water running from one conduit into another. Truly one can say of the Presocratics that their whole linguistic enterprise stands poised between the word acoustically delivered and the word articulated, written, and visible. Competition between mythos and logos has begun.

3. From Story to Statement

So far I have been defining Presocratic thinkers in terms of their style of composition. What then of their content? What are they trying to say? They are classed as philosophers, although this was not a title they applied to themselves. What then of their doctrines? Are these also of an intermediate quality, poised halfway between nonliteracy and literacy?

It is necessary first to be clear about what their purpose was. Unlike most poets of the intermediate period, they did not wish to please or entertain, but only to instruct. Upon what object or areas of human experience was this instruction concentrated? Evidently, from what they say themselves, it was what we would call the physical environment, the sky, sun, moon, and stars; the earth, seas, rivers, and mountains; its atmospheric and meteorological behavior: day, night, storm, sunshine, earthquakes, eclipses. To the naked and unsophisticated eye, these features occurred within an apparently self-contained area bounded by sky and horizon, a notion already expressible in Homer.

They wished to give a more coherent and we might say systematic account of this complex area of experience. In this enterprise they had a predecessor in the poet Hesiod. One of the poems attributed to him told a story of how the present complex came about by emerging from a "chaos"—a great "yawning gap," through the births of a succession of numerous gods and demigods ending in the triumphant overlordship of Zeus, symbolizing the natural features of what we would style the physical environment. The filiation which connects Presocratic speculation with Hesiod has lately been acknowledged by scholars. It may in fact be even closer than has so far been recognized.

What we must now consider is the precise linguistic forms in which the Greek experience of the environment had previously been clothed. I must here revert briefly, in summary fashion, to a connected theory concerning oral cultures which I have stated elsewhere in my published works. All cultures preserve their identity in their language, not only as it is casually spoken, but particularly as it is preserved, providing a storehouse of cultural information which can be reused. It is easy to understand how this works in a literate culture, where law, custom, values, and technologies—and even personal habits—are transmitted from generation to generation through a vast and increasing mass of documentation. But how is such information preserved in an oral culture? It can subsist only in the individual memories of persons, and to achieve this the language employed—what I may call the storage language—must meet two basic requirements, both of which are mnemonic. It must be rhythmic, to allow the cadence of the words to assist the task of memorization; and it must tell stories rather than relate facts: it must prefer mythos to logos. For the oral memory accommodates language which describes the acts of persons and the happening of events, but is unfriendly to abstracted and conceptual speech. Instead of stating that the angles of a triangle are equal to two right angles, it prefers to say that "the triangle stood firmly, its two legs astride the ground, stoutly defending its two right angles against the attack of the enemy."

As long as preserved communication remained oral, the environment could be described or explained only in the guise of stories which represent it as the work of agents: that is, gods. Hesiod takes the step of trying to unify these stories into one great story, which becomes a cosmic theogony. A great series of matings and births of gods is narrated to symbolize the present existence of sky, earth, seas, mountains, storms, rivers, and stars. His poem is the earliest attempt we have in a style in which the resources of documentation have begun to intrude upon the manner of an acoustic composition. But his account is still a narrative of events, of "beginnings," that is, "births," as his critics the Presocratics were to put it. From the standpoint of a sophisticated philosophical language, such as was available to Aristotle, what was lacking was a set of commonplace but abstract terms which by their interrelations could describe the physical world conceptually; terms such as space, void, matter, body, element, motion, immobility, change, permanence, substratum, quantity, quality, dimension, unit, and the like. Aside altogether from the coinage of abstract nouns, the conceptual task also required the elimination of verbs of doing and acting and happening, one may even say, of living and dying, in favor of a syntax which states permanent relationships between conceptual terms systematically. For this purpose the required linguistic mechanism was furnished by the timeless present of the verb to be—the copula of analytic statement. The angles *are* equal to two right angles. They are not born that way or become or are made so.

The history of early philosophy is usually written under the assumption that this kind of vocabulary was already available to the first Greek thinkers. The evidence of their own language is that it was not. They had to initiate the process of inventing it. To understand their dilemma it is necessary to discard the language in which the textbooks of later antiquity described their doctrines, for this language in effect became a meta-language, which now interposes itself between the modern mind and the original, and which to the modern mind becomes more congenial. It is only as antiquity happens to quote the earliest thinkers in their own words that a reliable foundation for assessing their contribution to the history of philosophical thought is provided. The doxographical tradition, sometimes extensive, sometimes meager, must be checked against the *ipsissima verba*, not vice versa.

Since in the case of the so-called Milesian school, by which it is supposed that philosophy was initiated, no coherent quotations survive which are indisputably authentic, but only a very few isolated scraps of vocabulary, a stringently critical account of early philosophy requires that they be considered only after the *ipsissima verba* of their successors have been considered first. Close as they were to the oral culture of Greece, it is not likely that they anticipated a level of conceptual abstraction which begins to become visible only in Anaxagoras and the Atomists.

Why did the Presocratics undertake this linguistic task? Aristotle replies, "out of curiosity"; but it is difficult to understand why such an instinct should have been aroused to action at this particular time, unless the prompting mechanism was the changing technology of the written word. Documented description of the environment, even at the Hesiodic level, tended already to separate what was described from the spoken speech of the describer. It rendered the logos in which it was written an artifact, an object separate from the describer's own consciousness. As this happened, the opportunity arose, and the desire with it, to render the object more explicit, to tie it down as a system or structure instead of a series of events issuing from the mouth of the poet or his muse. In short, while the environment had from our point of view always existed for the oral mind, this mind had not conceptualized and objectified it as an environment. The Presocratics not only had to invent a terminology suitable to describe an external world; they had initially to realize that such a "world" or a cosmos existed to be described.

4. The Presocratic Polemic

The initial evidence that they were in pursuit of a new vocabulary, and were aware of the fact, is furnished by the insistent polemic that they all direct against the language currently in use, which they sometimes identify as that spoken by Homer and Hesiod, and at other times by men generally.

Xenophanes leads the chorus by an outright condemnation of Homer and Hesiod. His strictures are in the first instance moralistic rather than philosophical: the gods of Homer and Hesiod behave disgracefully by human standards(B11 and 12). But he adds a critique which cuts deeper:

> Mortals suppose gods are born
> and have the same clothes, speech and shape as themselves.(B14)

In other words, the traditional account of the powers that rule the environment is inadequate. A single line, preserved without its context, states that:

> From the beginning according to Homer whereas all men have been instructed that . . . .(B10)

To what "instruction" does this refer? That the gods are immoral? Or is the phrase "from the beginning" (cf.B18) intended to refer to the kind of history, human or cosmic, conveyed in early epics? (Cf. Empedocles B39 below.) The syntax of the line is ambiguous, but it is relevant to compare Xenophanes' admonition covering the proper content of what is to be sung at a symposium:

> Let us commend that man among men who after drinking puts forth goodly matters to view, according to his recollection and his zeal for excellence with no mention of battles of Titans or Giants or Centaurs, those fictions of men of yore, nor vehement factional strife; these matters contain nothing good.(B1.19—24)

Xenophanes is closer to the orality of the poets than are any of his successors. He is too much of a poet himself, too proud of his own poetic skill (*sophia*), to wish to break with the language of the poets, although as we shall see later, in offering his own positive doctrine he comes near to doing so.

For Heraclitus, on the other hand, rejection of Homer and Hesiod becomes mandatory:

> The instructor of most men is Hesiod, whom they understand to be informed on most [things]—a man who did not recognise day and night as being one.(B57)
>
> . . . Hesiod, ignorant of the fact that the nature of every day is one-and-the-same.(B106)
>
> Multiple learning does not teach (a man) to have sense. Else it would have taught Hesiod and Pythagoras, as well as Xenophanes and Hecataeus.(B40)
>
> Homer deserves to be expelled from the contests and clubbed; also Archilochus.(B42)

The reference to "contests" (*agōnes*) exposes the oral situation in which the society of Heraclitus operates. The instruction to which he offers vehement objection is given by competitive recitation, which explains the social context of several more sayings:

> What sense or wit is theirs?
> They are persuaded by the bards of the peoples
> and take the talking crowd to be their instructor
> not knowing that the majority are no good
> whereas the good are the few.(B104)
>
> The most impressive knows [only] how to conserve impressions.
> But mark you, justice it is who shall arrest the
> artificers of falsehoods who also testify to them.(B28)
>
> The most excellent choose one [thing] in place of all [things], [namely]
> everlasting fame from mortals.
> The majority stuff themselves like cattle.(B29)

The inspiration behind these sayings is not simply the prejudice of an aristocrat who despises the commonality. More specifically, they attack the oral instruction offered by the poets to the society in which Heraclitus is living—the only instruction available. Such instruction relies on oral publication, which to be effective requires fame on the lips of men. It is offered by "artificers," that is, composers of the orally contrived word, whose recitations offer oral witness to what is not true. The word they speak is a beguiling word which fails to use the kind of language which Heraclitus will insist is essential.

As is the level of language, so is the level of consciousness. The mind of the poet is the mind of the populace. So Heraclitus extends his polemic to cover the prevailing modes in which men generally both speak and think:

> Human beings are without comprehension . . . most human beings are unaware of all the [things] they do when awake, just as they forget them when asleep.(B1)

Many do not use their wits about all the [things] they encounter, nor when in-structed do they recognise them, but nurse the impression that they do.(B17)

Human beings are deceived with regard to recognition of what is evident.(B56)

The human ethos does not possess discernments.(B78)

A human being is a dolt; any and every statement sends him soaring.(B87)

For the god all (things) are fair and good and just. Human beings however have made the assumption that some [things] are unjust and some just(B102.)

For human beings eyes and ears are not good testifiers in the case of those whose souls speak a barbarous language. (B107).

For human beings to have wishes fulfilled is not an advantage.(B110)

Once again, it is a mistake to understand these polemics as simply personal resentment aroused by the failure of his own doctrine to gain a popular fol-lowing. His critique is addressed to some fundamental flaw in present human experience, in the way men view their condition and react to it. One group of sayings are specifically worded to elucidate this penetration of the human condition:

They [that is, human beings] resemble the inexperienced, as they engage in ex-perience of words [verses?] and works such as I expound . . .(B1)

It is necessary to be a follower of the combinatory. The [my] statement is com-binatory, but most live as though possessing an intelligence private to themselves.(B2)

Many do not use their wits about all the [things] they encounter.(B17)

By that with which they most continually have converse are they set apart [alienated?](B72)

The [things] they daily encounter, even these appear to them as foreign.(B72)

We should not make [compose?] and speak like men asleep.(B73)

Intelligence means speaking and making [composing?] true [things] . . . (B112)

The human ethos does not possess wits.(B78)

Statements like these place emphasis upon modes not only of speech and thought, but of experience in the daily encounters of life, upon the way men live, their ethos. It is permissible to infer that Heraclitus' critique is directed against oral habit as well as oral speech. The ethos he wishes to correct is ac-tive but not reflective. Is it not therefore also Homeric? To accept and absorb the new language and mental habits is to accept a new way of life.

At a minimum, forty-two of the surviving sayings are so worded as to concentrate on modes of human communication, and upon the consciousness expressed therein. The proportion to the total is striking, and has not hitherto received the attention it deserves. As it is recognized, one realizes more clear-ly the basic continuity that exists in this regard between Heraclitus and Parmenides. The goddess whom Parmenides uses as his own mouthpiece, hailing the philosopher's arrival at his journey's goal, observes that the road taken

> is surely remote from the tread of human beings.(B1.27)

He will, however, be allowed acquaintance not only with the truth;

> but also with the impressions of mortals, wherein is no true reliance.(B1.30)

For, so we learn as the poem continues, the true objective requires us

> to keep away from the road along which mortal know-nothings
> wander two-headed. Incompetence [nursed] within their breast
> directs their wandering sense. They are carried along,
> as deaf, as blind, agape, countless tribes of them,
> who accept the convention that to exist and not to be [are] the same
> and not the same, all taking a path that is self-reversing.(B6.4–9)

The target of the polemic is not a rival school of thought (which some modern interpreters have mistakenly tried to identify), but the commonality of mankind, whose language is erroneous, whose thought is therefore erroneous and whose total experience of the environment is therefore erroneous:

> You must keep your sense away from this road of search
> nor allow the habit of multiple experience to push you
> along such a road....(B7.3–5)

Fundamentally, however, the trouble lies in the language used by the commonality to describe the environment. Viewed as it should be, as a system, this "being" is whole and unshaken, but

> There accrue to it all the names
> that mortals have proposed in conviction of their truth,
> [namely] to become, to perish, to be and not to be,
> to alter position, and exchange one complexion for another.(B8.38–41)

No Presocratic offers a more succinct analysis of the essentially fluid and mobile syntax in which the performative mythos of orally preserved speech seeks to describe the phenomena of the environment. It was the stringency of Parmenides' conceptual dialectic which enabled him to carry analysis this far.

The language of Empedocles is neither so stringent nor so conceptually oriented. In many ways his two poems mark a partial reversion to the concrete pluralistic imagery of pre-philosophic poetry; they tell stories. Yet he remains a philosopher, even if a conceptually flawed one, and accordingly he feels constrained to continue the same polemic directed against the modes of common thought:

Looking upon only a meager portion of livelihood in the course of their lives,
swift-fated, like smoke, they rise and are dissipated,
convinced of that alone which each may have encountered,
driven in all directions, yet each presumes to have discovered the whole.(B2.3–6)

The terms used in these lines variously recall the polemics of both Heraclitus
and Parmenides, suggesting that they are directed against the same target,
namely, the commonality, who are continually distracted by items in the passing show which catch their attention, preventing them from seeing steadily
and seeing the whole.

Mortal things do not have a [real] nature
...there is only mixing and exchange of [things] mixed;
"nature" is applied as a name to these by human beings.(B8)

This (namely, mixing) is what men call being born [becoming]
and when they are separated, [they call it] ill-fated doom.
It is not right so to call, but I too use convention in pronouncing the words.(B9)

The problem, hinted at by Heraclitus, asserted by Parmenides, is still one of
names, and of naming. We all as human beings use the wrong ones. Our
language of description must be reformed. There is an Empedoclean system
which requires this reform. Its particulars are a matter of separate investigation which need not concern us here. The point of initial importance to grasp
in his philosophy is his partnership with his predecessors in a denunciation of
the terms of common speech. Does he give any indication that this speech is
identifiable with the speech of poetry, and of poetry orally communicated?

Submit not to the pressure that the flowers of fair honour may bring to bear
to win them at the hands of mortals, at the price of speech that violates piety
by excess of presumption, and then forsooth rush to occupy the summit of
[poetic] skill.(B3.6–8)

Suppose forsooth that depths of earth were boundless,
as also the glittering atmosphere,
as comes vainly upon the tongues
and is poured forth out of many mouths of men who have seen a small bit of the
all.(B.39;cf. Xenophanes B10 above)

One perceives here a warning that the resources of poetry as commonly exploited in performance are unsuitable for the expression of philosophy. The
disciple to whom the poem is addressed may himself be a poet who is being
admonished in the manner of Heraclitus that bardic performance, with all the
prestige accruing to the performer, is an unworthy medium. Since Empedocles is himself a performer who assumes an oral relationship to his audience,
the difference must be in the quality of the vocabulary employed. Error of
thought has its parallel in error of language.

By the time we reach the Presocratic prose writers the issue as between philosophic language and the pre-philosophic has been formally reduced to a collision between the idiom of "common sense" and that of philosophy. So Melissus:

> If there exists earth and water and air and fire and iron and gold, and the living and the dead, and black and white and the rest—all that we say do exist as true; if I say these exist, and we correctly see and hear, then . . . (B8 [2])

The philosophic and dialectical argument which follows denies that such language has any validity. He then continues:

> The impression we have is that hot becomes cold and cold hot and hard soft and soft hard and the live [thing] dies and from not-being is born [becomes] . . . So it comes about that we do not [really] see nor recognise the [things] that [just] are.(B8.[3])

Once more, the target is not some rival philosophical school, but the idiom of common speech and thought, which narrativizes our experience, recounting it as a series of events, of becoming and perishing. These same impressions had been attacked by Heraclitus and identified by him with the hoarded repertoire of the poets. These have now been reduced dialectically to (erroneous) perceptions of apparent shift and change of quality or property or status, from life to death and vice versa. So he concludes:

> It becomes clear that we do not see correctly, nor is the impression formed of this many correct.(B8[5])

In this way, an attack originally launched against the vocabulary and syntax of speech orally composed and communicated is turning itself into an attack on the way our physical senses report the environment to us. The shift begins in Parmenides, although his main focus is still on the deceptions practiced by language; his disciples begin the process of shifting this focus to the deceptions practiced by the senses.

Anaxagoras sums up the issue tersely:

> Being born [becoming] and perishing [passing away] are conventions which are not correctly employed by the Hellenes. No thing either becomes or perishes, but is combined and recombined from existing things. So they would be correct if they called becoming combination and perishing recombination.(B17)

The target has now become the Greek language as such.

5. The Act of Integration

The Presocratics then unite in a chorus of condemnation directed against the modalities of the language used by their contemporaries, this language being partly identified with the kind of discourse supplied by Homer and

Hesiod. They would not have so condemned it if they were not prepared to suggest or supply an alternative. I have already from a theoretic standpoint indicated some of the requirements which this new language was to meet. It was to be documented, and therefore could begin to dispense with some of the pressures to memorize. Therefore it could be worded so as to replace personal agents by impersonal forces and replace the acts of agents performed upon other agents by statements of relationships between impersonal entities. Moreover, as the new statements in documented form began to separate themselves as visible artifacts from the consciousness of the speaker, who now could write them down, they became objects seen and contemplated, and so the notion was encouraged that what was being described also existed as an object which became single and unique. This object now did not just happen or perform, but existed, under two guises: as the total description, and as the total "fact," meaning the single physical fact which was being described. This became a cosmos, a system, a one and an all. This encouraged a corresponding urge to integrate the shifting panorama of events which constituted the content of orally memorizable mythos, replacing their discontinuous multiplicity by a single comprehensive statement which would somehow include them all by reducing them to aspects of the single whole. Finally, aside from whatever noun, or impersonal adjective standing for a noun, could be used to identify this single object, there would arise a felt need to replace the verbs of action and happening which crowded themselves into the oral mythos by a syntax which somehow stated a situation or set of situations which were permanent, so that an account could be given of the environment which treated it as a constant. The verb called upon to perform this new duty was *einai*, the verb to be.

Nevertheless, the Presocratics could not invent such a language by an act of novel creation. They had to begin with what was available, namely, the vocabulary and syntax of orally memorized speech, in particular the language of Homer and Hesiod. What they proceeded to do was to take the language of the mythos and manipulate it, forcing its terms into fresh syntactical relationships which had the constant effect of stretching and extending their application, giving them a cosmic rather than a particular reference.

The pioneers in this enterprise were possibly the Milesians, although the loss of their *ipsissima verba* makes any judgment concerning their role hazardous. The pioneer whose own language has been partially spared is Xenophanes, who offers the following key pronouncement:

One *theos*, among gods and men biggest.(B23)

The urge to unify the panorama has begun. The oral mythos had described events occurring in the environment as the acts of *theoi*--those supermen in the image of human beings. Xenophanes retains the term *theos*, but he insists that it be unified, or more correctly integrated. The emphasis falls on the numeral One, conceived not as one unit among a plurality of such, but as a unique single whole. The term with symbolic meaning which he attaches to this comprehensive figure is *megistos*. Admittedly this superlative can in epic indicate status or rank, but its primary reference is to physical extension, that is, "size." The noun *megethos* in this sense will recur in later Presocratic statements, and I think the presence of the adjective in this context indicates a *theos* who is coextensive with the physical environment. This conclusion is supported by the language of a second statement: "All of him sees, all of him senses, all of him listens"(B21).

The reiteration of the adjective *oulos* in this line seems to insist on a dimension of the *theos* that a later and more sophisticated language would call "spatial." Finally, Xenophanes tells us:

> Ever and always in the same [place] he abides in no wise disturbed,
> nor is it proper that he should at [different] times go from place to place.(B26)

Such language could be interpreted as a direct criticism of Hesiod's account in the *Theogony* of the actions taken by Zeus in the course of the struggles to establish his authority. More generally, it denies the propriety of any purely narrative account of the environment. The comprehensive unitary *theos* is himself the cosmos seen as a whole, and as a whole it remains a stable entity. "Propriety" here refers to what is linguistically proper.

The "shifts of position" which Xenophanes would exclude from such language refers to the dynamism of movement inherent in the acts of agents such as Zeus in the oral mythos. (Cf. *Theog.* 690, 855.) These have to be unified in description under the aspect of a single integrated whole.

To achieve such language requires a new effort of the Greek consciousness, an act of intellection. This effort is projected by Xenophanes into the cosmos itself:

> Far removed from [physical] toil by the wit of [his] sense he ordains all things.B25. (Cf. *Theog.* 656,881.)

As I have said, the twin notions of system as inherent in the cosmic environment, and as inherent in the new language describing that environment, are not at first disentangled (if indeed they ever are in Greek philosophy). Therefore, the new intelligence which is required to break with the mythos language becomes also that intelligence which informs the vision, if I may so call it, of that new physical system called into existence by the new language.

It became fashionable in later antiquity to divide the Presocratics into sects and schools which made it their business to propose doctrines in rivalry with each other, with the intention of correcting each other. According to one such arrangement, Xenophanes is assigned the role of precursor to

Parmenides, both of them being viewed as offering doctrines in contradiction to the doctrine of Heraclitus. Yet so much of the language used by Heraclitus, far from correcting or contradicting the pioneer efforts of Xenophanes, seems designed to expand and carry forward a common enterprise. This becomes evident in the first instance in the words he uses to describe the act of integration as it is performed within the human consciousness, and also upon the "facts" of the environment as perceived by that consciousness.

> Intelligence consists in listening not to me but to the statement and then to concur-in-stating that all [things] are one.(B50)

Every word in this compressed aphorism is weighted. An examination of its elements yields the following results. First, a statement designed to explain the environment is now recognized as existing in its own right apart from the speaker who pronounces it. It is still received orally by listeners, but is no longer the inspired voice of bard or muse. Second, its leading assertion or motif is that the entire plurality of the environment makes up a single system; it has to be viewed as an integral whole. Third, the term "all [things]," besides referring to the environment, refers also to the human experience of it. The subject to which the aphorism is addressed is "persons" in the plural. The unity of the environment as a single object must be matched by a unification of our experience of it. Fourth, it follows that the statement itself, as now formulated, forms a single linguistic system corresponding to the system of the environment which it describes. The philosopher drives home this congruence by a deliberate pun: the "statement" asserting that all things "concur" in unity itself requires a "concurrence" of "statement" on the part of those who pronounce it. Finally, to be able to use such language is an exercise of intelligence at a new level of understanding.

In Hesiod's vision, there was a "sense" (*noos*) exercised by Zeus on Olympus, variable, powerful, cosmic in extent, expressible also in Hesiod's verse. For Xenophanes, this "sense" becomes the unique possession of a unique god, who exercises it consistently, by his "wit." Heraclitus similarly accepts the predominance of this force, which he calls "intellection," but he discards the god symbol. The act of intelligence required to use this language is identified as such, without being projected onto the super-agent.

It is therefore not surprising to learn from another aphorism that

> Intellection [is] one and unique. To be stated as the name "Zeus" is not acceptable to it and is also acceptable to it.(B32)

That is to say, to identify this super-intelligence by giving it the name of Zeus, which Hesiod in particular had applied to a single super-power, a father of gods and men, may be a familiar oral convenience; but it is a matter of in-

difference. The one god of Xenophanes has truly now become an abstract
one.

The simple assertion of the existence of a total one, comprehending and
including all things, which I have called the act of integration, was an essential first step to take in the task of escaping from and superseding the narrative flux of previous language. But its full advantage, as ushering in a new
method of description, is fully realized only when it is spelled out with the
help of symbols which become more complex, by suggesting the concept of an
overall "order" or "system," implying that the one nevertheless has parts or
elements so related as to maintain a constant total identity of the system. In
one of his most familiar sayings, Heraclitus would appear to have taken a
step toward this realization:

> This order, of all-and-every the same,
> was not made by any individual of gods or humans
> but ever was and is and shall be fire ever-living
> kindling by measures and quenching by measures.(B30)

It is clear that the symbol fire, chosen here to identify the physical existence of the one whole, is intended to be a comprehensive one, not applied
analytically. Fire is not an element but a total and eternal condition of the all.
From the standpoint, however, of linguistic advance toward a conceptual
vocabulary, the presence of fire in this saying is less significant than the
presence of the term *cosmos*. Interpreters tend to pass over it lightly because
of an assumption that the concept of a physical cosmos preceded the
Presocratics and was taken for granted by them. It was doubtfully put
forward by the Milesians, but this is the first fully attested entry of the term
into philosophical language. It has been borrowed from the epic vocabulary,
in particular from previous application to the orderly array of an army controlled by its "orderer" (*cosmētor*); but it is now "stretched," so to speak, just
as the neuter of the numeral *one* is being stretched, to cover a whole world or
universe or physical system, and to identify it as such.

Once such a concept is accomplished, it becomes necessary to detach it
altogether from the style of previous narrative descriptions of the environment, for these portrayed the environment of sky and earth and sea as an
event or series of events which happened in time, contrived by the actions of
super-agents. The total order, by definition, because it is total, is inclusive of
its own past, present, and future: that is, it is not an event at all, but a self-
subsistent entity. What Heraclitus also succeeds in doing by using the fire
image is to suggest that this entity, this one, is also a process, although closed
and self-sustaining.

It is therefore appropriate that the "book" of Heraclitus' sayings
available to Aristotle should have begun as follows:

Of this statement which exists for ever
human beings are non-comprehensive
both before listening to it and initially after listening.
Of all things happening according to this statement
they seem to be without experience,
their experience being of utterances and deeds of that sort which
I myself expound
dividing each according to (its) nature and explaining how it is. (B1)

The statement (*logos*) like the system (*cosmos*) which it affirms, is itself a constant and a unitary construct, for it needs a "com-prehensive" intelligence (the play on words here is deliberate) to understand it after coming into contact with it. As a systematic statement it is not merely a one, an integration, but a one which once accepted makes possible the use of analytic language to describe the relationship of individual parts and particulars within the single system which includes them. These parts, however, are not the fleeting events of the narrative tale; they have their own analytic meaning: they become transformed into definitions retained within the overall definition.

Heraclitus is determined to assert the one while retaining the many, but the many have ceased to be those disconnected and ephemeral acts and events of the oral panorama.

Seen against the background of such linguistic endeavour, the route taken by Parmenides becomes a more stringent and urgent assertion that the One whole, as concept and as physical system, has an integrity which has priority over any attempt to analyze the parts. Yet this placed Parmenides in such a dilemma that he was forced to the step of offering a two-tier system of language—one for the One, and another for the Many. I have neither space nor leisure at this time to discuss Parmenides' *Way of Opinion*. I select for notice those portions of his own statement which can be connected directly with the linguistic experiments of his two predecessors.

For Heraclitus, the timeless identity of the order of things, prefiguring its conceptual character, is expressed by the formula "ever was, is and shall be," borrowed from Homeric speech, where the formula had covered the sequence of perceptions or of events perceived by a prophet.

Heraclitus is asserting that between "was, is and shall be" there is no distinction. By implication, the "is" (*esti*) remains the only verb needed in any language designed for theoretic purposes to describe the system as such. Parmenides grasps the implication firmly and applies it stringently. The "is" syntax is the only one appropriate to the task. It should replace the use of all other verbs and all other senses of the verb to be:

Neither ever was nor shall be since it is now together all. (B8.5)

In this pregnant line Parmenides corrects the Homeric and Heraclitean formula, and supplies the clue to the way in which the presence of *esti*, the unadorned "is," haunts his poem. The modern translator feels compelled to supply a subject, an "it," or "a thing." But the Parmenidean syntax insists that there be no subject, for it is asserting the naked proposition that any and every statement describing the environment or any part or aspect of it should be an "is" statement cast, as we might say, in the form of a theorem.

Yet does he wholly refuse to suggest what the subject might be, or what the reference of an "is" statement might be? Does he insist on a language which leaves *esti* suspended in mid-air with no referential function? The initial step toward supplying such a linguistic "subject," which would also be regarded as the "object" of thought, is taken when he allows the present tense of the verb to suffer replacement by the neuter participle accompanied by the article, and thus converted into a kind of noun:

> You will not cut off that-which-is from adhering to that-which-is,
> neither scattering in all manner of
> ways and means throughout [the] order,
> nor combining. (B4)

The one permanent god retained by Xenophanes and dismissed as a matter of indifference by Heraclitus here becomes a complete abstraction—"that which is." "Order" may have a double reference to the "*cosmos*" as a physical order externally realized—the *cosmos* of Heraclitus—and that orderly arrangement of language used to describe this *cosmos*. This ambivalence in Presocratic discourse has been previously noted.

The neuter participle now introduced as a noun is used in Parmenides' poem with the same regularity as the present indicative and tempts us to translate it by such terms as 'Being' or 'Reality', capitalized to give the words metaphysical status. But I do not think there is any metaphysics in Parmenides, properly speaking—any more than there is in any other Presocratic. What the philosopher does is to clothe his abstract noun with a physical, or at least spatial, dimension.

"Scattering" and "combining" are cast in the present tense; that-which-is does not undergo a process of continual dispersal and reunification. In this way the philosopher redefines in analytic terms the procession of events and acts which have constituted previous oral descriptions of the cosmos, while denying that such a process takes place. But the frame of reference is surely physical or spatial, not metaphysical. Elsewhere in the poem, and at length, the philosopher clothes his 'is' or his 'that-which-is' with a whole stream of epithets, the main burden of which is to suggest that this being is a physical continuum underlying the apparently separate and various phenomena of the environment. Taking the law of integration first partially expressed by

Xenophanes and applying it rigidly to the external world, Parmenides proposes in modern terms a conception of space-matter. As others of his epithets indicate, this permanent substructure of the universe also exists outside time; it is as timeless as it is indivisible. It admits neither of moments nor parts, as indicated in a passage already noticed which I shall now quote in full:

> Neither ever was nor shall be, since indeed it is [exists]
> now together, as an all,
> a one, a continuum. (B8. 5–6)

This constitutes one among many aphoristic statements in the poem. The last term in the Greek is a neuter adjective 'continuous' which I have ventured to transcribe into an abstraction. As a variant on this language, but with the same spatial reference, Parmenides offers the statement:

> All is filled up with what is
> therefore [it] is all continuous. For what-is
> closes with what-is.(B8.24–25)

Finally, and still adhering to the enterprise undertaken by his two predecessors, Parmenides discerns and affirms at a more stringent level the need for a new level of consciousness to achieve the new language. His assertion that the "is" cannot be cut off from the "is" was preceded by the following line:

> Fix your gaze on [things] absent yet also present to the sense [noos] steadily.(B4)

The Presocratics all search variously for terms by which to identify this kind of consciousness. They are seeking to isolate what we might describe as an act of cognition or intellection, directed toward grasping conceptual abstractions rather than narrating and describing events. The oral language, as exemplified in the Homeric epic, had offered a variety of terms to describe our awareness of things or people, without directing this awareness narrowly into such separate categories as perception versus thought, or intention versus reflection, or counsel versus purpose, and the like. To indicate the super-intelligence required to achieve an integration of all things, Xenophanes had used the two familiar Homeric terms *phrēn*—the "wits"—and *noos*—the "sense," and combined them, projecting them upon the one god. Heraclitus had preferred to conceptualize the purely human factor of skilled intelligence (*sophon*) and use this term to indicate the level of abstractive effort required. Parmenides selects the Homeric *noos* and *noēma* with their verb *noein*, comprehending, we might say, the total "sensibility" of man; but he uses them to describe that act of the consciousness which recognizes that only "is" statements carry the kind of validity required for a proper description of the universe. These are "present to the sense" and in fact constitute the context of what "is sensed," that is, thought, at the level of abstraction now required:

> An act of sense amounts to the same thing as having the sense that [anything] "is".(B8.34)

This would appear to be one way—perhaps the best—of rendering one of the most familiar but elusive statements in the poem, and I think we are rightly tempted to regard it as equivalent to saying "Thinking always means thinking about [something] real." The statement provides a basis for future questions about the relationship between what we call mind and the objects which mind thinks about. These lie outside Parmenides' purview. What is evident is that he is sharpening the insights of his predecessors by insisting that the new language of description, the "is" language, is itself the creation of a new level of intellection. The two are interwoven or interlock:

> Without that which is, within which it stands expressed,
> You will not find [the act of] sensing.(B8.35–36)

For Parmenides, this new mind, so non-Homeric, so conceptual, so abstract, is discoverable in the new language; the existence of either depends on the other. His poem is therefore not an essay in idealism, as though he were prepared to reduce the cosmos to a mental act, but more properly an essay in certain issues of linguistics and semantics which underlie all theoretic thinking.

6. The Act of Conceptual Analysis

With Parmenides the integrative effort is completed. The integrity and inviolability of the "is" are asserted on two fronts. This "is" represents both what "is there forever," or "stands there forever," a physical continuum; and also what "is so stated forever," a completed theorem. This biofocalism attests itself in two ways: by the two kinds of contexts in which the *esti* is placed, locative and copulative, and by the two kinds of attributes which attach themselves to the *on*, the physical (whole, full, continuous, etc., the predominant ones) and the epistemological (truthful, genuine, believable, thinkable, accompanied by the temporal ones: unending, everlasting, immortal).

This leaves future philosophical discourse at an impasse. The language is, as Parmenides admits, circular and so tautological. We can call his philosophy a "system" only in quotation marks, because a genuine system is such only in virtue of being a sum of categories or relations which, being themselves permanent, share in the nature of the permanent "is" which comprehends them. The linguistic need is for a one all which does not completely destroy the many but under whose aegis the many are reinterpreted in terms of categories which are as abstract and immutable as the one, and can be used in "is" statements which describe the one.

For the cosmic environment, this was to mean in practice a deployment of linguistic counters identifying such categories as matter (*hulē*), dimension (*megethos*), space (*chōra*), body (*sōma*), void (*kenon*), motion (*kinēsis* or *phora*), change (*alloiōsis*, *metabolē*), rest (stasis). Countless others could be named pertinent to the systems of individual philosophers of later antiquity. These are shared by all philosophers. In their philosophical or conceptual sense, none of them occurs in Greek literature before the end of the fifth century B.C. and some of them come into existence only in definitions supplied by Plato before being used by Aristotle. They have, however, previous linguistic histories of some significance and can be viewed as being forced into consciousness out of their original Homeric, imagistic reference and their original narrativistic context, out of the panorama and pageant of human experience as orally described and preserved, into the thought world of conceptual science and the speculative discourse of thoughtful men; as follows:

Dimension and Space

The reference of the noun *megethos* in Homer is confined to the bigness or stature of a human being. Correspondingly, the primary reference of the adjective *megas*, with its comparative and superlative degrees, is also to bigness whether strictly dimensional or extended by metaphor to big winds, big noises, big words, big leaps, big emotions (which fill the body), big rule (over extended territory); so that such senses as strong, loud, heavy, rapid, intense, and the like, are properly to be regarded as extrapolations of the basic reference to size. The second epithet in the Homeric formula of address, "O Zeus noblest, biggest" (*Iliad* 2.142, etc.), possibly refers to Zeus's tenure of the "wide heaven" as the "biggest" of the three allotments of the cosmos shared between himself, Poseidon, and Hades (*Iliad* 15.187–92).

When Xenophanes asserts that his one god is "biggest" among gods and men, he is in part repeating the Homeric formula, in part correcting the Homeric notion of any partition between three equals (though even in Homer Zeus is more "equal" than the two). Since Xenophanes's central concern is with the unity of his *theos*, the superior size becomes a property of this unity. This may overstate the degree of abstraction attained, but not by much; for in the next line as quoted it is stated that this god had a "frame" which fails to resemble that of a human or divine being. The language he repudiates is

Homer's (for example, *Iliad*, 5.801, 8.305, etc.). There, "size" possessed by this frame cannot be anthropomorphic either; but further implications of this are not explored in the meager text we have.

Parmenides once uses the comparative of the adjective to specify that his one whole "is" can be "neither bigger nor tinier either here or there" (8.44 —45). Since the terminal adverbs have a spatial reference rather than a qualitative one, he seems to be denying variation in size within the one which would occur if it were populated by varying physical objects. Is he arguing that the cosmos should be viewed as an absolute size; that is, as sheer "dimension"? He does not say so, but the use he makes of the epithet "continuous" twice (8.6 and 25; cf. 8.23), and his denial that the "is" is divisible, since "what is closes with what is" (8.25) point in the direction of this conception, as does his denunciation of language which uses such terms as "alteration of place" (that is, location) (8.41).

Zeno extrapolates his master's thinking by converting the specific *megethos* of a Homeric man into the "dimension" of the "is" (B1 init.) The noun, by being placed in this new syntactical relation, has been "stretched" out of its Homeric particularity into the name of a concept which has some approximation to the term "space." Zeno's dialectic addresses itself to the proposition that this "space" is truly continuous and indivisible: it is a comprehensive unity which contains no "units," no "many." Once the mind proposes to itself that the one does contain such a many, then that mind is forced to subdivide the many *ad infinitum*, producing self-contradictory propositions about what each member of this supposed many really is. Parmenides's epithets for the "one is" combined the notions of a plenum and a continuum. Zeno seized on the continuum and made it both explicit and absolute.

Melissus in this respect is his echo. He asserts dimension (still *megethos*) to be an attribute of "the unbounded is" (B3). The same "is" "cannot be divided"(B10). In the words of his interpreter Simplicius, "by dimension he means the sheer extendability (*diarma*) of the fundamental reality (*hypostasis*)"(B10).

Anaxagoras accepts Zeno's doctrine of infinite divisibility, but phrases it so as to retain big and small as usable descriptive terms: "Of the small there is never a least, but always a lesser—of the big there is always a bigger, equal to the small in number, and each being both big and small in relation to itself (B3)"; "There being equal portions of the big and small in number, all [things] would be in each [thing]" (B6). Correspondingly, he coins the abstraction "smallness" (*smikrotēs*) to represent a property of the "things" in his cosmos (but the smallness is always relative) (B1), making it available for use by Plato.

Such statements presume the existence of that physical dimension of "extendability" asserted by Melissus. But Anaxagoras was not interested in carrying this conception further, because the main thrust of his system was in the direction of defining and describing that "many" which the Eleatics had sought to deny. Hence the conceptual physical term which recurs in his language is *plēthos*, "number" (in Homer "multitude"; the abstract usage, however, predates Anaxagoras).

Actualization of the concept of "space" as a primary property of physical reality emerges in the Platonic *chōra*, meaning "area" on a cosmic scale, a "stretched" version of the Homeric term for a given "country." Parmendies forecasts this usage when he condemns the language which speaks of the "is" as though it "altered place (*topos*)." The linkage in discourse of "place" with the "is," albeit negative, assists in the conceptualization of a denied attribute.

Body and Matter

Despite their reputation as (for the most part) materialists, the surviving vocabulary of the Presocratics offers no Greek equivalent for "matter" or "material stuff," let alone "material substrate" or "element." Over eighty years ago, John Burnet, perhaps realizing that the materialist interpretation required some appropriate noun, proposed *phusis*, usually translated as "nature," as the Presocratic candidate for the meaning "primary stuff." For evidence he had to rely on a fragment of Euripides; the surviving Presocratic fragments which mention *phusis* do not support such usage.

Parmenides had asserted that all of the "is" is "filled up" (*empleon*) with "what is" (B8.24) and that it is "not short of anything," (*epideues*) (B8.23) words which Homeric man most readily applied to his stomach, in typically specific sense—what he "filled up" with food. When linked syntactically with what is, they suggest a physical and generic phenum, something close to abstract "matter," although Parmenides does not press the language further. The next step toward conceptualization is taken when Melissus, who repeats the notion that the "is" is "full," asserts also that it cannot possess "body" (*sōma*) for this would mean that it also had "thickness," and so possessed "parts," which would violate its unity. The fragment containing this sentiment is frustratingly brief (B9); he presumably found more to say on the subject, which we have lost. But the sentiment is linguistically significant, because it is the first on record to introduce "body," that is, corporeality, into the language of philosophy. It is instructive to see how this comes about. The selected term (*sōma*) has an Homeric sense appropriate to its new function, for in Homer (but not in post-Homeric authors) its reference is restricted to a dead body, a corpse—that is, something which while specifically imagined as human is nevertheless inert, ready for conversion to a piece of inert matter. The word is being "stretched," like so many other abstractions achieved by Presocratic thought, out of the specificity of a human being to the dimensions of cosmic reality: the change is achieved by altering the syntactical context; it is now brought into a statement which relates it to the *on*. This is done not by asserting it as a property of the *on*, but by denying that it is. In the moment of denial, it takes on abstractive force. It is therefore being prepared for the role it will play in the vocabulary of the atomists and of Plato and Aristotle where it is distinguished from matter by being qualified by the adjective *hapton*, "touchable body." This little history illustrates that law already referred to, operating in ancient Greek as in modern tongues, which could be styled the law of conceptualization of denied attributes. Parenthetically, it is instructive to note that the term adopted by Aristotle to signify undifferentiated matter which constitutes the raw material of touchable body was *hulë*, the Homeric word for a forest or its firewood, or timber, the Latin "*materies*," our "matter." However abstract may be the intention of this usage, its connotation is still that of solidity and touchability.

The Void or Vacuum

Popular thinking is prone to confuse "space" with "empty space"; but Greek philosophy was clear about the distinction. "nature abhors a vacuum" has become a cliché. Whether a vacuum has any real existence was a matter of dispute, in the course of which "The Void" entered the vocabulary of philosophy. It was another case of the conceptualization of denied attribute.

Once more, it is Melissus who codifies and conceptualizes the implications of Parmenides's Homeric language. To argue as the elder philosopher did that the "is" is not "short of anything"(B8.33) recalls, as we have said, the Homeric reference of the word to a shortage of food. To say that "what is gets close to what is" recalls the aggressive Trojan warrior "getting close" to the Greek ships. To say "the all is filled up with what is" again recalls Homeric food filling a stomach.

The language is still not conceptual; but Melissus, interpreting it as applying to physical space, converts the denial of the existence of a lack to a denial of existence of "the empty," and interprets the assertion of closeness and fullness as involving a similar denial:

> For the empty is nothing and nothing cannot exist. Nor is (that which is) disturbed. It has nowhere to give way in, but is full up. If the empty existed, it could give way into the empty. But since the empty does not exist it has nowhere to give way in.(B7.[7].)

The effect of this dialectic was to present the atomists with "void" as an established conception. Reversing the judgment that Melissus had placed on it, they promptly announce the "void" to be one of two fundamental elements of reality (Democritus B9, B125).

Change

Alloiōsis and *metabolē* as philosophical terms referring to physical alteration or "change" in a material object, or in "matter" itself, were brought into currency by Plato and Aristotle. Neither occurs in the Presocratics. *Alloiōsis* is a coinage of the fourth century B.C.; *metabolē* is post-Homeric but pre-Platonic, but not in its philosophical sense. The usage of both embodies an unusually strenuous level of abstractive effort on the part of the Greek mind.

Presocratic philosophy is often referred to as "a search for permanence behind change." The phraseology is in fact drawn from the prosaic language of the fourth and later centuries, not of the period when the Presocratics lived; still less does it represent the language of Homer and the early Greek poets. Elementary as the conception of change, or, for that matter, of process, in the abstract may seem, it would appear that its formulation presented some difficulty.

We can see retrospectively how it was arrived at by reflecting on the contexts in which the modern term 'change' can occur. We speak of the change from summer to winter, from boyhood to manhood, of an alteration from green to blue, of the difference between carrots and turnips. Yet, unless it be in the language of Alice in Wonderland, we do not speak of the change from summer to turnips, the alteration of boyhood to green, the difference between winter and carrots. Change and alteration acquire meaning as they are conceptually linked to two opposite poles which nevertheless enjoy a prior if unstated community between themselves. In simplest terms, the idea of change becomes meaningful as it occurs between pairs. The prior community of the pair is a form of unity which they share in part with the unity of the one, the whole, the all. Only as thought integrates itself around this all-embracing conception does it become possible also to conceptualize the principle of change and process within the one.

The linguistic experimentation of Heraclitus is here of central importance. On the one hand, he asserts the integrity of the one all; on the other, he continually tries to envisage a process taking place within the one which shall not be random (though he can occasionally slip into admitting the random (B124 with unamended text) but shall preserve unity. He apprehends this as achievable when the cosmos is viewed as consisting of or operating through corresponding but antithetical pairs. These can complement each other, exchange places with each other, swap identities with each other, become the negatives of each other. Many of his sayings are devoted to arrangements of such pairs operating or simply existing within the one all. They can be stated as interacting on each other, or as in simple confrontation with each other. The linguistic road he is taking can be plotted in successive stages of experiment:

> The cool is warmed up, the warmed up is cooled off,
> the liquid is dried out, the withered rain-drenched(B126)
> A potion unshaken parts asunder(B125)
> They do not com-prehend how self-divergent [it]
> is self-congruent(B51)
> Day and dusk are one(B57)
> War ex-ists as it con-sists(B80)
> Justice [means] contention(B80)
> Journey upwards downwards one and the same(B60)
> hewed-in two [means] brought-together(B8)
> out of dis-tractives fairest con-struction [*harmonia*](B8)
> brought together: carried apart(B10)
> dis-sonant con-sonant(B10)
> from all one from one all(B10)
> poverty feast(B65)
> famine feast toil rest(B80)
> day night winter summer war peace feast famine(B67)
> The same is there, living dead, waking sleeping, young old(B88)
> scatters and recombines, advances and withdraws(B91).

The import of these cryptic pronouncements becomes understandable when it is realized that the vocabulary is drawn from that Homeric and Hesiodic speech which describes human or environmental behavior or common objects and operations like splitting wood, attacking or retreating, mixing Circe's drink, singing a bardic song, or fitting the frames (*harmoniai*) of Odysseus's ship. The Homeric oral version of human experience, a panorama of narrativized actions and events, is being partly rationalized, brought into some sort of conceptual order, by being rearranged in these antithetical pairs.

It is tempting to see this kind of arrangement as a visual one prompted by the conversion of spoken speech to alphabetic shape. It may at the same time respond to the previous oral and acoustic habit of narrating events in patterns of echo.

The same kind of linguistic treatment is applied to the philosopher's own account of his own cosmic system:

> Reversals of fire first sea; of sea half earth, half hurricane(B31)
> Earth is dismembered [to be] sea and measured out into
> the same account as [it] stood prior to being born earth(B31)
> Living kindles from dead, waking kindles from sleeping(B26)
> Death for ghosts to be born water
> death for water to be born earth(B36)
> Immortals mortals, mortals immortals

living their death, dying their life(B62)
We live the death of them [namely, ghosts]
and they live the death of us(B77).

We need not explore what these mean for the details of his own cosmology, but only note that they continue to embody and manipulate the epic vocabulary in the interest of unifying phenomena in complementary pairs. Fire's "reversals" recall those of the Homeric and Hesiodic sun. Earth, in order to transmute into sea, needs to be "carved up" like a sacrificial animal at a Homeric feast. Tornado, playing a cosmic role as transmuter between elements, recalls the hurricane winds accompanied by lightning which were wielded by Hesiod's Zeus in his cosmic role (*Theog.* 846). The ghosts who exchange their condition for that of living men are from that realm reached by Odysseus's voyage (cf.B45).

As has been noted, the full conceptualization of material change and process implicit in these pairing arrangements was not achieved before Plato. The required terminology had to be extracted or adapted from the specifics of Homeric speech. Heraclitus comes near to making the extraction in the following examples:

reversals (*tropai*) of fire(B31)
construct reversed back (*palin-tropos*)(B51)
these being shifted over (*meta-pesonta*) constitute those
those being shifted over back again constitute these(B88).
Shifting round (*meta-ballon*) [it] is still(B84)
all [are] inter-change (*ant-amoibē*) for fire and fire for all
as things for gold and gold for things(B90).

Lurking underneath the concrete sense of "turning round" in *tropē* and *tropos* lies the philosophical sense of "alteration," and behind the participle *metaballon* lurks the philosophical sense of "metabolic" change. These, however, are unrealized; they lie in the future. The use of the prefix *meta-* in both *meta-ballon* ("that which shifts," used of a Homeric warrior turning his back; cf. Parm. 88, 41 below) and *meta-pesonta* "what is shifted" (apparently a Heraclitean coinage), is conditioned by the fact that the cosmic process is continually being "paired," for which the image of a move from one position to its opposite is appropriate. In the term "inter-change" Heraclitus successfully coins a pure abstraction to identify that concept of physical process which he is endeavoring to bring to birth.

Normally, his language stops short of such coinage. The impersonal verbs which he arranges in pairs are adumbrations of their corresponding abstractions, such as consonance versus dissonance, integration disintegration, union diversity, construction destruction, permanence change. These and dozens like them are not yet part of the Greek vocabulary, either philosophical or literary. The orally remembered idiom to which Heraclitus is heir supplies their place by verbs. He does his best by stripping the verbs of specific subjects, so that they become untranslatable, unless one adds the unwanted and misleading "it," or if one goes further by supplying "fire" or "the cosmos."

In one instance, the philosopher is credited with the statement that

> [it] is altered (*alloioutai*) even as when being commingled with ingredients (cf. Herod. II. 40) [it] is named according to the savour of each (67).

Precisely what he is talking about is disputable. Are the three verbs intended as impersonals, or should "god" be supplied as subject for the first (on the authority of the quoter) and "fire" for the next two? (So Diels, a restoration in the text.) Is he referring to a sacrificial ritual or to the preparation of a meal? Does "savour" mean smell or taste? These are not problems of present concern, which focuses on the initial verb *alloioutai*—"it is rendered other," otherwise attested first in Thucydides and used here to refer to physical "change" in an underlying substance, equivalent to the philosophical sense of the Aristotelian (and Platonic) *alloiōsis*. Does the word's presence mark a Heraclitean anticipation of philosophical vocabulary or does it represent the quoter's interpretative addition?

The latter seems more likely, since Parmenides, in a context which refers to the same significant connection between change and naming(B8), uses what may be the earlier equivalent form *allassein* (cf. Pindar *Nem*. 11.38) to express the same notion of "rendering other." Denying that this occurs (the object of the infinitive is "place" or "position"), he indirectly proposes that the Heraclitean positioning of interacting pairs is equivalent to an act of "alteration." The denied attribute of reality prepares the way for its conceptual recognition. The nouns *allagē* and *metallagē*, still indicative of "swapping," enter the vocabulary of fifth century drama.

This process accelerates in Melissus, who uses dialectic to intensify a denial of something which receives increasing linguistic definition even as he denies it:

> If it shifts sides, the one is done for.(8.6)

The statement revives the vocabulary of Heraclitus: *meta-piptein* is used four times in Melissus' preserved text. But this idiom, partially expressive of the dawning notion of "change," is raised to a more conceptual level when the action to be denied is reworded as "shifting order" (*meta-cosmein*), a verb employed three times. The coinage embodies a bold paradox: a cosmos by definition should not be subject to rearrangement. Once more, through denial, he has adumbrated an order which can be self-governing and contain a process of change within itself while remaining an order.

Anaxagoras, reversing the denial, and using its linguistic results for positive doctrine, takes up the conceptual challenge thrown down by Melissus and boldly asserts that a "re-ordering" (*diakosmein*) does take place, the product of a cosmic sense-intelligence. Like Heraclitus, he resuscitates that Homeric vocabulary which had applied "cosmos" to army ranks, so that *diakosmein* meant marshalling an expedition. The same "act" has now been given a cosmic dimension, another example of conceptual "stretching" through adjustment of syntactical context.

A companion linguistic development is perceivable in Melissus' exploitation of derivatives of the adjectives *heteros*, "other" or "second" of a pair. He uses the verb "othering" (*heteroioun*) four times to describe the process he is denying to the one. The verb expresses a rationalization of the pairing procedure, involving mutual interaction so characteristic of Heraclitus's attempt to conceptualize change.

Diogenes took the last logical step and completed the linguistic process by coining the crucial abstraction "other-ation" (*heteroiōsis*), a usable term to supply the concept of patterned change which he applies to describe the behavior of his cosmic "air."

Plato reuses the word, but its significance was too restricted for general use. *Alloiōsis* and *metabolē* generally took its place in the language of post-Socratic philosophy. But its preservation in what survives of Diogenes' text attests to the fact that, aside from the details of their cosmic machinery— what might be called their cosmic gimmickry—which have only antiquarian interest, the Presocratics faced a task of linguistic invention the performance of which was their chief contribution to later philosophy, and perhaps to science as well. If Empedocles appears to have been slighted in this account of what happened, it is only because while he was very strong on cosmic gimmickry he was very weak on conceptualization.

Motion

The word "motion" in English, like its equivalent in other modern tongues, is the name of a concept, identifying a property abstracted from the behavior of any "moving" body. As such "it" can be measured in terms of comparative varieties and velocities and assigned its own laws or rules mathematically stated. It becomes an object of thought in separation from physical objects as such. As a conceptual term, it has also entered common speech and written literature, regardless of whether it is used philosophically or scientifically.

The case is far otherwise in classical Greek: *kinēsis* and *phora*, two words available to render this conception, were not acclimatized to perform this semantic task earlier than in the writings of Plato and Aristotle. Neither of them is common currency among the remains of the Presocratics; nor is any substitute term offered which would fill the gap. *Kinēsis* emerges once at the end of the Presocratic sequence, in Diogenes. Its verbal ancestry is intriguing.

The Homeric verb *kinein* is used to refer to the "stretching" of one's arms and legs or "pushing open" a door or "prodding" a ghost to follow a guide or "shaking" one's head (in grief) or "disturbing" a wasp's nest, or of the west wind "swaying" a cornfield; or again, in the passive, of Apollo "swooping down" on the Greek army, or of the same army "swept" by emotion (like the cornfield, and in the same context). One catches from the contexts a sense of an organic dynamism in the archaic Greek tongue, preconceptual and preabstract. The modalities suggest that the dictionary definition of the word as "set in motion" (LSJ, s.v.) is for this period inappropriate. The Homeric speech, as well as the Homeric experience of the world, true to its narrativized genius, understands what we call "motion" only in its sensibly perceived form of "commotion" of any kind, a disturbance or dislocation inherent in any kind of action, pushing, prodding, shaking, and the like, not as an abstracted property of otherwise inert bodies.

Hence it is not surprising to find the adjective *akinētos* used by Hesiod (*WD*750) to refer to a grave which the trespasser must not violate by sitting on it; it is an "undisturbable," as also was the city of Camarina, later described in a famous aphorism. When the semi-abstract coinage *kinēsis* makes its literary appearance, in the poet Tyrtaeus and much later in Thucydides, the references are to a "dance" and to a political "movement."

When, therefore, Xenophanes asserts that his unitary *theos* "remains ever in the same (place) not distrubed (*kinoumenos*) at all," his target is not motion in the abstract, but "dislocation," as he goes on to say: "It is not appropriate that (he) should shift from place to place and time to time."

Parmenides, using more conceptual language to substitute the "is" for the *theos*, still describes in Homeric terms the behavior which must be denied to it. It is named, he says, by ordinary people as "altering place and exchanging complexion"(B8.41), as though it were a person, like the coward in Homer who shifts his stance and changes complexion in the ranks (*Iliad* 13.279–284; cf. 5.858). On the contrary, the "is" is "non-disturbable" (*akinēton*, and so perhaps also "inviolate" like any sacred spot, for example, a grave). The adjective hovers between the poetic and the abstract. Parmenides is not denying to the abstract "is" an abstract "motion" of which he has not yet clearly formed the conception, but asserting that the one all whole is as such undisturbable, as is true of any system which cannot suffer alteration in any part without losing its integrity—that is, its identity, as a system.

Yet Parmenides is aware of the rigidity of the mental impasse he has created. A one whole which always is a whole contains after all a series of related parts which all "are" in the sense that they constitute a permanent pattern of relationships, geometric or mathematical or philosophical, which can be expressed in "is" statements. By what descriptive language, other than the use of the tautological "is," do you describe them? Parmenides does not have such a language—not yet. Its adumbration will be the task of his successors. But he is aware of the need, and falls back on a second best resource—a picture of an "organization" (*diakosmos*, B8.60) which in effect, he ruefully admits, is in the idiom of the Homeric language he wishes to escape from. This is also expressive of the Homeric state of mind, the *doxai* of ordinary people(B8.51). The "way of opinion" accordingly is forced to revive the Homeric narrative language:

> You shall know the nature of the aether and in the aether all
> the signs, and of the all-holy Sun's
> clear flare the obliterating works(cf. *Iliad* 2.455, 5.757, 18.420),
>
> and out of whence they were born (cf. Hesiod *Theog.* 124).
> the works revolving of the circle-faced Moon you shall learn
> and its nature, and you will know the encompassing heaven
> (*Theog.* 127) whence it grew . . .(B10)
>
> . . . how Earth and Sun and Moon
> and aether the communal and the heavenly milk[y way] and Olympus
>
> last-and-uttermost (*Theog.* 113) and the hot might of the
> stellar [clusters] surged forth
> to be born(B11).

This language uses Homeric vocabulary and echoes the schematology of Hesiod's *Theogony* (as far as *Theog.* line 127). Parmenides has been compelled to revert to the syntax of the narrative series. The processes of being born (or "becoming") and growing and surging have intruded upon plain "being." The "is" has suffered dislocation. He knows that this is the language that his audience of "mortals" has been schooled to understand. Although describing a cosmology, it is being chanted to the strains of epic song(B8.52).

Parmenides's disciples Zeno and Melissus make further linguistic exploration of the consequences of denying and banning dislocation: "That which is shaken is not shaken within the place where it subsists (locative *esti*) nor in the place where it does not subsist" (ZenoB4). "[Existence] of necessity must be full [be a 'plenum'] if empty does not exist. If it is a plenum, it is not disturbed ('commoted') (Melissus B7.10). "If that which exists is divided, it (has to be) disturbed; once disturbed, it would not exist" (Melissus B10).

In statements like these, a language which began quite properly by seeking to banish the active dynamism of Homeric "commotion" is edging into an idiom which associates commotion with the "is" and embroils it in "is" statements; a thought habit is being encouraged which, in denying that commotion is a part of existence, will be tempted to suggest that a "motion" of another kind may after all be part of existence. Anaxagoras readies himself to propose that a special form of commotion does take place in the cosmos:

> . . . as these [things] rotate
> and separate out [impelled] by force and swiftness.
> The swiftness produces the force.
> The swiftness of them cannot be likened as to swiftness to
> any thing among the things now existing among men,
> but is swift many many times over.(B9)

What is this super-swiftness, unless it be the expression of a dawning concept of motion in the abstract, of inconceivable rapidity, dissevered from the erratic movements of objects of daily experience?

It is consistent with this inference that the "revolution" which possesses this swiftness is a creation of mind, that is, a mental object. To be sure, Anaxagoras does not quite say this, but only that "sense-mind" is its "master," and uses it to "set in order (or "organize") the (cosmic) revolution of stars, sun, moon, atmosphere, aether" (B12). "As sense-mind began to shift (sc. the content of the cosmos), it (had to be) separated from the entire shifting (area). . . . As things got shifted and divided up, the revolution made (them) divide up more and more"(B13).

In these aphoristic statements, Anaxagoras reuses in an abstract sense a Homeric name for swiftness of a dog or a runner, and coins the abstract term "rotation" (*perichōrēsis*). The conceptual direction of his thinking reveals itself in his insistence that this is a rotation with its own impetus, and also that it is something expressible in degrees of comparative measurement. His successor, Diogenes, offering a cruder and purely physical explanation of "sense-mind," as consisting of "atmosphere," adopts the same notion of a special kind of "movement" which this noetic air possesses. This he labels a *kinēsis*, a "commotion," which because of its noetic association is turning into the sense of abstract "motion," which it later became in the standard vocabulary of Aristotle. (It accompanies the coinage by Diogenes of "otheration," noted above [B5].)

Linguistically and conceptually, the breakthrough completes itself in the seventh book of Plato's *Republic*, in that passage which proposes to organize the sciences (as known to Plato) in a curriculum. Each is disposed within a set of coordinates, according to the abstract definition of ascending fields of operation. Within geometry we grasp the field of the plane "in two dimensions"(528a9). The "three dimensional" "partakes in volume"(528b2–3). Then comes the "three dimensional in motion (*phora*)" or "motion applied to volume" (528e1); its field is occupied by "swiftness that is" and "the slowness that is" (529d2). We hear in these terms an echo of the words of Anaxagoras (a debt which Plato's genius may have been disinclined to acknowledge). But now the collocation of the terms with the participle of the verb *to be*—a linguistic step which Parmenides might have taken but which Anaxagoras did not—has triumphantly identified a conceptual and abstract motion to be isolated and measured according to its own laws of comparative velocities and directions.

Phora, a "carrying," is the post-Homeric word preferred in this passage, although *kinēsis*, a "shaking," also occurs elsewhere in Plato's text; it became the symbol to which Aristotle gave preference as more inclusive of all types of physical alteration. Once enshrined in the doctrine of the four causes, it came to symbolize a conceptual standard by which the Presocratic philosophers could be classified. Did they accept or deny "motion"? And if they accepted it, was it eternal or temporal, and so forth? In this way, the doxographic tradition surrounding them tended to falsify the record and conceal from view the fact that their original task was linguistic invention rather than conceptual dogma.

For the modern philosopher the Presocratic enterprise as described offers two problems for possible debate and clarification. Since Kant, it has been commonly held by philosophers and laity alike that the categories of time, space, matter, motion, and the like, which we use to describe our experience of our environment, are innate. As thinking, sentient human beings, we have always had them. If, however, they had to be "invented" linguistically by the Presocratics, can this be true? Those who still reply yes are forced to rely on the assumption that although the equivalencies of such terms are not found in the period, this is a matter of accident: the concepts were there in their minds, and guided the thinkers' thinking, as is true of all thinking. To this one replies in turn: How do you know a concept or category exists except as the name for it tells you it exists? No supposition is commoner than that thought precedes language and is philosophically prior to it. Yet since thought is measurable only through words, the supposition violates a fundamental rule of empirical science. Is it possible that the Homeric mind (a shorthand term for a mental condition of which the Homeric poems are only one illustration) has existed and still exists within us, functioning as an alternative way of thinking and experiencing our environment?

This last question may receive some indirect illumination from an unexpected and very sophisticated quarter. One of the difficulties which the layman has in understanding modern physical theory is that it seems to require him to lay aside those neatly conceptualized compartments of matter versus "empty" space, body versus motion, space versus time, in which, since Aristotle, he has learned to think. What happens to the coordinates of his familiar world when (solid) matter can convert into sheer energy? Are the relations and relativities of modern physics demanding that we return, as by an ascending spiral, to a state of mind which the Greek philosophers tried to organize out of existence?

PART TWO:
THE LANGUAGE OF
THE MILESIAN "SCHOOL"

The historian who undertakes to write a history of Greek philosophy faces a crucial dilemma at the very beginning of his task. A philosopher considered as such is knowable only by the words he uses. But the story of Greek philosophy begins with the names of three men whose actual words are unknown. If the Preplatonic record deserves to be scrutinized as in the first instance a linguistic phenomenon, consisting in the invention by slow degrees of a new vocabulary and syntax of discourse, then the silence imposed by the passage of time upon these three pioneers—if that is what they were— becomes doubly embarrassing. The Milesian "school" has been identified under the names of Thales, Anaximander, and Anaximenes. The surviving record of what they taught, or wrote, is doxographical, dating from reports in Aristotle and his successor Theophrastus. It contains not a single coherent sentence which can be securely anchored as an authentic quotation. The difficulties thus posed for the historian are evident. In the first four editions of the *Fragments of the Presocratics* (1903–1922) compiled and edited by Hermann Diels—the standard collection upon which all historians now rely—the dubiety of any *ipsissima verba* attributed to Anaximander was, perhaps grudgingly, recognized. Revised editions of the same work, reflecting no doubt an understandable need for something to build on, have identified as securely authentic quotation a paragraph of thirty-six words which is radically suspect, but which has the effect of reinforcing a magisterial interpretation of the three Milesians taken together, as constituting a connected school of thought, a conception which seems to have originated with Theophrastus. Unwary readers of handbooks and histories of the period need to be warned against this practice. On the other hand, Kirk and Raven's *History of Presocratic Philosophy*, a recent treatment of the whole period, in an "Introductory Note" on the sources, states flatly that "it is legitimate to feel complete confidence in our understanding of a Presocratic thinker only when the Aristotelian or Theophrastean interpretation, even if it can be accurately reconstructed, is confirmed by relevant and well-authenticated extracts from the philosopher himself." Having so stated, the same history devotes to the Milesians eighty-nine pages of confident exposition in which are embedded one sentence of seventeen words attributed (wrongly, in my opinion) to Anaximander, and a second also of seventeen words partially attributed to Anaximenes (and again in my opinion, wrongly). The contrast between the stated principle of authentication and its practical application strikingly illustrates the dilemma confronted by all historians.

The prime source from which later antiquity formed its estimate of the Presocratic contribution to speculative philosophy was a textbook describing the *Physical Opinions* (Doxai), that is, doctrines concerning the nature of the cosmos and its contents, which had been promulgated by Greek thinkers prior to Aristotle. The text was compiled by Theophrastus, Aristotle's pupil in the latter half of the fourth century, and it can be speculated that it was produced to serve as a handbook for students in the Lyceum. It was the first of its kind, marking a break-through in historiography, as having called into existence the history of ideas as a recognizably learned discipline with its own rules. In this respect its appearance at this juncture, at the beginning of the Hellenistic Age, the age of learning, can be compared to that of Thomas Stanley's *A History of Philosophy in Eight Parts*, published in London in 1655–62, which reinstated the history of philosophy in England and (in translation) on the continent, and also to that of Hegel's *Lectures on the History of Philosophy*, which at the opening of the nineteenth century gave the discipline its own rationale as constituting an autonomous philosophical enterprise.

This work, soon epitomized, and also reedited and rearranged to suit a growing taste for biography, molded the ancient conception of what the earliest speculative thought was all about, particularly because the first chapter professedly sought to isolate and describe the conceptual "first principles" (*archai*) which were to be attributed to the period. The chapter (or "book" as it is commonly called, though it was obviously much shorter than a modern "book") was in fact, as will later appear, derived from a variety of notices touching on the early "physicists," many of them anonymous, which occur in the extant writings of Aristotle, and would not appear to enjoy an authority independent of this compilation. In the case of the Milesians, this means that the extant information available for inspection—so far as metaphysics is concerned—was put together well over two hundred years after they lived. Nevertheless, what Theophrastus said about them seems unambiguous and has effectively monopolized the attention of historians ancient and modern. It survives in a context which seems intended to connect them with Anaxagoras as his predecessors or even his philosophical partners. Accordingly, my translation will run to the point where Anaxagoras and his associate Archelaus have also been dealt with, but with this caution:

The passage in question has survived from Theophrastus's book only as excerpted in a commentary on Aristotle written by one Simplicius, a Neoplatonic philosopher of the sixth century A.D., who is presumed to have had access to a surviving copy or to excerpts from it already used by a previous commentator. It can be deduced that Simplicius quotes some parts of the text and paraphrases others, and that he certainly adds explanatory introductions and comments of his own. His categorical language, however, does not depart in spirit and substance from the language of the original, for both are written in a philosophical vocabulary—some critics would call it a jargon—which remains faithful to conceptual categories employed by Aristotle. The passage is accordingly here rendered without drawing those distinctions between the language of Simplicius and that of Theophrastus which modern scholarship has detected. The style of the text, though superficially continuous, is essentially disjunct, presenting lists of philosophical concepts and the various ways in which the various philosophers are supposed to have dealt with them. The effect is arid, not to say un-Homeric, and very unlike the style of those actual Preplatonic texts we happen to possess. The rendering here offered is arranged to correspond.

[1a   Of the group who stated the first-principle (archē) to be one and moving
1b   those whom Aristotle specifically (*idiōs*) names as "naturalists" (*phusikoi*)
2   one school states it to be finite (*peperasmenēñ*)
3a   for example] Thales the Milesian son of Examues
3b   and Hippon who is held also to have been an atheist
4   [who] stated the first-principle to be water
5   having been led on to this [conclusioñ] from appearances according to
         sensation
6a   for indeed the warm is alive in virtue of the moist
6b   dead bodies dry out
6c   seeds of all [things are] moist
6d   all nourishment is soupy
7a   by that out of which everything exists it also is constituted to be
         nourished
7b   water exists as a first-principle of the moist nature
[7c   and [is] constitutive of all [things]]
8   wherefore they deduced the first-principle of all things to be water
9   and published the opinion that earth rests upon water.
10   Thales is transmitted as the first to have expounded the "science" (*historia*)
         concerning nature to the Hellenes
11a   many others having gone before
[11b as indeed is the opinion of Theophrastus]
12   but Thales having been far enough superior to them as to have relegated
         all before him to obscurity.
[13   He is said in writings to have left nothing except the [work] entitled
         Nautical Astronomy].
14   Hippasus the Metapontian and Heraclitus the Ephesian—
15   they too [stated] one moving and finite
16   but they made the first-principle fire
17   and from fire they make all existing [things] by thickening (*puknōsis*)
         and rarefaction (*manōsis*)
18   and they dissolve [things] back again into fire
19   as this being the one substrate nature
20   for Heraclitus states all things to be an exchange for fire
21   and he also fashions a certain order

22   and a defined time of the change of the cosmos
23   according to a certain fated necessity.
[24   Of the school stating one and moving and non-finite (*apeiron*)]
25a   Anaximander the Milesian son of Praxiades
[25b   becoming a successor to and disciple of Thales]
26   stated the first-principle and element of existing [things] as the
           non-finite (*to apeiron*)
27   [being] the first to have provided this name of the first-principle
           [alternative version: first provided this name (namely) "first-principle"]
28a   he states it to be neither water nor any other of the named elements
28b   but some different nature non-finite
29   from which (he asserts) all heavens and the worlds (cosmoi) inside them
           to arise
30   and into those [things] out of which genesis exists for existing [things]
           [he asserts] destruction also to occur, according to necessity
31   for [he asserts] them to give "justice" and vengeance to each-other for
           nonjustice according to the order of time,
32   [using] in this way rather poetic "names" in saying so (for amended
           translation see below)
[33   [It is] evident that this [thinker], contemplating the change of the four
           elements into each other did not deem logical (*axioun*) to make any one of
           them the substrate, but instead something else extra to them.
34   This [thinker] produces genesis not by an element altering, but] by the
           opposites being separated-off (*apokrinomenōn*) through an eternal
           motion
[35   wherefore Aristotle connected him with the circle of Anaxagoras].
36a   Anaximenes, a Milesian son of Eurustratos
36b   becoming an associate of Anaximander
37   he too states the substrate nature (*hupokeimenēn*) (to be) one and non-finite as
           Anaximander [did],
38   not however non-determinate (*aoriston*) as he [did], but determinate
           (*hōrismenēn*)
39   stating it to be "air,"
40   and to differ by rarefaction (*manotēs*) and thickening, (*puknotēs*)
           according to its substances (*ousiai*)
41   when thinned (*araioumenon*) [he asserts it] to become fire
42a   and when thickened, (*puknoumenon*) wind, then cloud,
42b   then, further on, water, then earth, then stones;
42c   and the rest [of things] from these.
43   He too makes motion eternal, because of which [he asserts] change to occur.
44a   Diogenes the Apolloniate also
44b   having been practically the latest of that school giving [professional]
           attention to this [field] (*scholasantōn*)
44c   for the most part wrote in jumbled fashion
44d   [on lines] partly according to Anaxagoras partly to Leucippus
45   the nature of the all he too asserts to be air
46   non-finite and eternal
47   out of which as it thickens and rarefies and changes (*metaballontos*) in its
           affections arises the shape (*morphē*) of the rest [of things]

[48   this is the [scientific] information narrated (*historei*) about Diogenes by
        Theophrastus].
[49   Of the group asserting several first principles
50   one school posited them to be finite in number
51   another non-finite
52   of the school positing the finite number
53   one division [said] two
54a   as for example Parmenides in the [verses] related to opinion (*doxa*)
        [said] fire and water
54b   or rather light and dark
55   or again as the Stoics [said] god and matter
56a   evidently not meaning god as an element
56b   but as meaning one active versus one passive [factor]
57   another division [said there were] three, namely matter and the
        opposites, for example Aristotle
58   another [said] four
59a   for example] Empedocles the Acragantine
59b   who lived not much behind Anaxagoras
59c   and was a rival of Parmenides—
[59d   and near-neighbor (*plēsiastēs*)
59e   and still more of the Pythagoreans]
60   he makes the bodily elements [to be] four
61   fire and air and water and earth
62   [the four] being eternal
63   but changing in virtue of number and littleness
64   according to aggregation (*sunkrisis*) and segregation (*diakrisis*)
65   the first-principles properly speaking from which these are moved
        [being] love and strife
66a   for it must be that the elements continue moving
        cross-wise
66b   now aggregated (*sunkrinomena*) by [the agency of] love, now segregated
        (*diakrinomena*) by [the agency of] strife
67   so that according to him the first-principles are also six
68   for instance in one place he gives an efficient power to strife and love
69   "at one time all combining by love into one
        at another in reverse all borne asunder by strife's hate"
70   yet at another time he coordinates precisely these [two] with the
        four as coequal elements at the point where he says:
71   "at another time in reverse it [they] grew apart to be several out of one—
        fire and water and earth and the immense height of air—
        and strife destructive asunder from them each balanced
        and love among them equal in length and width."
[72   Of the school stating (the first-principles to be) non-finite in number
73a   one division stated (them to be) simple
73b   and of same kind
74a   the other division stated [them to be] composite
74b   of different kind
74c   and opposite
75   and characterised by the prevailing [factor]]

76a for [instance] Anaxagoras the Clazomenian son of Hegesiboulos
76b having formed community with the philosophy (*philosophia*) of Anaximenes
77   first produced a shift in the opinions (*doxai*) covering first-principles
78   and supplied the lacking cause (*aitia*)
79   having made the bodily causes non-finite (*apeiroi*)
[80 for all the bodies-of-like-parts such as water or fire or gold
81   he [stated] to be unbegotten and indestructible
82   but to appear-as-phenomena (*phainesthai*) becoming and destructing by
     aggregation and segregation alone
83   all [things] being [inherent] in all things
84   each several thing being characterised according to the prevailing
     [factor] in it
85   [that is] gold becomes evident as that in which much [of the] golden
     [factor] inheres even while all [things] inhere
86   anyway, Anaxagoras states
     "in everything inheres a share of everything"
87   and again
     "those (things) of which a majority inhere [in a thing]
     constituting the most evident [elements] are and have
     [always] been each several [thing]"].
[88a Theophrastus asserts that]
88b Anaxagoras in saying this [was] near-neighbor (*paraplēsios*) to
     Anaximander
89a The former states that in the segregation from the non-finite
89b [things] of related kind (sungenes) are conveyed to each other
90   and that what was inherent in the all [as] gold became gold and what
     earth became earth
91   similarly each of the other [things] not as becoming but as being
     inherently submerged principles (*enhuparchonta*).
92   Of motion and becoming Anaxagoras established mind as causal (*aition*)
93   from which he generated the segregated [elements] [to be] the worlds
     and the nature of the other [things]
94   "If we take it in this way" [(so Theophrastus says)]
95a "he would be held to make the material first-principles non-finite
     as I have said
95b and the cause of motion and becoming [to be] one
96a but if one were to take it that the mixture of all things were one nature
96b non-determinate as to form and magnitude
96c which is what he could be held to intend
97a it turns out that he states the first-principles to be two
97b namely the nature of the non-finite (*to apeiron*) and mind
97c so that in all respects he evidently makes the bodily elements in
     near-neighbor fashion (*paraplēsiōs*) to Anaximander"
98a Archelaus the Athenian
[98b who they say associated with Socrates]
98c having been a disciple of Anaxagoras
99   in the genesis of the cosmos and in the rest tries to contribute
     something individual
100 but produces the same first-principles as Anaxagoras.

[101a   The above then is that division which states the first-principles
              to be non-finite in number
  101b   and of different kind
  101c   positing the bodies-of-like-parts as first principles].

The terms "group," "school," "division" over-translate a series of
usages of the Greek generic article in the masculine plural accompanied by
verb or participle: "those who . . . " The choice of this translation device is
deliberate, to bring out the fact that the entire account is not historical but
analytic. The arrangement of Presocratic thinkers is schematic and proceeds
by classifying them under categories, or more precisely under genera, species,
and sub-species. The over-arching concept or term to be broken down in this
way is the philosophical "first-principle" (*archē*), itself a type of "substance"
(to use Aristotle's term). It is broken down into one versus several, finite
versus non-finite, and so on. That is to say, all the Presocratics mentioned are
explicitly presented as *archē*-specialists; this is their philosophical business.
Meaningful differences between them turn on the type or types of *archē*
chosen for their systems, subject to one limitation: the *archē* in all cases is a
moving one; an immobile one is not in consideration.

The types have been diagrammed according to a schema of some
elaboration, which emerges only as the text is comprehended as a whole. It is
then perceived to be partitioned by a main division into two groups consisting
of adherents of one first principle (items 1–48) versus more than one
(49–101), or in modern parlance, between monists and pluralists. Division is
then applied to the first group, producing School A, finite monists (item 2),
and School B, nonfinite monists (item 24), and is not carried further. The
second group, after being divided into two schools of finite pluralists (items
49, 50) versus nonfinite pluralists (items 51, 72), is further subdivided. Each
school is split respectively into three and two divisions, producing Division C
adhering to two finite first principles (items 52, 53), Division D adhering to
three (item 57), Division E adhering to four (item 58), Division F adhering to
nonfinite first principles which are simple (item 73a) and of same kind (items
72, 73), Division G adhering to those nonfinite (74a) and of different kind
(74b, 101b) and also opposite (74c). The text accordingly divides itself
unevenly between accounts of A, B, C. D, E, F, G, as follows:

A   items 2–23   monists finite
B   items 24–48   monists nonfinite
C   items 53–56b   pluralists finite two
D   item 57   pluralists finite three
E   items 58–71   pluralists finite four
F   item 73   pluralists nonfinite simple of like kind
G   items 74–101   pluralists nonfinite composite of different kind

The names of philosophers reported in accordance with this schema are distributed as follows:

School	A	Thales, Hippon, Hippasus, Heraclitus
School	B	Anaximander (connected once to Anaxagoras), Anaximenes, Diogenes (connected once to Anaxagoras and to Leucippus)
Division	C	Parmenides, Stoics
Division	D	Aristotle
Division	E	Empedocles
Division	F	no names listed
Division	G	Anaxagoras (connected twice to Anaximander)

In cases of E and G, the text reveals uncertainty surrounding the applicability of the category. Did Empedocles promote six rather than four *archai* (items 60 versus 67, 70)? Did Anaxagoras promote two rather than a non-finite number (94, 95a versus 96a, 97a)? Anaxagoras seems by implication at least to stray twice over from Division G into School B and Anaximander from School B to Division G (also twice). To these uncertainties is added the fact that item F is represented by nobody, while for D, E, and G, despite the pluralized group headings, only one representative apiece can be cited. An impression begins to form that the conceptual schema, if taken as a whole and not merely in detail, is artificial and may not have grown out of the actual preoccupations of the philosophers cited, or the language in which these were described. One also can observe that, aside from the rather mechanical dichotomy between supposed monists and pluralists, the schema is rather strikingly controlled by a conceptual dichotomy between the terms finite (*peperasmenos*) and nonfinite (*apeiros*) (items 2 versus 24; 50 versus 51 and 72 and 101a). Since both these dichotomies can be seen to exist a priori in the historian's mind, should we begin to suspect that the language in which both are expressed, after being fathered upon Presocratic history as a categorical arrangement, has also infected descriptions of their actual doctrines?

One may object that these awkwardnesses can be explained by assuming that the schema is not that of Theophrastus' text, but an artificial creation superimposed by the Neoplatonist Simplicius who is quoting it. The references to the Stoics in Division C and to Aristotle in D certainly postdate Theophrastus, for it seems evident that his textbook did not go beyond Plato. All the headings which I have translated in terms of "groups," "schools," and "divisions" are usually assigned to Simplicius, but not the striking reference to a professional "school" of philosophy in item 44b. I have indicated by square brackets the total amount of text segregated from the Theophrastean original as printed in *Doxographi Graeci*. But this does not remove the underlying critical problem, namely, that the rendering of the early history of ideas in categorical terms is a convention already established in Aristotle, inherited from him by Theophrastus, and converted into standard procedure thereafter, and that the main leading dichotomies of the schematism, monist versus pluralist and finite versus nonfinite, with their elaborations, had already been employed by Aristotle, either as directly applied to the Presocratics, or as illustrated by citations from them (see below). Simplicius, if he has improved upon Theophrastus, has done so because he has been guided by the methods adumbrated not only in the *Metaphysics* but the *Physics*, the treatise to which his own commentary is devoted.

Our present interest in this diagrammed account of Presocratic philosophy is directed toward what it says about the Milesians, simply because we have nowhere else to turn (aside from anything Aristotle may say) for information coverning their speculative activity. In the case of the post-Milesians who are named (excluding the obscure personalities of Hippon, Hippasus, and Leucippus) we can resort for guidance to a body of surviving *ipsissima verba*. These can be compared in individual cases with the Theophrastean judgment that Heraclitus (along with Hippasus) made fire a first principle (item 16: misleading and essentially false), and that he made all out of fire by thickening and thinning (item 17; certainly false); that an approximate model for Diogenes' philosophy was provided by Anaxagoras (item 44d; comparison cannot support this judgment) and that his air thickens and rarefies to produce physical change (47: his own words do not supply this formula); that Parmenides seriously promoted two first principles (54a, b: in face of the fact that Parmenides' own poem states that to name a second is a mistake); that Empedocles names four elements plus two really valid principles (items 60, 65) or alternatively six coeval first elements (70), a confusion of terms and of judgment which is of the historian's own making, since only the first alternative can be reconciled with any plausibility with the original; that Anaxagoras promoted a doctrine of "bodies-of-like parts" which were eternal (items 80, 81, 101c; Anaxagoras does not use this terminology and attributes permanence to the components of bodies).

The views attributed to three philosophers, and perhaps four, are illustrated by quotation. The Heraclitean one (item 20) is very casual, a fragment of a fragment, and is used carelessly to support an inapporpriate interpretation. The first Empedoclean quotation (item 69) is appropriate to its purpose, albeit the conception of an efficient cause (68) is Aristotelian. The second, however (71), is inappropriate to the doctrine (70) that it is supposed to illustrate, and the phrase "each balanced" in the third verse is a misquotation of the original text designed to assist the notion that strife and love are coeval with the other four elements. Anaxagoras is also quoted twice

(86 and 87). So far as these quotations are intended to support items 83–85, they are appropriate; so far as they are also intended to illustrate items 80 and 81, they are not. They are also used to support a linkage with the speculations of Anaximander (88b), which, however, were described earlier in terms which have nothing in common with the two Anaxagorean quotations.

Such manipulative use of quotation, in the case of Heraclitus, Empedocles, and Anaxagoras, raises the possibility of similar manipulative use of whatever Anaximander may himself have said—a problem which historians have tended to ignore, and which becomes more acute when it is realized that no independent source exists by which to check Theophrastus' words and the way he uses them. Although the standard edition of the Presocratic fragments, as previously noted, is prepared to segregate items 30 and 31 as authentic quotation, it has been pointed out (a) that their syntax is that of reported speech; (b) that item 31 as worded seems intended to offer a quotation in support of item 30, which would imply that item 30 is offered as interpretation and is not a quotation; (c) that in any case the support seems lacking: items 30 and 31 appear to describe quite different cosmic situations. Doubts thus raised are increased when the text of item 32 is scrutinized. The expression "in this way" (*houtōs*) does not occur in four of the seven MSS of Simplicius' commentary: the phrase "in saying it" (which KR renders "as he describes it") more accurately means "in saying them," which would most naturally refer to the "them" of item 31. The comparative "more poetic" has always been rendered less literally as "rather poetic." Thus, an amended translation of item 32 would read "using more poetic names (sc. than I have used) to identify them" (sc. the "them" of item 31). On this view of the passage, (a) the historian was confessedly not quoting but paraphrasing a more poetic original, (b) his text has been amended by the addition of "in this way" to suggest otherwise. A motive for this can perhaps be detected. The term "names" finds its echo in a previous reference to providing a "name" (item 27) for the first principle. The combination suggests an interest in the nomenclature of the original. In what survives of Theophrastus' textbook, the only close parallel appears to be a reference to Plato "styling the substrate as pan-recipient" (*Dox. Gr.* 485.2), where the historian could have had the text of Plato's *Timaeus* before him. Otherwise the issue of nomenclature employed by the Presocratics is ignored.

*The non-finite (*to apeiron)

Item 27, translated as "the first to have provided this name (sc. the non-finite) of the first principle" in fact reads ambiguously as the alternative translation offered suggests. Uncertainty is increased by a second version given by Simplicius elsewhere, which most naturally reads "first called the first principle the substrate" (where, however, object and predicate could be reversed). A third version occurs in Hippolytus: "he stated the first principle and element of existing things [as] the non-finite, first having called the name of the first principle." Modern historians have usually chosen our first translation of the first version as the preferred one. Rather than do this, one might conclude that this competition reflects the uneasy result of tampering with an original (see also on Aristotle below) in order to read into it a meaning which it did not contain. The motive, again, was to provide a precious scrap of quotation, even if only an authentic "name." The immediate excuse had been provided by Theophrastus' reference to the "more poetic names" of the original. And if this had occurred, may not the actual use of this "name," namely, "the non-finite," in item 28 be likewise suspect? This possibility is supported when one notices that items 28a and b are worded not as an explanation of 26 and 27, but as an alternative version. The introductory "he states" of 28a replaces the introductory "stated" of 26, and introduces a terminology, in the words "different nature non-finite" which is incompatible with "the non-finite" expressed absolutely in item 26, since it has a different conceptual implication. The hypothesis must be entertained that Theophrastus' text on Anaximander, beginning with item 25a, did not include items 26 and 27, but did perhaps include the original, whatever it was, of Simplicius' alternative version, "called the first-principle the substrate" (or vice versa): that is, Theophrastus identified Anaximander as having used language which could imply that he in some sense developed the Aristotelian doctrine of matter adumbrated by Thales, an interpretation supported by what is said in items 28a and b. What is said in 28b could be read as suggesting to an Aristotelian-minded copyist the propriety of adding a gloss, isolating "the non-finite" in the neuter absolute as an expression used by Anaximander in anticipation of Aristotle's use of the same expression. He may have had a second excuse for doing so, if the text of Theophrastus included (as Diels assumes) items 89a, 97b, for these father the abstraction upon Anaxagoras to support the opinion, attributed to Theophrastus, that a community existed between Anaxagoras and Anaximander (items 88b, 97c). The expression "the non-finite" does not appear in Anaxagoras' extant text; indeed it would appear to be incompatible with his otherwise attested use of the term as a plural adjective. Theophrastus has used loose but understandable language, identifying Anaxagoras' original mixture as "a non-finite" because it contained "non-finite" ingredients. But this would not prevent our hypothetical "copyist" from misreading 89a as a reference to Anaximander (as have some modern historians) and so justifying him in adding the "non-finite" to the text of item 26. (The less likely alternative is that "the non-finite" in item 89a has been contributed by Simplicius. He cannot be held responsible for item 26, which is attested by Aetius, though item 27 is not.)

For good measure our copyist has added the inference that in using the term "the non-finite" for the first principle Anaximander was a "first" (item 27); Anaxagoras presumably being understood to be the second, on the strength of 89a, 97b. We say "our copyist" because the same distinction in a different context is applied to Thales in item 10, where it appears as a correction of 11a, that is, of Theophrastus (item 11b): a common author for both is probable. The device of initiating histories of the arts, sciences, and religious cults by first identifying their inventors, originating in the Lyceum, became a Hellenistic habit, and is here applied to the history of ideas. The "first" in item 77 is usually attributed to Theophrastus (*Dox. Gr.* p. 478) and indeed is traceable to the influence of Plato's *Phaedo*. However, 77 and 78 interrupt an otherwise logically connected exposition beginning with 76b and continuing with 79 (where a participle may have been substituted for a finite verb) and running through to 91, at which point description shifts to the role of mind (92) as the second main item in Anaxagoras' system. I suspect that 77, together with 78 cited in support, constitute an interpolation by the author of the other two "firsts," he being anxious to get this one in ahead of Theophrastus' exposition, and anticipating the information of 92, 97b for this purpose.

This dissection has the important result of casting discredit upon the view shared by all modern historians of philosophy that an important philosophical advance was achieved, as early as the Milesians, by introducing a conceptual abstraction, in essence metaphysical, into the language of philosophy, and using it in a fundamental sense to explain material existence. That is to say, the term "the non-finite," identified as a term by the generic article in the neuter singular, a device uniquely Greek, was, it is supposed, offered as identifying a philosophical idea in its own right, as opposed to the mere adjective "non-finite" used to qualify something else, whatever that something may have been. An alternative possibility, that the term was used by Anaximander only in an adjectival or adverbial sense (see more on this below), gains credence when we review the overall schematism of the passage. It is controlled by the two dichotomies: one principle versus more than one; and finite principle (or principles) versus non-finite principle (or principles); with further subdivision according to the dichotomy determinate versus non-determinate.

Within the first half of the first dichotomy, the term "finite" is used attributively, applied as an adjective to one moving first-principle (items 2, 15); within the second half, to several first-principles (50), and number (52).

Correspondingly, within the first half the term "non-finite" is also used attributively applied as an adjective to something (unnamed) "one and moving" (24) to "some different nature" (28b), to a "substrate nature" (37), to "air" (45, 46); and within the second half, in the plural, to "first principles" (51, 72, 95a, 101a) and to "bodily causes" (79).

Commentators have been slow to grasp the fact that the attributive usage on the one hand, in which infinity is treated only as a property of something else, and the conceptual expression "the infinite" on the other, which treats infinity as an identity in its own right, considered as noetic phenomena, are mutually exclusive. Putting it another way, if a Presocratic described something as "non-finite" this did not mean, in Platonic terms, that he thought of this statement as involving the assumption that "non-finite" existed separately as some sort of Platonic form. The rare exceptions in the Hellenistic Presocratic record where the expression is used pose the possibility that they are intrusive, reflecting the effect of linguistic habits developed in Plato and Aristotle; whereas an item like 28b represents the kind of language Anaximander may have used, consistent with the attributive usage in his Presocratic successors. Items 26 and 27 may be historical inventions foisted upon him, just as items 89ab, 97b are foisted on Anaxagoras (see below).

There is no Milesian text against which to test this supposition as it applies to Anaximander. But the texts of Zeno, Melissus, and Anaxagoras strengthen the possibility that it is correct. It is with them, in Presocratic history, that the term *apeiros* comes into its own, and exclusively in the attributive usage. Zeno applies it twice to describe "the many" and "existing (things)" (*onta*). His attitude to the term is negative; it signifies something that is the result of error: it is not a property of reality. Melissus applies it three times in the singular to "what is" (*to on*) and once in the plural to describe what a "two" lacks. Interestingly, his use of the term is positive; it is a property of reality, primarily temporal (non-finite in time) but also apparently spatial. Anaxagoras applies it attributively three times in the singular, to "the containing," to "the small," and to "mind," and twice in the plural to "things" (*chrēmata*) and to "seeds" (*spermata*). One has to ask, in face of these consistently attributive usages by sophisticated thinkers, whether it is likely that the absolute use with the generic article had been in existence for a hundred years before their own speculations were proposed. Why, if it had been, do they linguistically ignore it?

Prior to the Eleatics, the term in its epic form, *apeirōn*, had been used by Empedocles, positively in the singular to describe his cosmic god or "sphere," and negatively in the plural, to deny that the "depths of earth," and "shining aether," are "non-finite." The context is a polemic, apparently directed against Homer's cosmic imagery (*Iliad* 20.58) as rationalized by Xenophanes (B28), who draws a contrast between "this finite limit (*peras*) of earth above at our feet" and "the below that reaches into non-finite (*es apeiron*)" using the term adverbially to qualify a verb of motion. It would seem likely that, like Empedocles, he is using the epic form *apeirōn*, but in the neuter singular. One can hazard the guess that Anaximander spoke of an *apeirōn phusis* (item 28b), recalling the Homeric (and Hesiodic) formulas *gaian apeiresiēn* and *ep 'apeirona gaian*. An alteration in the quantity of a single terminal vowel would transpose the word into philosophic terminology.

Bruno Snell has pointed to the conceptual advantage given to Greek by the use of the neuter singular with neuter adjective. Here it becomes crucial, converting the notion of some object which happens to be non-finite into the notion of "infinity" (or something approximate to this) in the abstract. What is the history of this neuter device in general, leaving aside the application to *apeiron*, so far as illustratable from surviving language? For Xenophanes the idiom "the intelligent" (*to sophon*) is attested once; Heraclitus uses it twice, as also "the common" (*to xunon*) twice and "the discordant" (*to antixoun*) once. Philosophically it becomes acclimatized when in Parmenides' verse the article is used to accompany the neuter singular participle of the verb to be: "the being" (*to eon*) occurs five times, "the not-being" and "the full" and "the nothing" once each, leading to a usage which in the case of *eon* can even drop the article, as in the phrase "being borders on being." Empedocles, who reflects Parmendies' linguistic influence, appears to have been the first to express the integration of the cosmos under the simple idioms "the all" (*to pan*), three times, and "the whole" (*to holon*), once, as well as using "being" without its article. Following along what will become a mental track, Zeno speaks of "the being," "the subtracted", "the moved," and "the added" (twice). Melissus multiplies the device. Aside from using "the being" and "the not being" a total of nine times, and "the full," "the not full," and "the nothing" once each, in the manner of Parmenides, he adds "the healthful" (twice), "the painful" (once), "the empty" (twice), "the living" (once) and "the one" (once), and also takes the pioneering step (intellectually speaking) of introducing coinages arranged in contiguous antithetical pairs, the famous "opposites" of Presocratic thought: namely, "the thin" versus "the thick" (*to araion*; *to puknon*) twice, "the alive" versus "the dead," "the hot" versus "the cold," "the hard" versus "the soft" (one each). Anticipations of this device in Heraclitus are confined to its expression in antithetical verbs. Such pairing of opposites is taken up by Anaxagoras. In the context of his system overall, it would appear likely that his primary "opposition" (a word he does not use) is between "the great" and "the small," but this is extended to include the hot versus the cold (four times), the wet versus the dry (three times), the bright versus the dark (twice) and the thin versus the thick (*to araion*; *to puknon*) twice. Historians are so used to these devices as employed in Plato and particularly in Aristotle that they incline to take them for granted as available at the time of the Milesians. The Presocratic record suggests otherwise. The idiom of "the finite" versus "the non-finite" as a particular case would appear to be a coinage of Aristotle's, adumbrated in the earlier antithesis between "finite limit" (*peras*) versus non-finite (*apeiron*) in Plato's *Philebus*. If then the employment of the neuter generic article to conceptualize an entity is to be regarded as an Eleatic invention, growing out of Parmenides' dialectic of the "is," the credentials of "the non-finite" as authentically Milesian (already impaired by the absence of this particular combination in later Presocratic vocabulary) are further undermined.

The testimonies covering the three Milesians commonly appear in textbooks as segregated from each other, as though the evidence for each were independent of the two others. This is misleading, because the accounts of all three share a common sophisticated vocabulary which may have suffered a common contamination of the sort already made perceptible in our analysis of the usage of the adjective *apeiros*. In the original textbook it is fairly clear that the first philosophers were grouped, so far as their *archai* were concerned, in a single account which included Hippon, Hippasus, Heraclitus and Diogenes, as far as item 48. The terminology employed, so far as it is preserved in Simplicius' epitome, deserves to be scrutinized under the following criteria: What proportion of it does not otherwise appear at all in Preplatonic philosophic vocabulary? What proportion does appear, but only after Parmenides? What proportion does appear, but never in a philosophic context?

Professional Vocabulary

The thinkers who are the subject of Theophrastus' history are styled "naturalists" (*phusikoi*, item 1b, usually rendered "physicists" or "physical philosophers"). The choice of the title is correctly attributed to Aristotle. It is not one they use themselves, nor in fact does any Presocratic use a title either for himself or his peers which would indicate an awareness that they offered a professional discipline or claimed professional status. Xenophanes contrasts the intelligence (*sophia*) of his own poetry, at present unrewarded, with the rewards allotted to athletic prowess; Parmenides refers obliquely to himself as "the man who knows," another Odysseus; Empedocles claims to be a reincarnated diety (*daimōn*). No doubt such sentiments presage the future claims of "philosophers," but they are not professional. The word *philosophos* occurs in an apothegm of doubtful authenticity and interpretation attributed to Heraclitus, where it might reasonably be read as a new coinage meaning "those who embrace *to sophon* (sc. as this is identified in my system)." The verb *philosopheō* occurs once in the first book of Herodotus and once in Thucydides' *Funeral Speech*, in non-professional contexts. The noun *philo-sophia* appears in Plato's *Charmides* and *philo-sophos* in his *Apology*. None of these words occur in Old Comedy before the fourth century. It is likely that they first became professionalized in Plato's Academy. It is reasonably certain that Athenians would regard Presocratic intellectuals such as Anaxagoras or Diogenes as "sophists" (the word already occurs as a term of disparagement prior to Old Comedy, in the *Prometheus Bound*), or as "meteorologists" (in Comedy and Gorgias), never as "physicists" or "philosophers." The word "physiologist" occurs in a notice of Diogenes, but it is probably contributed by the author of the notice. Self-conscious claims (whether or not historically authentic) to professional status and professional content of teaching are put into the mouth of Protagoras in Plato's dialogue. In contrast, the Presocratic "cosmologists" (another anachronistic title) speak like poets (or orators) addressing audiences. Their wisdom is in a sense "Homeric," or couched in Homeric terms. Once labeled professionally by Aristotle as physicists, they are assigned doctrines suitably professional and cut down to size. The language in which the doctrines of the Milesians are reported cannot have been the speech they used. The reference to "science concerning nature" (*historia*) credited to Thales (item 10, another "first") is indeed professional, but the professionalism belongs to the language of Theophrastus (item 48, *historei*) and has been read back into the Milesians. By this I mean the words as applied to identify an academic discipline or activity. The *historia* practiced by Herodotus was not of that kind, and indeed he shows some contempt for Milesian geographical speculation, which he would not put in the same category as his own type of inquiry. The same critique applies to the language of that "school of professionals" (item 44b) of whom Diogenes is represented to have been a member.

For good measure, the terms "associate," "disciple," "successor," liberally applied in all the textbook histories (items 25b, 36b, cf. 59cd, 76b, 88b, 97c, 98b) find no echo in the extant Presocratic language, nor does it employ such professionalisms as "contemplate" (of theoretic inquiry) and "think logical" (*theorein, axioun,* item 33). Such vocabulary subtly distorts the story of early Greek thought by presenting it as an intellectual game dealing with problems already given and present to the mind, rather than as a groping after a new language in which the existence of such problems will slowly emerge, as language emancipates itself from the oral-poetic tradition. From this point of view, a Milesian "school" of materialist monists is in danger of dissolving into a phantom.

First-principle (archē), element (stoicheion), *substrate* (hupokeimenon)

As noted earlier, *archē* as a philosophical term dominates the entire account of the Milesians and their successors to Anaxagoras and Diogenes. None other offers such a crucial instance of the need for correct perception of semantic evolution in order to understand Presocratic history. Despite its ubiquity (items 1a, 4, 7b, 8, 16, 26, 27, cf. 65, 67, 72, 95a, 97a, 100, 101a, 101c), it is to be noted that it can be replaced by equivalents, in the Milesian case, by "some nature," "substrate nature," "nature of all" (28b, 37, 45), and by "element" (26), as well as by unnamed neuters (15, 24); and in the case of Anaxagoras, by "cause" (79, 92). "Element" and "cause" (in contrast to "nature," as noted above) were introduced into the language of philosophy by Plato ("cause" in particular connection with Anaxagoras); and "substrate" (both as epithet, item 37, and as noun) by Aristotle. It is anachronistic to attribute theories of element, or substrate, let alone cause (as sometimes in modern textbooks), to the Milesians. Is the case any better with *archē*? It is at least more complicated. The word is part of the Presocratic vocabulary (Xenophanes, Heraclitus, Empedocles, Anaxagoras, Diogenes, probably Democritus, and the sophists) but it is precisely the syntax involved in their use of the term, when contrasted with the syntax required to convert it into a "principle," that illuminates the way in which a surviving narrative level of Presocratic thinking was later converted to a conceptual level. According to the Theophrastean version, all the Presocratics used the *archē* as the subject or predicate of the verb "to be." The monists state it "to be one and moving" (1a), "to be finite" (2). Thales and Hippon state it "to be water" (4,8). Water "exists as a first principle" (7b). Anaximander states it "to be some different nature" (28ab). The idiom is sustained through the coverage of Anaxagoras, with the variation that a thinker is sometimes said to "make" the *archē* equivalent to a given substance.

The usage treats *archē* as representing a present and inherent (cf. item 91) and permanent factor in the present cosmos. Accordingly, if material, it can be equated with that *out of which* bodies or phenomena may emerge or be constituted, either to return back into it or to contain it permanently within themselves. The idiom "out of," in the sense of material or metaphysical extraction, though not applied to the *archē* itself, is used freely to govern its material equivalents: "that out of which everything exists" (7a); "from fire" (17); "from which" (29); "out of which" (30, 47). Now, such expressions of material extraction do occur in Presocratic language, especially in that used by Empedocles and Anaxagoras. But they are never associated with the term *archē*. On the contrary, when *archē* occurs, the sense shifts backward to the idiom of Hesiod's *Theogony*: "from the beginning." The reference is to succession in time, not derivation from principle. So far as I know, there is no instance prior to Plato's *Timaeus* of *archē* being shifted over into the sense of *present reality*, an *archē* that "is." The word provides a case history to illustrate the rule that in the evolution of the Greek language toward abstraction, coinage of new terms is less important than the conversion of traditional ones through conversion of syntax in which they are used; the main instrument of conversion being the use of the verb "to be," as fostered by Parmenides' dialectic. It is difficult to escape the conclusion that what the Milesians may have said, following and correcting Hesiod, was something like "from (or in) the beginning all was water, or air," or "from the beginning the nature of the all was, is, and ever shall be non-finite." The ambiguity of the prepositions *ek* and *apo* supplied support for a transposition of *archē* into the new sense of material principle fostered in the Academy and Lyceum, which historians could then read back into the Milesians.

motion, moving (1a, 15, 24, 43) change, altering, differing (33, 34, 40, 43, 47) sensation (5)

These examples, unlike *archē*, must be rated as artificial additions to the original Milesian vocabulary, despite their prevalence in the language used by modern historians. As in the case of *archē*, however, their formal codification as philosophic terms takes place in Plato. I have earlier reviewed the semantic history of "change" (*metabolē alloiōsis*) and "motion" (*kinēsis, phora*).

Thales is described as being guided to his choice of first principle by (physical) "sensation," which does not seem in itself inappropriate language for him until one realizes that the abstract noun "sensation" (*aisthēsis*) does not appear in the Greek vocabulary before Thucydides, and that its philosophical use to express "sensation" as opposed to "intellect" is not earlier than Plato; so also the usages of the plural referring to the physical "senses." Even the verb "to have [physical] sensation of " (*aisthanomai*) does not occur in extant Presocratic vocabulary before Democritus and Critias. This is not to deny the obvious, namely, that the Presocratics continually indulge in language which suggests a split between the superficial and the speculative, and that Parmendies formally separated "truth" from "opinion," and that Democritus distinguished "genuine" from "bastard" knowledge. From what they actually say, however, the general target of the Presocratics was erroneous language, not sensation. The epistemological distinction between sense perception and intellect is first codified in Plato's writings. Milesian thought, at the initiation of Greek philosophy, by being linked to "sensation," is thus implicitly placed in a category which might appear reasonable two hundred years later, but one which the Milesians themselves would not have recognized.

opposites separated off (34 cf. 57), heavens and worlds (29) thickening and thinning (17, 40, 41, 42a, 47), stones (42b)

All these terms, unlike the previous ones, avoid abstraction (or seem to), and sound as though they were responding to actual Milesian language. However, although the doctrine of separation of opposites is credited to Anaximander, later in the exposition it is correctly assigned, and uniquely, to Aristotle (57). As already noted above, while the arrangement of antithetical pairs, hot, cold, etc., emerges in the language of Melissus and Anaxagoras, their formal designation as "opposites" is lacking, as also the term "opposition" as a formal element of philosophic vocabulary. For good measure, the action of "separating off" of antithetical pairs is found explicitly only in the language of Anaxagoras, with whom, in Theophrastus' history, Anaximander was conflated. One concludes that "opposites" have been foisted on the Milesian without original authority. The case of heavens and worlds is a little more subtle. The *ouranos* in the singular furnishes a common image in epic verse and without doubt reappeared in Presocratic vocabulary. The cosmos, a commonplace of philosophic textbooks ancient and modern, is in a different case. As noted above, its first recorded philosophic usage is in Heraclitus. Did the Milesians invent the usage? If so, certainly not with the intention of putting it to the use recorded. The plurals, "heavens" and "worlds," do not occur in Presocratic language until Democritus (Anaxagoras refers only to other regions of the earth besides ours). The intellectual powers (one may say the courage) of the atomists first allowed the Greek consciousness to penetrate beyond the visible firmament hitherto embracing (so it had seemed) a self-contained geocentric "world." It was a revolutionary conception, firmly rejected by Plato and Aristotle, and revived by the Epicureans, creating a contest between the doctrines of one cosmos versus infinite cosmoi which was finally and decisively settled in favor of one, until Copernicus and Galileo. The issue, so fundamental as it seemed in later philosophy, and involving as it did an apparent clash between materialism and idealism, was read backwards into the beginnings of philosophy, on the assumption that the challenge to the one-world doctrine must have arisen at that time.

A doctrine of "change," itself non-Milesian, is in the case of Anaximenes fleshed out by ascribing to him an apparatus of thinning and thickening, applied to air, to produce different "substances" (40), ranging from fire at one extreme to stones at the other. The explanation has a pleasing systematic quality about it, mechanically easy to grasp, which has always appealed to historians of the period. But is it authentically Milesian? Suspicion is kindled by noticing that the same system has previously been foisted on Heraclitus (item 17) where it obviously does not belong (though his aphorism Death to ghosts to be born water: death to water to be born earth" might provide an excuse for the attribution) and will later be foisted on Diogenes (item 47) where it probably does not belong either (he makes one isolated physiological remark which could be forced into implying the doctrine, but the forcing is artificial). Is this another instance of a doctrine assumed a priori to be early and so foisted on the record indiscriminately? The philosophical issue turns once more on nomenclature. The adjectives *araios* thin (cf. item 41) and *puknos* thick are part of the epic vocabulary. Anaximenes, fastening his attention on the role of *aēr* in Hesiod's cosmic architecture (*Theog.* 721, 729, 776, 757, 807) may well have argued to the effect that "in the beginning all was air which became thick and thin" (thus replacing Hesiod's Chaos and also Thales' water). This would be a theory based on empirical observation of the behavior of the atmosphere extended to cover all things. But did he develop an abstract vocabulary, so as to conceptualize "thickening" and "thinning" as a comprehensive principle of material "change"? The same pair of epic adjectives, as noted above, are exploited by Melissus and Anaxagoras, but not the actual abstract nouns "thickening" (*puknōsis*, item 17; *puknotēs*, item 40) and "rarefaction" (*manōsis*, 17; *manotēs*, 40), not even the participle "thickening" (*puknoumenon*, 42a, 47) and "thinning" (*araioumenon*, 41; *manoumenon*, 47). All of these words used analytically to describe degrees of material density otherwise emerge only in the philosophic language of the second third of the fourth century. Plato's *Timaeus* again is the pioneering source. But once equip Anaximenes with a complete system of mechanical mutation, and one gets the system extended to "stones." It may be indeed that the insertion of "further on" in item 42b betrays the fact that the whole item is a doxographical addition to an original description of purely atmospheric phenomena; the aether is thin air, and the clouds are thick air. However that may be, the striking climax of "stones" is suspicious. A theory of mutation from water to earth to stones first appears in Melissus, where the connection seems to be taken for granted but is not associated with any theory of compression. In Anaxagoras the sequence is completed:

> for out of cloud water is separated out
> and from water earth and from earth stones are compacted because of
>   the cold (that is, coldness)
> these evacuate themselves to a greater degree than water" (B.16)

The last stage is accounted for by a metaphor which is probably medical. The antithesis rare versus dense otherwise exploited in Anaxagoras' language in connection with the separation of the qualitative but invisible constituents of the cosmos is not associated with this mutation series. Does the reference to degrees of compacting justify connecting them? Then why the medical metaphor? And why the reference to temperature (as though earth were analogous to ice)? The question arises: if the doxography foisted upon

Anaximenes a theory of material mutation based on degrees of rarefaction and condensation exhaustively applied, did it also fasten on him the conclusion of "stones," in the plural, a noun otherwise first encountered in the singular in the *ipsissima verba* of Melissus and, in the plural, of Anaxagoras? Why does such a geologically simple idea not occur earlier, for example in Empedocles (who it seems did have a theory of temperature)? The first systematic account of mutation from fire at one extreme to stones (plural) at the other occurs in the cosmology of Plato's *Timaeus* (49b–d; cf. 59 bff). Has it been transferred backward to the Milesians?

There remain those two sentences in the account which have been treated with special respect by historians as enclosing actual quotation (items 30, 31). Reasons for doubting parts of them have already been adduced. A more extended scrutiny of their vocabulary will enlarge doubt to cover the whole.

genesis exists [*is*] . . . *destruction occurs (item 30)*

Genesis is Homeric, and may recall language used by Anaximander. But the formal antithesis "genesis" versus "destruction" (more often translated becoming and perishing) is linguistically speaking post-Socratic. This is not to deny the obvious, that the verbs "to be born," (or "become") and "to perish" become commonplaces after the Eleatic dialectic made them so, and occur together. But the abstraction *phthora*, "destruction", used philosophically in antithesis to *genesis*, is Platonic, and as such became naturalized (along with cf. item 92) within the Aristotelian vocabulary (a single instance in Democritus is not philosophical). Should it properly be applied to interpret the words of a thinker who lived two centuries earlier, particularly when given syntactic, that is, conceptual, identity as the subject of the verb "to be"? The substitution of a metaphysical noun in place of a verb replaces a language of narrativized process by a system of conceptual relations. This is precisely the kind of linguistic change which might not appear until Presocratic linguistic experimentation had done its work.

[*Genesis exists*] *for existing things (item 30)*

The neuter participle of the verb "to be" in the plural, accompanied by the generic article, is used here, (as also in item 26), to refer to the actual objects, things, or phenomena of the (presumably) visible world, the existence or presence of which Anaximander's theory is designed to explain. The same usage had appeared in the case of Heraclitus (item 17). In Homer and Hesiod this particular idiom occurs as the first third of a hexametric formula, "the [things] being present, being about to be, and being before," where the sense is temporal, referring (as would be natural in narrativized speech) to events, "happenings," present, future, and past. The same temporal sense recurs in a sentence of Empedocles' poem: "He easily saw each (thing) of all existing [things] in ten and twenty life-times of men." It was again Parmenides, the pivotal figure in the development of philosophic syntax, who first exploited this participle with generic article, but in the singular, to convey the sense of "what exists" or "existence" in general. Zeno and Melissus (perhaps by inadvertence?) pluralized the usage to refer to "beings" or "existences," meaning the separate "things" in the environment (which for Zeno paradoxically had no "existence"). The occurrence of the idiom in a saying of Heraclitus (B7) reads like an addition to the original. Anaxagoras more accurately used the phrase "existing things" (*eonta chrēmata*), this time meaning the permanent physical constituents of the cosmos. *Ta onta* becomes a linguistic coin of common currency in the sophistic period. It is the ambiguity hovering between event and thing that gives piquancy to Protagoras' aphorism: "Man [is] measure of all [things], of the existing [things] that they exist, of the non-existing [things] that they do not." If for "things" we substitute the Homeric "events" (neither noun is present in the original) the sophist is asserting, in effect, that man makes his own history, an assertion which could be read as part of his anthropological theory. But if *onta* can be read post-Homerically in its Eleatic sense, this gives Plato the excuse to interpret and attack the saying as a relativist theory of reality and/or knowledge.

Strictly speaking, Greek has no equivalent for the English word (or the German or French for that matter) "thing," and in the singular it was not easy to designate "a thing," for (*to*) *on* meant "what really exists," and what this was depended on the metaphysics of the speaker. *Ta onta* did double duty, meaning "things" and also "realities," and both senses grew out of the Eleatic dialectic. To attempt to describe what Anaximander may have said by using such terminology is to commit an anachronism. These same observations apply to the term *ousiai*, translated "substances" (item 40) with the difference that *ousiai* in the fifth century carried a concrete reference (typical of the pre-conceptual stage of language) to "real property."

according to necessity (item 30, cf. 23); according to the order of time (item 31; cf. 21, 22)

The phraseologies of these two expressions should be considered together. First to be noted is the earlier presence in the account of equivalents ascribed to Heraclitus. This is not the first time we have seen identical doctrinal statements ascribed to disparate philosophers, where there is reason to think the ascription is improper in both cases, and results from the desire to seek analogues for fourth century doctrines in the sixth century. The repetitious syntax of the two formulas (in items 30, 31) leads one to suspect that the second is a variant of the first, perhaps intended as an interpretation of it. The use of the preposition *kata* in the sense of "according to" in both betrays the philosophic climate in which these expressions are used. The idiom recurs in item 5 "according to sensation," item 23 "according to . . . necessity," item 40 "according to substances;" compare "according to Anaxagoras, according to Leucippus" (44d), "according to aggregation" (64), "according to the prevailing factor" (84). The preposition is of course used in this sense from Homer on, especially governing specific symbols of human behavior, like spirit, purpose, law, envy, and the like. The point to make here is that the present usage transfers the direction of relationship toward an abstraction. This became a common device of philosophical language in the fourth century to express rather loosely a logical or philosophical connection between the abstraction and the sense of what has preceded; for example, Thales was "led to water according to sensation:" meaning that sensation logically conditioned the conclusion drawn. The recurrence of the device in the Milesian account (five times) suggests that its twofold occurrence in the supposed quotation does not represent the original language of Anaximander; it is absent also from the language of his successors. (It has been supplied, once more for Heraclitus, and once more mistakenly, in an amended text B 112.)

As to the "*necessity*" used with the article (*to chreōn*), the combination otherwise occurs first in Euripides to express the sense of "fate" or "death." On the other hand, the idiom "there [is] necessity (no article) [that] . . .," (often without the verb "to be") is common in Greek literature and is used several times by Parmenides. Homer uses a parallel formula "[there is] need that . . ." or "need of . . .," though neither Homer nor Hesiod use the form *chreōn*, used here, and supposedly antique. One is tempted to infer that while Anaximander may have said something like "It is necessary that these [things] exchange . . ." (to which Parmenides may have intended to reply directly "It is necessary that the "is" exists always"), the present report has converted the original poetic formula into that logical form preferred by later philosophy. As for "*order of time*," the term "time" in Preplatonic quotation (Xenophanes, Empedocles, Melissus, Democritus) identifies historical duration whether linear or circular, and the Milesians may well have used the word in the same sense. Considerable play is made with the concept in the sophistic period (Critas, Gorgias, Thrasymachus, Antiphon, The Anonymous; some sixteen instances). Since, however, the term "order" or "arrangement" (*taxis*) so far as we know is not Presocratic, the combination in which it here appears would again seem to reflect a fourth century level of thinking. The suggestion that the phrase might refer to an assessment imposed by a personified "Time" is too artificial to be plausible.

*Give justice (*dikē*) and vengeance (*tisis*) to each other for non-justice (*adikia*)*

Few can be found to doubt that this phraseology is authentic. But is it? If, as argued above, Theophrastus' text unamended said that the original was "more poetic than this," his textbook for once was right. "Vengeance" alone provides epic flavor and may well represent a genuine reminiscence. The Homeric and Hesiodic formula runs "Vengeance awaits . . ." or "There will be vengeance for . . ." On the other hand, the idiom "give justice" (with vengeance here added on) came into vogue in the latter half of the fifth century, perhaps in response to the increasing formalization of legal procedure under conditions of growing literacy. "Non-justice" is metrically speaking not poetic but prosaic (it could not fit into epic or elegiac verse). Since diurnal or seasonal alternation could be rendered either as exchange of location or as alternating surrender of territory "unjustly" monopolized, Anaximander may well have expressed some such sentiment as that "Vengeance awaits one and the other in turn, for justice so demands (this would be the "Justice" of Hesiod's *Works and Days*); perhaps adding that "there is a necessity" that this be so. An image of the Milesian original, one suspects, has been compressed into the prose of an epitome, and in the process given abstract formulation.

The literary hacks who in the Hellenistic Age supplied students with textbooks of the history of philosophy could not of themselves have invented that screen of doctrinal language which the said students were required to place between themselves and the originals. Its source was formidable—nothing less than the powerful mind of Aristotle. From his notices of the "physicists" or the "first philosophisers" (his terms) Theophrastean and post-Theophrastean accounts derive by direct descent—so far at least as concerns the supposed metaphysics of these men. The first book of his treatise now named *The Metaphysics* introduces his subject with a survey which runs as follows (983b7ff.):

1   Of those who first philosophized
2a   the majority considered the first-principles
2b   in the class (*eidos*) of matter (*hulē*)
2c   to be the only first-principles of all (things).
3   For that out of which all existing (things) exist
4   and out of which first they come-to-be and into which they
           destruct finally,
5   the substance substantially remaining
6   but changing (*metaballousēs*) in its affections—
7   this they state to be the element
8   and this the first-principle of existing (things)
9   and because of this they consider nothing to become
           or perish (*apollusthai*)
10   as (assuming) this kind of nature to be always preserved
11   as we do not say of Socrates that he "becomes" absolutely

whenever he becomes handsome or educated
nor perish whenever he may lose these dispositions,
because [of the fact that] the substrate
remains the substrate [namely] Socrates himself
and similarly with all the rest [of things].
12   For there must exist some nature
13   either single or more than one
14   from which the rest [of things] become, the
        nature being preserved.
15   Now, the number and the class of this kind of first principle
16   all fail to agree on
17   Thales however the principle-leader (arch-ēgos) of this kind of philosophy
18   states [it] to be water
19   wherefore he expounded (the opinion that) the earth also exists upon
        water
20   perhaps having formed this assumption
21a from seeing the nurture of all [things] to be moist
21b and the hot itself (sc. heat) to become from this (sc. the moist)
        and live by this—
21c and (of course) that out of which all [things] become is [also] their
        first principle—
21d so then, having formed this assumption both because of this,
21e and because of the [fact] that the seeds of all things
        have a nature [which is] moist
21f and that water is the first-principle (or beginning?)
        of their nature (growth?) for moist [things].
22   There are those who consider the all-ancient ones,
        [those who] theologized first and much before the present generation
23   to have formed assumptions (hupolabein) on similar lines concerning
        nature.
24   [For example], they made Ocean and Tethys fathers of genesis
25   and the oath of the gods water
26   the one called Styx by them, [that is], by the poets
27   for the eldest is most honored, and what is most honored is an oath—
28   Well, whether this opinion (doxa) concerning nature is really antique,
        such as it is, and quite old, may perhaps be unclear.
29   Thales anyway is said thus to have expounded [his opinion]
        concerning the first cause on these lines.
30a Hippon would not logically be placed among these
30b because of the low level of his mentality
31   Anaximenes, and also Diogenes,
32   posit air [as] prior to water
33   and as the preferred first principle of the simple bodies
34   Hippasus the Metapontine assigns fire
35   and also Heraclitus the Ephesian
36   and Empedocles the four
37   adding earth to the [previously] mentioned as fourth
38   these [he asserts] to persist always

39   and not to become except (in terms of) number and smallness
40   being congregated (*sunkrinomena*) and segregated (*diakrinomena*) into
          one and out of one.
41   Anaxagoras the Clazomenian
42   by age prior to him but in activities posterior
43   states the first principles to be non-finite
44   practically all the bodies of like parts, such as water or fire
45   he states become and perish in this sense
46   in other respects they neither become nor perish but persist eternal.
47   From the above (list) then, we would hold
48   the sole "cause" (*aitia*) to be the one expressed in the class of matter.
49   But as they pushed forward in the above fashion,
50   the enterprise by its very [nature] created a path which
          they were compelled to follow accompanying their search . . .
51   (the result, continues Aristotle, being the incomplete "discovery"
          by some of the second cause, namely that of motion).
52   After them and after such causes as these—
53   these not being sufficient to generate the nature of existing
          [things]—
54   once again being compelled, as described above, by the very
          nature of truth,
55   they sought the first principle next-in-order
56   (this is then described by Aristotle in terms which suggest the
          final cause, though his meaning is uncertain)
57   and so at last when [there came] one pronouncing that mind, even
          as it is present in animals
          so also [is present] in the nature [of all]
58   as causal of the cosmos and of all order (*taxis*)
59   (here) was one offering a spectacle of sanity and sobriety alongside
          of babblers—namely those preceding him.
60   On the evidence we know [for a fact] that [it was] Anaxagoras [who]
          engaged in arguments (*logoi*) to this effect
61   (Aristotle then adds that prior credit can go to a Hermotimus,
          otherwise obscure,
62   and summarizes this position as proposing a final and an efficient
          cause simultaneously)
63   One might suspect that the first to investigate this sort of problem was Hesiod . . .

Seen in conspectus, this account can be divided as follows: Items 1–14 put forward a philosophical category which is Aristotelian, and by implication warns us that what follows is to be accomodated to it, as indeed is stated later in items 47, 48.

Items 15–19 introduce the first Milesian as being within this category.

Items 20 and 21 supply some tentative interpretation of why he chose to belong there.

Items 22–28 interrupt with a tentative suggestion that certain pre-Milesian "*theologoi*" be included in the same category.

Items 29–33 resume with the first Milesian and add a second, adding some non-Milesian names as well.

Items 34–46 proceed with subsequent thinkers to Anaxagoras.

Items 49–51 introduce a second category. The text, summarized in our conspectus, refers to "other thinkers," otherwise anonymous, except for a muddled reference to Parmenides.

Items 52–56 introduce a third category.

Items 57–62 introduce Anaxagoras (again) as being within this category.

Item 63 adds the tentative correction that Hesiod might be included too.

This conspectus extends considerably beyond what is said about the Milesians in order to bring out five facts:

(I) The particular category to which the Milesians are assigned (items 2, 15) forms the initial portion of a more extended scheme covering two more (49–51 and 52–56). Each of these three depends for its analytic validity on its relationship to the other two.

(II) Both accounts share a common critical pattern, which has the effect of placing the Milesians in close connection with their successors, and presenting their doctrines as a function of this connection (but with the conspicuous absence of Anaximander in the prototype).

(III) Within the deployment of such dichotomies Anaxagoras recurs more than once, as occupying a dominant place in the story.

(IV) There is betrayed a lingering view (items 22–28 and 63) that the history of speculative thought began not with the Milesians but with Homer and Hesiod.

(V) These four taken together demonstrate a close relationship between this account and that of Theophrastus.

A primary Aristotelian dichotomy had been supplied in a context which immediately precedes our conspectus (and is not included), namely, the doctrine of the four causes (*Met.* I, 983a24ff.). Of these, the logically first, the material (items 3–6, 11–14) is here put forward as the historically first (items 1, 17) The language used treats the terms "cause" and "first principle" and "element" as logically interchangeable (cf. items 7, 8, 29). That is, as in Theophrastus, so also here, the Presocratics are presented as *archē*-specialists.

A secondary dichotomy is implicit; it occurs between a single material cause supposedly offered in historical sequence in three different versions, namely water, air, fire, versus *the* four. That is, earth as fourth is added to the three previous single ones to produce a combination of four replacing a previous list of three. The analytic character of such a sequence emerges when it is realized that it is accomodated to the

Aristotelian doctrine of the four primary or simple bodies or elements here represented as emerging historically in response to philosophical logic (items 32, 33, 37).

As before in the case of Theophrastus, statements covering the post-Milesians can be tested against the *ipsissima verba*. Some identical distortions occur in both sources. Thus it is asserted that Heraclitus espoused a doctrine of elemental fire; that the four "elements" of Empedocles were "congregated and segregated" (item 40); when in fact these two terms belong to the system of Anaxagoras ("separated off" (*apokrinesthai*), a common Anaxagorean term, is used once by Empedocles); that Anaxagoras taught a theory of "bodies of like parts." The phraseology of the whole account is either post-Eleatic or lacks Presocratic credentials altogether. The thinkers concerned are "philosophisers" (items 1, 17. cf. Theophrastus items 1b, 10, 44b, 76b) dealing with *archai* (2a and *passim*: cf. Theophrastus *passim*), which are classified as "material" (*hulē*, an item of the Aristotelian vocabulary which Theophrastus avoids); their project is to explain "existing (things)" and the "underlying substance" of these and their manner of "change": this "substance" being the "element" or "substrate." Anaximenes chooses air among "the simple bodies" (item 33). The language of items 20 and 21 is by Aristotle's own admission post-Milesian. Similar phraseology continues to haunt the account of the post-Milesians.

When one discounts all this Peripatetic baggage, what is left of the "Milesians," so-called? (They are not here so named.) So little, one may say, that their entire position in the history of philosophy becomes doubtful. All we can be reasonably sure of (extracting from the account what seems beyond invention) is that Thales in whatever context asserted that the earth was on top of water (Did he call this "the deep sea"?) or more likely "extended downwards into water" and perhaps added that "from the beginning all was water." Anaximenes replaced water by "air," assigning it the same function of supporting the earth (Aristotle, *de Caelo* II, 13, 294b13), perhaps adding "from the beginning all was air" as a variant on Thales. Xenophanes in turn replaces both these theories of "what is under the earth" (*ta hupo gēs*) by asserting that "the underneath extends to non-finite" (B28). All three theories would represent successive attempts to rationalize the cosmic architecture of Hesiod's *Theogony*, where "the beginning" was Chaos.

Doubts surrounding the credentials of a Milesian "school" of philosophy espousing material "first principles" are reinforced when one notices the total silence that prevails concerning these men as philosophers in Aristotle's sense prior to Aristotle himself. Thales, though a familiar figure in Herodotus and Old Comedy, is remembered as an astronomer, mathematician, and inventor, and possibly also as a statesman; and for these accomplishments gained a place among the seven wise men. The post-Milesian Presocratics either mention each other or are referred to by Plato, or both, or (in the case of Diogenes) are satirized anonymously for their doctrines. But no one before Aristotle has ever heard of Anaximander and Anaximenes and no one before Theophrastus has heard of all three together as constituting a Milesian "school." (Plato *Hipp. Mai* 281c offers no exception.)

The anticipatory language of the introductory paragraph (items 5, 6) leads us to expect that the "first philosophers," in addition to furnishing a variety of material first principles, are going to equip them with mechanisms for change. For Thales, Aristotle supplies the mechanism himself (items 20–21e). Why is it not supplied for Anaximenes? Why no mention of the Theophrastean formula of thickening and thinning? He is equally silent on this matter in the case of Heraclitus, but has no hesitation in attaching theories of change to Empedocles and Anaxagoras. Was it because neither Anaximenes nor Heraclitus could furnish satisfactory evidence of the required mechanism? The tendency of the Theophrastean version to improve upon the Aristotelian original has been already noted. Does the ascription of thickening and thinning (or rarefaction) represent such an improvement? Where did Theophrastus get it from? Its initial inspiration lies in that fatal phraseology (fatal, that is, to history) used in items 32 and 33. The assumption behind the use of this kind of language is that all the Milesians were already confronted with the Aristotelian doctrine of the four simple bodies, and that one of them chose air as having priority over water, the choice being governed by a philosophical relationship between the two. There seems to be an implication that the relationship depends on a scale of degrees of some sort within which the four position themselves. What sort of scale was this? For an answer, Theophrastus supplemented the introduction to the *Metaphysics* by resorting to the introduction to Aristotle's *Physics*, (I.2. 184b5ff) which includes a similar though less systematic review of preceding theories. It responds again to a priori categories with which we are familiar:

1 There is necessity that
2 there exist one first principle
3 or several
4 if one, either unmoved
5 as Parmenides and Melissus assert
6 or moving
7 as the physicists ("naturalists") assert
8 some alleging the original first-principle to be air
9 others water.
10 If several
11 (they have to be) finite or non-finite
12 Aristotle follows this with a long polemic against authors of doctrines
      described in items 4 and 5 (184b27–187a12)

13 and then returns to the "physicists" (above item 7) (*Phys*. I. 4)
14 according to whose statements there are two "ways" (*tropoi*)
　　　(sc. of defining first principles).
15 One division, having made the existing and substrate body
　　　(*to on sōma to hupokeimenon*)
16 (to be) one
17 (that is) (one or) the other of the three
18 or (yet) another which is thicker than fire but finer than air,
19 generate the rest (of things) by thickening and rarefaction (*manotēs*)
20 (thus) producing (a) many;
21 these are opposites,
22 but in a more generic sense, excess and deficiency
23 for example Plato speaks of the great and small
24 except that he makes these (into) matter (*hulē*)
25 and the one (into) form (*eidos*)
26 whereas "the others" (all the physicists?)
27 make the one
28 [into] substrate matter
29 and make the opposites
30 [as cause] of differences and forms
31 and others (another division?) [again state]
32 the inherent oppositions
33 to be segregated out of the one
34 as Anaximander says
35 and all who say
36 that one and many exist
37 as Empedocles and Anaxagoras
38 for they too segregate the rest from the mixture (*migma*)

In the dichotomies established between monists and pluralists (items 2, 3) and "finite" versus "non-finite" (item 11) the reader will recognize the source of similar dichotomies in the Theophrastean account, exercising similar control (item 1) over the disposition and interpretation of Presocratic doctrines as these are fitted into appropriate conceptual slots. The application of a third dichotomy, that between unmoved and moving first principle, has the effect of separating the Eleatics (items 5 and 12) from the "physicists" (items 6, 7). The bulk of the passage is devoted to monists (items 8, 9, 15–34) without regard to the dichotomy "finite" versus "non-finite" previously proposed. The account given of them is highly confused. On the one hand they are initially (and unexpectedly) lumped together as proposing either air or water, with no further option (8, 9). But after interruption (items 10–12) they are split into two divisions (item 14), one of which (its members unnamed) is credited with the purely Aristotelian doctrine of material substrate (15), linked, by implication, to another canonical doctrine of the four elements or simple bodies subsumed under the expression "the three" (17). What are these? Presumably air and water (8, 9) and fire (18). The figure "three" replaces a previous two (items 8, 9) The implied presence of the canonical elements is then confirmed by the addition of a fourth (18), which completes the required number. The role of this mysterious fourth will be considered in a moment. Aristotle, perhaps stimulated by its alleged intermediate density between fire and air, then makes the astonishing statement that this whole division of the Presocratics utilized the mechanism of thickening and rarefaction to produce multiplicity. We know this is false for Heraclitean fire, and there is otherwise no evidence to apply it to Thales' water. The allegation occurs in a context which has insisted that these unnamed predecessors anticipated the doctrine of the indeterminate substrate from which the four elements emerge or within which they undergo mutation into each other. Being determined to find an anticipation of this mutation, he supplies it by a Presocratic theory of thickening versus rarefaction. On the evidence of Presocratic *ipsissima verba*, he could have derived this from a strained interpretation of Anaxagoras where, as earlier noted, the terms of such an antithesis are first exploited. He simply extends it into generic Presocratic doctrine. He reveals a further dogmatic motive for doing so. He wants to find historical anticipation for two more items in his own system, namely, the qualitative interaction of contraries within the substrate and the formula whereby generation can be described as the removal of deprivation in the substrate. Accordingly, he proceeds to equate each of these (items 21, 22) with the antithesis he has constructed between thickening and rarefaction (using the connective adjective "these" in item 21 for this purpose).

Theophrastus takes him seriously enough to assume that this theory of thickening and thinning should at least be assigned to a specific philosopher. But to whom? Aristotle has already said (*Metaphysics*, items 32, 33) that Anaximenes chose air as "prior to water and most preferred" (sc. of the four). That was enough for his disciple to draw the conclusion that this air, like the unnamed fourth, was an intermediate between water and fire, passing into both by alternately thickening and thinning. So the doctrine, equipped with a terminology otherwise unsupported before Anaxagoras, becomes firmly embedded as a doctrine of the Milesian school.

So at last we come to Anaximander (item 34). The initial list of early philosophers presented in the introduction to the *Metaphysics* had been addressed explicitly to those who proposed a material first principle. If the list omits an "Anaximander," placed by Theophrastus in a key position after Thales, the safe inference is that Aristotle was unaware that Anaximander had proposed anything of the kind, or occupied any such key position in the history of materialist philosophy. But in this *Physics* preamble, he does introduce the name in a linkage with Empedocles and Anaxagoras (its chronology not otherwise indicated; items 34–38), and, reverting once more to his own doctrine of oppositions (or contraries) inherent in the substrate (item 32), puts such a theory into Anaximander's own mouth, as he had previously put it into the mouths of a prior division of physicists (item 21) which had presumably included Thales and Heraclitus. For good measure he also tacks on the assignment of a doctrine of segregation, as though Anaximander could speak not only with the voice of Aristotle, but with the voice of Anaxagoras. Presumably there was a record of Anaximander having said something which could be interpreted to excuse this extraordinary *tour de force* of interpretation, but what it was is not revealed and possibly we shall never know.

Here, however, is a candidate for inclusion in Theophrastus' textbook of authors of first principles. But what precisely was this first principle? Aristotle here calls it a "one." In Theophrastus (items 26–34) this term is avoided, perhaps because he recognized that it was Eleatic. Aristotle, identifying as historical "the three" elements, had added an unnamed fourth intermediate in density between fire and air (item 18). Modern scholarship has failed to identify this mysterious reference. If it is to be historically justified from the *ipsissima verba* of the Presocratics, it could refer to what they called aithēr (Xenophanes, Empedocles, Anaxagoras). Aristotle would have a strong motive for avoiding the name, since its presence as a "fifth wheel" awkwardly compromises the exclusiveness of his canonical four. However that may be, Theophrastus adopted this "extra" (above, Theophrastus, item 33) to supply an identification for Anaximander's *archē*, and for good measure, in his item 34, added an adaptation of *Physics*, items 32, 33, to supply an alternative explanation.

Theophrastus probably drew further support for this ascription from a second reference by Aristotle to Anaximander, this time in the twelfth book of the *Metaphysics*, when, however, the context is even more glaringly unhistorical. It need here only be briefly summarized:

1 Change, argues Aristotle, is of four kinds (*Metaphys.* XII, 2., 1069b10) involving mutation between contraries;
2 matter is capable of such oppositional shift in either direction.
3 Hence everything is generated from an existing reality, but this reality ["what is"] is a potential, not actualized (sc. until change occurs).
4 This potential [is] the one of Anaxagoras (1069b21)
5 since, adds Aristotle, it is better to call it this, rather than use the expression "all were together,"
6 and also (is) of Empedocles the mixture and (the something) of Anaximander
7 and, as Democritus says, all were together potentially but not actually.
8 This means (*hōste*) they would (all?) have touched on matter.

The pseudo-historical character of these notices is obvious. Items 1–3 establish the analytic, not to say dogmatic, context within which they occur. To reinterpret Anaxagoras (4) he has to edit his language (5), and he appears to do the same for Democritus (item 7) assigning him a combination of the language of Anaxagoras and his own.

Anaximander's name occurs in a pendant genitive (item 6), so located as to encourage the reader to suppose he is mentioning a "mixture," but without actually saying so. More importantly, the context seeks to include him in a category of materialists (item 8) who anticipated Aristotle's theory of matter and of material (that is, qualitative) change (item 2). Once more we cannot tell what it was Anaxaimander may have actually said to encourage such manipulation. But we can point to the contradiction between the suggestion here that he was one of those who "touched on matter" and his omission in the first book of the *Metaphysics* from the list of those who did. This will not prevent the later tradition from suggesting that his first principle was a "mixture" of elements.

Anaximander so far has been supplied by indirection with a fictitious material first principle which has been connected with the terms "one" (*Phys.* I–4 items 33, 34) "mixture," (*Metaphys.* XII, 2; item 6) both otherwise lacking linguistic credentials earlier than Parmenides and Empedocles. Theophrastus has associated it with an unnamed extra element. Authorship for such an element was all the more urgently needed, since this same unnamed is mentioned four more times in Aristotle (*Physics* 189b3, 203a18; *Metaphys.* 988a31, 989a14), though always without reference to Anaximander.

However, this mysterious *archē* has still not acquired a name, an identity of its own. Can Theophrastus find one that may seem plausible? Perhaps yes, if recourse is had to one more passage in Aristotle devoted to pseudo-historical reminiscence.

The fourth chapter of the third book of the *Physics* (202b30) opens as follows:

1 Since the subjects of physics are magnitudes, motion and time
2 and since each of these can be placed under [the dichotomy of] non-finite versus finite
3 it follows that for him whose business is with [the investigation of] nature
4 it is [logically] appropriate to give theoretic attention (*theōrein*)
5 to [the] non-finite (*apeiron*)
6 does it exist
7 and if so what is it?

"Non-finite" appears here in the neuter singular without an article, but in the course of the long analytic argument that follows it soon acquires one. The argument running through to chapter 8, which terminates the book, furnishes the first Greek text we have (so far as I know) which establishes the linguistic credentials of "the non-finite" (or "infinity" or "the unlimited"—and there are other modern variants) as a philosophical abstraction conceptually central to cosmology—the first, that is, if we discount the similar language hitherto attributed to Anaximander. However, it can safely be deduced from the wording of items 3 and 4 that the argument will require Aristotle to discover, if he can, some rudiments of his own conception of the non-finite in his predecessors, and we have now acquired reasons to think that he will discover them willy-nilly. However, his aims in forming such a conception are complicated—one is tempted to say contradictory. Their complication had arisen in certain philosophical discussions of the fourth century which preceded the formation of his own system. It seems fairly clear from the developing terms of his argument that the problem of the term "non-finite" was set for him by Plato and by arguments in the Academy. The *Philebus* had proposed a dichotomy between finite limit and non-finite (*peras* versus *apeiron*) and either Plato or Platonists added a corresponding dichotomy between a "one" and an "indeterminate dyad." (Aristotle, *Metaphys*. XIII, 1081a22). In addition, certain Pythagoreans" (a school whom I here would assign not to the sixth century but the fourth, and possibly to a faction within the Academy) had proposed to arrange the substance of the universe under a series of contraries, of which "finite" limit versus "non-finite" was the prime instance (*Metaphys*.. I, 986a23) and had also spoken of (the) non-finite, as existing "outside heaven" (*Phys*. III, 203a8)—a view he also ascribes to the physicists (206b24)—and as being drawn into the cosmos and made finite (that is, given Platonic form through limit) (*Metaphys*. XIV, 1091a 17–19). Inherent in these formulas were two complementary but distinct meanings for the term *apeiros*. Did it refer to the indeterminacy of infinitely divisible matter or the indeterminacy of infinitely extendable matter, that is, beyond the visible heaven? Aristotle's formal position, reached at the end of chapter seven (*Phys*. 203a13), is that the first is correct; but in the present instance he tries to have it both ways, by arguing that a doctrine of a non-finite existing external to the heavens has relevance to his own cosmology.

For the argument continues (*Phys*. III, 4. 203a1ff.):

8 There is evidence that
9 the theoretic investigation of it is germane to the science (sc. of physics)
10 namely [the fact that] all those held (*dokountes*) to have engaged reputably in philosophy of this kind
11 have all produced discourse concerning the non-finite (*to apeiron*)
12 and all posit it as some sort of first-principle of existing [things].
13 The Pythagoreans and Plato posit the non-finite as existing *per se* as a substance (*ousia*)
14 except that the Pythagoreans [assign] the non-finite among the visibles

15 and to exist [as] what is outside the heaven
16 whereas Plato [asserts] there is no [material] body existing outside
17 not even the forms
18 because they are not anywhere (sc. in space).
19 Aristotle then adds a brief disquisition on the role of the non-finite
          in Platonic and Pythagorean number theory, and resumes
20 The entire school [dealing] with nature on the other hand (203a17)
21 always subsumes some other nature under the non-finite (sc. make
          non-finite a predicate of some other subject)
22 [namely one] of the stated elements
23 for example water or air or that between them
24a one division [within this school] makes the elements finite
24b none of its members makes [them] non-finite.
25a There is also a division which makes the elements non-finite
25b for example, Anaxagoras and Democritus.
26 Aristotle here adds a short disquisition on both these philosophers
          which seems to lack historical foundation.
          He then continues (203bff.):
27 The above makes it clear
28 that a theoretic investigation (sc. of the non-finite)
29 [is or was] an appropriate one for physicists.
30 It is logical (*eulogōs*) for them all to posit it as a first-principle
31 it cannot exist (sc. as a philosophic term) for no purpose
32 nor can any power other than first principle pertain to it
33a for everything is either a first principle or
33b [derives] from a first principle
33c and [there is] no first principle of (behind) the non-finite.
33d (if there were) "it" (or "there") would be a finite limit of it
34 again (the non-finite) is unbegotten and indestructible
35 as being a kind of first-principle
36a for that which has become must necessarily find an end
36b and [correspondingly] every [process of] destruction [must]
          also have a conclusion
37 therefore, following (the line of) our argument
38 there is no (further) first principle of this first principle
39 on the contrary, this first principle is held to be the first-principle
          of the "others" (sc. of principles? or things?)
40 and to "contain" all things
41 and steer all things
42 as say all who do not make other causes alongside of the non-finite
43 for example mind or love
44 moreover this [appears] to be "the god-like"
45 for [it is] immortal and imperishable
46 as says Anaximander and most of the physiologists.

The first thing to observe of this passage is that it accords "the non-finite" an elevated character and status flatly inconsistent with that reduced definition of the term finally reached in the same third book of the *Physics*, in chapter seven (206b32ff.): the non-finite exists on the basis of subdivision (*diaeresis*) but not extension (*prosthesis*); it is contained (*periechetai*) as (being) matter (*hulē*), but (only) form (*eidos*) can contain; it is causal (*aition*) in the sense that matter is, *per se*, a sensible continuous substrate (208a1–5). For this meaning of the term he then claims universal precedent: "all the others utilize it as matter." The reference is sweeping and is surely meant to include not only Platonists but Presocratics.

In the present passage, on the other hand, "the non-finite" is presented as a cosmic controlling power, the first principle of all other principles (items 32–39) and no objections are offered to counter this view. A motive for such indulgence is supplied when we consider its relationship to Aristotle's cosmic theology. Clues lie in two terms: "contain" (*periechein*, item 40) and "the divine" (*to theion*, item 44). The first is Presocratic (Diogenes and Anaxagoras); the second is his own. His own geocentric cosmology, as adumbrated at the close of the treatise (*Physics*, VIII, 267b1ff.) calls for an unmoved mover situated not in the center (where motion is slowest) but at the circumference where it is fastest; "there therefore is the mover," actuating a series of inner continuous circular motions.

In the conclusion of the twelfth book of his *Metaphysics* (the famous *Metaphysics Lambda*) this system is elaborated. The prime mover, now a "first principle" and a "substance," actuates responsive circular and perfect motion in a unique eternal heaven, one which is transmitted successively to a series of eternal celestial bodies revolving within and below it. The prime mover now becomes a "living creature" (*zōion*) which is also "eternal" (*aidion*), and is equivalent to "mind" (*nous*) and given the title "god-like" (*theion*) and finally called "[a] god" (*theos*).

The terms of this complex physical-theological formula had been prepared for him in Presocratic speculations, but they are post-Milesian and late-Eleatic. Melissus had asserted of "what is" (which Aristotle could style substance, *ousia*) that in addition to being "non-finite as to magnitude," it is "eternal" (*aidios*). Anaxagoras (to whom Aristotle's theology owes a debt rarely acknowledged) offered the doctrine of an autonomous intelligence mixed with nothing else, but existing apparently in a "non-finite container," itself being "non-finite," and controlling cosmic revolution. Diogenes, asserting that his cosmic air was "an eternal and immortal body," which "contains the whole cosmos," added a notable analogy, "just as our own psyche being air combines-and-controls us." (That tradition which by an understandable confusion assigned this to Anaximenes has fortunately been corrected by recent scholarship.) Finally, Democritean atomism more radically disrupted the single cosmos altogether, placing other non-finite worlds outside it.

In combination, these authorities (or "witnesses" as Aristotle sometimes likes to think of them) offer many anticipations of the terminology required:

an eternal substance which is also an eternal mind controlling the circular motion of a "container" which is identifiable with the heaven, and which also exercises control in the likeness of a psyche controlling a person; that is, it resembles Aristotle's living creature.

But in the language of his predecessors, the substance is non-finite, the container is non-finite, the mind is non-finite. Aristotle could have chosen to repudiate the linkage. But he cannot easily do this, for the non-finite is to be incorporated into his own cosmology, although in the sense of "matter." (Was he aware that both Melissus and Anaxagoras may have anticipated him in this?) He has no choice in this part of his *Physics* but to identify "the non-finite" (his own creation) as itself a prime principle, a "substance," loosely analogous (in this context only) to his own prime mover.

But all these precedents were materialistic, or at least non-theological. The eternal air of Diogenes was still air, and for Anaxagoras even the sun was just a red-hot stone. Further precedent is needed for Aristotle's "god-like." He searches backwards toward Parmenides and Heraclitus for the verb "steer," with its associations of personal control, and remembers that Parmenides spoke of a divinity (daimōn) "steering all" (B12) and Heraclitus of an intelligence (*gnōmē*) "steering all through all" (B41). Then, recalling Diogenes's formula "immortal and eternal body," he adds two adjectives "immortal and imperishable (item 45), the latter a philosophical term (*anōlethron*) probably coined by Parmenides. The two are left syntactically pendant, linked by association only to the previously mentioned "non-finite" (item 42) but more properly to "first principle" (items 39, 40). Finally, reaching back to the Milesians, he credits the use of the two adjectives to Anaximander (item 46). On independent evidence, it is possible that Anaximander used the word "ageless" (*agērōs*), which, like immortal (which he may also have used), has epic authority. But to what did it apply? We know that the verb "steer" as actually employed had no connection with "the non-finite," though Aristotle attempts to suggest it had (item 42). It seems improbable that Anaximander's "ageless" had any such connection either. But the citation of the two adjectives has given him the support needed for a precedent for his "god." "And this (appears) to be the god-like" (item 44). (The Greek to theion is referable to his own theology, "my god-like," not to the language of the Presocratics.) He adds for good measure, and improperly, that steering was a function of the non-finite adopted by all Presocratics except Anaxagoras and Empedocles (items 42, 43). The thread of Aristotle's argument when unravelled, just as it reveals no support for the notion that there was a Milesian "non-finite" which had powers analogous to those of Aristotle's god, also fails to support the notion that Anaximander ever used the conception at all as a first principle of anything.

Space forbids further analysis of the pseudo-historical methodology of this passage, except for one central observation. Aristotle offers his own evidence against himself; that is, against his linkage (if it is a conscious one) between Anaximander and a doctrine of the non-finite as a first principle. For in item 21 he has asserted explicitly that all physicists without exception restricted their use of *apeiros* to the attributive function. Used philosophically, it was applied as an adjective to describe something else. Usage already tested in the Eleatics and Anaxagoras has confirmed this, and if Aristotle is thinking of them when he says this (he often uses the word "all" loosely), it may mean that Anaximander never used the word at all.

For Theophrastus, however, still searching for a "name" for (a) the mysterious supposedly "intermediate element," (b) the "mixture" or "one" ascribed elsewhere by Aristotle to Anaximander, this passage of the *Physics* was enough. It must have been "the non-finite," and seizing on the inference that "immortal" and "imperishable" were adjectives used by Anaximander, and were meant to refer back to "the non-finite," he identified the latter as Anaximander's "first principle." An Aristotelian conception and vocabulary was transferred backwards in his history to the Milesians and, like the "thickening and thinning," it has remained embedded there ever since.

To trace the labyrinthine record of the Milesian school through to its end is to realize that such a "school" as portrayed since antiquity never existed. It is not a matter of a mistaken word here or there. A whole elaborate structure of interlocking conceptions has collapsed—a structure which has enjoyed a life of its own for so long in the history of European philosophy. One recalls the strange case of Monsieur Valdemar, as narrated in the story by Edgar Allan Poe. A corpse has been kept in a state of suspended animation by the mesmeric spell of an antique and revered tradition. Remove the spell and the body of evidence disintegrates.

Are these names then to be removed from the history of thought? Surely not; but their role in it must have been other than the one ascribed to them. If the language in which they are reported is not theirs, what was their language? An initial clue surely lies in the language used by their immediate successors, who were poets, or, like Heraclitus, spoke the language of poetry. If Milesians were still so close to orality, still composing their thought for listening audiences, is it likely that they were more sophisticated than their successors? Is it likely that they were capable of composing the kind of prose suitable for the manufacture of such abstract conceptions and mechanisms as are attributed to them?

It is true that their fellow Milesian, Hecataeus, who followed closely upon them, composed an Hellenic genealogy and an Hellenic geography in Ionic prose—the first Greek prose we know of. The same kind of prose has been credited to Anaximander's "book," as constituting a pioneer geographical treatise, the first of its kind. It is possible that Anaximander, if he constructed a first geometric world map, attached a prose commentary to it. Indeed, judging from the remains of Zeno and Melissus, the impulse to compose prosaic dialectic may have arisen from the need to supply written explanations of geometric figures which by definition had to be seen and not just heard. In any case, Hecataeus uses a narrative format in expounding his subjects. The exposition of ideas, which involved a break with narrative, being mentally a more difficult undertaking, tempted its first expositors to avoid the extra effort of breaking with the easy rhythmic continuities of verse.

That verse (and epic verse at that) may have been the Milesian medium is supported by some small scraps of evidence. Thales, according to a single precious notice (Theoph. item 13) left behind him in writing nothing except "a Nautical Astronomy in verse." Anaximander (if the text is corrected) used "more poetic language" than the terms used in Theophrastus' report of his doctrine would indicate. Even in what he does report, the phrase "and vengeance to each other" (Theoph. item 31) composes the first half of an epic hexameter, though this may be fortuitous. "Vengeance," "immortal," and "ageless," three words among others credited to him, all have a Homeric flavor. If, as reported, he compared the earth to a stone pillar, the original Ionic Greek (Diels, *Dox. Gr.* p. 219) could have been contained in epic phraseology (for example, *kioni toi litheēi*). The doublets *apeirōn, apeiresios,* meaning "boundless," if he employed them, are authentically epic.

These are scraps of hints, no more. The overriding reason for supposing an epic format for Milesian compositions lie in the further presumption that they enjoyed a close relationship with Homer and Hesiod. *Iliad, Odyssey, Theogony,* and *Works and Days,* whatever the original conditions of their composition, had in the sixth century become transcribed as the founding documents of Greek culture—a culture still mainly oral. The Milesians could read them and reflect on them and begin to improve on them. It is surely a safe deduction that Thales' versified *Nautical Astronomy* was a revised geometer's version of Hesiod's star map as narrated in the *Works and Days.* Philosophy proper arose as a commentary upon and correction of the cosmic imagery of Homer and the cosmic architecture of Hesiod's *Theogony.*

These are not mere presumptions. Aristotle, however reluctantly, bears testimony to the truth himself, when he allows himself to say that Milesian speculation had an ancestry in the "Theologians" and quotes both Homer and Hesiod in support (*Metaphys.* I, items 22–27, 63). Admission of Hesiod's priority in cosmology is repeated in *Physics* IV 208b30; *Metaphys.* 1,989a10; III, 1000a9. Nor does he hesitate to suggest or at least imply that the first principles of the physicists replaced the Hesiodic Chaos and Night and Earth.

But he must grant the connection grudingly, because it conflicts with his non-historical assumption, made a priori, that "architectonic" or "first philosophy" (*Metaphys.* I, 1; VI, 1; *al.*) began with a search for the first of his four causes, the material one. This requires that the connection between the epic-oral cosmologies and the Milesian ones be fractured, with the further result that the motives for metaphysical speculation be represented as a break with the past (*Metaphys.* 1.981b23,*al.*). One concludes that the style of Milesian composition would have resembled that of Xenophanes, Parmenides, and Empedocles, but perhaps with even closer reference to the epic models. Can any simulacrum of it be imagined? This is not the place to attempt a reconstruction of the Milesian contribution to Greek thought. To clothe the ghost with some vestige of flesh and blood, however one may be permitted the indulgence of a few imaginary hexameters after the style of the post-Milesians. Doggerel stuff, no doubt of that, but maybe offering an echo, however contrived, of what their original compositions may have sounded like:

A. (concerning the nature of the all)

ek gar apeironos aiōnos[1] phusis estin hapantōn[2]
athanatos[3] te menei kai agerōs[4] ēmata panta
hen[5] d'ar' aei toi tauta pelei kai pampan apeiron[6]
panth' hos' horōmen anō[7] xunechei[8] t'ara dapsilos aithēr[9]
gignomen' ex archēs[10] kai phtheiromen'[11] aien apeirou[12]
allēloisi chronōi tinota dikēn en agerōi[13]

for from a life without-end does the nature of all things exist
and immortal it remains and ageless all its days
[as] one therefore always do these things exist, even altogether boundless—
all that we see above and that the shining aether contains
becoming and destructing ever from boundless beginning,
to each other in circle of seasons paying justice in retribution

B. (concerning the earth):

kionos hēde menei litheēs[14] evalinkios onkōi[15]
messothen isopalēs pantēi[16]

Here it remains like to the mass of a stone pillar
from the center evenly balanced in all directions

Eric A. Havelock

Yale University

NOTES

1. Diels-Kranz, *Vorsok.* I, p. 83, line 31.
2. Emped. B8,1.
3. Aristotle, *Physics* III, item 45.
4. Diels-Kranz, *Vorsok.* I, p. 84, line 2.
5. Aristotle, *Physics*, 1. 4. items 33, 34.
6. Emped. B. 28, 1.
7. Xenophanes, B28, and 29.
8. Aristotle, *Physics*, III.4, item 40.
9. Emped. B. 39, 1.
10. Hesiod, *Theog.* 45, 115.
11. Theophrastus, item 30.
12. Theophrastus, item 26.
13. Theophrastus, item 31.
14. Diels, *Doxog. Graeci*, p. 219.
15. Parmenides, B8, 43.
16. Parmenides, B8, 44, and Diels-Kranz, I, p. 84, lines 6–8.

ORALITY AND SEQUENCE

Eric Havelock has done more than anyone to reveal the persistence of oral ways of thought and composition into the era of written Greek literature. Few of the challenges presented by early Greek poetry in particular—and one thinks not only of Homer and Hesiod but also of early lyric, of Pindar, even of tragedy—can be faced without a searching consideration of their oral dimension. The Presocratics present different kinds of problems, but I welcome Professor Havelock's renewed interest in them, for even the alternation between poetry and prose as favored means of exposition focuses attention on the choice of style and language as intimately connected with the mode and limitations of the thinking they express.

Much of the quality of life and thought in the eighth century B.C. must remain speculative, however hard we try to press the evidence, and differences in individual assessments are inevitable. There are a few special topics over which I would tend to adopt a slightly different position from that urged in these pages by Havelock: over the persistent after-effects of Mycenaean social and religious organization, for instance, or the reasons for seeing the early eighth century B.C. as one important period for the development of the alphabet (see p. 7 of Havelock's "The Linguistic Task of the Presocratics"); or over that fashionable conundrum the causes and effects of the early *polis* (p. 7); or over the functions of a "storage language," particularly in its most obvious poetical forms, as distinct from unformalized instruction within the family circle (p. 13). What I should like to do now, rather than discussing such points as these, is to present a slightly different version—complementary to Havelock's in certain respects—of the factors that might have drawn thinkers and composers from Hesiod on away from a mythical approach to the world and toward a rational one—old Cornford country, this, in which I have found myself wandering before in relation both to myths themselves and to the possible sources of Presocratic thought.

First, then, a few words about differences between the oral and the literate approaches themselves. Havelock is eloquent on rules of composition that are acoustic not visual (p. 8 *fin.*), and alludes more than once to an "echo principle" that he describes most fully in his chapter on "The Alphabetization of Homer" in *Communication Arts in the Ancient World*;[1] a principle which is opposed to the "visual patterning of paragraphs and themes" in literate composition (p. 8, "Linguistic Task"). For my part I am not so sure that such echoes mostly work in so pervasive and so determinative a manner. Havelock is surely right that there is a significant relation between the priest on the seashore complaining to Apollo early in *Iliad*, book 1, and Achilles on the seashore complaining to his mother the sea-goddess Thetis later in that same book (see "Alphabetization," p. 14); but the relation may be a conceptual as much as a verbal one. For although there is a certain formular overlap between the two scenes, as Havelock acutely observes, it is not as great as it could be according to regular Homeric style and conventions—the thematic parallelism itself is more strongly marked. To take a further example of his, it seems doubtful whether the famous dual forms in the apparently three-man embassy to Achilles in *Iliad*, book 9, are to be explained merely as an "echo" of the two heralds (and their associated dual forms) who fetch Briseis at *Iliad* 1, 320–47. Emissaries to Achilles are involved in both cases, to be sure, but once again I see that as a thematic redevelopment, at most, rather than as a primarily aural response on the singer's part. Themes may or may not be restated in similar words; they tend to be so, in an oral poem; but the oral composer's use of the narrative idea, the motif or theme, is often as important as his use or reuse of "echoed" language. There is, moreover, a question of how far formular phraseology is repeated in accordance with any kind of aural rule, tendency, or reaction, and how far it depends on memory in a more intellectual phase, of the kind that might be equally involved in literate composition also; but that is a problem that is easier to raise than to resolve.

In short, the old chimera of an "oral poetics" begins to raise its oddly articulated head, demanding to be told once again what sort of rules, principles and discriminations it must try to embody. Does the oral poet, for instance (as distinct from the oral reciter of prose tales), work differently from the literate poet primarily because he is to some degree controlled by, or is ever ready to exploit, the poetical phrases and sequences that echo in his head? But Pindar, who is to a large degree, at least, a literate composer, can have undergone no less, and even Sophocles (one suspects) was susceptible to that kind of influence; so indeed, to a lesser degree, were most other ancient poets, and so too are many modern ones, lyricists in particular. Turning to the typical marks of literate composition, on the other hand, Havelock writes of a "visual patterning of paragraphs and themes" ("Linguistic Task," p. 8) that does not affect the oral poet. But that, too, is far from self-evident. Prose-writing, presumably, is the primary medium envisaged here; but is it too simple-minded an objection that *paragraphoi* were inserted in (or applied to) most ancient texts long after the act of composition, not for visual reasons so much as for logical and organizational ones, to mark the new directions of argument or narrative? A modern writer may "put in" a paragraph for primarily visual reasons, even where there is no strong interruption in argument, but that is because he knows that the printed page will otherwise look too dense; that is an entirely different matter. As for themes, they are perhaps the crucial factor; for themes are not distinguished visually in a written text any more than in an oral performance, but intellectually (helped in the latter case by emphasis, intonation, even gesture)—except of course where theme coincides with paragraph, which is what Havelock must have in mind. But in the first instance their identity and limits are revealed by their own inherent meaning and coherence, and that is so as much for oral composition as for literate, despite the possible refinements I have just mentioned. The distinction between these two modes of composition cannot be satisfactorily reduced to or expressed in terms of physical differences between the audible and the visible; it is the different ways of deploying themes on the one hand, and language on the other, that are relevant here—for example, exact repetition is often necessary for the oral/aural singer/audience, but never so for the writer or reader; the same with foreshadowing and reminiscence; variation, on the other hand, can be a stylistic requirement in a written work but is almost never so, or only in a very limited degree, in oral literature.

That being so, does the transition from oral/aural to literate/visual have quite the effect on the development of new ways of *thought* that Havelock suggests? Or is it primarily some other change, one that accompanied the aural/visual transition and perhaps even conditioned it? I believe that that is so, and that the change was very much what Havelock has in mind in his heading for section III, "From Story to Statement." His brilliant characterization on pp. 13–14 of Hesiod's *Theogony*, and of the uneasy combination there of "narrative" and "documentation," brings out much that is important in the transition from *muthos* to *logos*, from an oblique and allegorical way of looking at things to a direct and analytical way. In itself that polarization is too extreme and can be misleading, especially since in ancient Greece, at least, there was an intermediate stage of some duration and great significance. I have inveighed elsewhere against the facile concept of "mythopoeic thought," a panacea that others, but not Havelock, are tempted to introduce here; what can be rescued from the idea is well presented by Walter Burkert in his Sather Lectures.[2] It might seem safer and more practical to start from the idea of the traditional society. Admittedly some of the common applications of that idea, too, have been castigated, this time by Ruth Finnegan.[3] It is true that romantic overtones can creep in, and that certain societies classed as traditional (or "primitive") are incompletely so; yet the fact remains that many tribal societies *were* wholly traditional, in the sense that they were not substantially changing, that the present was seen to be completely rooted in the past, and that ancient traditions were to be preserved at all costs, through religion, myths and rituals as well as in other ways. Folk-memory and traditional tales (folktales and myths) were usually the most important means of maintaining as well as explaining that connection between past and present.

On p. 14 ("Linguistic Task") Havelock well writes that the *Theogony* "is still a narrative of events, of 'beginnings,' that is, 'births.' . . . From the standpoint of a sophisticated philosophical language . . . what was lacking was a set of commonplace but abstract terms which by their interrelations could describe the physical world conceptually; terms such as space, void, matter, body, element, motion . . . the conceptual task also required the elimination of verbs of doing and acting and happening . . . in favor of a syntax which states permanent relationships between conceptual terms systematically." That could hardly be better stated, but I want to add an important gloss on the process of "elimination"; for only when the inbuilt sequentiality of myths has been replaced, as what matters in viewing the world in a general way, by the ability to express things in their own terms, can the formation of abstract descriptions and concepts pertinent to "permanent relationships" proceed very far. It is not because the *Theogony* has something of the "manner of an acoustic composition" (p. 14, "Linguistic Task"), but because, being mythical (that is, sequentially narrative), it reduces the world to a genealogy, that it is philosophically rather sterile. Myths are usually oral or "acoustic," indeed, but it is their diachronic aspect itself rather than the secondary consequences of oral technique that make them so limited with respect to the development of a philosophical language or, in broader terms, a philosophical world-view.

The gradual replacement of oral tales as the regular mode of interpreting society to itself and relating it to the world outside is likely to have had multiple effects on the idea of that world, quite apart from the removal of the imagination-block imposed by the strict operation of the traditional society. For oral tales, whether they be classed as myths or as folktales, impose their own limitations on any view of cosmic and social organization. Being narrative, they are also sequential; it is events, not permanent relationships, that are their currency (even though relationships in a crude sense are implicit in the limited number of "functions" which Vladimir Propp saw operating in certain classes of folktale). That means that, when tales concern themselves with the nature of the outside world, they do so in personal and genealogical terms of the kind used by Hesiod and his sources in the *Theogony*. That is not only because of the inclination of tales (and their tellers) to animate, to anthropomorphize (which has its own special reasons), but also because the development of action requires the complexities of seasonal changes (say) to be represented in diachronic not synchronic terms, as history rather than as philosophy or science. There may be a quasi-philosophical motive too, insofar as aetiological and charter-type myths elicit causes and sanctions from mythical history; but that is a dead end with respect to conceptual progress. The language of the *Theogony* is, typically, the language of sequence; aorist rather than present tenses predominate; even in the prologue there is no sense of the world *now*, and the Muses there are preoccupied with how it came to be as it is, in a state which hearers and readers are left to judge for themselves. The emergence of Zeus as supreme ruler is what counts; how he rules, and exactly what he rules, are passed over, taken for granted—or at best left to the probably later poem *Works and Days* to explore. Yet even that poem, based as it is on the concept of Zeus ruling the world through Dike, justice in a sense (and on that additional concept of a "good" strife existing alongside the bad one which causes the lapses on which Dike and her agents report), presents the permanent working of the world, very awkwardly, in a series of story-like vignettes: not only the actual myth of Prometheus, the theft of fire and Pandora or the quasi-myth of the five races, but also the parables of the just and unjust cities (225–47) and the ravishing of Dike herself (217–24). Thus even when Hesiod is trying to set out the conditions of the present world, he is constantly driven back on personification and myth—on personification indeed *because of* the need for myth, not just because he is taking refuge with tradition but rather because he simply does not know how to describe (quite apart from vocabulary matters) a dynamic complex without interrelating its components in a historical manner.

The longstanding habit of myth-telling, protected by society itself and resistant to the onslaughts even of a Plato, is an important factor here, although there are obviously other elements in the complex and fascinating intermediate stages toward the achievement of a groundwork for philosophy, whose limits and possibilities I have barely indicated. What I have tried to do is to show that the development of a non-sequential *language* is only part of the problem. Yet one point has to be made in the defense of myths, especially as we consider the transition to the Presocratic stage; and that is that the tales and genealogies do lead in the end to a fixed state, even if that state is not analyzed. There is an element of interrelationship even between the myths, parables, and fables of *Works and Days*; above all sits Zeus in glory with Dike at his right hand—if only we could keep him there, without the petty interferences and gallivanting and rushing to and fro, from Olympus to Ida to the Aithiopes, that characterize his rule over the world in the *Iliad* at least, and which Hesiod has really done little to dispel!

It was against this background of confusion that the Presocratics turned their attention to the world at large, still dominated in certain ways by the traditional viewpoints, even as modified by Hesiod and Homer, but struggling to reach out to something more permanent, less anthropomorphic and frenetic. Havelock sees Heraclitus as a key figure in the development of new means of discourse, and I agree, though with a slightly different emphasis. I would also be inclined to bring Anaximander into the argument, despite the tiny harvest of *ipsissima verba*—frag. 1 alone, and there are of course doubts even about the extent of that. But in the opposition between the effects of injustice and the restitution of regularity according to the "ordinance of Time" we can perhaps see the beginnings of the modified opposition between permanence and change that was to preoccupy Heraclitus. That was firmly stated in the opening of his treatise ("This *logos* always exists . . . all things come-to-be according to this *logos*": τοῦ δε λόγου τοῦδ᾽ ἐόντος ἀεὶ . . .γινομένων γὰρ πάντων κατὰ τὸν λόγον τόνδε . . . , frag. 1, where λόγος implies an objective rule, among other things; for even if it referred to Heraclitus' own "word" it would amount to a statement of such a rule.

The maintenance of permanence through change, of unity in plurality, lies at the center of Heraclitus' vision of the world, and is exceedingly difficult to express even apart from exigencies of vocabulary and language. In his surviving statements he ranges from particular symbolic instances (frag. 60, "road up and road down is *one and the same*"; frag. 12, "upon those who step into *the same* rivers *different and different* waters flow") to general statements about large-scale physical change (frag. 31, "the *turnings* of fire: first sea . . . and [earth] is dispersed as sea and measured into *the same* proportion as existed before it became earth"). The difficulties of defining such a relationship between same and different are most clearly shown in frag. 88: "as the same thing there exists in us living and dead, the waking and the sleeping, young and old; for these things having changed round are those, and those having changing round are these"—τάδε γὰρ μεταπεσόντα ἐκεῖνά ἐστι κἀκεῖνα μεταπεσόντα ταῦτα. That these are those is due to their (successive) changes into each other; the mere juxtaposition of the language of physical change (μεταπεσόντα) and that of permanent existence (ταυτό τ᾽ ἔνι) leaves too much unexpressed—even, in this case, the Heraclitean agency of λόγος or μέτρον itself. More than difficulties of language are involved, however—there is insufficient precision in categorization, for example, as is shown by the different kinds of succession entailed by young-old-young and waking-sleeping-waking.

I have already suggested (in *The Nature of Greek Myths*, pp. 298–300) that Heraclitus at least, despite his attacks on Homer and Hesiod in particular, may not have been so much interested in rejecting the whole of the mythical and religious world-view (inadequate as that might have been) as in shifting the emphasis from one aspect of it, the diachronic succession-myth approach that dominates the *Theogony*, to another, the succeeding stage of

Zeus' stable rule assisted by Dike, and described, fleetingly to be sure and with much injection of mythical paradigm, in *Works and Days*. That still seems to me to be a fruitful way of looking at things, and to be supported to some degree by Heraclitus's interest in Dike even in the extant fragments. In 28 and 94 she is very much the Hesiodic figure, with the Erinyes (also Homeric) as her agents in the latter. In 23 she is set into an opposing relationship with *injustice*, without which her name would not be known. In 80 she is actually equated with *eris*, strife; that is, with the tension that under the name of Polemos, War, is universal (80) and father and king of all (53). The "wise thing" that according to 32 is both unwilling and willing to be called by the name of Zeus implicitly rejects the Zeus of *Theogony* and accepts the Dike-partner of *Works and Days*. Clearly the argument can be developed further; but what I want to stress here is that Heraclitus seems to be developing the παλίντονος ἁρμονίη of 51, the "back-stretched connexion" between succession and simultaneity, not by wholly rejecting the historical and genealogical language of myths, but by seeing in it the same elements of unity-in-diversity that he detects in the world as a whole. That attitude, containing as it does a brilliant reinterpretation, rather than a total dismissal, of tradition, is promising in itself, perhaps, and especially congenial to a modern reader; but it had to be shattered by Parmenides before the painstaking, prosaic, and almost gruesome construction of a proper vocabulary for physics (even) could begin.

   To return, finally, to orality itself: the Greeks were peculiar if not unique in maintaining orality far beyond the ordinary limits of the "traditional society." There may have been traditional elements in Mycenaean culture, although with its elaborate socio-economic structure, its documentary system, its comparatively rapid development and collapse, it was far from traditional overall. With the end of the Bronze Age and the fall of the Mycenaean "empire" came the obsolescence of Linear B writing, and such tradition as there was maintained itself by purely oral means. The reduced and depopulated post-Mycenaean world retained something, no doubt, from the past, notably in certain religious practices and the myths themselves; perhaps the scattered and disorganized rural groups inherited the traditionalism of peasant preoccupations, at least; but change, political, economic, and architectural, was in the air. These were the people of the tenth, ninth, and even the early eighth centuries, and they were apparently still wholly non-literate. The social and political foundations of historical Greece were laid down at this time, and yet similtaneously the oral epic tradition was under imposing development and the mythical detritus of the Mycenaean era was being licked into shape—a metaphor which may be mixed but which has the advantage of stressing the similarity to British schoolboys who used to be so licked; that is, to be disciplined, organized, and imaginatively much diminished in the process. In one way or another Greece retained its contacts with Egypt, the Levant, and the Near East, all of them literate regions with developed if peculiar economies and religious systems. Perhaps it was precisely their innocence of writing during these centuries, at the same time as they were digesting the relics of Mycenaean sophistication and observing the structures of other cultures, that set the Greeks going— that enabled them to maintain the tradition of earlier myths and tales and yet subject them to new styles of analysis and organization that were highly untraditional in themselves. For that is what Hesiod did, and what in a rather different way some of the earlier Presocratics continued to do.

G. S. Kirk

Trinity College, Cambridge University

NOTES

1. Edited by Eric A. Havelock and Jackson B. Hershbell (New York: Hastings House, 1978), p. 14f.
2. *Structure and History in Greek Mythology and Ritual*, ch. 1 (Berkeley and Los Angeles: University of California Press, 1980).
3. In *Oral Poetry: Its Nature, Significance and Social Context* (Cambridge: Cambridge University Press, 1977), esp. pp. 46–51.

APHORISM AND ARGUMENT

I

Aphorisms are memorable. When books are rare, when they come in rolls, when they lack page-numbers and indexes, when they are written for an audience rather than for a readership, authors have all the more reason to cultivate a memorable style. Versifiers have an advantage over the writers of prose; for the rhythms of verse lodge in the memory more readily than the rhythms of prose. Even so, in poetry as well as in prose the neat apothegm, the well-turned maxim, and the sententious gnome will serve as useful *aide-mémoire*.

And aphorisms are striking. They catch the attention and capture the mind: an author uncertain of his audience and eager to be heard will advisedly indulge in a little aphorizing.

All that applies to philosophy no less than to other literary trades. The earliest Greek philosophers had a variety of good reasons for being gnomic.[1] Indeed, they had better reasons than most of their contemporary men of letters. Herodotus no doubt wished his histories to be remembered; but it was his narrative, not the particular language in which it was expressed, that mattered. In philosophy, content and language are not so easily severed; or rather, the particular words a philosopher chooses, and the particular order he chooses for them, are often essential to the content of what he is saying in a way in which the words and syntax of an historian are not.

On the other hand, philosophy is nothing without argument: a philosopher who avoids argument is like a cook who omits the meat; and un-argued philosophizing is as insipid and unnourishing as a nut cutlet. Arguments characteristically require complex syntax: *if* is the philosopher's most important word, and his discourse will be crammed with particles and other sentential connectives—with *but* and *and*, *either* and *or*, *so* and *because*, *for* and *therefore*.

Aphorism and argument are uneasy fellows: the particles and connectives which are the linguistic marks of argument do not satisfy the brisker requirements of an aphoristic style. Gnomic philosophy may not involve a *contradictio in adjecto*; but it surely must be a *rara avis*.

Those general reflections may idly lead the mind to pose a pompous question: Must there not have been an inner tension in the souls of the

Presocratic philosophers? The external constraints on their writing—in particular, the need for literal memorability—must have urged them toward a crisp and apothegmatic style, the more so if they determined to write in prose. The intrinsic demands of the subject—in particular, their professional commitment to argument and to reasoning—must have inclined them to long periods and a style full of particles and connectives.

II

Γνώμη and ἀφορισμός are Greek terms. Aristotle discusses the place and purpose of "gnomology"; and he offers a description of the nature of a gnome: "A gnome is a statement—not about particulars (as saying what sort of a man Iphicrates is) but universal, and not about anything whatever (for example, that straight is contrary to curved) but about the things with which actions are concerned and which are to be chosen or avoided with regard to acting. Thus, since enthymemes are usually deductions about things of that sort, the conclusions and the principles of enthymemes, with the deduction removed, are gnomes. For example, 'No sensible man should ever have his children taught to be excessively clever.' That is a gnome; but if the cause and the reason why are added, the whole thing is an enthymeme" (*Rhet.* B 21, 1394a21–31).[2]

Aristotle's gnomes are a species of aphorism, not the genus itself: gnomes are practical maxims—and though the requirement that gnomes be connected with action does not impose a very severe restriction on their range, still it is plain that not every philosophical apothegm will count as a gnome. Ἀφορισμός is a wider notion than γνώμη. Galen, for example, defines "the aphoristic form of instruction" as that which "marks out in a very few words all the special features of the subject" (*in Hipp. Aph.* XVII B, 351–52 K). Galen stresses brevity, which Aristotle does not explicitly mention but surely takes for granted; Aristotle stresses that gnomes carry no reasons or explanations with them (add reasons to a gnome and you change its nature, turning it into an argument); and although Galen does not explicitly make the point, it is a natural corollary of his requirement of brevity.

Aristotle thinks of gnomes in a rhetorical context, and he sees them as devices for winning over an audience (in particular, an uncultivated audience: *Rhet.* 1395bl); maxims are occasional embellishments to a discourse; a decent discourse is not a sequence of maxims. Galen has something different in mind: in the "aphoristic form of instruction," pithy maxims are not rhetorical adornments superadded to a technical exposition; rather, the exposition is itself constituted by a string of maxims.[3]

For Galen is commenting on one of the most celebrated of early medical treatises, Hippocrates' *Aphorisms*. That work, a substantial part of which is generally agreed to go back to Hippocrates himself, consists of more than four hundred medical maxims, arranged into seven sections. Some of the maxims are very short— "Convulsion after hellebore is lethal" (V 1), "If a man with dropsy gets a cough, his case is hopeless" (VII 47); a few amount to whole paragraphs (for example, I 3, on the purging of athletes, III 12 on the effects of wet winters); but most of the entries run to three or four lines, and present a snippet of medical information or advice in a single carefully turned sentence.

Aphorisms may strike the modern reader as a tedious little work; nor is he likely to esteem it as a textbook for the general practitioner—others of the Hippocratic writings are more fun to peruse and scientifically more instructive. Yet *Aphorisms* appears to have been the most popular and the most admired member of the Hippocratic *corpus*; and surely its style had something to do with that popularity.

There are other gnomic works in the Hippocratic canon—*On Nutrition*, for example, and *On Dentition*, and parts of the *Epidemics*—and the aphoristic mode no doubt had value for busy medical men. But the doctors did not have a monopoly of the *genre*: according to a disreputably late source, "no one could produce a work of that sort as well as Hippocrates, whom philosophers have called the Friend of Nature—Democritus did indeed try to produce one, but he did not finish it as Hippocrates had done" (pseudo-Oribasius, 68 B 308).[4] And Galen cites a couple of lines written by Critias "in the first book of Aphorisms"[5] (*in Hipp. off.* XVIII B, 656 K = 88 B 39), thereby implying that Critias had penned at least two gnomic volumes.

Of Critias' *Aphorisms* we know nothing beyond the two quotations in Galen; on Democritus we are better informed. For there have been preserved, under the heading "Gnomes of Democrates," some eighty practical maxims, introduced by the following preamble:

> If anyone listens with intelligence to these gnomes of mine, he will perform many deeds worthy of a good man and he will avoid performing many bad deeds (68 B 35).

The catalogue of sentences which follows in our manuscripts is probably a late Byzantine compilation; but it is plausible that the selection is an abridgment of a Presocratic collection of adages, and that Democritus lies behind "Democrates."

The Democritean gnomes are all of an ethical, or at any rate of a practical, nature. They are brief, rarely running to more than a couple of lines; and they are pithy. Their content is homiletic and depressingly sober—"The man who is wholly subservient to material goods will never be just" (68 B 50), "Neither art nor wisdom is attainable if a man does not learn" (B 59), "Inopportune pleasures breed displeasures" (B 71). Taken together, the maxims

cannot be said to constitute a moral system, still less a philosophical ethics—
that, after all, was never their pretension; but they do convey a reasonably
coherent body of practical advice, and Democritus' promise in B 35 is not
wholly absurd.[6]

Democritus probably had a Presocratic model before him. For that
group of Pythagoreans who came to be labeled *acousmatici* encoded their
thoughts in a series of sentences: "the philosophy of the *acousmatici* consists
of *acousmata*, presented without proof and without argument" (Iamblichus,
VP 82 = 58 C 4—*acousmata*, or *sumbola* as they were also called, were
aphoristic remarks). Those Pythagorean sentences, according to Iamblichus,
fell into three groups; "for some of them signify what something is, others
what is most such-and-such, others what ought to be done or not done"
(Iamblichus, *l.c.*). "What are the islands of the blessed?—the sun and the
moon"; "What is most wise?—Number"; "One ought to have children,"
"One ought not to walk in the public highways."

Democritus' gnomes are practical sentences. The Pythagorean
catechism includes a practical section, but it also covers the theoretical side of
Pythagorean thought; and it may be regarded as an attempt to express the essence of Pythagoreanism in the aphoristic mode. We do not know exactly
when lists of *acousmata* were first written down: our main sources are
relatively late, and, like everything Pythagorean, the *acousmata* enjoyed a
long history during which their contents no doubt changed and developed; but
it is certain that many of the existing *acousmata* are Presocratic in origin, and
it is highly likely that Pythagorean collections of *Aphorisms* were in circulation in the fifth century B.C.[7]

A characteristic of the *acousmata*, as Iamblichus observes, is their innocence of any proof or reason: they are presented as dogmatic pronouncements, not as the rational conclusions of philosophical argument.[8] Some of
the *acousmata*, it is true, are tricked out with short justifications—"Do not
help anyone with a burden; for one should not become responsible for
someone's not working" (Iamblichus, *l.c.*—two of the Democritean gnomes
carry similar brief explanations); but Iamblichus says that such justifications
were appended only by some of the *acousmatici*, and it is clear that they were
not found in the original Presocratic *corpus*.[9]

III

Some of the Presocratics went in for the aphoristic style: they did not
merely bedizen their writings with sententious gems; they undertook to present their beliefs, or some substantial parts of them, through the medium of
maxims. Against the supposed inclination to aphorism stands the tendency to

argumentation. There is no need to demonstrate the argumentative urges of the Presocratics; for it is evident to the most superficial glance that their surviving texts bristle with ratiocination. Elsewhere I have tried to show how pervasive and how important was that characteristic trait of Presocratic thought; here I want to illustrate the argumentative *style* of some of the Presocratic writings.[10] I shall take Melissus as my paradigm.

Melissus wrote a concise account of Eleatic thought; he presented in clear and articulate prose a modified version of Parmenides' metaphysics, which had originally been published in rude hexametrical form. Of his treatise we possess some eighty lines: to judge from the various paraphrases and reports of Melissus' work in the later doxography, those lines must represent at least half of the lost original. The eighty lines are systematic and argued. They formed part of a continuous exposition. Melissus' treatise *On Nature* was not a sequence of aphorisms, and the fragments we now read are organic parts of a logically connected whole. The twenty or so theses which constitute Eleatic metaphysics form a systematically articulated body of doctrine, and each constituent is explicitly supported by argument.

Melissus' prose is regularly pointed with the linguistic marks of reasoning—with inferential connectives and particles. The surviving fragments contain twenty-five occurrences of the word γάρ, *for*; there are more than twenty *if*/*then* sentences, the staple syntax of argument; *since* and *because* are common; *therefore* appears a dozen times; *necessarily*, marking the conclusion of an inference, crops up in five places.

Fragment 7 contains twenty-one lines, a quarter of Melissus' surviving words. The fragment begins with an οὖν, *therefore*, and its first sentence summarizes the conclusions of the argument so far. Next, Melissus explicitly states the theses he is about to prove: "And it will neither be destroyed, nor become larger, nor change in arrangement, nor suffer pain, nor suffer anguish." Then, an argument for those theses, expressed in an *if*/*then* sentence and introduced by *for*, γάρ: "For if it underwent any of those things it would no longer be one." That conditional sentence is next justified, *seriatim* for each thesis, in a long string of arguments: the logical structure of those arguments is in some places uncertain (the Greek text is not always perfect), and Melissus does not invariably argue validly (he is indeed notorious for one particular fallacy); but it is utterly clear that he is *arguing*, and the sixteen lines which the arguments occupy are framed within the familiar grammar of ratiocination. The final thesis, that "it does not suffer anguish," is justified by the remark that "as for its suffering anguish, the argument is the same as for pain." Fragment 7 continues with a brief argument for the thesis that "it is not in any way empty"; that is followed by Melissus' most famous piece of reasoning, his argument against locomotion—an argument which became a standard part of philosophical debate, and the subtlety of which has rarely been properly appreciated. After that comes the attack on rarity and density; and the fragment ends by pulling its last three strands together: "*Necessarily*, then, it is full, *if* it is not empty. *If, then*, it is full, it does not move"—ἀνάγκη τοίνυν . . . , εἰ . . . . εἰ τοίνυν . . . .

Fragment 7, which I take to be typical of Melissus' treatise, is a subtle and intricate piece of prose; from beginning to end it hangs together as a continuous logical progression; and Melissus' prose style is perfectly matched to the needs of his thought. Whatever the philosophical merits of Melissus' arguments may be,[12] his linguistic achievement is surely noteworthy: Parmenides' verses are indeed as rigorously articulated as anything Melissus wrote; but, for all that, the lines of his thought often remain dark and obscure; Melissus freed Eleatic metaphysics from the straitjacket of bad verse, and in doing so he invented a prose style uniquely adapted to the ends of logical and philosophical thought.

It is worth dwelling a moment longer on that feature of the Greek language which Melissus so well exploits. For Greek is peculiarly rich in little words—in connectives and particles; and those little words enable Greek authors to make quite explicit, in a fashion not imitable in more lapidary languages, not only the nuances of an orator's persuasion but also the subtlest articulations of a philosopher's reasoning. Most of the work done in Greek by its various particles can indeed be done in other languages—in Latin, say, or in English. But in Greek such things are natural, a part of the ordinary language; in Latin or in English they are cumbersome and indecent—anyone who has studied the Latin translations of Greek philosophical texts, or who has labored to put Aristotle or Sextus into English, will grasp the point at once: the translator must often choose between a rebarbative version which is pedantically faithful to the Greek and a natural version in which the reader must himself supply the subtleties and connections which the Greek makes explicit. Students of Greek literature are familiar with the peculiar power and flexibility which particles give to a literary text;[13] students of Greek philosophy, reflecting on the same linguistic phenomenon, might be pardoned for thinking that Greek is the most philosophically satisfactory of languages.[14]

IV

Democritus and Melissus illustrate opposite tendencies in Presocratic prose style: Melissus opts for the logical style, with long periods, complex syntax, integrating particles; Democritus, in his Γνῶμαι, prefers the aphoristic style, with snappy sentences, simple grammar, few particles. Those brief characterizations of Melissus and Democritus are neither of them controversial: the Presocratic to whom I now turn, and who will be the hero for the rest of this paper, is no stranger to controversy—I mean, Heraclitus of Ephesus, Heraclitus the Obscure.

Much has been written on Heraclitus' style, and on the connection between his art and his thought.[15] There is no perfect unanimity on the matter among scholars (*facilius inter horologia quam inter philosophos conveniet*); but there is, I think, a view which can appropriately be called orthodox. According to that orthodoxy, Heraclitus was an aphorist; he did not produce periodic prose or write in continuous chapters; rather, he unburdened himself in the aphoristic form of instruction, by way of a series of short and allusive sentences. No doubt he wrote "a book."[16] But his "book" was no treatise; rather, it had the outward look of the Hippocratic *Aphorisms* or of Democritus' collection of gnomes.[17]

A quick perusal of Heraclitus' surviving fragments must appear to confirm that orthodoxy; for the fragments—or at least those of them which stick in the mind—are nothing if not aphoristic. "The way up and the way down are one and the same" (22 B 60); "The invisible harmony is stronger than the visible" (B 54); "Poor witnesses for men are the eyes and ears of those who have barbarian souls" (B 107). And in Heraclitus' Greek the force of such sentences is all the greater: B 60, for instance, which I have turned into twelve English words, contains only six words in the original—the verb is elided, "up" and "down" are antithetically juxtaposed, the epigram is as neat as you could wish.[18] Here, surely, is a writer who deliberately chose Galen's "aphoristic sort of instruction."

But are we really justified in drawing that conclusion from the fragments? Should we not be wary of judging the style of a man's work on the basis of short passages quoted from it by later authors? Scholars have shown themselves acutely conscious of the dangers of interpreting Heraclitus' thought from the glosses put on it by Sextus or by Hippolytus: there are equal dangers in interpreting Heraclitus' style from the fragments preserved by those later authors. Most of the fragments we possess—in all, they number less than a hundred[19]—are very brief: only four stretch to five lines of text; many consist of a mere half dozen words. The authors who quote or allude to Heraclitus are seldom interested in his philosophy: many of them filch a Heraclitean phrase for polemical use in their own intellectual battles; many of them cite a bit of Heraclitus in order to brighten their prose with a learned allusion. Heraclitus, like Shakespeare, had an eye for the quotable phrase: it would be absurd to judge Shakespeare's style on the basis of those lines and half-lines which later authors have turned into clichés; it is equally absurd to judge Heraclitus' style in a similar way. We should expect short quotations

to be snappy and aphoristic—that, after all, is how they come to be quoted—
and the fact that many (not all) of the surviving fragments are sententious is
no indication of the general style of Heraclitus' book. Many of the fragments could indeed have come from an anthology of epigrams; equally, they
could be stray poppies picked from an extensive acreage of corn.

I shall return to the fragments. But if we are to form a judgment about
Heraclitus' philosophical style it is helpful to start not from Heraclitus' own
words but rather from the indirect evidence. That evidence falls into two
parts: there are "imitations" of Heraclitus, and there are ancient judgments
on Heraclitus as a writer.

V

Heraclitus founded no formal school; but he had many followers
(Diogenes Laërtius, IX 6, 15), and later men imitated his writings.[20] In the
Theaetetus Plato comments, in a mocking vein, on some of Heraclitus' followers who battled violently in support of their theory of flux but who would
not stand still in an argument; "and if you ask any of them anything, they
pluck, as from a quiver, riddling little sayings ($\dot{\rho}\eta\mu\alpha\tau\dot{\iota}\sigma\kappa\iota\alpha$) and fire them off;
and if you try to get an account of what they mean, you will be transfixed by
another one, newly reworded" (180 A). This passage has been used to support
the orthodox view of Heraclitus as an aphorist; for his followers were surely
imitating him in pulling little sayings or aphorisms from their quivers, and in
falling back on things "newly reworded" or newfangled metaphors.

That will not do. First, Plato is in a playful mood, and we may hardly
take those paragraphs from the *Theaetetus* as serious history. Second, Plato
is talking about men who lived at least half a century after Heraclitus, and
whose relation to his style and thought is very uncertain. Third, Plato is referring to the debating habits of those latter-day Heracliteans: he is not speaking
of their written style, and the fact that they talked in "little sayings" hardly
implies that Heraclitus wrote in "little sayings." Finally, Plato probably does
not mean to say that the Heracliteans were metaphorical and aphoristic: his
point is rather that, in response to questions, the Heracliteans would produce
riddling catchphrases;[21] and if you asked them to explain a catchphrase they
would simply produce another one, "newly reworded"—they would repeat
themselves in different words. The Heracliteans are being accused not of being strong on aphorism but of being weak on argument.

None of Plato's Heracliteans is known to have written anything; and no
writings by any have survived. One imitator of Heraclitus whose writings
have survived has already been mentioned. For one or two of the surviving
fragments of Democritus are patently pastiches of known Heraclitean say-

ings (compare 68 B 64, "Many polymaths do not possess understanding," with 22 B 40, "Polymathy does not teach a man to possess understanding"); and several others are probably to be construed as allusions to Heraclitus. Those imitations of Heraclitus—and there were surely more which we are no longer in a position to recognize—come among Democritus' gnomes: his maxims are colored by allusions to the writings of Heraclitus. Does that not suggest that Heraclitus too wrote in the aphoristic mode? Thus Democritus, compiling a text of maxims, will have gone back to an earlier aphoristic compilation. That is hardly a convincing argument: Democritus was quite capable of extracting aphorisms which Heraclitus had embedded in continuous prose—that, after all, is the sort of thing which collectors of *bons mots* regularly do. Democritus' imitation tells us nothing about Heraclitus' style.

Perhaps there is more to be learned from a different source: various passages from the Hippocratic *corpus* are regularly cited among the imitations of Heraclitus; and editors of certain Hippocratic treatises commonly describe them as being Heraclitean in style.

Now some of those treatises are characterized as Heraclitean simply in virtue of their style: *On Humours*, for example, or *On Dentition*—or, for that matter, *Aphorisms*—contain nothing that is peculiarly Heraclitean in matter; there are no known allusions to Heraclitus' words, no recognizable references to Heraclitus' thoughts. If we knew that Heraclitus' work was an aphoristic compilation, then we might properly describe *On Humours* as Heraclitean in style; but evidently we cannot infer conclusions about Heraclitus' style from the style of *On Humours*.

There are, however, two treatises in the Hippocratic *corpus* which are more directly Heraclitean: in *On Nutriment* and *On Regimen* there are unmistakable allusions to Heraclitus, and indeed those works contain paraphrases of surviving Heraclitean fragments. It is thus not implausible to look to those tracts for evidence about the style of Heraclitus' book. Yet when we look, we find conflicting indications; for the style of *On Nutriment* is quite different from that of *On Regimen*. *On Nutriment* is a short and curious pamphlet; it consists of a connected string of aphorisms, and it illustrates clearly and briefly what Galen calls the "aphoristic form of instruction." *On Regimen* is a longer and more ambitious treatise: it certainly contains aphoristic passages, but it is essentially a continuous prose essay; it is not richly argumentative (its content demands exposition rather than argument), but neither is it a sequence of snappy sentences. Which, if either, of those two works should we take as Heraclitean in style?

On Nutriment is a purely medical tract: its aphorisms all belong to the physician's art, and it does not attempt to set the phenomena of nutrition within a larger scientific or philosophical context. Its Heracliteanisms strike me as extrinsic—they do not belong to the core of the work, and the work itself is only superficially Heraclitean.[22] *On Regimen*, on the other hand, is more "philosophical"; and those chapters of its first book which are cited as imitations of Heraclitus are concerned to set forth a summary account of the nature of things, and specifically of the nature of man: parts at least of *On Regimen* deal with subject-matter which is familiarly Presocratic, and indeed Heraclitean.

Diels-Kranz print *On Regimen* I 5–24 as "imitation" of Heraclitus; and I 5 is indeed a cento of paraphrases of Heraclitean sayings. But I 6–24 are not plainly Heraclitean: there are, to be sure, a few allusions to Heraclitus, as there are to Anaxagoras; but I see no reason to claim the paragraphs in general as Heraclitean.[23] As for I 5, it is false to call that section an *imitation* of Heraclitus: rather, as I have said, it is a brief sequence of paraphrases; and from that breathless and muddled farrago, it would be rash to draw any conclusions about the style of Heraclitus' original book.

VI

Heraclitus' imitators are untrustworthy. Let us turn now to the few ancient comments on Heraclitus' style which we possess; for the ancients, unlike us, could read the whole of Heraclitus' book, and their judgments were made on a sounder basis than ours can claim.

Heraclitus was a by-word for obscurity: Timon of Philus, the fourth-century satirist, called him "the Riddler"[24] (DL IX 6; cf. Plato, *Theaetetus* 180 A—above, p. 98); and at some date he won his standard sobriquet, "the Dark" or "the Obscure"—ὁ σκοτεινός (for example, Strabo, XIV 25 = 22 A 3a). Lucretius calls him *clarus ob obscuram linguam* (I 639); and Cicero has an explanation: "But see whether, if I don't understand what Epicurus says although, as I think, I know Greek pretty well, the fault is not partly his for speaking in such a way as not to be understood. That can happen blamelessly, in two ways—if either you do it on purpose, like Heraclitus 'who is called the Obscure by nickname because he has written too obscurely about nature,'[25] or when an obscurity in the subject-matter, not in the words, makes the language not understood, as in Plato's *Timaeus*" (*fin.* II v 15). And according to Diogenes Laërtius, "Theophrastus says that through melancholy he wrote some things in a half-finished state and others in different ways at different times" (DL IX 6).[26] Finally, there is a celebrated anecdote: "They say that Euripides gave Heraclitus' book to him [sc. Socrates] and asked 'What do you think of it?'; he replied: 'What I have understood is splendid, and I think that what I have not understood is so too—but it requires some Delian diver' "[27] (DL II 22 = A 4).

Cicero's assertion that Heraclitus was obscure on purpose we may leave to one side.[28] Many modern scholars, it is true, implicitly endorse it; for they find a reference to such deliberate obscurity in B 93: "The god whose is the oracle at Delphi neither speaks nor hides but signifies." Is not Heraclitus here acknowledging, and justifying, his oracular style? But that interpretation of B 93[29] is supported neither by the words of the text itself nor by any doxographical comment; and the Ciceronian charge was no doubt a pure speculation—a speculation as ill-grounded as Theophrastus' diagnosis of "melancholy."

A second point in Cicero's text is worth bringing out: Cicero distinguishes between verbal obscurity and obscurity of subject-matter—the *Timaeus* is obscure because the topics it deals with are intrinsically tough; Heraclitus' subject was on the whole plain—it was his language that imported the obscurity. Thus Cicero stresses that Heraclitean darkness is a stylistic feature; and his remark is at least consistent with the rest of the ancient tradition. Diogenes, it is true, says that "sometimes in his book he expresses himself with brilliance and clarity, so that even the most stupid easily understand and gain an elevation of soul—and the brevity and weight of his style are incomparable" (DL IX 7). But those flashes of lucidity were intermittent: the ancient sources give a uniform impression of stylistic gloom. No wonder that "there are very many who wrote commentaries on his book" (DL IX 12).

To say that Heraclitus' style was obscure is to say little enough—and nothing that helps with our current question. Why, and in virtue of what, was he obscure? Two texts do something to answer that question. "In general, what is written should be easy to read and easy to speak (that is the same thing); and that will be the case if there are many connectives and not if there are few,[30] nor if the text is not easy to punctuate, like that of Heraclitus—for it is a job to punctuate Heraclitus' writings because it is unclear whether a word is connected to what precedes it or to what follows" (*Rhetoric* Γ 5, 1407b11-15 = A 4).

Aristotle's complaint is that Heraclitus' writings are syntactically ambiguous—they are hard to punctuate, you cannot tell which word goes with which. Aristotle illustrates his complaint with a celebrated example, the first line of B 1, where it is uncertain whether ἀεί goes with ἐόντος or with ἀξύνετοι. Other examples can be found among the surviving fragments;[31] and presumably Aristotle thought that the phenomenon was widespread in Heraclitus' book. Note, however, that Aristotle does not say that Heraclitus was deliberately obscure and ambiguous in this way.

In the passage I have just cited Aristotle mentions the use of particles as an aid to the reader; but he does not say that Heraclitus was sparing with par-

ticles, nor does he ascribe Heraclitus' obscurity to that fact. The next passage
to be cited does precisely that. It comes from Demetrius' treatise *On Style*:
"Clarity depends on several points: first, on the use of words in their proper
sense; then, on the use of connected words. What is wholly unconnected and
loosened is always obscure; for the beginning of each colon is unclear because
of the looseness—as with Heraclitus' writings; for it is for the most part
looseness which makes them obscure" (192).[32] Here "connected" translates
συνδεδεμένοις, "unconnected" ἀσύνδετον: συνδεσμός is Aristotle's word for a
connecting particle;[33] and when Demetrius says that clarity depends on
words' being "connected," he means that it depends on their being tied
together with connectives or connecting particles. Demetrius, in sum, claims
that the main reason for Heraclitus' obscurity is that he did not use connecting particles: he preferred asyndeton, and as a result it was hard to tell
where one thought began and another ended.

The evidence surveyed in this section contains in effect three specific
judgments about Heraclitus' prose style: Heraclitus was enigmatic, a riddler;
his sentences were syntactically ambiguous, hard to punctuate; he was sparing with connectives. The first two judgments do not bear upon the question
of the aphoristic form of instruction—riddles and ambiguities are not
peculiarly characteristic of the aphorism. The third judgment, with which one
ancient critic particularly associates Heraclitus' celebrated obscurity, is more
pertinent; for a hallmark of the aphoristic style will be an infrequent use of
connectives,[34] and logical, Melissan, prose is distinguished by its richness in
inferential particles.

VII

With Demetrius' assertion in mind, let us now return to the surviving
texts of Heraclitus himself; and let us ask to what extent those texts support
Demetrius' judgment that Heraclitus was sparing with his connectives.

If we ask of each of the surviving fragments, "Did this sentence originally contain connectives?", our answer must often be a *non liquet*; for many of
the fragments are short sentences or phrases, molded to the syntax of the
author who quotes them, and we cannot tell from the context whether the
original Heraclitean colon was connected or not. At first glance it seems possible to give a more positive answer to the question in about fifty cases; but in
a dozen of those cases closer inspection again leads to a *non liquet*: a dozen of
the fragments are introduced by a connecting γάρ which is plainly due to the
author who is quoting Heraclitus and not to Heraclitus himself; and here it
remains an open question whether the quoter's γάρ masks a Heraclitean connective or a Heraclitean asyndeton.

In the forty-odd fragments which remain, the following features may be observed: καί (as a sentential connective) occurs twelve times; δέ occurs about twenty times, twice with a preceding μέν; γάρ occurs nine times; διό occurs once; and there are eleven cases of asyndeton.[35] Since we are here interested in argument, it is the ten inferential connectives which are of primary concern.

B 40 is a simple case: "Polymathy does not teach men to possess understanding; *for* it would have taught Hesiod . . . ." B 78 is more interesting: "*For* human character does not possess insights, divine does." The initial γάρ does not belong to the syntax of Origen, who quotes the line: it must be original—though we cannot say what the fragment was produced in explanation of.[36] B 88 is of greater significance: "The same thing is living and dead, and what is awake and what sleeps, and young and old; *for* these having changed about, are those, and those, having changed about again, these." I have elsewhere stressed the importance of this fragment; for it shows us that, in a particular instance at least, Heraclitus *argued* for one of his characteristic theses—the so-called Unity of Opposites—from another—the Theory of Flux.[37]

B 114 is one of the longer fragments, and it exhibits a clear logical structure: it consists of three sentences; the second is introduced by a γάρ and explicitly offers a justification for the first; the third is a conjunction, its three components linked by two occurrences of καί, and it also overtly parades in justificatory dress, being again introduced by a γάρ. B 2 is often supposed to have followed immediately upon B 114.[38] The text of B 2 is controversial: on the version which seems to me the most plausible, it consists of two sentences; the second is tied to the first by an adversative δέ, the first is introduced by an inferential διό.[39] Take B 2 and B 114 together, and you get seven or eight lines of continuous prose, molded into an argument and explicitly articulated as such.[40]

What is the upshot of all this? In three quarters of the forty fragments we can properly consider, Heraclitus uses connecting particles; and in one quarter he uses inferential particles. In one case, at least, there is reason to think that he constructed a moderately complex and logical piece of prose. On the other hand, Heraclitus allows asyndeton in a quarter of the forty cases; and, since that is a high proportion, Demetrius' judgment on Heraclitus' style receives some support from the surviving texts.[41]

VIII

Heraclitus' prose style was not like that of Melissus: Melissus abjures asyndeton; inferential particles are his stock in trade. Heraclitus rather favors asyndeton; his connectives include inferential particles but are not dominated by them. The contrast is unsurprising: Melissus, like Parmenides before him, was concerned to develop, in axiomatized fashion, a deductive system of metaphysics; Heraclitus—like most philosophers—was not. Philosophy can be rich in argument without being relentlessly deductive in the Eleatic fashion; and philosophical prose, though it will be well supplied with the linguistic signs of argumentation, need not be as unremittingly inferential as the tract of Melissus.

On the other hand, Heraclitus' prose style was not like that of the most aphoristic of the Hippocratic writers: *On Humours*, for example, has been called Heraclitean; but that treatise is wholly different in style from the book of Heraclitus. *On Humours* contains only a couple of dozen particles in its fifteen pages of text; asyndeton is employed everywhere; inferential connectives are almost totally absent. Nor is *On Dentition*, or the seventh book of *Aphorisms*, Heraclitean in style: those treatises consist of sequences of short entries, most of them amounting to a single brief sentence, none of them tied to its predecessor by any particle, few of them containing internal particles. If those works are paradigms of the aphoristic form of instruction, Heraclitus was no aphoristic instructor.

Advocates of an aphoristic Heraclitus may, I suppose, retreat to a more defensible position: the first book of the Hippocratic *Aphorisms* contains several longer entries; and in some of them a little argument, and a number of inferential particles, are found.[42] Perhaps Heraclitus' book was comparable to that: perhaps it consisted of a series of entries, each syntactically and logically independent of its neighbours, some of them simple maxims or sentences, others evincing a degree of internal complexity and a scattering of inferential connectives?

I doubt if that hypothesis can be conclusively falsified; but I find it highly implausible. The surviving fragments contain too many particles, and in particular too many inferential particles, for the hypothesis to be persuasive. More importantly, in one or two cases at least—B 88 and B 114 + B 2—the inferential particles connect substantial parts of Heraclitus' philosophy: they are not comparable to the low-level internal connections within the Hippocratic *Aphorisms*.

We are not in a position to reconstruct any substantial passages from Heraclitus' book.[43] Could we do so, we should certainly find riddles and ambiguities in its exposition; and we should find a prominent use of asyndeton. But we should also, I suspect, discover a continuous and argued prose treatise: in many cases the direction of argument would be explicitly indicated by the standard devices of particles and connectives; and if asyndeton sometimes left Heraclitus' reasoning in darkness, that would not always be so—often enough the connection of thought is visible despite the lack of connectives.[44]

If that is so, Heraclitus was not a man apart, standing aloof from the traditions of Presocratic thought: his philosophy had its idiosyncratic moments, and his prose had its peculiarities; but for all that he is recognizably a Presocratic, his major interests and his mode of exposition falling within the newly established canons of philosophical science. Scholars may properly attempt to establish the outlines and interconnections of Heraclitus' thought: whether they can ever hope to succeed in that attempt is another question.

Jonathan Barnes

Balliol College, Oxford

NOTES

1. If, as Havelock says, the Presocratics "expect an audience of listeners," the appeal of aphorism will have been all the stronger. And though the Presocratics, from Anaximander (if not from Thales) onward, certainly wrote their thoughts down, there is reason to believe that listening rather than reading was the normal way of becoming acquainted with what they had written.

2. Cf. Theophrastus, *apud* Gregory of Corinth, *Comm. in Hermog. meth.* V 44, p.1154 Walz; ps. Aristotle, *Rhet. ad Alex.* 11, 1430a40–b29. For the later rhetorical definition see, for example, Hermogenes, *Progymnasmata* 4: "A gnome is a summary statement in the form of a universal assertion dissuading from or persuading to something or indicating what sort of thing something is" (cf. Aphthonius, *Prog* 4; Sopater, *Prog* 4; and—on the Latin *sententia*—ps. Cicero, *ad Her* IV 24). LSJ s.v. γνώμη cite five passages for γνώμη in the sense of "maxim": apart from *Rhet.* 1394a22 and 1395all, these are Sophocles, *Ajax* 1091, Xenophon, *Mem.* IV ii 9, and Heraclitus, 22 B 78. In none of the last three passages does γνώμη mean "maxim." (Mouraviev, in his survey of pre-Aristotelian uses of γνώμη does not recognize the sense of "maxim"—he even classifies the examples from *Rhet.* under the sense "piece of knowledge, thesis." See S. Mouraviev, "Gnome," *Glotta* 51, 1973, 69–78.) See rather, for example, Isocrates, II 44; Aristotle *Soph. El.* 17, 176b18–20; Quintilian, VIII v 3; Sextus, *M* I 279 (perhaps also Aristophanes, *Clouds* 896, 924, 948). On the nature and history of gnomology see K. Horna, "Gnome, Gnomendichtung, Gnomologien," Pauly-Wissowa, *RE* suppt. VI 1935, cols. 74–90; W. Spoerri, "Gnome," *Der kleine Pauly* II, cols 822–9 (with rich bibliography and references); on gnomology as a philosophical *genre* see M. Untersteiner, *Problemi di filologia filosofica* (Milan, 1980), pp. 51–53.

3. For γνωμολογία see also Plato, *Phaedrus* 267C. As well as γνώμη and ἀφορισμός, there are such terms as ἀπόφθεγμα, ὑποθήκη, χρεία: in technical rhetorical contexts the senses of those words are held distinct, but for present purposes the technical typology does not matter.

4. References in this form are to chapter, section, and item in Diels-Kranz, *Die Fragmente der Vorsokratiker.*

5. Reading Ἀφορισμῶν (with Wilamowitz).

6. On the "Democrates" passages see F. K. Voros, "The Ethical Fragments of Democritus: the Problem of Authenticity," ΕΛΛΗΝΙΚΑ 26, 1973, 191–206; A. Brancacci, "Democrito e la tradizione cinica," in F. Romano, ed., *Democrito e l'Atomismo antico* (Catania, 1980).

7. On the *acousmata* see Walter Burkert, *Lore and Science in Ancient Pythagoreanism* (Cambridge, MA: Harvard University Press, 1972), ch.II.4. Note also the gnomic verses of Theognis, Phocylides, and the rest, the saws of the Seven Sages (see Barkowski, "Sieben Weise," *RE* IIA, 1921, cols. 2255–61), and the Delphic maxims (see *SIG*³ 1268), which were later taken as far as Afghanistan by the Peripatetic Clearchus (see the inscription published by L. Robert in *Comptes Rendus de l' Académie des Inscriptions*, 1968, 422–31).

8. "Are presented as," not "are." The aphoristic style is a mode of presentation or a form of instruction, and the fact that beliefs were presented without argument does not imply that they were arrived at without argument. Behind the Hippocratic *Aphorisms* there lies a mass of detailed observations and a quantity of theorising; and not all the Pythagorean *acousmata* were mere dogmas or expressions of instinctive taboos.

9. The most celebrated example of the aphoristic mode of instruction in philosophy is given by Epicurus' Κυρίαι Δόξαι; compare, from a later age, the Epictetan maxims or the sentences of Sextus. A closely related *genre* is that of the *florilegium* or anthology, among the better known examples of which are the monostichs of Menander and the pseudo-Epicharman γνῶμαι (for which see 23B8–54, A 10, Pap.Hibeh I 1 [Diels-Kranz, I 193–4]—see Untersteiner, *op. cit.*, pp. 123–27, with references). For the practice of excerpting see, for example, Isocrates, II 44; Plato, *Laws* 811A; Aristotle, *Topics* A 14, 105b12–8; Diogenes Laërtius, VI 31; Marcus Aurelius, II 14. Collections of χρεῖαι were made by numerous philosophers: Aristippus (DL II 85), Diogenes (VI 80), Metrocles (VI 33), Zeno (VI 91 = SVF I 272), Persaeus (VII 36 = SVF I 435), Ariston of Chios (VII 163 = SVF I 333). See the learned paper by J. Barns, "A New Gnomologium: with some remarks on gnomic anthologies," *Classical Quarterly* 44 (1950), 126–37; 45 (1951), 1–19.

10. In *The Presocratic Philosophers* (London: Routledge and Kegan Paul, 1979) I urged that the rational approach to science and philosophy (in a fairly relaxed sense of the term "rational") should be seen as the primary feature of Presocratic thought and as the Presocratics' greatest gift to posterity. In that book I paid too little attention to another great gift, that of conceptual innovation, which Havelock rightly emphasizes in his paper "The Linguistic Task of the Presocratics" in this volume. I also tended to disregard the stylistic features of Presocratic exposition: in the present paper I hope to do something—not much—to repair that omission.

11. "When the prose of Zeno, Melissus, Anaxagoras, and Diogenes is scrutinized closely, it can be seen to be built up out of a succession of sentences in which the shape of the aphorism is detectable. That is. to say, the earliest philosophical prose is contrived out of the original genius of the self-contained maxim, now remodeled to produce a continuous argument" (Havelock, "Linguistic Task of the Presocratics," p. 11; cf. p. 40, for aphorisms in Anaxagoras; p. 27, for aphorisms in Parmenides' philosophical verse). Havelock rightly stresses the argumentative continuity of the prose of Zeno and Co.; but the claim that that prose is built from a succession of aphorisms seems, to me at least, wholly false: perhaps there are a few aphoristic phrases in these authors (Anaxagoras' ὄψις τῶν ἀδήλων τὰ φαινόμενα and ὁμοῦ πάντα

χρήματα are, I think, the *only* celebrated *mots* there); but for the most part the constituent sentences of their prose are not at all aphoristic.

12. For an attempt to assess Melissus' arguments see Barnes, *The Presocratic Philosophers*, vol. I, pp. 180–230; on fragment 7, see pp. 214–19.

13. "The contribution which these particles make to the force and vividness of Greek has been universally recognized. Often they cannot be appropriately translated into a modern language, and their effect must be suggested by inflections of the voice in speaking, or by italics, exclamation marks, or inverted commas in writing" (J. D. Denniston, *The Greek Particles* [Oxford: Oxford University Press, 1954], p. xxxix).

14. The Stoics, I think, were the first philosophers to reflect on the use of connectives (cf., for example, Diogenes Laërtius, VII 57; Galen, *Plac. Hipp. Plat.* VIII 3 = SVF II 148; Posidonius, F 45 EK, F 192 EK); and the Alexandrian grammarians, who paid subtle attention to particles, were influenced by Stoic grammar (see Apollonius Dyscolus, περὶ Συνδεσμῶν ad. *init*). Denniston's *Greek Particles* is indispensable for the study of the ancient philosophers (although Denniston himself is more interested in purely literary texts, and his study ends at 320 B.C.); but there is still much work to be done on the use of particles by the Greek philosophers. A student might well start with the works of Sextus Empiricus: the prose style which Sextus perfected derives ultimately from the writings of such men as Melissus; and for clarity and explicitness of logical articulation I know of no rival to Sextus' prose.

15. See, for example, Bruno Snell, "Die Sprache Heraklits," *Hermes* 61, 1926, 353–81, and "Heraklits Fragment 10," *Hermes* 76, 1941, 84–87 (both in Snell's *Gesammelte Schriften* [Göttingen, 1966]); U. Hölscher, "Heraklit," in his *Anfängliches Fragen* (Göttingen, 1968); C. H. Kahn, *The Art and Thought of Heraclitus* (Cambridge: Cambridge University Press, 1979).

16. The most important reference is Aristotle, *Rhetoric* Γ 5, 1407b16 (quoted below); see also Diogenes Laërtius, IX 1, 5, 6, 7, 12.

17. "The one hundred and twenty-nine statements assigned to him as authentic are properly speaking not 'fragments' excerpted and quoted from a continuous prose work, but self-contained sayings designed for memorization and containing elements of rhythm to further this end" (Havelock, "Linguistic Task of the Presocratics," p. 11). For a trenchant statement of the aphoristic view of Heraclitus, see G. S. Kirk, *Heraclitus: The Cosmic Fragments* (Cambridge: Cambridge University Press, 1962), pp. 7–8; *contra*, for example, W. K. C. Guthrie, *A History of Greek Philosophy*, vol. I (Cambridge: Cambridge University Press, 1962), pp. 406–08.

18. ὁδὸς ἄνω κάτω μία καὶ ὡυτή.

19. Havelock (see above, n17) speaks of 129 authentic statements: I am not sure where his figure comes from. Diels-Kranz print 130 passages under the heading "Fragmente"; Marcovich prints 111 (*Heraclitus*, Merida, 1967); Kahn prints 125 passages, remarking that "only 89 qualify as fully verbatim citations, and even this figure may be a bit too generous" (*op. cit.*, n15, p. 25).

20. See the texts collected in R. Mondolfo and L. Tarán, *Eraclito: testimonianze e imitazioni* (Florence, 1972).

21. The weight falls on αἰνιγματώδη; as for ῥηματίσκια, that does not mean "aphorism"—it is a derogatory diminutive, meaning "little phrases" ("pet phrase, phraselet," LSJ, who rightly compare Aristophanes' use of ῥημάτιον: *Acharnians* 444, 447; *Clouds* 943; *Knights* 216; *Peace* 534).

22. I agree here with the Budé editor of the treatise (who dates it to the third, or more probably the second, century B.C.).

23. I 4 is thoroughly Anaxagorean: I 6–24 are more Anaxagorean than they are Heraclitean, and we should beware of regarding the author of the *de victu* as a simpleminded Heraclitean. See R. Joly, *Hippocrate: du Régime* (Paris: Budé, 1967), who holds that the influence of Heraclitus on the *de victu* is superficial (Joly dates the treatise to c. 400 B.C.).

24. τοῖς δ' ἐνι κοκκυστής, οχλολοίδορος Ἡράκλειτος αἰνικτὴς ἀνόρουσε (frag. 43 D).Ὀχλολοίδορος, "reviler of the mob," is easy enough: see B 104 (quoted by Proclus, *in Alc* p. 117 Westerink, who refers to Timon); and cf. e.g., B 2, B 17, B 29. The sense of κοκκυστής is less clear: LSJ give "crower, screamer" (for κοκκύζειν used of cocks cf. Stephanus, s.v. κόκκυξ, and see, for example, Aristotle, *HA* I 49, 631b9); LSJ say that κοκκυσμός is used of "the sound of a very high voice" (see also Hesychius, s.v. κοκκύζει), and they think that κόκκυξ can be used of a stammerer (citing Σ Pindar, *Pyth.* IV 1 [II p. 93 Drachmann]—but that is not the implication of the passage: Battus was nicknamed "Cuckoo"—ironically—because he had a soft voice). None of those suggestions is appropriate to Timon, where a reference to Heraclitus' mode of speech is out of place. Nauck proposed ἐπικοκκαστής for ἐνι κοκκυστής, and compared ἐπικοκκάστρια at Aristophanes, *Thesmophoriazusae* 1059, which the Scholiast explains as "mocker." "Mocker" is surely the sense we want; and I guess that κοκκυστής itself can convey the idea.

25. Apparently a quotation from a poet: see Madvig *ad loc.*

26. The commentators explain μελαγχολία by reference to Aristotle, *EN* H 8, 1150b25. Theophrastus does not actually imply that Heraclitus' writings were *obscure*; rather, he says that some were "half-finished" and that others were ἄλλοτε ἄλλως ἔχοντα. The latter phrase does not mean that Heraclitus was inconsistent; it means that he changed his mind. The surviving fragments provide no illustration of either criticism, and I find nothing relevant in the doxography; nor is it clear what evidence Theophrastus could have possessed to ground his judgment.

27. One of Pythagoras' many incarnations was as a Delian diver (Heraclide Ponticus, fr. 89 W = DL VIII 5); does Socrates mean that only a Pythagoras could understand Heraclitus?

28. See DL IX 6: "He [sc. Heraclitus] placed it [sc. his book] in the temple of Artemis, having planned (as some say) to write somewhat obscurely, so that those in power might have access to it and it might not be easily despised by the vulgar." The text may be corrupt (there is no δέ answering the μέν in ὡς μέν τινες); but it is clear that "having planned . . . obscurely" is parenthetical: Diogenes means that Heraclitus placed his book in the temple so that only those in power should get at it; he does not mean (as most scholars suppose) that he wrote obscurely so that only the nobs should understand it.

29. The interpretation is perhaps implied by Lucian, *vit. auct.* 14 = C 5.

30. I accept Diels' supplement ⟨ἔχουσιν, οἱ δ' ὀλίγοι⟩. Kassel, *ad loc.*, thinks to defend the received text by reference to 1407a24 and 27ff (he misreports Diels' conjecture); but those passages are not parallel, and Diels was right to compare Demetrius (quoted above, p. 17).

31. E.g., B 15 (see Kahn *ad loc*); B 18; B 32 (Kahn *ad loc.*); B 55 (see Marcovich *ad loc.*); in general, see Kahn, *op. cit.*, pp. 91–95 (although Kahn is as much concerned with lexical as with syntactical ambiguity).

32. A "colon" is a sentence or phrase; for Demetrius' explanation of this important notion see *On Style* 1–2.

33. Συνδεσμός is the regular term for "connective" in the Greek grammarians (for example, in Apollonius Dyscolus' treatise on connectives); it normally covers both

what we call particles (γάρ, δέ, ἄρα, οὖν) and what we call sentential connectives (ἤ, εἰ, ὅτι).

34. But asyndeton is not proprietory to the aphorist: see, for example, Aristotle, *Rhet.* Γ 12, 1413b2–1414a7, Demetrius, *On Style* 193, Longinus, *On the Sublime* 19–21, for the use of asyndeton as a stylistic device in rhetorical and literary texts.

35. Asyndeton: B 10, B 34, B 45, B 51, B 52, B 53, B 57, B 62, B 67, B 111, B 126.

36. ἦθος γὰρ ἀνθρώπειον μὲν οὐκ ἔχει γνώμας, θεῖον δὲ ἔχει (see Marcovich *ad loc.*).

37. See Barnes, *The Presocratic Philosophers*, vol. I, pp. 72–73.

38. See Marcovich *ad loc.*; for the argument see Barnes, *The Presocratic Philosophers*, vol. I, pp. 132–35.

39. I follow Marcovich's text. Some scholars think that διὸ δεῖ ἕπεσθαι τῷ ξυνῷ (or κοινῷ) belongs to Sextus, who quotes the passage, and not to Heraclitus (see esp. M. L. West, *Early Greek Philosophy and the Orient* [Oxford: Oxford University Press, 1971], pp. 118–19). But διό certainly does not belong to Sextus, who quotes it as though it were from Heraclitus. Διό is rare in early prose; but there is no good reason to deny it to Heraclitus.

40. Other occurrences of γάρ: B 1, B 56, B 57, B 85. B 48 is puzzling: as quoted by the *Etymologicum Magnum* it is introduced by οὖν, as quoted by Tzetzes it is introduced by δέ (text in Marcovich *ad loc.*); neither particle belongs to the quoter, and each quoter implies that the particle he uses is Heraclitean. Is either right? See further Kirk *ad loc.*

41. How far, in any case, should we trust the judgment of Demetrius? My colleague Carol Clark has drawn my attention to a letter written in about 1602 by the learned French lawyer Estienne Pasquier. Pasquier is describing Montaigne's *Essais* (he was a friend of Montaigne's and presumably knew the *Essais* well): "Mais, sur tout, son Livre est un vray seminaire de belles & notables sentences . . . [he excerpts eighteen such maxims] . . . Tout son Livre n'est pas proprement un parterre, ordonné de divers carreaux & bordures; ains comme une prairie diversifiée, pesle-mesle & sans art, de plusieurs fleurs. Vous n'y rencontrerez que sentences" (E. Pasquier, *Choix de Lettres*, ed. D. Thickett [Geneva, 1956], pp. 47–48). According to the scholarly Pasquier, the *Essais* exhibit the aphoristic form of instruction: there could scarcely be a less accurate description of Montaigne's prose style.

42. See, for example, I 3: οὐ γάρ . . ., ἐπεὶ δέ . . ., λείπεται οὖν . . ., τούτων οὖν εἵνεκεν . . ., σφαλερὸν γάρ . . .; I 5: πᾶν γάρ . . ., διὰ τοῦτο . . ., διὰ τοῦτο οὖν . . . .

43. For two valiant attempts see West, *op. cit.*, pp. 113–14; D. Holwerda, *Sprünge in die Tiefen Heraklits* (Gröningen, 1978), p. 122.

44. For trivial cases where asyndeton does not mask the connection of thought see, for example, B 34 and B 51; a non-trivial case is supplied by B 10, where the difficulty of the fragment is not, however, caused by the asyndeton. Compare Philostratus' description of Antiphon's Περὶ 'Ομονοίας: . . . ἐν ᾧ γνωμολογίαι τε λαμπραὶ καὶ φιλόσοφοι σεμνή τε ἀπαγγελία καὶ ἐπηνθισμένη ποιητικοῖς ὀνόμασι καὶ τὰ ἀποτάδην ἑρμηνευόμενα παραπλήσια τῶν πεδίων τοῖς λείοις (*vit. soph.* I 15 4 = 87 B 44a).

PHILOSOPHY AND THE WRITTEN WORD:
SOME THOUGHTS ON HERACLITUS
AND THE EARLY GREEK USES OF PROSE

The Egyptian god Theuth, who invented writing, thought it would bring the Egyptians wisdom (*sophia*) and good memory. With Plato's obvious approval, King Thamous objected that it would give them the appearance of wisdom but actually make them more forgetful, because of their reliance on an external text: writing would serve not for memory but only for reminding.[1] And of course the Egyptians knew more about writing than the Greeks. Herodotus reported that they had written records going back 15,000 years.[2]

The Greeks, on the other hand, had a rich tradition of oral minstrelsy which preserved the memory of Mycenaean power and wealth in heroic poems sung across the centuries, so that both the material and the stylistic form of Homeric poetry were fully prepared for the two great artists who composed the *Iliad* and the *Odyssey* in the early age of alphabetic literacy, toward the end of the eighth century B.C. The traditional *sophia* of these poets—their learning and their skill—was a true gift of memory from the preliterate age. What we will never know is just what role writing and the relatively new alphabet played in the composition of such monumental works.[3] My own guess is that writing was indispensable for the composition of both epics and was actually used for this purpose in the eighth century. The poet would need some kind of text precisely as a reminder of what he had done, in order to complete the work in a consistent way and then to preserve it in a recognizable state from one performance to another.[4] On my view, the authors of the *Iliad* and the *Odyssey* are no longer strictly oral poets: writing in some form has become a part of their *sophia*. But for a long time the written text would probably be the privileged possession of professional singers—perhaps the guild property of the *Homeridae*. Even in a later age, for anyone except schoolboys learning to read, familiarity with the epic poems would be primarily a matter of public performance and extensive memorization. When literacy became commonplace, poetry probably continued to be more often performed or recited than read in silence. And when prose works began to circulate, they too would typically be read aloud before one or more listeners. Thus in the pages of Plato, Lysis reads to his parents, Phaedrus reads Lysias' new speech to Socrates, and Zeno introduces his own paradoxes to Athens in a public reading before a select audience.[5]

We must be grateful to Eric Havelock for emphasizing this long predominance of the oral element in Greek culture and its importance for the understanding of Greek literature. He is surely right to insist that the Presocratics played a special role in developing a new type of prose literature, designed to project their new "scientific" vision of the world, and directed in various ways *against* the older oral-poetic tradition for which Homer and Hesiod were the spokesmen. I want to focus attention here on some evidence for the early stages of this development and to specify the place of Heraclitus in the creation of genuinely literary prose.

I

One quotation from Heraclitus implies that sixth-century treatises of a quasi-scientific type were more common than we might otherwise suppose.

> Pythagoras son of Mnesarchus pursued inquiry (*historiē*) further than all other men and, choosing what he liked from these compositions (*syngraphai*), he made a wisdom of his own: much learning, artful knavery. (DK 129 = Marcovich 17)

Since Zeller and Diels the authenticity of this fragment has been contested, not only because of the difficulty of identifying the written works referred to but also because of the puzzling syntax of the phrase "choosing what he liked from these compositions" (*eklexamenos tautas tas syngraphas*). Although it is now generally agreed that the beginning and the end of the quotation must be genuine, there is still some doubt as to whether the phrase in question is correctly preserved. But although we cannot guarantee their literal accuracy, we must certainly recognize these words as prima facie evidence for the existence of *syngraphai* in the sixth century, numerous enough for Pythagoras to make a selection from and connected somehow with his practice of "inquiry" or research (*historiē*). But what writings could Heraclitus have in mind?

In the later fifth century *syngraphē* is the standard term for a written report of Ionian *historiē*, either for history in the narrow sense[6] or for a scientific treatise. Thus Diogenes of Apollonia refers to his own book as "this *syngraphē*" (fr. 4), while Herodotus uses this noun and its cognate verb in reference to his work as historian.[7] But the term can designate the "writing up" of any material: it can apply to written contracts, legal agreements or proposals, even to architects' specifications. (See LSJ s.v. *syngraphē* II.2; cf. *syngrapheus* II.) The common thread is the documentation of any report, proposal, or decision of which it is desirable to keep a written record.

Such a record will normally be in prose. I have found no examples of *syngraphē* referring to poetic texts. Herodotus does use the cognates *syngramma* and *syngraphomai* in reference to versified texts, but only where it is a question of recording an oracle that has already been formulated in hexameter verse.[8] In that case the term *syngramma* refers not to the poetic composition itself but simply to the written version of a text that happens to be in verse. There seems to be no normal use of *syngraphē* or *syngramma* to designate a *composition* in verse.

Hence there is no good reason to take seriously the old suggestion, recently renewed by Burkert, that the "writings" used by Pythagoras would be Orphic texts.[9] For Orpheus was a poet, and the compositions ascribed to him are in hexameter verse. Furthermore, the term *historiē* points not to Orphic theology but to Ionian research. So the implications of fr. 129 are quite clear. The question is: can we believe in the existence of any substantial body of semi-technical literature in the sixth century?

The evidence is fragmentary and frequently neglected, but there is more of it than might be supposed. In the first place, we hear a good deal about old didactic poems of a practical nature, studied by Nilsson in an article in 1905. Against the skepticism of nineteenth-century scholarship Nilsson defends the antiquity (though not the authenticity) of (1) a *Gēs periodos*, a Geography or World-description ascribed to Hesiod, (2) an *Astronomy* with inaccurate information on star-settings, also ascribed to Hesiod, (3) the famous "Nautical Astronomy" handed down under Thales's name (but also attributed to Phocus of Samos), and (4) an astronomical poem of Cleostratus of Tenedos, containing the first Greek mention of the signs of the zodiac. There is also some evidence for (5) a *Kataploi* or versified description of harbors.[10] These would all be practical works, of use for agricultural calendars (like Hesiod's own *Works and Days*) but above all for the mariners of Miletus and other Ionian cities so active in colonization and commerce in the sixth century and even earlier.

These texts were composed in hexameter verse for easy memorization, and hence they do not strictly qualify as *syngraphai*. But they do attest to a tradition of technical literature going back well into the sixth century, if not to Thales himself. More securely dated and pretty certainly in prose are the descriptions of several famous archaic temples recorded by their architects.[11] Among the examples of this genre mentioned by Vitruvius (Book VII, Preface 12) at least two belong in the middle of the sixth century in the region that concerns Heraclitus: an account of the Heraion at Samos by the eminent sculptor and architect Theodorus (of Samos), and a parallel report on the other colossal Ionian structure of this period, the so-called Croesus-temple of Artemis at Ephesus, by Chersiphron and Metagenes. Here we have definite evidence of technical prose literature in sixth-century Ionia: the treatises of Anaximander, Pherecydes, Anaximenes, and Hecataeus were not as isolated as might at first appear. The original affinities between this architectural literature and Milesian *historiē* can be illustrated by a later example, from the mid-fifth century: the strange and somewhat anachronistic figure of Hippodamus of Miletus, the last representative of the Milesian "school." Hippodamus was a kind of Doxiades of his day, the city-planner who rebuilt Rhodes, laid out the Piraeus, and probably designed the ambitious Periclean colony of Thurii. Our sources describe him as a *meteōrologos*, that is, a natural philosopher, as well as a social theorist and a master builder. His distinctive contribution to city planning seems to have been the imposition of a complex pattern of streets and neighborhoods, based upon the grid-plan but developed as a system, "derived from principles of geometrical and political theory and carefully fitted to the demands of function and site."[12] In the breadth of his interests and theoretical vision, and in his taste for geometric construction, Hippodamus seems to have been a true Milesian. Furthermore, he must have left a prose treatise behind, since Aristotle could give a detailed account of his theories a century later.

Geometry and architecture were linked from the start, and a similar concern is characteristic of early Greek sculpture. (Theodorus, the architect of the Heraion, was also a sculptor and a painter.) The study of *symmetria* or proportions was fundamental, for example, in the use which the Greeks made of Egyptian canons in developing the standing male statue or *kouros* in the seventh and sixth centuries B.C.[13] The earliest surviving fragment from a treatise that represents this tradition, the famous *Canon* of Polyclitus from the middle of the fifth century, speaks of achieving success "by way of many numbers" (*dia pollōn arithmōn*, DK 40. B2). Some have looked for Pythagorean influence in Polyclitus' doctrine of proportion.[14] But since canons of this sort characterize archaic sculpture as well and apparently go back to Egyptian precedents, we might invert the question of influence: perhaps it was technical treatises of this kind, applying principles of number and proportion to sculpture, architecture, engineering, and the like, that Heraclitus had in mind when he accused Pythagoras of fabricating his own "wisdom" from a selection of earlier writings, writings that belonged in a general sense to Ionian *historiē*.[15] The plans and proportions of the master builders belong here, as do the astronomical diagrams and the land-and-sea charts of Anaximander and Hecataeus.

I suggest, then, that we understand Heraclitus as attacking Pythagoras' originality by claiming that his ideas depend upon earlier Ionian science, including the development of applied mathematics and the study of geometrical proportions in the arts. So understood, Heraclitus' claim may contain a good deal of historical truth. "The purely practical canons of proportions long employed by Greek artists,"[16] and employed in particular by Pythagoras' older compatriot Theodorus (who was active around 570–560 B.C.), together with the applied mathematics of the building trades and the numerical astronomy long practiced in Babylon and now being cultivated in Miletus, all of these—together with the new geometric cosmology which was largely the work of Anaximander—may have provided Pythagoras with the basis for his own generalized theory of nature in numerical terms, a generalization which will have included the new and specifically Pythagorean discovery of the ratios of musical concord, and which was (from the beginning, or soon afterwards) to be extended to the "music of the spheres"—which only Pythagoras himself is said to have heard.[17]

II

We have found sufficient evidence to support the claim, implicit in Heraclitus fr. 129, that there existed in the sixth century a body of technical literature, primarily Ionian in origin, which by the end of that century would have been almost entirely in prose.[18] Since such treatises were designed for practical use, they would soon go out of date; and it is natural that few traces of them have survived. If we happen to know more about the treatises of Anaximander and Anaximenes than about the others,[19] that is because their works contained more general theories about the origin of the world and the structure of the heavens. It was these doctrines which their successors found worth copying and which thus survived to attract the interest of Aristotle and Theophrastus two centuries later, when the papyrus of most sixth-century treatises had long since moldered into dust.

Heraclitus is writing when this Ionian tradition was still fresh, and if he has chosen to write in prose it is certainly not in imitation of Pherecydes' theological story-telling,[20] the only other form of literary prose attested for the sixth century. We must see his use of prose as a deliberate acceptance of the medium of Ionian *historiē*, for a report of his own observations. The nearest parallel is probably the *Historiai* or *Genealogies* of his older contemporary Hecataeus, which begins: "Hecataeus of Miletus says as follows: I write these things as I judge them to be true; for the accounts (*logoi*) of the Greeks are, in my opinion, many and ridiculous" (fr. 1, Jacoby). The *logos* of Heraclitus begins in a similar vein, with the scornful rejection of the views of most Greeks, indeed of most men; Heraclitus too will, unlike his predecessors, tell it like it is (fr. 1). But this superficial resemblance joins two works that differ profoundly both in scope and in quality. Whereas Hecataeus' production was soon overshadowed by the literary achievement of Herodotus and supplanted by later writers, Heraclitus' book became the first Greek prose classic, the oldest book in prose worth preserving both for its style and for its content. And the form must have been as important to him as the matter. No author of antiquity has composed his sentences with greater care; no philosopher except Plato can match Heraclitus' command of the words and rhythms of Greek.

The question arises: How far does this first major work of artistic prose still reflect the forms and modes of communication of an oral culture? Since Havelock has lent some support to Kirk's theory that Heraclitus did not originally compose a book at all but a series of independent sayings "framed not to be read but to be heard and memorized,"[21] I must review once more the evidence against this view of Heraclitus' work as essentially non-literary. But first of all it is important to recognize that Heraclitus does in fact present his *logos* as if it were a word addressed by a speaker to an audience, just as he refers in turn to his predecessors as "those whose *logoi* I have heard" (DK 103, M. 83). So men do not understand Heraclitus' own *logos* "even after they have heard it" (fr. 1); they are like the deaf (DK 34, M. 2), "knowing neither how to listen nor how to speak" (DK 19, M. lg). But I think it would be a mistake to take these expressions literally as a reflection of face-to-face verbal contact between Heraclitus and his audience. This is, I suggest, part of the *literary* convention of early prose. Of course we know that some prose works were actually read aloud before an audience. But there is no reason to suppose, when Heraclitus complains of "those whose *logoi* I have heard," that his complaint is *limited* to those doctrines he has listened to in oral presentation. (Of the four authorities criticized in DK 40 = M. 16—Hesiod, Pythagoras, Xenophanes, and Hecataeus—Heraclitus may have literally *heard* none of them, except for the recitation of Hesiod's poems.) It is an essential feature of the literary form that Heraclitus should engage his readers *as if* they were being directly addressed. And what he means by "listening to the *logos*" (DK 50 = M. 26) is anything but conventional. But it is important to recognize that oral phrases were part of the natural terminology for communication in writing, then as now. Thus "Hecataeus of Miletus says (*mytheitai*) as follows: this is what I *write* (*graphō*)." A century later Diogenes of Apollonia speaks of "beginning a discourse (*logos*)" in proper form, with simple, dignified style (fr. 1), but, as we have seen, he refers to his work as a written treatise (*syngraphe*) in fragment 4. We find an amusing example of this automatic use of oral terminology in the episode in Herodotus where Croesus is testing a series of oracles by comparing *written* reports of their utterances. Herodotus first describes the Lydian king as "unfolding the texts and inspecting them," but he immediately lapses into the oral mode: "When Croesus *heard* (*ekouse*) what the oracle from Delphi said . . ." (I. 48. 1). The point is not whether Croesus could read Greek, but that Heraclitus feels no inconsistency in passing from the language of visual reading to that of oral communication. Just so, if I ask you, "Did you hear the news from

Poland today?," I do not mean to distinguish between information from the radio and from the newspaper.

Important as it is, then, the language of speaking and hearing in Heraclitus is not to be taken at face value. A closer look at the fragments will show that they do not lend themselves to lecture use or to sustained public reading (though they are of course *quotable*, and in this sense memorizable). Furthermore, all the external evidence points to communication in writing. The doxography knows nothing of any circle of personal disciples or "hearers" of Heraclitus; Diogenes Laërtius speaks rather of his isolation and his misanthropy (IX. 3). By contrast, we are told that it was his *book* which "acquired such fame that it produced followers of his doctrine who were called Heracliteans" (Diogenes IX.6). In the famous anecdote where Euripides asks Socrates for his opinion, it is the *book* which is passed from hand to hand, and there is no suggestion that Socrates will read it (or have it read) aloud (ibid. II.22; cf. IX. 11). The need for close and repeated study, which is implicit in the Socrates story, is made explicit in the epigram quoted by Diogenes (perhaps from Cleanthes?), which warns the reader not to roll up the papyrus scroll too quickly but to consult an initiate first (which probably means a written commentary). (Diogenes IX. 16.) And it is of course the written text that Aristotle has in mind when he mentions the difficulty of punctuating the first sentence (*Rhet.* III. 5, 1407b 13–18). Such evidence as we have, then, confirms the impression that this was from the beginning a book for readers rather than for hearers. The fifth-century echoes of it that we find in Democritus, Cratylus, and the Hippocratic Corpus, as later in Plato, Aristotle, and Cleanthes, are due to careful study of the text rather than to any continuous oral tradition going back to Ephesus.[22]

Adopting the form of an Ionian *syngraphē*, Heraclitus' book is nonetheless a momentous innovation. Earlier Ionian treatises are like practical instruments for recording and transmitting the results of research, part of the apparatus for technical advance. The signatures which are attached to the work, as in the case of Hecataeus (or later Alcmaeon and Ion) and apparently in the Samian and Ephesian temple descriptions as well, certainly make a claim for personal accomplishment on the part of the author. But for the architects the accomplishment is not the book but the temple. To some extent we can imagine that the same is true for Anaximander and Hecataeus: the pride with which the latter announces what he has to say seems to attach to the content and not to the book as such. We know nothing of the form of his work that suggests any intrinsic significance, beyond the fact that it is the device by which Hecataeus is making his discoveries available to the public. If we look ahead at Herodotus, on the other hand, we see that "the display of his *historiē*" has become a major literary art work. This is visible not only in the scale and style of Herodotus' work but in his express motive: to insure that the great and marvelous deeds of Greeks and Barbarians do not lose their glory (*kleos*). As with the heroic epic, so with the history of the Persian wars: the great fame of the subject will be preserved by the durable success of its literary monument.

Heraclitus is less interested in glory than in understanding and communicating the truth. But quite apart from the crucial fact of literary talent, he has both a social and a philosophic reason for crossing the line that separates a simple research report from a work of art. The social reason is that he is presenting his work as a serious rival to the "wisdom" of Homer and Hesiod, the major poets. The philosophic reason lies in the sense in which the *logos* he has to offer is true forever; everything happens in accordance with it, and so it is public or "common" before he has said a word. Yet his audience is not expected to understand at first hearing. So the book is designed, if not as an oracle, at least as a riddle, which will require much thought and reflection if its meaning is to be grasped. I speak here not of the philosophic content as such, but only of the book as an object carefully contrived and intended for careful study.[23] It is a "sign" to be interpreted, a field in which we must dig in order to come up with any gold. In this perspective Heraclitus' little book is the paradigm of a philosophic classic, to which one returns indefinitely for deeper understanding, while other early prose treatises are like our scientific textbooks which become obsolete as the discipline advances.

Could such a work originally be communicated in the oral mode, by memorizing it and reciting it to one's friends and colleagues? The answer must depend to some extent on taste and talent. But I think that, in addition to the external evidence already cited, the book bears internal signs of having been composed with readers rather than with auditors in mind. One obvious point is the problem of punctuation in the first sentence: we must read that sentence *twice* in order to see that the adverb *aiei* "always" may be construed either with what precedes ("this *logos* is so") or with what follows ("men fail to understand"). Now it is one of the chief advantages of reading to oneself that it is easier to go back and start over. And this will be necessary for the comprehension of many of the fragments. For example, fr. 62 (M. 47) contains six statements, only four of which can be grasped on a single reading: (1) immortals are mortal, (2) mortals are immortal, (3) the latter live the former's death, (4) the former live the latter's death, (5) the former are dead in the latter's life, (6) the latter are dead in the former's life.[24] Now statements (3) and (4) exclude one another on first reading, as do (5) and (6). As a written text for study this is hard enough. As an oral text, spoken but not repeated, it would be sheer mystification. The same can be said for the four fragments on *sophon* "what is wise" and *hen to sophon* "the one wise" (DK 108 = M. 83, DK 50 = M. 26, DK 41 = M. 85, DK 32 = M. 84). Even if these four texts are read one after the other, the complex interconnections (what I have called their density and resonance) can only be teased out bit by bit. Perhaps for some auditor with the gift of total recall no written text would be needed. But for most students of Heraclitus it must be the book and not an oral reading that is the object of study.

I do not think the same can be said for the poems of Xenophanes, the only earlier *philosophic* author whose work is accessible to us. Here it is the doctrine and not the specific verbal expression which seems to be primary; and Xenophanes' poems are clearly composed for public performance. So we may reasonably count Heraclitus not only as the first major prose author of Greece but also as the first philosopher for whom *the written word* is the essential mode of communication. This is probably less true of his fifth-century successors in prose: it is my impression that in the continuation of Ionian *historiē* Anaxagoras, the atomists, and Diogenes employ writing more as a tool of research and publication than as a literary art. (In the case of Democritus, however, the evidence is too fragmentary and ambiguous for any confident judgment.) The situation is more complicated for the two poet-philosophers, Parmenides and Empedocles, who make use of Homeric techniques in entirely new ways, to project radically different views:[25] part of their literary power derives from the fact that they are working against the grain of the medium they have inherited. In any event, the poems of Parmenides and Empedocles are clearly exceptions to the new rule, brilliant examples of the age of experimentation. After Democritus and Plato the language of philosophy became, as it remains, consistently prose. In this regard Heraclitus, for all his apparent isolation, points the way to the philosophic mainstream. I conclude with some general considerations as to why prose came to supply this function.

We began with a survey of the technical literature that precedes Heraclitus, where the earliest specimens were in hexameter verse. Although versified representatives of this tradition do not strictly require writing, they are already post-oral in one sense: the institution of public performance is no longer essential for poetry in this vein. If by the oral mode we mean forms and structures tied to conditions of performance, there is nothing more "oral" about Thales' *Nautical Astronomy* than in our own use of rhyme in "30 days hath September/April June and November/. . ." It may be natural to recite such a poem aloud, or just under one's breath, but only because the rhythmic mechanism of recall works best that way. In such cases verse functions precisely like an internal equivalent of writing: as a reminder. But when it comes to noting detailed observation for later reference, whether of star risings, harbor entrances, temple dimensions or the symptoms and progress of a disease, there is no substitute for writing and, in the end, no substitute for prose.

This use of written prose for recording the facts of observation and planning points to something more fundamental: the essentially "realistic" or mimetic tendency of prose. Whereas the archaic language and traditional formulae of the Homeric hexameter help to create a fictive world, and the powerful rhythms and unusual vocabulary of lyric poetry contribute to an expressive reshaping or ritual celebration of experience, prose represents language in its most natural state, as a vehicle for information and command. Oversimplifying a bit, we may say that whereas poetry tends to produce an art work as a kind of substitute for the everyday world, prose serves on the one hand to record and preserve the world as it is and, on the other hand, to draw up a blueprint for *changing* the world (in legislative proposals, decrees, contracts, or architects' plans). On the one hand we have *historia* as a report of the facts; on the other hand we have *technē* as a capacity to rearrange the facts according to some plan. In either case the writing is intended to be transparent, in that it clearly refers to something else beyond: we look *through* the written word in order to see the world as described or direct the action as enjoined. This is typical of the early uses of prose; it probably applies as well to the lost Ionian verse treatises, and even to some parts of Hesiod's *Erga*. For the *Theogony*, however, and above all for the Homeric epic, poetry has a quite different function which Plato refuses to recognize:[26] not to mirror the world of nature and action but to transmute it into a new realm of brighter and darker colors, sharper relief, and more dramatic moments of emotion and decision, a fictive realm which is essentially opaque in that there is nothing behind it, no more basic "reality" to which it can be referred.[27]

The contrast I have in mind between what we may call the creative and the mimetic or representational functions of literature, between opaque and transparent uses of discourse, does not at all coincide with the distinction between oral and literate modes of composition or presentation. On the one hand, the fully literate worlds of Vergil and Shakespeare are just as opaque and self-sufficient as that of Homer. On the other hand, some "scientific" treatises of the Hippocratic Corpus, which are essentially transparent insofar as they attempt to capture aspects of the nature of things, are at the same time oral in their mode of communication, since some are clearly designed for public reading. Similarly, practical oratory, which uses language to change the world, can normally succeed only by its oral impact upon a company of hearers. But note that there is a secondary use of the oratorical mode as a conventional form for strictly literary publication, as in the case of Isocrates, which parallels the formal use of speaker-hearer framework which we find in Heraclitus. These complex interactions between oral and literary modes are of great interest in their own right; but they are basically irrelevant to the distinction between poetry and prose to which I want to draw attention. This distinction depends upon whether the literary work projects its own reality by creating as it were its own subject matter, or whether it essentially refers, by way of description or intended influence, to the ordinary world in which the audience and the author have their everyday existence.

This contrast between the creative role of poetry and the mimetic function of prose will be clearest if we take two authors such as Homer and Herodotus, whose themes and stylistic resources are to some extent comparable. The epic poet conjures up (with the aid of a centuries-old tradition) a self-sustaining world of heroes, who live a life of their own. For all his heroic inspiration and liberty of invention in detail, Herodotus presents us with a picture of Greece and Persia as he thinks they really were, not a fictive world with its own standards of truth. When he creates or shapes an episode, Herodotus is concerned to bring out the true factors—social, psychological, theological—which decided the actual course of events. Even if some of the events told by the poets are, like the Trojan War, believed to have taken place, everyone knows that bards can "tell many a lie." For the epic poet, as for the later dramatist, the traditional plot or myth is only a flexible framework to be filled in with a meaningful set of episodes that is the poet's job to create. The only real world behind the poem is the artificial world of the epic tradition itself. But for Herodotus his pictures, no matter how skillfully elaborated, are always pictures *of* something that is the real thing: the antiquities of Egypt, the invasion of Xerxes, the Athenian response. So Herodotus is a mimetic artist in a sense that Homer is not. The point would be even more obvious if we took Thucydides as our prose specimen, since the originals of his imitation are so much closer and more familiar to his audience. The relative remoteness of Herodotus' subjects in time and place allows him more freedom of a quasi-poetic sort. But even in his case we can see that the work of *historiē* is essentially representational and "realistic," not creative and self-contained.

What is true for the use of prose in history is also true, *mutatis mutandis*, for its use in philosophy. The philosophic author does not transport his audience into another realm with its own standards of verisimilitude. Even more than the historian (who may be concerned with a distant past), the philosopher must reveal to his readers a world with which they are in some sense already familiar, for it is his aim to tell them the truth about the world in which they live. In this sense his discourse too is supposed to be transparent: the audience is invited to look *through* his words in order to recognize the reality which he describes. That is, perhaps, one of the deeper reasons for the philosophic (and scientific) preference for prose: this more relaxed and natural form of discourse tends to make for less opacity; it provides less of an artificial screen to interfere with the ordinary descriptive and referential functions of language.

But prose too has its opacities, to which Heraclitus was not insensitive. The enigmatic texture of his discourse must have been intended, at least in part, to disabuse the reader of any temptation to assume that his utterances might be taken as entirely transparent, as if the truth about the world could be stated in an unambiguous description. But at least the truth that he wants to manifest is already "common" and public: his auditors will recognize it as familiar if they can only wake up. The problem is more acute for Plato, who insists upon a conception of reality entirely remote from ordinary experience. The unchanging truth he has to reveal is bound to be distorted by the flux of words men use to talk about their day-to-day affairs. And for Plato the written word is doubly cursed, because of its inflexibility (which makes it unable to respond to the specific and variable state of mind of the reader) and also because of its apparent dogmatism: the sentences *look* as if they were bare statements of the truth, as if it were possible in writing "to bring forth the nature of things into the light for all to see," whereas in fact philosophical understanding "is not at all stateable like other kinds of knowledge."[28] Hence Plato's genial invention of the philosophical dialogue. Here the written word will not serve to state the truth directly (and hence deform it in the attempt) but rather to depict men in the process of seeking wisdom and working to clarify their insights by argument and analysis. The formulae for depicting the nature of things are neatly relativized to a particular stage of the discussion with a particular interlocutor under given circumstances, thus allowing the reader to correct for his own intellectual latitude and longitude. By combining the arts of the poet and the historian, Plato has created a semi-fictive world around the historical Socrates, thus neutralizing the distorting tendencies of the literary medium by making this medium plainly visible, in the carefully drawn characters and situations of the speakers in the dialogue. Because he knows that his own prose cannot be fully transparent, Plato has as it were put a picture frame around the window, so that we know in looking through it that what we see is not the naked truth but the human attempt at discovery and formulation.

Heraclitus' artistry is less elaborate, but its motivation is not dissimilar: to guarantee that the relative opacity of the written word will not go unnoticed, and thus to stimulate the reader to make the effort of understanding that will permit him to appropriate some of the author's insights for himself.

Charles H. Kahn

University of Pennsylvania

NOTES

1. *Phaedrus* 274E–275A.
2. Hdt. II. 145.
3. For some interesting speculation see E. A. Havelock, "The Alphabetization of Homer," in Eric A. Havelock and Jackson B. Hershbell, eds., *Communication Arts in the Ancient World* (New York: Hastings House, 1978), pp. 17–19. My own assumptions are closer to those of J. A. Davison, "Literature and Literacy in Ancient Greece," *Phoenix* 16 (1962), pp. 147–51.
4. What M. L. West says of the early book will apply to the epics as well: "The written book was a record of the spoken or sung word and subordinated to it. It was primarily valuable to the author himself, as an aide-memoire, a way of fixing his liquid thoughts" (*Early Greek Philosophy and the Orient*, [Oxford: Clarendon Press, 1971], p. 5). But the longer the poem, the more indispensable writing becomes to preserve some constancy from performance to performance, and from generation to generation.
5. Plato, *Lysis*, 209A–B, *Phaedrus*, 228D ff., *Parmenides*, 127C. In *Phaedo*, 97B8, Socrates hears someone reading from a book of Anaxagoras; but then, it should be noted, he goes on to read it for himself (98B).
6. See Thuc I. 97.2 for "the Attic *syngraphē*" of Hellanicus of Mytilene.
7. Hdt. I. 93.1: "the land of Lydia does not have many marvels worth recording" (*es syngraphēn*); cf. *syngraphō* in III. 103; VI.14.1.
8. Hdt. I. 47.1, 48.1.
9. Walter Burkert, *Lore and Science in Ancient Pythagoreanism*, tr. E. L. Minar, Jr., (Cambridge: Harvard University Press, 1972), p. 13ff., 210 (= *Weisheit und Wissenschaft*, p. 107f., 143). The fact that a third-century poet can use *historiē* to refer to the "learning" of Hesiod is scarcely evidence for Heraclitus' use of the term. Contrast Eur. fr. 910N and Pl. *Phaedo* 96 A8.
10. See Nilsson, "Kataploi," *Rheinisches Museum* 60 (1905), pp. 178–86, who points out that the *Kataploi* are the least well attested. For Hesiod's *Astronomy* see DK 4; for Cleostratus see DK 6, Burkert, *Lore and Science*, p. 333 (= *Weisheit und Wissenschaft*, p. 312), and my article in *JHS* 90 (1970), p. 104. For Thales' *Nautical Astronomy* see Dk 11.B.1 and 11.A3a.
11. For *syngraphai* in this sense, as architects' specifications, see LSJ s. v. II. 2.
12. J. M. McCredie, "Hippodamos of Miletus," in *Studies Presented to George M. A. Hanfmann* (Mainz, 1971), p. 100. Aristotle, in reporting his social theory, emphasizes that Hippodamus systematically divided everything into three parts (*Pol.* II. 8). As Newman observed in his commentary on this remark (1267b 31), there is a striking parallel here to the contemporary speculation of Ion of Chios, whose basic principle is that everything comes in threes (DK 36 B 1).
13. See J. J. Pollitt, *The Ancient View of Greek Art: Criticism, History, and Terminology* (New Haven: Yale University Press, 1974), p. 12ff. with notes p. 88ff. In the archaic period architecture and sculpture, like engineering, navigation, and astronomy, represent major forms of applied mathematics. For the high technical level achieved in the proportions of the Heraion, the tunnel of Eupalinus, and other products of Samian skill, see H. Diels, *Antike Technik*, 2nd ed. (Leipzig: Teubner, 1920) pp. 6–11; K. von Fritz, *RE* 24 (1963), s.v. "Pythagoras," 185f.
14. So Pollitt, *Ancient View of Greek Art*, pp. 18–20.

15. This a less speculative alternative to the suggestion of M. Marcovich (*Heraclitus editio maior* [Mérida, Venezuela: Los Andes University Press, 1967], pp. 69 f., following Wilamowitz and von Fritz) that "some oriental (Babylonian) mathematical treatises are meant." The existence of treatises by early Greek architects and sculptors is attested, whereas translations from the cuneiform are not. Of course we can infer (but not confirm) Egyptian and Babylonian sources for this technical tradition.

16. Pollitt, *Ancient View of Greek Art*, p. 258.

17. For the early evidence, see my "Pythagorean Philosophy Before Plato" in A. P. D. Mourelatos, ed., *The Presocratics* (Garden City, NY: Anchor Press, 1974). It is worth recalling the mysterious relationship between our Pythagoras and the sculptor of the same name, also from Samos, who is said to have been "the first one to aim at *rhythmos* and *symmetria*" (Xenocrates, cited by Pollitt, p. 21); and one is reminded of Seltman's thesis that it was our Pythagoras who designed the new coinage of Magna Graecia. (For a favorable view of this extraordinary possibility, see W. K. C. Guthrie, *A History of Greek Philosophy*, I, (Cambridge: Cambridge University Press, 1962), p. 176f.) I mention these insoluble historical problems only because they tend to reinforce the importance of the technical tradition in the arts for understanding Pythagoras' own brand of *sophia*, and for appreciating Heraclitus' attack upon him.

18. For more information on early scientific prose see A. Lesky, *Geschichte der griechischen Literatur* (Berne: Francke, 1957), pp. 203–209 (English translation by James Willis and Cornelis de Heer [New York: Crowell, 1966], pp. 216–22), who also notes early work in medicine (Alcmaeon of Croton) and the *Periplous* ascribed to Scylax, the navigator who explored the Indian Ocean and the Red Sea for Darius in the late sixth century.

19. With the exception of Pherecydes. See the following note.

20. For Pherecydes see, DK 7 and M. L. West, *Early Greek Philosophy and the Orient*, chapters 1 and 2. Heraclitus could have no sympathy with Pherecydes' project of using what Havelock has called the god-apparatus to tell an entertaining story with cosmological allusions.

21. E. A. Havelock, "Pre-Literacy and the Pre-Socratics," *Bulletin of the Institute of Classical Studies* 13 (London, 1966), p. 55, referring to G. S. Kirk and J. E. Raven, eds., *The Presocratic Philosophers* (Cambridge: Cambridge University Press, 1957), p. 185. See also Kirk, *Heraclitus: The Cosmic Fragments* (Cambridge: Cambridge University Press, 1954), p. 7.

22. For details, see my *The Art and Thought of Heraclitus* (Cambridge: Cambridge University Press, 1979), p. 3ff. Of course the study of such a text will often have been a group activity, with reading done aloud. Xenophon describes Socrates as "unrolling with his friends the treasures of wise men of old, which they have written and left behind in books" (*Memorabilia* I. 6. 14). Myles Burnyeat has recently depicted an imaginary but plausible "reading" of Heraclitus' book before an audience gathered for this purpose (*The New York Review of Books*, May 13, 1982). My point is simply that such public readings or study groups presuppose the written text as the vehicle for Heraclitus' thought. Compare the evidence for Anaxagoras' book in n.5 above and in *Apology* 26D.

23. This is intended as a non-controversial claim, reflecting those features of the fragments which justify Heraclitus' reputation for obscurity. I assume that no one believes this obscurity is accidental or uncontrived. So my point here is independent of

the further claim that the over-all arrangement of the fragments was in turn artfully designed.

24. For exegesis, see *The Art and Thought of Heraclitus*, pp. 216–20.

25. We happen to know by a chance remark of Aristotle (*NE* VII.3, 1147a20, b12) that the poems of Empedocles were frequently memorized and recited by rote, a century after they were composed. It is not clear what this tells us about the original system of communication, but it does point to a continuous interaction between written and oral modes in the transmission and study of difficult texts.

26. See above all *Ion* 537C–541A, where Socrates systematically reduces the subject matter of Homeric poetry to the objects studied by the other arts and crafts.

27. As historians, of course, we may be interested in the Mycenaean (or post-Mycenaean) origins of the Homeric world, and this historical dimension will add to our enjoyment of Homer's art. But such knowledge or speculation is largely irrelevant for the immanent understanding of the heroic world which is created by the poems themselves. By contrast the modern novel, though in some ways successor to the epic, has in virtue of its prose medium an inherently "realistic" tendency which makes the historical novel a paradigm of the genre. To some extent a quasi-historical tendency is also characteristic of the ancient novel or romance. But the novel as a literary genre is a complex secondary development, heavily influenced by poetry and drama, and it can only be partially accounted for by the view of prose presented here.

28. *Epistle* VII, 341 D7 and C5. I have no doubt that these words were written by Plato himself. But those who suspect the authenticity of the *Seventh Epistle* may find essentially the same view of writing expressed in the *Phaedrus*, 275C–276E, immediately following the passage quoted at the beginning of this essay.

THE ORAL-POETIC RELIGION
OF XENOPHANES

In "The Linguistic Task of the Presocratics," E. A. Havelock considers Xenophanes an "oral composer" who expected "to be listened to rather than read," and whose thought must be understood against the "oral mythos" of Homer and Hesiod.[1] According to Havelock, Xenophanes' "key pronouncement" is "one *theos*, among gods and men biggest" (B23), and this "comprehensive, unitary *theos*" is co-extensive with the physical environment or "cosmos seen as a whole."[2] These observations of Havelock provide a basis for this essay, which, after consideration of Xenophanes' style, will focus on his much-vexed views about the divine. In both matters, attention will be given to ways in which the poetic tradition of Homer and Hesiod influenced Xenophanes' "thought," his *phrontis* (B8, 2), and his own poetic "skill" or "craft" (*sophia*, B2, 12–14).[3]

The claim that Xenophanes was an oral poet is not new. There is the ancient testimony of Diogenes Laertius who at IX.18 of his *Lives of Famous Philosophers* reports:

> He |Xenophanes| wrote in epic meter, also elegiacs and iambics against Hesiod and Homer, reproving them for what they said about the gods. But he himself also recited |*errapsōdei*| his own poems.

Diogenes gives no source for his last remark, which, because of the verb *errapsōdei*, has been taken to mean that Xenophanes was a rhapsode who gave public recitations of the Homeric epics.[4] But in view of Xenophanes' attacks on Homer and Hesiod, it seems unlikely that he was a rhapsode whose main function was to uphold Homer's renown.[5] Probably Diogenes' report means no more than that Xenophanes recited his own poems, as the rhapsodes recited those of Homer. Whatever Diogenes meant, it is clear that he or his source believed that Xenophanes gave public recitals of his poems.

Diogenes' testimony is supported by the extant fragments of Xenophanes' works, and these provide the chief evidence that he was an oral poet. Certainly B1, an almost complete elegiac poem, seems to have been sung at a symposium when Xenophanes was in charge, and gave advice on how much wine to drink and how to hymn a deity.[6] In B8 (also elegiac) Xenophanes may allude to his career as an itinerant poet relying on contact with audiences which heard rather than read his verses in written circulation.[7]

Xenophanes' style also suggests that he was an oral poet who sought to impress his beliefs on a listening audience. In particular, the repetitiveness of several fragments deserves attention. B11–12, for example, contain an identical line:

> Both Homer and Hesiod have ascribed to gods all
> things that are a shame and disgrace among mortals:
> *stealing, adultery, and mutual deception.* (B11)

> They |Homer and Hesiod| have told as many lawless deeds of gods as possible:
> *stealing, adultery, and mutual deception.* (B12)

Similar repetitions are frequent in the Homeric epics, and Xenophanes may simply be imitating or even parodying their style. Less obvious though equally interesting repetitive patterns are found in other fragments. For example, in B30 Xenophanes proclaims:

> Sea is source of water, and
> source of wind; for neither
> in clouds |would there be any strength
> of wind blowing forth| from within
> without mighty sea, nor streams of
> rivers nor rain-water from sky. But
> mighty sea is begetter of clouds,
> winds, and rivers.

Not only does the fragment consist of repeated words, for example, *pēgē* ("source"), *pontos* ("sea"), *potamōn* ("rivers"), but its concluding verse essentially repeats the thesis of the first verse: sea is the source of water and wind.[8]

B2, one of the largest fragments, has a more complex repetitive pattern which B. A. Van Groningen described as a gradually narrowing or shrinking spiral ("Le développement suit . . . un mouvement en spirale. Ici c'est une spirale qui va en se rétrécissant."):[9]

> What if a man win victory in swiftness
> of foot, or in the *pentathlon,* at
> Olympia, where is the precinct of Zeus
> by Pisa's springs, or in wrestling,—
> what if by cruel boxing or that fearful
> sport men call *pankration* he become more glorious in the citizens' eyes,
> and win a place of honour in the sight of
> all at the games, his food at the public
> cost from the State, and a gift to be an
> heirloom for him,—what if he conquer in the
> chariot-race,—he will not deserve all this
> for his portion as much as I do. Far better

is our art than the strength of men and of
horses!
These are but thoughtless judgments, nor is
it fitting to set strength before goodly art.
Even if there arise a mighty boxer among a people,
or one great in the *pentathlon* or at wrestling, or
one excelling in swiftness of foot—and that stands
in honour before all tasks of men at the games—
the city would be none the better governed for that.
It is but little joy a city gets of it if a man
conquer at the games by Pisa's banks; it is not
this that makes fat the store-houses of a city.

(J. Burnet's translation)

After mentioning six main events at the Olympian games, Xenophanes maintains that his *sophia* (Burnet translates 'art') is far superior to success in these. He then mentions only four of the six events, omitting the *pankration* and chariot-racing, with the remark that these do not bestow good order on a community. Finally, he summarizes all events in the single word *aethleuōn* (Burnet translates "conquer at the games"), and concludes that such activity does not enrich a community's "store-houses."[10]

"Far better is our art than the strength of men and of horses . . . nor is it fitting to set strength before goodly art"—the main point of the elegy is essentially repeated in these verses which themselves are preceded and followed by varied repetition, a catalogue of the Olympian games by Pisa's springs (or banks): swiftness of feet (*podōn*), the "five exercises" (*pentathlon*), wrestling (*palaismosunē*), boxing (*puktosunē*), wrestling and boxing combined (*pankration*). When recited aloud the alliterative enumeration, combined with other repetition, produces an intense and vigorous acoustic effect; when read silently in translation, this long fragment of a poem seems tiresome, even clumsy. Its appeal, in brief, is to the ear and not to the eye.

Attention has thus far been confined to repetition of phrases, words, and the ideas fashioned from them. But Xenophanes' choice of these, his shaping of language into a now permanent form, was determined by a still more basic repetitive pattern, the "flow" (*rhythmos*) or succession of long and short syllables of words, and so the fragments are in identifiable meters: hexameters and elegiacs, with one example of an iambic trimeter followed by a hexameter (B14). Generally, however, metrical form inhibits or restricts what can be expressed. For example, hexameters are not well suited for an easy use of Greek, and many words, because of their scansion, are excluded.[11] Why, then, if a prose style existed which would have better served his philosophical purposes, did Xenophanes use poetry as the medium for conveying his thought? Perhaps the question has no decisive answer, but given the previous evidence, Havelock's thesis about Xenophanes' "orality" provides a convincing explanation. In essence, this thesis is that Xenophanes composed in a predominantly oral culture in which "publication" was by means of recital and not by manuscript. His probably semi-literate audiences were accustomed to hear, for example, the Homeric epics sung by rhapsodes, and what was orally presented depended on memory for its preservation and transmission. Yet memory depended, in turn, on rhythmic words organized in metrical and verbal patterns having a high degree of regularity. Conscious, then, of his *sophia* and the need to correct and replace Homeric-Hesiodic conceptions of the cosmos and the gods, Xenophanes used poetic composition as the most effective way of communicating with his audiences and guaranteeing that his own teaching would not be forgotten as he wandered throughout the land of Hellas.

Unfortunately, much of Xenophanes' work *has* been forgotten, and only some forty-odd fragments, or a total of about 119 lines and part-lines of his poems, survive.[12] The content of these fragments, like their style, is perhaps best understood against the background of early Greek poetry, especially the epics of Homer and Hesiod. Certainly in B10 Xenophanes versified: "from the beginning in accord with Homer when [since] all learned. . . ." What was learned is not stated,[13] but presumably Xenophanes included himself among all who learned, and he explicitly attacks his "teacher": "both Homer and Hesiod have attributed to the gods all things that are a shame and disgrace among mortals: stealing, adultery, and mutual deception" (B11). Imputation of these same "lawless deeds" (*athemistia erga*) to the gods is implicitly criticized in B12, and with very probable reference to Hesiod and other epic composers, Xenophanes considers the narrated battles of Titans, Giants, and Centaurs as "fictions of those of former times" (B1, 22).[14] Similarly, he criticizes mortals who have learned from Homer and Hesiod to believe that the gods are born or come into being, and have their own clothing, voice or speech, and body or shape (*demas*) (B14);[15] for example, Aethiopians say their gods are black and snub-nosed, Thracians that they are red-haired and blue-eyed (B16). But if oxen, horses, or lions had hands, they would depict gods in their own shapes (B15). In sum, contrary to the beliefs of Homer, Hesiod, and mortals under their sway, Xenophanes does not think the gods are "immoral" or like human beings in appearance.

Nowhere in the previous fragments does Xenophanes question the existence of many gods, and in other verses: B1, 13, B18, 1, B34, and B38, "god" is used in the singular and plural with apparent indifference to number. In B1, 13, for example, the singular can be explained as a reference to a particular god, perhaps Dionysus, and the singular in B38 seems to be conventional: "if a god had not made yellow honey . . ."[16] In sharp contrast to these uses of "god," however, stands B23, which, when taken in conjunction with B24–26, presents a conception of divinity at variance with that of the Homeric and Hesiodic epics:

> One god, among gods and humans greatest,
>   in no way like mortals in body or mind. (B23)
> Entire it sees, entire it thinks, and entire it hears. (B24)
> But apart from toil it shakes all things with
>   the center of its mind. (B25)
> And being disturbed in no way it remains always
>   in the same place nor is it fitting for it to go
>   elsewhere at other times. (B26)

These fragments, especially B23, have received considerable attention from modern interpreters of Xenophanes' thought.[17] Their translation, however, is by no means certain, and since they come from different sources—B23 is quoted by Clement of Alexandria, B24 by Sextus Empiricus, and B25–26 by Simplicius—[18] it is also uncertain whether the order of Diels-Kranz is correct.

Havelock and others[19] have rightly seen these verses as directed against Homeric-Hesiodic conceptions of deity. For example, the phrase "in no way like mortals in body" (B23) seems to contradict Homeric descriptions of mortals like the gods in body (*Iliad.* VIII, 305; *Odyssey* viii, 14); B24 strongly suggests that a god needs no special organs to see or hear; B25 is probably meant to recall the way Olympus shook when Zeus nodded his head (*Iliad* I, 530); and B26 seems directed against gods who are constantly moving about in the cosmos. But what was the meaning of these verses for Xenophanes? Did he believe in the existence of one and only one god? And was this god coextensive for him with the cosmos so that his thought can be labeled "pantheistic monotheism"? A brief review of interpretations of B23–26 seems apposite.

B23 is preserved only by Clement of Alexandria, who in his *Stromateis* quotes it before B14 and B15 in a rambling account of how the Hellenes stole from barbarian (that is, Hebrew) philosophy. In citing B23 Clement views it as a declaration that god is one and incorporeal (*asōmatos*), and Diels and others accordingly punctuate with a comma after *theos* so that the first two words mean there is one god, or that god is one. Clement's interpretation, together with reports by other ancient authors, for example, Cicero, Hippolytus, pseudo-Aristotle (in the *De Melisso, Xenophane, Gorgia*), have probably influenced modern scholars who think that B23 is an affirmation of monotheism.[20] But besides the ambiguous *heis theos* there is the phrase "greatest (*megistos*) among gods and men." Proponents of a monotheistic interpretation regard this as a "polar expression" (or "polarische Ausdrucksweise") used primarily for emphasis and not to be taken literally, and so the phrase means no more than "greatest of all."[21] This is a possibility, but M. Stokes has questioned whether a convinced monotheist in an unreceptive polytheistic society would "cloud the issue by mention of plural gods which is at best ambiguous, in the very context where he is firmly stating his revolutionary view."[22] Moreover, as M. Nilsson observed, Xenophanes is never included among the *atheoi* by the ancients.[23]

Perhaps the key term in B23 is not "one" (*heis*), but *megistos*, for *heis* is often used in Greek to reinforce a superlative, and so the emphasis is on a one god "greatest" among gods and men.[24] Havelock would render *megistos* "biggest," noting that the primary reference of *megas* (hence its superlative) is to size or quantity.[25] But whatever the nuances of *megistos*, Xenophanes is using an Homeric epithet often applied to Zeus: Zeus is "most glorious, biggest (or "greatest")" . . . *Il.* II, 412, III, 278, 296, etc. Cf. *h. Hom.* XXIII, 1 where Zeus is "best and biggest of gods" (*Zēna theōn ton ariston . . . ēde megiston*). It would seem, then, that Xenophons' biggest god is being singled out or contrasted with something, probably Zeus in particular or the mythological gods in general. In any case, unlike these gods, it is no way "like mortals in mind or body."

Perhaps as Havelock and others[26] have maintained, this god is to be identified with the world, and the repeated adjective *oulos* ("entire" or "whole") of B25 has a spatial connotation.[27] Certainly beginning with Theophrastus, if not before, the later doxographical tradition equated Xenophanes' god with the cosmos.[28] But if this is correct, what is to be made of Xenophanes' references to other deities? Is their mention simply a concession to conventional usage or to the poetic tradition in which Xenophanes was composing? B32 provides a clue: "and she whom they [presumably Homer and mortals under his influence] call Iris, she too is actually a cloud, purple and flame-red and yellow to behold." In other words, a deity such as Iris is only a rainbow. The "stars" appearing on ships, that is, St. Elmo's fire, which sailors call the "Dioscuri," are "small clouds glimmering on account of a certain motion" (DK, A39).[29] Thus, according to Xenophanes, some of the deities of mythology were "names" that mortals used for what are, in fact, metereological phenomena. Was Zeus also for him a name mortals used, say, for the wide sky or the world itself?[30] No fragment or ancient doxographer suggests such a notion, but clearly in Xenophanes' mind something was amiss with the way mortals spoke and thought about the divine.

To return to Havelock's thesis, there is strong indication that Xenophanes was an oral poet engaged in creation of a new language, a language which will replace that of the Homeric-Hesiodic epics in the attempt to think about the cosmos. If this is correct, an interpretation of Xenophanes as the earliest Greek monotheist tends to obscure his place in the history of ancient thought.[31] Indeed there was nothing striking in his time in the existence of one greatest or biggest god among gods and men—the Zeus of Homer and especially of Hesiod already played such a role.[32] Their Zeus, however, needed in Xenophanes' mind to be divested of human characteristics if it was to be worthy of awe, and if the nature of the world were to be properly understood. His attack is thus not so much directed against a plurality of gods as against anthropomorphism. When he speaks of other gods, for example in B23, B34, he may have been thinking of what to-day would be called "natural phenomena." These are "appearances" of the one god or the cosmos itself.[32] Admittedly the relation between the one god and many gods in Xenophanes is obscure, but then Xenophanes was not writing a "summa theologiae," and Havelock's thesis puts Xenophanes' thought in a proper historical perspective.

J. P. Hershbell

University of Minnesota

NOTES

1. E. A. Havelock, "The Linguistic Task of the Presocratics" (cited hereafter as "Linguistic Task") in this volume, pp. 9–10. See also Havelock's earlier study, "Pre-literacy and the Pre-Socratics," *Bulletin of the Institute of Classical Studies* 13 (1966), pp. 44–67, esp. pp. 51–54 on Xenophanes.

2. Havelock, "Linguistic Task," p. 22.

3. For a survey of the various meanings that have been suggested for *phrontis* and *sophia*, see Mario Untersteiner, *Senofane, Testimonianze e frammenti* (*Biblioteca di studi superiori* 33), Florence, 1956 pp. 113–14 and 127.

4. See Theodor Gomperz, *Greek Thinkers: A History of Ancient Philosophy*, tr. L. Magnus, I (London: J. Murray 1901), p. 155.

5. John Burnet, *Early Greek Philosophy* (New York, 1957), p. 115, maintained that Diogenes' statement "has no foundation at all." His view was later shared by Werner Jaeger, *The Theology of the Early Greek Philosophers* (Oxford: Clarendon Press, repr. 1948), p. 41.

6. See C. M. Bowra, *Problems in Greek Poetry* (Oxford: Clarendon Press 1953) p. 1ff.

7. Havelock, "Linguistic Task," p. 10.

8. On the structure of the fragment, see Untersteiner, *Senofane*, p. 139. W. K. C. Guthrie notes that a scholiast quotes the fragment on lines in *Iliad* XXI, 196 which describe Oceanus as the source of all water-rivers sea, springs, and wells (*A History of Greek Philosophy* I |Cambridge University Press, 1962|, p. 391).

9. B. A. van Groningen, *La composition littéraire archaïque grecque* (Amsterdam: Noord-Hollandsche 1960), p. 89.

10. On this fragment, see especially Bowra, *Problems in Greek Poetry*, (see n6 above), pp. 15–37; and Untersteiner, *Senofane*, pp. 109–16.

11. This has led to speculation that the Greeks adopted hexametric verse from some other language such as Minoan or Hittite. See C. M. Bowra, "Metre," in *A Companion to Homer*, ed. A. J. B. Wace and F. H. Stubbings (London: Macmillan, 1962), p. 23.

12. The extent of Xenophanes' poetic production can no longer be determined. Diogenes Laertius (IX. 20), relying probably on an Alexandrian source, reports that Xenophanes wrote poems on the foundation of Colophon and on the settlement of a colony of Elea in Italy in 2,000 lines. If this is any indication, his poetic output, especially given his longevity, was probably considerable.

13. Diels, thinking of Plato, *Resp.* 600E, completed, the verse with "the gods are most wicked." Havelock, "Linguistic Task," p. 15, queries whether Xenophanes was referring to the kind of human or cosmic history conveyed in early epics.

14. See Untersteiner, *Senofane*, pp. 106–08.

15. *Demas*, derived from *demein* ("to build" or "to construct"), means something like "Körperbau, äussere Gestalt,"; see Halmar Frisk, *Griechisches etymologisches Wörterbuch* (Heidelberg: C. Winter, 1960–72), s.v. *demō*.

16. Guthrie remarks, "It is a conventional phrase in which a Greek might use either singular or plural, and means no more than 'if honey had never existed.'" *History of Greek Philosophy*, I, p. 376. (Cited hereafter as *History*.)

17. To the bibliographical references in Untersteiner, *Senofane*, may be added G. Kirk and J. Raven, *The Presocratic Philosophers* (Cambridge: Cambridge University Press, 1957) p. 168 ff.; Guthrie, *History of Greek*, p. 373 ff.; Walter Pötscher, "Zu Xenophanes, Frgm. 23," *Emerita* 32 (1964), pp. 1–13; Michael C. Stokes, *One and Many in Presocratic Philosophy* hereafter *One and Many* (Cambridge: Harvard University Press, 1971), esp. p. 76ff.; and Jonathan Barnes, *The Presocratic Philosophers* I (London: Routledge and Kegan Paul 1979), p. 84ff.

18. Clem. *Strom.* V 109 (II 399, 16 St.), Sext. *Adv. math* IV 144, and Simpl. *Phy.* 23, 19. B24 is quoted also at Diogenes Laertius IX, 19 in *oratio obliqua* without attribution to Xenophanes and with omission of *holon noein*. *Mē mentoi anapnein* is quoted instead: "it certainly does not breathe." See Guthrie, *History*, I, p. 374, n2, on the version in Diogenes Laertius.

19. For example, Jaeger, Kirk, Guthrie, and Stokes.

20. The doxographical reports are neatly tabulated and discussed in detail by Stokes, *One and Many*, p. 68ff. The doxographers tend to be late. One of them, Hippolytus of Rome, is already a Christian apologist. The date of pseudo-Aristotle, *De Melisso, Xenophane, Gorgia*, is by no means certain, but most modern scholars consider it late and probably not before the first century B.C. Guthrie, *History*, I, p. 367; and Burnet, *Early Greek Philosophy*, p. 126, n1.

21. Ulrich von Wilamowitz-Möllendorff seems to be the originator of this interpretation in his *Euripides, Herakles* I (Berlin, 1895), p. 231. Burnet in reference to Wilamowitz's explanation of the phrase in Xenophanes coined the term "polar expression." *Early Greek Philosophy*, p. 129. See also Guthrie, *History*, I, p. 375, n2 and Stokes, *One and Many*, p. 76.

22. *One and Many*, p. 76.

23. Martin Nilsson, *Geschichte der griechischen Religion* I (Munich: Beck, 1967), p. 743.

24. See Stokes, *One and Many*, p. 77.

25. Havelock, "Linguistic Task," p. 22, See also 29f.

26. For example, Burnet and Guthrie.

27. Havelock, "Linguistic Task," p. 22. *Holos (oulos* is the Ionic form) comes to be used as a substantive, *to holon*, in Plato, for example, at *Grg.* 508A. In this usage it refers to the world or universe.

28. As Stokes pointed out, the evidence in Theophrastus is not wholly clear. In any case, Theophrastus was not the first, but was preceded by Aristotle. Aristotle, however, does not claim at *Metaph.* 986b2 that Xenophanes equated god and the world. He says that Xenophanes "looked up to" the whole heaven and "said" the one was god. See Stokes, *One and Many*, p. 66 ff. and p. 82 f.

29. J. Lesher, "Xenophanes' Scepticism," *Phronesis* 22 (1978), pp. 1–21, argues convincingly that Xenophanes' scepticism is best understood as a response to religious and poetic ways of thinking and is thus closely tied to his criticism of Homer. He sees these passages as having an "anti-divinational flavor" (p. 8).

30. Havelock, "Linguistic Task," pp. 29–30, maintains that when Xenophanes asserts his god is biggest, he is thinking of Zeus' allotment of the "wide heaven" in the distribution of the cosmos described at *Iliad* XV, 187–92. Zeus' name is, of course, clearly connected with the sky. See, for example, Emile Boisacq, *Dictionnaire étymologique de la langue grecque* (Heidelberg: C. Winter, 1916), s.v. *Zeus*.

31. Terms such as "theology," "monotheism," and "polytheism" belong to later Greek vocabulary. For example, Jaeger noted that "theology" and "theologian" are not attested before the works of Plato and Aristotle (*Theology*, p. 4f. and 194, notes 13 and 14; *polytheia* appears first in Philo (see *LSJ*), s.v.; *monotheia* appears rather late, probably in the 5th–6th century A.D. See G. W. H. Lampe, *A Patristic Greek Lexicon* (Oxford: Clarendon Press, 1961), s.v. To be sure, Xenophanes' religious beliefs anticipate later reflection about the divine, but they need continually be seen against the background of his predecessors, in particular Homer and Hesiod, not that of his successors, Plato, Aristotle, and later Christian opponents of polytheism.

32. See, for example, Havelock, *Bulletin of Classical Studies* 13 (1966), p. 53; and Stokes, *One and Many*, pp. 78–79.

33. C. H. Kahn, *Anaximander and the Origins of Greek Cosmology* (New York: Columbia University Press, p. 156, n3, observed that "In all probability the plural 'gods' of Xenophanes are the elements and the sun, moon, and stars. . . ." Pötscher, *Emerita* 32 (1964), p. 12, refers to the existence of gods in Xenophanes as "eine legitime Erscheinungsform des Gottes."

HERACLITEAN CONCEPTS AND EXPLANATIONS

Curiosity is part of human nature. In some cases curiosity can be satisfied by the mere gathering of information, but in other cases it demands explanations. Philosophical speculations guide curiosity by showing puzzling aspects of things that we have previously taken for granted, and by formulating new types of questions and molding new types of explanatory patterns. One of the key strands in the history of Pre-Socratic philosophy is the development of new types of questions, and explanatory patterns. First I shall sketch what I take to be the main outline of this series of developments, and then will attempt to locate Heraclitus' thought within this framework. In the course of doing this I shall show how this outline places certain recent debates into proper perspective.

I

Origin, Stuff, and Attribute

In this section I would like to suggest that Pre-Socratic speculation goes through three stages of explanatory patterns. These are: explanation solely in terms of origin, explanation in terms of stuff or constituency, and explanation in terms of entities and their attributes. The movement through these three stages should be thought of as progress, since without it science and logic as we know them would not have been possible. I do not claim that the progression goes through distinct stages with sharp breaks. On the contrary, much of the difficulty in understanding Pre-Socratic thought can be alleviated when we locate various thinkers as in between these stages, or as not being fully aware of the pattern of explanation within which their thoughts move.

There are other developments in Pre-Socratic thought as well. The break with the mythical and the move toward literal logical explanations—"from myth to logic," in Bruno Snell's felicitous words[1]—as well as the push to seek explanation for the observable in terms of unobservable underlying entities, and the effort to comprehend the unity of nature that underlies seeming diversity,[2] are enormous conceptual steps in the development of Western thought. I wish, however, to concentrate on changes in explanatory patterns. The particular three-stage development that I posit has not been—to my knowledge—pointed out before, and the understanding of Heraclitus' unique place among the Pre-Socratics primarily requires locating his ambiguous position with regard to this three-stage development of explanatory patterns. The main claim of this interpretation is that Heraclitus' thought is characterized by a shift from the second to the third stage of explanatory patterns, and that this shift is, to a large extent, responsible for ambiguities that run through many of the fragments.[3]

What is it to explain something solely in terms of origin? Today we separate the question "What is it?" from the question "How did it come about?"—though in some contexts we think of the answers to these questions as having relevance to each other. For example, historical accounts are viewed at times as helping to understand the nature of political institutions. There is no evidence, however, that at the dawn of Greek thought these two questions were sharply separated. Both Homer and Hesiod see natural phenomena, or the feats of some human beings as calling for account in terms of origin. A hero is said to have had a divine mother, one generation of gods is explained in terms of a previous generation, natural phenomena are explained as the outcomes of divine actions, etc.

If one thinks that to know that x comes from y helps to understand x, one is likely to assume some similarity between the two entities: x comes from y and is thus similar to y. Nowadays we would immediately ask: "Similar in what respect?" But at the stage of development with which we deal here similarity has not yet been analyzed as two entities sharing an attribute or property. That account is made possible only by stage three. There are remnants of this form of explanation in our culture today. Only we do not call them explanations, but label them prejudice. For example, "He must be so-and-so because he comes from such-and-such a family (or religious, or racial background, etc.)."

Explanations solely in terms of origin are primitive because they lack the analysis of an entity into its attributes, and lack also a concept of causality adequate enough to allow the formulation of causal laws. For these explanations involve a primitive, undefinable, notion of "x coming from y" where both "x" and "y" stand for particular entities. It was an arduous struggle in the subsequent history of thought to get away from the temptation to analyze every instance of "x causes y" as "y comes from (is originated by) x."

Another limitation of this type of explanation is its vagueness. Since not all instances of origin can be explained in terms of the process of human reproduction, one does not know which range of processes will count as "generation." A further defect is lack of generality. As long as "x" and "y" stand for particular entities, one cannot form a law based on these explanations. In order to form a law, one has to analyze both x and y as falling under certain properties. Once this is done, the burden of the explanation will be carried by the relation between the properties. This type of explanation places a minimum burden on the vocabulary required for its expression. It requires only a set of names, and the unanalyzed relation "*x* is originating *y*." As we shall see, other types of explanation demand an expanding vocabulary.

Reflection on explanations claiming that we can understand much about some entity if we know how it came about shows that this type of investigation needs supplementing. We tend to think today that origin can indicate something about an entity but only when we have the notion of an attribute that is inherited from one entity to another, as well as the notion of a causal mechanism by which the inheriting takes place. But these notions are only in inchoate form in the minds of those who play roles in the first chapters of Greek thought.

Explanations in terms of origin were initially mythical. The start of philosophy can be marked at the point, presumably with the Milesians, when explanations in terms of origin turn from the mythical to the speculative; that is, from identifying the originative source with some mythical entity to the identification of this source with some element known from nature.

Once we turn to non-mythical speculative explanations in terms of origin, it is easy to see why the shift toward explanations in terms of stuff or constituency should have taken place. "Where does it come from?" and "What is it made up of?" seem to us quite distinct questions. But when the answer to the first is given in terms of some natural stuff, such as water or air, then one can see how gradual transition to the second might have taken place. If it comes from water, then, maybe, it still is, in some sense, water. After all, where did all that "originative" water go?

Once we construe as our main question: "What is its stuff?" we are forced to analyze the entity we investigate into parts or ingredients. This is not necessary in the case of explanations solely in terms of origin. In the schema "*x* came from *y*" both *x* and *y* can be left, for the purposes of the explanation, as simple unanalyzed entities. But when we investigate stuff or constituency, we must distinguish as least minimally between the entity and what it is made of. The schemata "*x* is made of *y*" and "everything is made of *y*" require that we construe the elements of nature that we investigate as complexes. They also require an extension of the vocabulary; for we must add kind terms, and terms denoting varieties of relations of constituency. We will call this kind of explanation *compositional explanation*.

There are many kinds of compositional explanation. The underlying stuff posited as basic can be observable or unobservable. Again, they may be denoted by mass terms such as "water," "air," etc., or by count nouns such as "atom." Thales' explanation involves observable kind that is named by a mass term, while that of the atomists involve unobservable entities denoted by count nouns.

This type of explanation comes close to being, at least in part, testable. It offers empirical explanations of the sort "things are so-and-so because they are made up of *this*," where the demonstrative picks out some observable stuff. This form of explanation forces us to introduce types of causal mechanisms (for example, rarification, condensation) that are responsible for transforming one kind of stuff into another.

Still, compositional analysis is relatively primitive. It can only link entities to kinds of stuff, without referring to attributes of the entities under investigation and attributes of the posited stuff, and any laws interrelating these attributes. But anyone reflecting on this type of explanation would want to start asking questions about what kind of entities we explain and what kind of things the underlying elements are; thus pushing toward stage three. Without stage three, we are restricted to saying that common sense objects have in them such-and-such ingredients, and the best way to account for this is to construe them as really manifestations of a certain kind of fundamental stuff.

At the third stage of this development we analyze entities into their properties. The "What is it?" question is now taken to call for an analysis into a set of attributes. Within this framework questions about origin, composition, and the natures of entities can be sharply separated; geology does not become a substitute for physics. Exact and detailed analyses of entities can be given only within this framework, since even the positing of minute unobservable underlying parts of matter is done in terms of the explanatory attributes that such elements are supposed to have. We shall label this the *attributional* level of analysis. On this level we list a number of attributes that can be linked in causal and other types of explanatory laws. As Havelock remarked, change is not analyzed adequately until late in Greek thought. I would say that change can be analyzed adequately only on the attributional level; that is, as an entity gaining and losing attributes. There are, however, two ways of viewing change and predication on the attributional level.[4] On one view, which we might call the "coat-hanger" view, we think of attributes as attaching themselves to some underlying entity that is more than the mere sum of attribute instantiations. It is like a coat-hanger on which the "coats," that is, attributes, hang. This model reaches its explicit formulation in Aristotle's work. The other is the "onion"-theory of predication. The entity under analysis is simply the mere sum of attribute instantiations. Once we have given a complete description of the entity, and thus listed all of its attributes, there is nothing left over; once we remove all of the leaves of an onion, the onion disappears. This other way of construing the attributional level reaches its explicit formulation in Plato. In the *Phaedo* (100d) he maintains that the proper way to explain why something is of a certain kind is to exhibit the entity as partaking of a certain Form, or attribute, and that an attribute, such as equality, is a distinct entity, over and above all instantiations

(74a,b). But even Plato tends to slide back to the compositional model; or at least he feels the need to explain what we would call various types of attributions or predications in terms of the peculiar abstract terminology of his Method of Division.

One might speculate why it was so difficult to achieve a mode of explanation that we today take for granted. One possible reason is that the key relationships in the other two models, achieved at stages one and two, are analogous to something observable. Certain types of births or other generations, as well as certain types of constituency can be analyzed in terms of what we observe. These relationships are, at least in some cases, observable. But, as Plato is so anxious to point out in the first half of the *Parmenides*, the relationship between an entity and an attribute—even if the attribute is some observable feature such as shape—is neither observable by the senses nor analogous to an observable relation. Partaking needs to be detected by intellect alone, and the relationship is *sui generis*. Hence the move from stage two to stage three, the move from the compositional to the attributional level of analysis, requires a "quantum-jump" in abstract conceptualization. It also introduces a distinction between appearance and reality not encountered before. Within the other two patterns the observable elements are explained by unobservables; but these, for example, the "indefinite" or atoms, are construed as being in space and time. They are "underlying" elements in a literal sense. On the attributional level, however, the reality contrasted with the appearances is not causally related to them, but consists of timeless, abstract entities.

It is easy to see why the rise of the third stage should bring with it Platonistic ontology. For when a new pattern of explanation is discovered, it is natural to assume that there is an isomorphism between the key parts of the new types of explanation and key elements of reality. But the explanatory pattern of the third stage, the attributional analysis, stands on its own with or without Platonistic ontology. In fact, the insight that one can keep this pattern as fundamental without Platonistic ontology was one of Aristotle's key contributions.

The shift from physical constituent to attribute was a gradual one. The reason for this is that many of the elements posited by the compositional analysis of stage two, as well as some of the elements posited by the new attributional analysis, were named by mass terms. The distinction between the attributes of being hot, being water, etc., and all of the heat, or water, etc., in the world, is a fairly subtle one. It is forced on us not so much by everyday discourse, but by reflections on the explanations we offer. Water can be caused to freeze, but the attribute of being water cannot freeze. On the other hand, the attribute of being water enters into definitions and causal laws. Laws and principles govern the spatio-temporal, but should not be confused with the latter.

Let us consider now two concepts, that of "archē" and "enantion," as illustrations of concepts straddling stages two and three.

"Archē" means "origin," or "source"; but with the latter meaning it can refer to constituency as well as to some originating factor, There are no clear linguistic criteria separating the meanings; one can easily shade into the other. Furthermore, by the time we come to Aristotle, we see that "archē" can also mean "fundamental principle." Again, one has to infer from the context in terms of content rather than form, which meaning the term has in any given occurrence; and again one meaning can shade into the other. Thus we have vagueness and ambiguity in works such as the products of the Milesians, and even later. One cannot ascribe to the author clearly which sense of the term he uses, or even a clear awareness of ambiguity in each case.

The "enantia," or "opposites," too, can be interpreted on different levels. As one interpretation, opposites such as heat or cold can be seen as natural forces, with important causal powers. They shape the conditions of the human environment and those of the human body as well.

A more sophisticated conception represents these opposites as partly unobservable elements that are contained in everything, and whose mixture underlies a number of natural potentialities. This is the dominant conception of opposites at stage two. Once we leave the compositional level, and arrive at stage three, or the attributional level, opposites are construed as attributes. They include natural attributes like coldness, heat, dryness, and moisture, but also abstract ones like odd and even. We can treat opposites in terms of the laws of logic, rather than merely in terms of causal laws, only when we construe these as abstract elements, or at least abstract features of natural entities. Thus at stage three we treat the opposites in terms of contrariety, and contradictoriness. Above all, we can apply to them the logical operation of negation. It is a long leap from causal laws governing opposite forces to the logical laws of negation and contradiction.

Once we have arrived at stage three, we can return to questions of origin and composition, and formulate more adequate answers to these. The results are developmental laws, positing successions of attributes and causal mechanisms of inheritance, as well as the compositional laws of the natural sciences; laws that formulate complicated interactions between the having of certain attributes and relationships of composition. On the attributional level of explanation there need not be anything primitive about explanations of evolution or that of physical constituency.

The movements from stage one to two, and from two to three, were long and difficult. They were no doubt influenced by the kinds of cultural factors that Professor Havelock has been emphasizing in his writings.

This sketch of three stages can be applied to the whole development of Pre-Socratic philosophy. This, however, would have to be a major undertaking, beyond the scope of this paper. A caveat is, however, worth mentioning. We should not construe progress through the stages as linear. There were "relapses," or misunderstandings of what had been achieved, in terms of explanatory framework, by predecessors. The history of this development, like that of most conceptual developments, more nearly resembles a succession of waves than it does a straight line.

The opposites play a key role in Heraclitus' philosophy. One of the main contentions of this paper is that Heraclitus is a transitional figure, between stages two and three. His straddling of the compositional and attributional levels accounts for many of the puzzles and ambiguities that interpreters have encountered.

II

Common Sense and Tradition

To be a pioneer is not necessarily to formulate new answers. It can also consist in forging new explanatory patterns. Given the framework developed in the previous section, it is natural to think of Heraclitus in this second role. Once we have this viewpoint, we can place into proper perspective the recent controversy between Karl Popper and G. S. Kirk.[5]

Popper is intent on maintaining that Heraclitus proposed bold new theories. He ascribes to Heraclitus the following theses: (a) Everything, individually and collectively, is in flux. (b) Many of the changes making up this flux are unobservable. (c) What we take to be solid bodies are really processes.[6]

As we noted above, boldness and novelty need not be located in the actual content of theories alone. Furthermore, if the hypothesis that Heraclitus represents the transition between stages two and three is sound, then claim (a) becomes difficult to assess since it cannot be given a precise formulation. Without stage three, no clear analysis of change can be given. Hence it becomes impossible for the historian to say, in terms of our concept of change, what precisely the nature and extent of the Heraclitean flux was. Heraclitus might have had the idea that in some sense everything is always perishing and being reborn. This does not translate into any precise statement in terms of the gaining and loss of attributes by the various elements of reality about how thoroughgoing the Heraclitean flux is supposed to be.

Claim (b), on the other hand, is not only ture, but follows from the general considerations adduced above. Formulations of speculative answers about origin on a large scale, and the attempt to formulate general compositional explanations, require going beyond mere observable changes. Speculations about cosmic origin must involve the positing of unobservable changes since we have no witnesses to tell us about these alleged events. Furthermore, some of the compositional hypotheses of the Milesians make sense only if some of the modes of transformation, for example, condensation, are taken to be partly unobservable. Unobservable changes were posited by Heraclitus' predecessors; they are essential to their explanatory patterns. Hence it is highly likely that unobservable changes were also posited by Heraclitus.

Claim (c) is fraught with the same difficulties as claim (a). Given what was said about Heraclitus' place in conceptual development, it is anachronistic to ascribe to Heraclitus a sharp distinction between solid bodies and what we would call processes. Popper, however, could have argued for the lesser claim—one that does not entail claim (c)—that Heraclitus did not accept the common sense view of bodies as solid and compositionally enduring things. As we shall see in the following sections, this claim has much to recommend it.

Finally, Popper also maintains the interpretative principle that gross departures from tradition should be made only when backed by very strong evidence.[7] The difficulty with this claim is that it does not distinguish between different contexts for traditions. Some traditions span periods during which there are no drastic shifts in the concepts and explanatory patterns used. In these cases Popper's principle seems reasonable. For example, we trust the oral traditions on the basis of which many ancient epics were preserved. One of the reasons for such trust is the assumption that in terms of mode of dissemination, explanatory pattern, conceptual and technological changes, etc., the periods in question were basically stable. But in cases in which the traditions cut across periods in which explanatory patterns, and hence concepts, change drastically, what tradition reports must be taken with a great deal of caution. For later links in the traditions will represent the theory transmitted from generation to generation within their own explanatory and conceptual frameworks. In the case of the tradition transmitting Heraclitean doctrines we face a situation in which shifts across radically different explanatory patterns have taken place. Thus we can expect a Plato or an Aristotle to report what they take Heraclitus to be maintaining within their own respective conceptual frameworks. These reports are hardly trustworthy from the point of view of determining the degree of conceptual sophistication attained by the original Heraclitean doctrines.

In sharp contrast with Popper we find Kirk arguing that one should not ascribe to the Pre-Socratics views that fly against common sense unless one has very strong evidence backing such an ascription, and that even when the Pre-Socratics reached conclusions opposed to common sense, they based the arguments backing such conclusions on common sense and empirical observation.[8] Kirk's principle is even more suspect than Popper's. For what are we to take as common sense? Is it the common sense of a twentieth-century Oxford or Cambridge don, or is it what might have passed as common sense in Heraclitus' time? We have no justification for assuming that there is a set of common sense views and attitudes that transcend historical context and cultural differences. What we call stage three type of analysis is by now deeply embedded in the common sense of today. We have difficulty trying to imagine what it must have been like to think of the elements of one's environment without analyzing these into entity and attribute. But for an average person living in the seventeenth or eighteenth centuries it was probably also inconceivable that one could view matter and natural phenomena in any except a mechanistic way.

We have, in fact, very little evidence on the basis of which to reconstruct the common sense of Heraclitus' time. Furthermore, Heraclitus insists that not only his views but also his explanatory patterns fly in the face of common sense.[9] Thus there is really very little to recommend Kirk's methodology.

The main point of this section is not to criticize Kirk and Popper, but to show that we need not opt for either. The framework developed in the first section of this paper enables one to view Heraclitus as a conceptual pioneer, neither shackled by common sense nor formulating theses that could be compared in a precise way to modern views, but marking significant changes in modes of thought.

III

Epistemology

It is pretentious to talk of Heraclitus' epistemology, since the fragments contain no precise doctrine about evidence or justification. Still, the fragments do leave us with suggestions about ways of knowing and understanding. In this section I would like to present an interpretation of the relevant fragments, and suggest that Heraclitus' views on knowledge and understanding are in many ways similar to Plato's views, and mark significant progress in Pre-Socratic thought.

For the purposes of exposition I shall follow the numbering of the fragments presented in the widely used collection of the Pre-Socratics by G. S. Kirk and J. E. Raven, with Diels's numbering in parentheses. Using that numbering, the relevant fragments are: 197–201, 211, and 253 (B1, B2, B50, B55, B107, B114, and B123. Without linking these to fragments in any isomorphic way, I list the following points as the gist of these passages on knowledge.

(1) It is necessary to follow the "common" (Logos).
(2) The average person lives as though understanding were something private.
(3) One must listen to the common Logos, and not to Heraclitus as a person.
(4) Heraclitus prefers things that are perceptible (heard, seen).
(5) Eyes and ears are false witnesses for those with uncomprehending souls.
(6) Nature likes to hide itself.
(7) Those speaking sensibly must rely on the "common" as the city must rely on its law, and even more so.

These points raise a number of problems. What is the "common," and what is the private understanding that people usually assume they have? What is the distinction drawn in (3)? How do we reconcile the tension between (4) and (5)? How does (6) relate to what has been said about understanding and perception?

One possible line of interpretation is to be found in various writings of Kirk. According to it, Heraclitus favors perception, and accepts the common-sense account of things. He trusts perception provided that it is interpreted correctly.[10] He accuses the average person of accepting some sort of relativism or subjectivism, and warns against this.[11] He wants human beings to follow the common principle or principles operative in perceptible things,[12] and is not contrasting his own views with an impersonal notion of truth.[13]

This line of interpretation runs into a number of difficulties. Why would Heraclitus ascribe to the average person some form of relativism? Such ascription might be plausible in twentiety-century England or America, but hardly for Heraclitus' environment. We have no evidence to support such a claim. Relativism, as an articulated view, emerges—as far as we know—with the rise of the Sophists. Heraclitus could have hardly had this in mind here. Secondly, if perception is to be trusted, how does one account for the claim that nature likes to hide itself? If this means that nature is perceptible but requires an untangling of perceptual data, then it would be more natural for Heraclitus to suggest that nature is enigmatic and manifests itself in a puzzling way. The notion of hiding, however, suggests strongly the break between the observable appearances and the underlying unobservable reality. Thirdly, why would Heraclitus say that it is not his person that should be listened to?

How does this interpretation explain the contrast drawn in (3)? Finally, why call the Logos common, and why should Heraclitus say that we should follow the "common"? Kirk's suggestion[14] that the commonality of the Logos is its being operative in all things hardly answers the question. The fact that something is operative in all of nature does not explain why it should be processed in human minds as a common principle in contrast with private understanding. The contrast that Heraclitus draws is in types of thought or cognitive processes, and this would not be entailed by the contrast between the globality or limitedness of the applications of Logos.

These difficulties suggest the need for an alternative interpretation. Let us start with fragment 200 (B55) in which Heraclitus expresses his preference for things that are perceptible. The fact that he wants, in explanations, to investigate and use entities that are perceptible, does not indicate that it is perception that he prefers as a mode of knowledge. One might wish to regard perceptible things as the most fundamental part of reality and still believe that some of the essences of such things must be grasped by reason alone. Furthermore, the fact that Heraclitus refers to some entities as perceptible does not indicate that he thought those things to be perceptible in their entirety. As we would say, some of their attributes might not be given in perception.

Given that Heraclitus is drawing here a distinction between two kinds of entities and not between two modes of knowledge, how are we to interpret this distinction? There is no evidence that mathematical objects entered into Heraclitus' philosophy in any significant way; nor is there evidence, as Vlastos pointed out,[15] that Heraclitus is influenced by Pythagorean thought. Thus the elements contrasted with the perceptibles cannot be the types of elements we encounter in Plato's philosophy. Given Heraclitus' transitional role between stages two and three, it is much more plausible to suppose that he is contrasting fire, air, etc., both with the non-perceptibles posited by mythical accounts of origin, and with some of the non-observables posited by the semi-compositional accounts of some of the Milesians, as, for example, Anaximander.

We seem to be led to the conclusion that Heraclitus wants to investigate things that are perceptible at least in terms of some but not necessarily in terms of all of their attributes. Attribute-talk is not yet present in Heraclitus' conceptual scheme. So he might say that some entities are perceptible, but not completely. We see them and hear them partially; they are also in some ways hidden. This is, of course, exactly what fragment 211 (B123) says: nature likes to hide. The interpretation, then, that Heraclitus' preference is for partially perceptible and partially hidden elements of nature makes sense of a number of fragments. We can have information about these favored entities by way of sight and hearing, but some of their compositional or attributional structure (this is a transition stage, as we said) is hidden from the senses. Thus we need something other than perception to understand the fundamental unity and functioning of these entities. This is not to say that perception is useless; rather, that it is not sufficient. We need also nonperceptual cognition, or rational insight. This is likely to be some form of understanding. We need not assume that Heraclitus thought of knowledge as primarily propositional.[16] On this reading we can make good sense also of fragment 201 (B107), in which perception is described as a false witness to those who lack understanding.

The Logos, then, must be grasped by the mind, not by the senses. It governs the underlying nature of things that are partly perceptible. Thus we have in Heraclitus a contrast between perception and intellectual comprehension. This contrast helps to explain additional fragments.

Fragment 198 (B2), among others, contrasts the common with the private. This contrast can be linked naturally to that between rational understanding and perception. Perception is private. We see and hear things with our own eyes and ears. Like witnesses at a scene, we cannot really present our evidence to the public, we can only testify about it. Perhaps no two people hear or see exactly the same thing. In contrast, cognition is common. A principle like that of opposition can be stated in public, and the argumentation backing it is public. Proofs, unlike sensory perceptions, are not private and incommunicable.[17]

This interpretation helps to make sense of the Heraclitean claim that the average person acts as if he had private understanding. Everyone who primarily trusts the senses acts this way. Such a person relies chiefly on what each of us has separately, and rests his case on evidence that cannot be laid on the table. It is indeed plausible to ascribe the view that perception by itself yields knowledge to the average person of Heraclitus' time. The notion of intellectual insight was hardly developed. Heraclitus is one of its pioneers, the Eleactics develop it further, and it reaches its final culmination in Plato's thought. Thus a "seeing is knowing" attitude is likely to have been held by the "hoi polloi" that Heraclitus chastises.

We are now in a position to explain Heraclitus' contrast between listening to him and listening to the Logos. To listen to a person in the context in which Heraclitus writes is either to want a particular person's eyewitness testimony, or to require a special person's prophetic announcements. In both of those cases we rely on sayings for which we cannot have direct evidence, and thus we trust specific persons. The Logos is different from prophecy or eyewitness accounts. It is impersonal. Its grasp is a common matter for which we need not accept someone's hidden evidence. Plato and Socrates go to considerable lengths to point to the impersonal nature of rational argument and insight. Since Heraclitus is wrestling with similar data, it is plausible to construe him as a pioneer, pointing toward the same thing, though still somewhat "darkly." Given this interpretation of the contrast, we can see why Heraclitus thinks of common persons (fragment 197 [B1]) as if they were asleep. When we are asleep we take things at face value, and do not use our critical faculties. This is also the main flaw in the person who trusts perception alone. The exercise of critical faculties, that is, rational understanding and discrimination, is missing in such a person. Finally, the same interpretation explains also the analogy in fragment 253(B114), drawn between the law that a city must rely on, and the "common." The law represents what is common and can be exhibited as such. It contrasts with the private interests of the citizens. The law gives the city its structure and cohesion. Likewise, intellectual comprehension makes sense of and thus weaves into a cohesive unit what is otherwise merely a scattered collection of private perceptions.

This interpretation shows Heraclitus holding some views about knowledge and understanding that pave the way toward views that become crystallized in Plato's thought. One does not want, however, to overemphasize the similarities. Heraclitus has neither the conception of a Platonic realm as objects of understanding nor a carefully worked out methodology for mathematical argumentation. For Plato cognition includes not only argument but also insight. Heraclitus paves the way toward the acknowledgement of the special position of rational insight and its contrasts with both perception and prophecy. Working out a methodology of proof and argumentation of the sort that becomes later embedded in deductive logic requires thinking on the level of stage three; and this Heraclitus has not attained yet.

This interpretation of Heraclitus' epistemology fits in well with the hypothesis that he is a transitional figure between stages two and three. For someone who represents a move away from purely compositional thinking toward attributional thinking, it is natural to emphasize the need for conceptual thought in addition to perception. That there are sick and healthy people is a matter of perception. But to see that the contrast between disease and health enables us to see the goodness in health is a matter of intellectual insight and not a matter of perception. Furthermore, once one asks what makes health good, one is only a step away from treating goodness or badness as attributes of various states and agents; attributes whose ascription depends on certain contrasts.

We see also that although Heraclitus wants to explain common sense phenomena and not "hidden" facts, both his explanatory patterns and what he posits within the new explanations go beyond common sense. To see entities evolving as a result of warring opposites is to construe the unity of common sense entities beyond the common sense level, and to posit these "wars" as constant is to posit processes that are not on the level of the observable. But to formulate clearly laws governing opposite attributes would have required for Heraclitus to have arrived at level three, distinguishing clearly compositional from attributional relations. There is no evidence that Heraclitus reached that level.

IV

Unity and Sameness

The Logos of Heraclitus governs relationships between opposites. There is, however, a restricted domain of such relations within which certain logical questions emerge, albeit only in embryonic form. For in some fragments Heraclitus is concerned with the *sameness* and *unity* of certain entities. There are two aspects of these questions. One can ask about conditions of identity: What makes a certain entity identical with itself? In a compositional framework this question is likely to emerge as: What gives a collection of parts unity? The other aspect of sameness is identity across time, or persistence. What enables an entity to be the same entity at two different times T′ and T″? Kirk in his arrangements of fragments—for example, in his numbering of 202–205—leaves the fragments dealing with these questions scattered among fragments dealing with various quasi-physical or at most semi-conceptual relationships among opposites. Questions of identity, however, have a different logical character from that of general questions about how opposites contrast or can succeed each other or inhere in the same entities.

Needless to say, questions of persistence have special relevance to questions about change. If something changes, then it also persists through the change. Thus in an adequate account, both change and persistence need to be explained side by side.

Heraclitus does not have the means of an abstract vocabulary to say all this. He does not mark off explicitly, with a preamble, the fragments dealing with identity and persistence from the others. But if the most plausible interpretation shows him to be offering interesting comments on these topics, and we note the linguistic fact that oneness and sameness together figure prominently and uniquely in these fragments, then it is not arbitrary to claim that Heraclitus was a pioneer exploring these issues; issues that in fact still haunt logic and philosophy today.

Two fragments deal prominently with sameness. One of these is the road fragment, (203) (B60), and the other the fragment or group of fragments that deal with the task of stepping into the same river twice.

It is clear from these fragments that Heraclitus acknowledges the legitimacy of such common sense unities as a road or a river. He does not deny that one can talk truly about the same road or the same river. But the texts in question challenge the grounds of such assertions, at least as such grounds are ordinarily thought of. What grounds could one give for identity claims either in a purely compositional framework, or in a framework not including any reflections on explanatory patterns? Compositional thinking might assume that *a* and *b* are identical as long as they have the same parts. Unreflective thinking, not concerned with explanatory patterns, might assume that each of our descriptive labels singles out an entity. In this naïve conception of the relation between language and reality it might seem plausible that, for example, each species term labels a single entity, with more generic terms labeling complexes made up of these simples. In fragment 203 (B60) Heraclitus focuses on a case in which we not only have two descriptions and only one entity, but in which the descriptions form a pair of opposites. The conclusion of the fragment is basically negative. We cannot assume that every time we have two opposing descriptions, we will not have the same underlying entity. This is taken by Heraclitus as a point mainly about reality rather than about language. It is seen as a metaphysical point also by Plato, who develops this Heraclitean insight into a general account of sameness and difference in the *Sophist*, but at a higher level of abstraction. In modern times the problem is reformulated into semantic terms and becomes the focus of much of contemporary philosophy, starting with Frege's famous example about the Evening star and Morning star. (Heraclitus would have liked the Fregean example since it involves opposites.)

We should note that Heraclitus' example involves opposite descriptions rather than forces of nature. Nobody could have taken, even in Heraclitus' time, the contrast between the road up and the road down as a contrast between clashing natural forces. The fact that the example and the resulting puzzle deals with things and descriptions furnishes additional evidence for the hypothesis that Heraclitus is a transitional figure between stages two and three.

Heraclitus' example, then, points to the negative conclusion that the one label—one designatum theory—will not work, and that even opposite labels can pick out the same entity. There is, however, no specific positive solution to this problem in Heraclitus' writings. He talks in general about how tension between opposing forces or constituents, or what we would call attributes, underlies the unities of things that we know by way of perception. A solution to the logical puzzle that his example points to would have required the full apparatus of the third, or attributional stage, in the development of thought.

The fragments dealing with stepping into a river deal with a related problem, namely, that of persistence. They show the difficulty of spelling out

conditions for identity across time. Kirk has argued for eliminating some of
the alleged fragments dealing with this issue from the corpus, while Vlastos
defended keeping B12, B49a, and B91 as part of what we ascribe to
Heraclitus.[18] Although my sympathies lie with Vlastos, I shall bypass this issue, since the key points I wish to make will stand up even if we restrict
ourselves to what Kirk regards as genuine. For on any account, even if one
takes only Kirk's 217 (his version of B12 and B91), the main point raised here
is that of stepping into the same river repeatedly, over time, while water is
flowing downstream. Thus the problem is that of the river remaining the
same entity between the two times that we step into it, even though it does not
contain the same water. There is no evidence that Heraclitus is questioning
the legitimacy of the river as a unit. To this extent he agrees with common
sense. What he questions, however, is the ground for the persistence of the
river. On the compositional level, the most plausible candidate for the ground
of persistence is sameness of parts. Heraclitus seems to use the example of
stepping into a river to show that this compositional account is inadequate.
The river is made up of its bank, and of the water it contains. Both bank and
the water have parts, or stages. Thus spread across a time-slice bounded by T'
and T" we have the following situation.

1	A
2	B←
3	C
4	D

	A
1	B
2	C
3	D

T'   T"

In this figure the numerals mark the river stages while the letters mark
the parts of the river bank, with the arrow indicating the point at which we
step into the river at time T'. If someone stepped into the river at T', at point
B, as indicated by the arrow, then he is at the combination 2B. If he steps into
the river again in the same place, at time T", he will be at combination 1B;
thus identity in terms of sameness of parts is lost. Alternatively, we can
imagine someone chasing water stage 1, from time T' to time T". In that case
he steps into the river at T' and meets combination 1A. When he follows the
river stage 1, and steps into the river again at T", he will meet combination
1B, and the principle of identity through sameness of parts fails again.

Having demonstrated that sameness of parts cannot be what guarantees
persistence, Heraclitus offers little if anything in terms of a detailed analysis
of persistence. All we can do is to refer back once more to the various general
descriptions of the tension between warring opposites. This is not surprising.

It takes an elaborate abstract vocabulary developed on the attributional level, with a sound apparatus of logic thrown in as well, to state these matters clearly. Although Heraclitus lacked these means, his treatment of the problem of the persisting river shows that he was dissatisfied with the conceptual framework within which such questions would have been treated in his time. One can imagine subsequent generations seeing the negative result and not finding any positive solution, concluding that Heraclitus must have abandoned the claims that common sense objects like rivers have sound principles of identity and persistence underlying them. This (rather understandable) misconception of Heraclitus' speculations could have given rise to reports about extreme Heraclitean views according to which "everything is always in a flux."

Thus we see that while there is no evidence that Heraclitus held the extreme flux view, neither did he uphold the common sense view of things, as Kirk would have him do.[19] The passage about the river shows also that some of the changes posited by Heraclitus are unobservable. The constant flow of water is not distinguishable by human beings down to minimal parts. The possibility of constant change is compatible with Heraclitus' framework, but we simply do not have enough evidence to know how far he would have wanted to carry this view.

What Heraclitus says about the river also has important consequences for change. Without the attributional level of analysis of stage three, change can be seen only as parts coming and going. Heraclitus' thought shows that such generation and perishing is not a sufficient condition of change; hence we need something beyond the compositional level of analysis in order to analyze change adequately.

*　　*　　*

In summary, the following general view of Heraclitus' speculations on understanding, identity, and persistence emerges. Popper complained that interpretations like that of Kirk took away the philosophically exciting parts of Heraclitus, and left nothing behind to replace them.[20] Real accomplishment, however, comes not only with new answers to old questions, but also with undermining traditional answers, and groping for new ways of asking questions. It is an unsound as well as a conceited view that an earlier philosopher thought up something exciting only if he thought of something that we today might want to uphold. The interpretations presented in this paper do show Heraclitus as having made philosophically exciting advances. These came primarily in his seeking to define knowledge in new ways, and seeking to formulate new frameworks for explanations. He emphasizes the need for rational insight in addition to perception, and undermines both a naïve view of how language relates to reality and as purely compositional analyses of identity and persistence.

Heraclitus was the first pioneer to search for proper formulations of principles of identity and persistence. We might think that we have more highly developed abstract conceptual frameworks within which one can handle these problems. Issues of identity and persistence, however, remain to some extent unresolved even today. Identity and persistence seem to have become parts of the perennial scope of philosophy. We can thank Heraclitus' dark sayings for that.

Julius M. Moravcsik

Stanford University

NOTES

1. Bruno Snell, *The Discovery of the Mind*, tr. T. G. Rosenmeyer, ch. 9 (Cambridge: Harvard University Press, 1953).

2. Edward Hussey, *The Presocratics* (London: Duckworth, 1972), p. 35.

3. The role of ambiguity has been emphasized recently in Charles Kahn, *The Art and Thought of Heraclitus* (Cambridge: Cambridge University Press, 1979).

4. I am indebted at this point to discussion by my colleague Bruce Rosenstock.

5. The main papers are: Karl Popper, "Back to the Pre-Socratics," *Proceedings of the Aristotelian Society*, n.s. 59 (1958–59), pp. 1–24, and G. S. Kirk, "Popper on Science and the Presocratics," *Mind*, n.s. 69 (1960), pp. 318–39. They will be referred to in terms of pagination as they are reprinted in *Studies in Presocratic Philosophy*, ed. David Furley and R. E. Allen, vol. 1 (London: Routledge and Kegan Paul, 1970).

6. Popper, "Back to the Pre-Socratics" (cited in n5, above) pp. 140–41.

7. Ibid., p. 146.

8. Kirk, "Popper on Science and the Presocratics," pp. 170–73.

9. John Burnet, *Early Greek Philosophy*, 4th ed. (London: A. & C. Black), p. 168.

10. G. S. Kirk and J. E. Raven, *The Presocratic Philosophers* (Cambridge: Cambridge University Press, 1957), pp. 188–89.

11. Ibid.

12. G. S. Kirk, ed., *Heraclitus: The Cosmic Fragments* (Cambridge: Cambridge University Press, 1954), p. 43.

13. Ibid., p. 67.

14. Ibid., p. 55.

15. Gregory Vlastos, "On Heraclitus," *American Journal of Philology* 76(1955), pp. 337–68.

16. In fact not even Plato thought of understanding as primarily propositional. See J. M. Moravcsik, "Understanding and Knowledge in Plato's Philosophy," *Neue Hefte für Philosophie* 15/16 (1979), pp. 53–69.

17. For a very different account see Burnet, *Early Greek Philosophy* (cited in n9, above), p. 168.

18. Vlastos, "On Heraclitus," part 1.

19. Kirk and Raven, *Presocratic Philosophers*, p. 197.

20. Popper, "Back to the Pre-Socratics," p. 14. 141.

PRELITERATE AGES
AND THE LINGUISTIC ART
OF HERACLITUS

On a Philosopher's Style

Among the prose masters of Greece only Plato was his equal; on this the world's scholars agree, but, in the matter of the celebrated Heraclitean style, on little else. The linguistic artistry of Heraclitus is universally admired, but it has eluded definitive analysis and so baffles us even as it continues to intrigue us. Fundamental questions still divide expert opinion: Are his statements true sayings? What manner of prose is this? Or is it prose at all?

In the work of an older generation of scholars one reads over and again that the obscure or dark words of the great Ephesian philosopher were "oracular" and deliberately "riddling," characterizations repeated from antiquity and traceable to supposed hints in the fragments themselves. But neither term, as a description of the Heraclitean verbal artistry, is very complimentary or even accurate. Indeed, for centuries after Heraclitus' death special officials of Apollo's temple still converted the revelations of the Pythia to hexameters—increasingly bad ones as the centuries wore on— before the oracles were delivered to the temple's clients.[1] But the hexameter is precisely what Heraclitus has abandoned; his statements are not epic verse but local dialect, Ionic prose. Or are they?

Many scholars, Eric Havelock prominently among them,[2] would hesitate to designate them "prose" without serious qualification, preferring instead to consider them something like prose-poetry or poetized speech. Faced with a similar difficulty in the Egyptian genre known as Instruction, Miriam Lichtheim, in a recent anthology of Egyptian literature, argued that the Instructions, although not poetry in the more obvious sense of a sequence of lines of similar meter, were nevertheless not prose either. They were composed in a "third style," which the Egyptologist termed "orational."[3] It is a term not without appeal as a designation for the preserved composition of Heraclitus.

The statements in the Instructions to which Lichtheim was referring were sayings, oral in remoter origin but preserved in written collections and showing evidence of literate reworking; they remain true sayings, however, designed to be heard and memorized even if read by composer/scribe to auditors. The sayings in the Instructions are a form of memorable utterance which is rhythmed in ways other than by meter—mainly by parallelism—but systematically rhythmed none the less, and therefore removed from the proper domain of prose. The distinction is of course crucial for understanding any thinker's words and intentions, and Heraclitean scholars will at once recognize a close affinity to issues which have bedeviled and divided Heraclitean studies.

The suggestion that the fragments in their original form were maxims or sayings was proposed by the great editor Diels, vigorously defended by Kirk[4] in work of enduring importance for Heraclitean scholarship, and adopted by Marcovich and Havelock, among others. Equally reputable scholars remain skeptical; indeed, at a recent philosophical congress the remark was made that again to address an audience of Heraclitean scholars on this issue may now be to confront two hardened camps: the converted and unconvertible. In this paper, I hope, perhaps rashly, to bring some new support to the side of the converted in the form of evidence which may not as yet have been weighed by the unconverted.

I propose to examine the nature and component parts of the saying, and some of its long history as a device for oral storage in preliterate and protoliterate societies, admittedly a novel prelude to an examination of the Heraclitean statements. My hope is to reach a somewhat better understanding of Heraclitus' verbal artistry, its compositional parts, and its author's philosophical purpose, by considering how the saying is forged and why it survives in oral cultures. That such an endeavor is, at the very least, congenial to the approach to Presocratic philosophers advocated by Eric Havelock in the leading paper of this volume, as well as in his other writings, should be evident. My debts in this paper to those writings are many, even though in what follows my own journey through much foreign territory, at times no doubt blundering, remains solitary.

Certain of my conclusions about the shape of the Heraclitean statements should be stated at the outset. Allowing for some garbling in transmission, and for some partial quotations reflecting the special interests of later writers, two features nevertheless emerge with a consistency which argues for the premise that the fragments are not pithy sentences excerpted from a continuous prose exposition. The two features are (1) a maximum economy of words ("terseness"), combined with (2) one or more rhythmic or mnemonic or echo elements buried in virtually every Heraclitean saying ("density"). If the argument of this paper proves correct, then these two features, taken together, indicate that the body of Heraclitean statements preserves a group of true sayings modeled by their author on oral originals of a sort familiar to us from studies of oral cultures and which we may be sure were familiar to Heraclitus from his own society, and probably from neighboring Semitic societies as well.

It should be noted that such conclusions say nothing about how or when the original collection was put together, whether the collection(s) quoted by the writers of antiquity was the same one compiled by the author, or whether in the construction of an individual saying the author made use of writing. Those questions, while fascinating, are not affected by my thesis. Nor do I directly address the reasons for the sustained polemic of the author as he so elegantly castigates *anthrōpoi*, most men, his fellow Hellenes. What he clearly advocates is no less than a new mentality and a new type of rational investigation and argument for Greek thinkers, an endeavor which makes him, in this regard, also Plato's greatest predecessor.

Ephesian Preliteracy

For the purposes of this paper I must assume that readers will accept at least a portion of the thesis offered by Professor Havelock in the leading paper—a position which most scholars of Greek literacy would not now dispute in any case—namely, that Heraclitus lived at a time and in a city which was protoliterate at best. This means that despite the sophistication of commercial Ephesus, one of the three great cities of Ionia, the general manner in which its citizens conducted their daily lives and absorbed their literature and culture remained oral and aural—as, for example, Heraclitus attests when he bitterly complains about his fellow citizens' weakness for wandering singers. Cultural continuity and indoctrination were, it seems, governed by the enticements of the ear and the efficiency of highly trained preliterate memories. On the basis of extant evidence we can imaginatively reconstruct some of the occasions, but not all. These include festivals, many local, but some no doubt on the scale of the old Pan-Ionia, a great musical panygris held in honor of Apollo on Delos for all Ionians. These national festivals were curtailed in years of occupation but a description from about a hundred years earlier gives us the flavor of such occasions at which the Ephesians would have constituted a large and proud delegation.

> For it is in Delos, O Phoibos, that your heart delights the most,
> for Ionians with trailing garments gather there
> in your honor together with their children and modest wives.
> And with boxing matches, dancing and song,
> they delight you and remember you whenever they hold the contests.[5]

So splendid were these contests of sport and sung poetry, attended by "the fair-girded women and the men with their swift ships and many possessions," that the anonymous author, a blind singer who reveals his island of origin, Chios, thinks that an observer would conclude that the Ionians were virtually gods, "forever immortal and ageless." Or so the singer, perhaps with a wisp of trepidation, tells us the Ionians thought themselves in their hours of youth, beauty, wealth, and success, ever the things prized by Greeks.

We know also, from Heraclitus himself, that in Ephesus there were continuing recitations of older material in epic language and meter; he uses the present tense in describing the activities of long-dead figures: Homer, Hesiod, and Archilochus.[6] Bards "of all the peoples" (the plural[7] suggesting itinerant singers) were, the philosopher complains, enormously popular; the occasion could have been anything from a small gathering in the market place to a great agōn in a theatre with an audience of thousands, twenty-thousand being the number reported in attendance on the occasion when another Ephesian, Ion, won first prize for reciting Homer at Epidarus.[8] The dramatic date of Plato's Ion is during the closing years of the Peloponnesian War, and thus, roughly a century after Heraclitus, Homeric recitations by the professional rhapsodes were still major events. In addition, there were the assembly and the law courts, ceremonies at the Artemisium, instruction at the parental hearth, and perhaps even musical schools for the sons of successful merchants. But information on all such occasions (and this through the period of the philosopher's life) was absorbed by the ear, retained in memories, and remembered in great quantities. Not a scrap of evidence has survived to indicate that as yet in Ephesus any of it depended on the silent labor of the eye, although my subjective judgment is that some of it, mainly the law, was being transferred to written form in Heraclitus' lifetime. If we take nomos in his sayings to include written law, then clearly he applauded this development.[9] But whatever the case, the fundamental continuities of cultural preservation were, as the sixth century was drawing to a close, still secured aurally, in performance and in living memory. It would be only in a later age that these would repose securely in stacks of scrolls awaiting consultation by a body of literate citizens.

It requires historical imagination to grasp how deeply such a fact of technology penetrates every aspect of life and, as Heraclitus seems to have intuited, even affects the critical (or uncritical) reflections of a whole people. Few historians possessed greater sensitivity to this difference between early Greek life and the later achievement of popular literacy than did George Grote. His work is of course now little read because any history published before the excavations at Troy is hopelessly out of date, but his perception of the oral and aural way of life in Archaic Greece remains more astute than that of many successors. I cite below some connected passages from a section in Volume II of his great History of Greece in which Grote explains that before Herodotus and the development of a body of prose literature no Greek composition was privately read. All literature was poetic and was performed. Of these compositions—epic, lyric, hymnic, choric—Grote observes that

"how they were circulated and brought to bear upon the public deserves particular attention."

> They were not read by individuals alone and apart, but sung or recited at festivals
> or assembled companies. . . . In appreciating the effect of the poems, we must
> always take account of this great difference between early Greece and our own
> times—between the congregation mustered at a solemn festival, stimulated by
> community of sympathy, listening to a measured and musical recital from the
> lips of trained bards and rhapsodes, whose matter was supposed to have been in-
> spired by the Muse—and the solitary reader with a manuscript before him; such
> manuscript being, down to a very late period in Greek literature, indifferently
> written, without division into parts and without marks of punctuation. . . .
> Originally, the bard sung his own epical narrative . . . his profession was separate
> and special, like that of the carpenter, the leech [physician], or the prophet . . . all
> the variations superinduced on the original hexameter, beginning with the pen-
> tameter and the iambus, and proceeding step by step to the complicated strophes
> of Pindar and the tragic writers, still left the general effect of the poetry greatly
> dependent upon voice and accompaniments, and pointedly distinguished from
> mere solitary reading of words . . . poetry, as such, is and has now long been, so
> exclusively enjoyed by reading, that it requires a special memento to bring us
> back to the time when the Iliad and the Odyssey were addressed only to the ear
> and feelings of a promiscuous and sympathising multitude. Readers there were
> none. . . .[10]

No one can say with certainty how many adults in the Ephesian populace
ca. 510 B.C. could make sense of the undivided and unpunctuated strings of letters
which was their script, or what, especially in the way of prose, there was
around for anyone to read. A safe conclusion is that "books" of any sort,
with the possible exception of some technical manuals, architectural and
medical primarily, were few and read by not many. A mature adult populace
prepared to read Heraclitus or any other author would have been born in the
mid-sixth century, scarcely 150 years after the Phoenician script had so
casually, and with so powerful a rival in oral habit, entered Greece.[11] When
we turn to a yet greater city for which we have far more evidence, Athens, the
controversy has come down to whether the populace made its first significant
strides toward literacy early in the fifth century, or in the last quarter of that
century. I know of no evidence which would place a popular reading habit
anywhere in the sixth, which for Ephesus we would be required to do, and not
late in the century, in order for any significant number of Heraclitus' adult
audience to have been habituated in the ways of literacy by ca. 500. What
would have been the corpus of literature on which a reading habit must be
formed? Copied by whom for what purpose at whose expense and distributed
how?

Public inscriptions we know there were, although Ephesus is not especially rich in early ones. Inscriptions are, however, notoriously two-edged

as evidence for popular literacy (for example, in Egypt), as are law codes carved in stone. Papyrus there must have been from busy trade with Naucratis, or even Al Mina, but only craftsmen had much incentive to learn the letters to put on it. These would be minstrels, who had use for a single prized copy of Homer which they memorized for recitation; the decline in spontaneous oral composition in the Archaic period indirectly argues for such a procedure. Like the book of Michael Scot, however, this was read by one only, and probably buried with the singer unless it was given to a loyal apprentice, or to a daughter for a dowry. Next would be the singer's fellow craftsmen—potters and vase-painters and masons—who could be commissioned to put some letters on funeral markers, statues, vases, bowls, and the like. Ionian architects,[12] the best in Greece, are a special case because their probable use of letters, to produce manuals and to supplement drawings, would be on a perishable material, no doubt papyrus. However, when we recall that, like other craftsmen, they traveled extensively,[13] sometimes to serve Persian masters, or to places like Syracuse where recently were found the ruins of a gigantic temple which was modeled on the great Ionic temples at Ephesus, Samos, and Miletus,[14] it is difficult to imagine that they traveled without some sort of technical memoranda, affording them motive to learn letters. Commerce and administration of the city and temple are less likely motives, reversing our literate expectations.[15] Identification and cylinder seals, backed by witnesses and good memories, had for centuries been adequate for commerce and perhaps preferred; we underestimate how much the ever-secretive Levantine businessman (to this day) can keep in his head of his accounts and transactions, thus retaining control. A word given was kept if a man wished to stay in business; or, if the stakes were high enough, private vengeance was understood and calculated for. The system worked well and thus the business document and contract were less necessary than in a society where oral habit, and the self-motivated trust that it engenders, have been eroded. The same analysis would be true for civic and temple administration, although documents in the form of lists and inventories are probable. Whatever the case, education for the upper classes remained oral, poetic, and musical long after 500 B.C., and its core remained poetry sung and memorized, as the argument of Plato's *Republic*, unless an elaborate anachronism, makes incontrovertible. As late as Xenophon, as Athenian gentleman is said—this as routine, and not the exception—to know Homer by heart.

At what period in Ephesus all this began to change, when schools and books and a literature written to be read, or even the law in written form, became part of daily life, and when a philosopher could address an intelligent literate public in the written word and expect that word to be privately read rather than recited, or hope that his thought if neglected might survive in writing to be copied and read in a more sympathetic age, we simply cannot say, but it would have been long after Heraclitus deposited his scroll in the Artemisium and retired. In Athens, one would not confidently place the prose book as the medium of philosophical instruction earlier than Aristotle, who first put the instructing book at the heart of Western education, where it remained. In order to understand Heraclitus in an earlier century, a protoliterate century, to appreciate how he must anticipate addressing and impressing his audience and how that might affect his celebrated style, we must understand the ways of communication in the long preliterate ages which so closely preceded his labor and which so strongly impinged on it. Above all, we require some understanding of his chosen medium, the saying.

The Shape of the Saying

A saying is a self-contained item of deserving wisdom which has been linguistically framed in such a way as to be repeated as uttered. Unlike a more extended composition, such as a parable or a fable, the saying is designed to lodge "as is" in popular memory, the words fixed in a certain order which resists all but superficial manipulation. As a self-contained linguistic item, the saying becomes the smallest—and the primary—item of speech designed to survive in memory as an independent unit of meaning. It is this fact which determines its form or unique shape.

Sayings are universally recognized to be terse expressions; they are, as we say, "pithy," and do not ramble on. But economy of word (generally the fewer the better) is a direct function of the requirement of self-containment, namely, that the saying must survive in a kind of mnemonic vacuum. It cannot reach out for the support of relevant context in a narrative to which it would then become attached essentially, for it must be free to be applied to a thousand situations. Collections can of course arrange independent sayings in some arbitrary order, for example, by subject matter, or even in the form of an acrostic; but the exercise which produces such fixed collections betrays the influence of at least craft literacy, as in the Egyption genre, Instructions, or in the biblical Book of Proverbs, a collection which includes an internal acrostic. Suppose it is agreed that self-containment and terseness are indispensable to a true saying. Have we not slighted impressiveness or profundity, or at least cleverness of meaning? Is that not, after all, why we remember a saying, for the reputed wisdom (or information or instruction) contained in it? But the question as phrased is less than precise. The bit of hoarded wisdom or ancestral advice carried in the saying may indeed be the motive for expending the mental energy necessary for its retention in a crowded human memory, but it is not what lodges it there. For ten thousand human utterances have been terse and wise and deserving of repetition down through the generations, but nevertheless died on the lips of the utterer. An added requirement of the saying is that, unlike other wise human pronouncements, it must normally contain one or more elements of rhythm, or, less common, have embedded in it a related mechanism to aid recall, such as word play.

Such devices are present in sayings because they assure retention in memory and reasonably faithful repetition. I have called them mnemonic devices, and such they were in historical origin, although in later literate societies they are seldom recognized as such. Rather, they are taken—or mistaken—for poetic figures or stylistic ornaments; as an earlier age of literate criticism phrased it, "Dame Posey doffing and donning her jewels." Such dandified description makes of them something trivial and ornamental and effectively obscures their original technological purpose. However, as the writings of Eric Havelock remind us, viewed in the historical context of man's management of the preserved utterance, the genus of poetry is the rhythmic utterance, rhythm being a wider concept than meter or rhyme. The subordinate devices of rhythm create the subordinate species of the rhythmic utterance. The devices are, on the acoustic level, meter or rhyme or alliteration[16] or assonance, or even onomatopoeia and other forms of sound-word-play; and on the level of meaning, antithesis or chiasmus or parallelism. They are in fact man's most ancient mnemonic devices of easy and accurate recall. They serve to create the subordinate species of poetized speech, an important part of the broad genus of poetic utterance; like poetry itself, the saying is fundamentally a mechanism of cultural storage and recall.

Such humble items as "waste not, want not" roll off our lips without conscious recognition that the repeated "wa . .t", followed each time by the decisive "not," sets up an almost nursery-rhyme rhythm. It is a simple example of a balance of parts, or rudimentary parallelism, which at the simplest level can be the repetition of a word. Additional examples are furnished in many epic formulas, sometimes termed polar expressions, which combine opposites, a slightly more complex parallelism because it is antithetical. For example, the phrase "of all gods and of all men" combines the familiar opposites human/divine; moreover, in Greek the unit is reinforced as memorable because the words constitute a sequence of genitive plurals which repeat the ending ōn four times in close sequence, and moreover the whole phrase is metered. Parallelism as the principal device of rhythmic construction in Hebrew poetry becomes more obvious in the longer oral saying preserved in Deuteronomy: "The heavens show forth the glory of God/the firmament declareth the work of his hands."

Other examples of unrecognized buried mnemonic devices might be etymological or acoustic word play, or resort to rhyme or alliteration, and the like; no saying or self-contained aphorism which survives in oral memory on its own merits will likely be without at least one such device. In more clever and more complex sayings, we normally find some mix of them which may betray deliberate individual and not popular manufacture, as in Heraclitus.

In summary, poetry was called into existence in preliterate ages to subserve the needs of oral memory, what Havelock calls cultural storage; the self-contained saying is an important but neglected instrument or device of oral memory, which in turn is compounded of parts which are ancient mnemonic devices. Moreover, we should be prepared to discover that parallelistic construction, long neglected in Western critical analysis (it was rediscovered in biblical scholarship as constituting the dominating poetic unit of Hebrew poetry only in the eighteenth century) may emerge as an important, perhaps the dominating, rhythmic device of longer sayings. In pursuing this thesis by citing diverse examples in various cultures and historical periods, we may gain further appreciation of the linguistic art and formidable accomplishment of Heraclitus.

Before we explore this diverse evidence, however, a personal experience put into the record by the classical scholar and student of classic Celtic poetry, George Thompson, may prove instructive. It involved Thompson's living in remoter villages of Ireland and listening to (and learning) the inhabitants' speech. He reveals that he had gone to Ireland puzzled over the extensive repetitions in the Homeric text—whole verses, part lines, phrases; it was, he notes, before he had encountered the work of Milman Parry. He had attributed the repetitions to being a "primitive" element in Homer, which term in retrospect he acknowledged was a covering label the meaning of which he did not at all understand.

> Then I went to Ireland. The conversation of those ragged peasants, as soon as I learned to follow it, electrified me. It was as though Homer had come alive. Its vitality was inexhaustible, yet it was rhythmical, alliterative, formal, artificial, always on the point of bursting into poetry . . . it had all the qualities noted by Radlov in the conversation of the Kirghiz."[17]

One day Thompson heard from a villager an expression which was strikingly poetic in both imagery (in fact, an eloquent instance of kenning) and acoustics, the words in Gaelic being musically alliterative. Thompson reports that his first reaction was one of some surprise at such eloquence from illiterates, but that before long he was to hear the same saying used in diverse situations from many villagers, along with many other expressions of equal

eloquence which seemed to bubble up in daily speech. Finally, Thompson
realized that in this illiterate village poetized speech was "common property
. . . these gems falling from the lips of the people, so far from being novelties
were centuries old—they were what the language was made of."[18] What of
course he had stumbled upon was an enclave of genuine preliterate speech,
the everyday poetry of a people whose tradition in song and verse was rich
and whose daily conversation reflected it. Thompson was to draw the obvious
connections with Homer.

> His language was artificial, yet, strange to say, this artificiality was natural. It
> was the language of the people raised to a higher power. No wonder they were
> enraptured.[19]

Thompson was correct in concluding that such poetized vernacular (the
cross-fertilization between the poetized culture language and the daily vernacular being natural, continuous, and unconscious) is a universal
phenomenon of preliterate and protoliterate societies. The explanation
evidently is that among such peoples poetically charged speech becomes
linguistic "common property," often the peoples' patrimony in the absence of
any other; and so everyone draws on it freely. Could it be that the vernacular
prose to which Heraclitus is often thought to have reverted and
imitated when he elected to eschew the artificial speech of the hexameter was,
in large doses, a very special kind of prose, perhaps (at least to a later generation of Greeks) somewhat artificial and formal, perhaps closer to poetized
speech than we have heretofore imagined? The evidence of his surviving sayings, when joined to what we discover of the daily converse of preliterate peoples who have a rich oral tradition—and none was more sophisticated than
the Greek—indicates that it may have been.

Nyanga Proverbs: The Saying in Oral Africa

The lesson of Thompson's Irish experience was, in part, that while
orality may be total, as in pre-Alphabetic Greece, literacy never is; the oral
way of life is gradually eroded before the advance of a superior technology, a
script, but is never vanquished. What is of special interest, therefore, is an opportunity to record the oral ways and language of a society not as yet infected
by literacy, or barely so; that is, a society which is as yet embedded in its own
preliterate ages.

A valuable example, recently made available to the world's scholars, is
that of the oral literature of the Nyanga, some 27,000 Bantu-speaking people
who live in a largely isolated mountainous rain forest in the eastern part of
the Congo Republic, Kinshasa. Daniel Biebuyck is the leading authority on
Nyanga literature and social organization, as well as the anthropologist

mainly responsible for recording and translating (with the help of a native Nyanga, Kahombo Mateene) the tribe's epic material.[20] Biebuyck reports that the diversification of the Nyanga's oral literary forms is remarkable, especially when contrasted with their limited, but very efficient, technology. An important form of Nyanga oral literature is the saying, "mushumo," defined as "proverbs, maxims and other terse statements" which, in Biebuyck's understanding, collectively represent the Nyagna's code of values.[21] A first indication of the importance of the saying is the fact that, in the tribe's initiation ceremony, virtually all teaching and precept is given in the form of sung or chanted sayings.

The shape and instructional use of the saying or proverb deserves careful notice. First, as Biebuyck points out, no proverb is in prose; all are poetic.[22] In form, most of them consist of two verses or cola separated by a caesura, a word-break. The rhythm is created in one of two ways: quantitatively, by a balancing or parallelism of the number of syllables or words, a form of rhythm utilized in, for example, Hebrew, Ugaritic, and Egyptian poetry, and of course in Heraclitus. Or else the rhythm is set up by acoustic repetition—specifically, by alliteration, assonance, rhyme, word or partial word repetition, and the like—devices also familiar from the above-mentioned traditions, and Heraclitus.

Normally the Nyanga bard or leader sings the first colon or verse of a saying, often leaving the task of phrasing and/or actually singing the second verse to his audience. Biebuyck and Mateene observe that all Nyanga know the proverbs and can improvise variations on them; moreover, both men and women actively participate in this recreational and educative exercise, although often separately.[23] Proverb singing thus becomes an indirect means of enforced collective memorization, since the ability to participate is a function of superior memory as well as of musical endowment. In this it bears comparison to the sung *skolia* of the Greek male *symposion*. In addition to being a feature of initiation ceremonies, the singing and dancing of proverbs is a special interlude in the performance of their epic. Biebucyk reports that on these occasions there is much miming and acting out of parts by the bard, in which the audience does not sit passively but fully participates and imitates. He writes that a "percussionist and members of the audience act the refrains of the songs or repeat a whole sentence during each short pause made by the bard. In this capacity they are called *barihsihya* (those who agree with . . .; those who say yes)."[24] Moreover, the audience continually enters into the performance with clapping, rhythmic movement, short exclamations (including, significantly, onomatopoeia) and even "whooping."

Music and dance are obviously indispensable to the performance of Nyanga oral material. The musical instruments consist of three kinds of drums; percussion stick, antelope horn, flute (bamboo or reed), rattle (wicker), anklet bells, and a zither-like instrument, to mention only those which seem to have recognizable analogues in the Western repertoire. But the verbal material, although equally varied, never seems to be subordinated to the music, a feature also of Greek poetry in all periods. Of course in the absence of written preservation, regular performance is required and the communal occasions of performance are eagerly awaited, no doubt in large measure for the music and dance. The anthropologists stress the audience's enthusiastic and mimetic participation in this tribal act of collective renewal and reinforcement of traditional ways; could they be supplying us a clue to Heraclitus' censorious attitude toward the Ephesians' enthusiastic—and to him mindless—addiction to listening to bardic reciters?

Nyanga proverbs, in addition to being sung and performed at initiation rites and epic recitals, are also quoted in legal contexts as well as in more casual discussions and arguments.[25] Biebuyck reports that they form part of discussions which go long into the night at the men's meeting place where groups—agnates, affines, friends—gather to relax, drink and smoke, discuss the work of the day and the next day's projects, and in general seek to conform the daily habits and expectations of the group, especially of the young, to ancestral ways. What emerges is that *mushumu*, the Nyanga saying(s), is as close as the group gets to a collective body of law and precept which governs every aspect of life and which is available for daily consultation.

A final and related form of Nyanga literature deserves brief notice in light of its presence in all oral literatures and societies and of its recurrence in Heraclitus' preserved sayings: the riddle, in Nyanga, *iondo*.[26] The mnemonic utility of the humble riddle, like that of its near relative the nursery-rhyme, is sometimes overlooked by historians of cultures. But the riddle, once learned, is highly memorable because some unusual or secret meaning/association has been discerned and therefore firmly established; the association is reinforced by the admiration, and hence the pleasure, which the command of the secret brings to its possessor. Use of the riddle becomes a competitive game, a miniature contest, and, not unlike the exciting struggles of epic heroes, it focuses concentration by exploiting confrontation and conflict. Children will remember even complicated riddles for this reason. The riddle, or more specifically the association embedded in it, thus becomes available for cultural mnemonic and instructional purposes.

Riddles, however, have less potential for storing culturally important information than do true sayings, of which in fact the riddle is a kind of poor cousin. Biebuyck notes that the Nyanga riddles are "less rich in content" than proverbs, although one gifted reciter claimed to know 268 of them. Nevertheless, the Nyanga sing and perform riddles in a manner similar to proverbs, to which they are similar in form, each having two verses. The first verse invites audience response by challenging auditors to provide the completion, or answer.

The first verse contains a statement, possibly a name, or more rarely, an onomatopoeic utterance, and Biebuyck reports that the entire riddle can be introduced by expressions which betray its instructional and mnemonic purpose: "Tell me," "Teach me," "May I know," or "Beware." The answer, which often repeats a part of the first verse, normally begins with an expression meaning "It does not surpass," "It is not difficult."[27] In the accepting cadences of such speech we can detect the authentic sounds of oral life.

The Sayings Attributed to Solomon

Modern biblical scholarship in form criticism took a first step toward focusing attention on the saying, or, more accurately, on collections of them, as an important part of a separate genre which came to be known broadly as wisdom literature. The biblical Book of Proverbs is perhaps the example best known to Western readers and it can serve as a useful introduction to what many Semiticists now believe was a "floating body" of poetry and poetized speech which was common to many Semitic cultures (the languages are sufficiently close to permit material to transfer easily) in the ancient Near East both in Heraclitus' time and much earlier. Some recent discoveries also provide indirect evidence that this floating body may have been known to Heraclitus, at least in oral translation, but this is not a primary reason for undertaking an examination of this literature. For apart from the *ex oriente* issue, always a tantalizing one, what is significant is that, in this vast body of Semitic literature, the shape of the rhythmic saying again emerges intact along with the standard subordinate mnemonic devices which are found in the literature of the Nyanga and other oral cultures, especially the device of parallelism.

Greek scholarship, and above all Heraclitean scholarship, is in permanent debt to Semitic studies for the rediscovery of parallelism as creating a shorter poetic unit, and for the realization that its origin lies in the techniques of oral verse-making. The first part of the discovery was made in the eighteenth century, while the latter has been mainly confined to the research of recent years, led by the so-called Harvard school under Frank Moore Cross (see below). In later sections of this paper we shall suggest that parallelism is Heraclitus' primary device for constructing the extended saying, although he also makes generous use of the other subordinate devices of rhythm as well. These, like the shape of the saying itself, are not his invention; it must be stressed that they, too, are old and universal mnemonic devices. As we expand the number of cultures examined, we shall find alliteration, assonance, chiasmus, word-sound-play, parallelism, onomatopoeia, meter, rhyme, and the rest emerging over and again as indispensable mnemonic tools utilized by preliterate and protoliterate man to forge the rhythmic, and hence memorable, self-contained statement. It is hoped that enough evidence will be surveyed to suggest that the Heraclitean statement, in compounding the saying from these same devices, should not be viewed as an isolated phenomenon, however brillant the individual product. Rather, it should be put into the broad perspective of the ancient saying and its component parts viewed as devices of preliterate preservation. That does not of course directly address the question of why the philosopher elected to compose in this ancient and exacting medium; but it puts the product of his labor, his extant sayings, in historical perspective.

Early in modern biblical scholarship, experts established that Proverbs was a composite work, a fact evident even to the lay reader. There is also general agreement that there is literate reworking throughout, that one part is dependent on an Egyptian source, and that Chapters 10:1–22:16, the so called Sayings of Solomon, was the nucleus of the composite collection. This section is the oldest part; the contents are short pithy couplets, mostly composed in antithetical parallelism. They are attributed by the redactor back to Solomon, famous for his wisdom, as is the whole collection at the outset of the book, a fact later overlooked when various internal attributions are made.

The parallelisms (A is like B, even as a is like b; or, assuming opposites, the antithetical pattern A//C :: B//D, A is opposite to C as B is to D) and repetitions are evident even in translation. Many proverbs in the collection need no exegesis for the reader once attention is drawn to parallelism as the principle of construction. In the two examples below, Proverbs 16:8 and 19:28 respectively, A parallels a, B/b.

> Pride (A) goeth before a disaster (B)
> A haughty spirit (a) before a fall (b)

> Even a fool if he keeps silent (A) is thought wise (B)
> if he closes his lips (a), intelligent (b).

Antithetical parallelism, a more complex pattern of "likenesses" is evident in Prov. 12:28:

> In the path of justice (A) there is life (B).
> but the abominable way (C) leads to death (D).

In this case the path of justice is to life as the way of sin is to death, and the path of justice is opposite to the way of perdition as life is opposite to death: A/B :: C/D and A//C :: B//D. Memory is led from like to like, or reaches across opposites; having once trod the path, the way is easier the second time the journey is taken, especially when the path follows a known or anticipated design. Such examples of true oral sayings, taken at random from the oldest section of the book, reveal the Hebrew *mashal* or proverb in its purest form. The word originally meant "likeness" and at first referred to maxims and wise sayings such as those above; in time, the meaning of *mashal* was extended to include riddles (an ancient and neglected form of oral memory and instruction, as noted above), and, finally, even parables and allegories.

The reader of the collection is soon aware that the *mashal* is often not particularly religious, especially in the oldest sections of Proverbs. Indeed, most are as secular as their Greek counterparts which became attached to the names of the Seven Wise Men. It may be worth noting that the earliest literary reference to the famous (and Delphic) "Know thyself" is in Heraclitus; and in another fragment he refers to a saying of one of the sagacious Seven, Bias;[28] Heraclitus seems to be intrigued by successful sayings whatever their manufacture. The manufacture in both the early Hebrew and Greek cases is in fact totally secular, in the practical "wisdom" or skill of getting on in life. Both the Hebrew word for wisdom (*hokmah*), and the Greek (*sophos* = "wise": *sophie* the Ionic noun) carry in their etymological root the meaning of "skill." An unmistakable example is found in such common early inscriptions as "Critobolus by his *sophie* made me," the item being an admirable pot. The Hebrew word, like its Greek counterpart, came early and naturally to mean skill in living, wise in practical matters, wisdom. In Greek we have the final transformation memorialized in the name of a great cathedral, Aya Sophia, Holy Wisdom, in Istanbul.

Thus the wise man (*hakam* = the *sophos*) knew how a man lives skillfully and could impart this skill to others. His primary medium was the *mashal*, although the riddle was early recognized as an appropriate form. Word play, including pun and exploitation of acoustic likenesses, etymological fact or invention (including elements of name-magic), and so forth, were also favored, and are often made parts of sayings and riddles; the examples are too numerous and too well-known to biblical scholars for citation.[29] The point is that the *hakam* knew how to make wise and lasting sayings, or how to unravel and explain them. Just as in Greece famous sayings early became attached to The Seven, no *hakam* could be without his *mashals*, and collections of ageless and essentially anonymous sayings were attributed back to appropriate figures such as Solomon, famed for his wisdom.

The Book of Proverbs may serve as an introduction, later to be supplemented, to the widespread character of Near Eastern wisdom literature, to the origin and purpose of the genre, and its relation to literacy, but especially to the fact that the saying or aphorism is its primary item, the heart of the genre, and to parallelism as the primary (but not the only) poetic-mnemonic device of the saying. In Near Eastern collections the sayings are put into the mouths of fathers or sages or legendary kings and recited to (and memorized by) appropriate sons, pupils, or subjects. This creates a convenient narrative framework and permits arranging the sayings in a certain order. Both features, narrative and order, are regarded by most scholars as invention, essentially conveniences of a scribal school. In the Egyptian, Akkadian Babylonian, Ugartic (Ras Shamra texts) and Hebrew texts (related Semitic languages), to which could be added Indian (Indo-European), there is internal and external evidence that this was in fact the circumstance of composition and communication for the genre.

Thus the collections of sayings called wisdom literature found in all the Near Eastern cultures which share the Semitic languages are the product of a later craft literacy which has supervened on the older oral forms. The sayings in them may or may not have received some literate reworking. This does not, however, alter the fact that the genre itself was addressed to ears and memories, for internal evidence in the texts confirms what analysis of the unvocalized script (reader supplying the vowels from context, with some dispute even yet) strongly suggests: any degree of literacy in the ancient Near East remained scribe literacy. The origin of the shape of the saying lies in mnemonics and is to be traced to preliterate ages, but this is not true of the several collections of them known as wisdom literature; they are the product of scribal schools and will vary in form as scribal traditions vary.

Parallelism and the Principle of Acoustic Responsion

M. L. West, in an introduction to a recent critical edition of Hesiod's *Works and Days*[30] (which West rightly sees as related to the genre of wisdom literature) offers a wide survey of collections of sayings from many cultures and periods. West's book provides valuable testimony for the importance of the saying in all cultures unlettered and partially lettered; it can also serve as additional warning that what is old and of oral origin tends to become reworked in written collections; poetic original is often blurred into prose and paraphrase as later scribal (for example, the biblical deuteronomists) interests select and arrange material, often making it difficult to determine what is genuinely poetic.

Biblical scholars have long faced such difficulties, and their steps toward solutions may shed unexpected light on Heraclitus' remarkable style. In order to detect or restore a poetic original (let us say, an instance of garbled chiasmus in Jeremiah) a biblical exegete would of course have to be familiar with chiasmus as a poetic unit. However, as noted above, the major key to appreciating Hebrew verbal rhythms was relatively a late discovery in European scholarship; namely, parallelism, Semitic literature's most pervasive poetic device. As a direct result, much Hebrew poetry in the older translations of the Bible, notably the great King James Version, was mistaken for prose and printed as such. The full discovery did not come at once in Semitic studies and may not be fully appreciated yet; it may prove instructive to trace some of the steps. The discovery of parallelism as creating a poetic unit is attributed to the eighteenth century scholar, Bishop Robert Lowth. (Or perhaps this should be designated a discovery only by scholars, for in the world's synagogues the proper chanting of the texts must have made the point evident to the ear?)[31] Lowth published *De sacra poesi Hebraeorum praelectiones parallelismus membrorum* in 1753.[32] In this work he called attention to what he termed a parallelism of members, in which the thought in one verse is repeated—oralists might now prefer "echoed"—in a following verse in different terms. We explored incidental examples in a previous section, but these now require supplement which more clearly exposes the basic mnemonic principles at work.

At the simplest level we easily detect the parallelism present in such verses as Isaiah 1:10:

Hear the word of Yahwew
you rulers of Sodom
Give ear to the teaching of our God
you people of Gomorrah.

The echoing repetitions and contrasts in meaning between hear/give ear, rulers/people, and so forth, are not complicated. However, the infamous cities remind us that parallel word pairs can be basic building-blocks of Canaanite and Hebrew poetry; these can be divine names, or cities, metals, colors, or whatever. All that is required to set the echo going is that the mind or ear perceive a link. The prophet is here linking the first two in the list of the five cities of the plain from Genesis 14:2, a word pair of such lasting association that it will be used throughout the writings of the prophets and even by Christ himself.

Semitic scholarship has duly and usefully catalogued various types of parallelistic construction, e.g., synonymous, antithetical, emblematic, introverted, and so on, terms which might have vaguely bemused the singers who made the verses. A noted example of synonymous parallelism is the impressive verse:

The heavens (A) show forth (B) the glory of God (C)
The firmament (a) declareth (b) the work of his hand (c).

In this case, A/a as B/b as C/c; once the mind grasps the principle, which again is the echo (analyzed further below), then in hearing A-B-C it can anticipate a-b-c, because the latter echoes the former. The members thus become, in literates' terminology, patterned, or, preferably, rhythmed.

Bishop Lowth's discovery that parallelism creates a poetic unit has resulted in a gradual re-evaluation of all biblical texts which are not obviously metered or rhymed (or in books called Songs, Psalms) with the result that whereas only about 15 percent of even the American Version of the Old Testament was printed as poetry, in the Revised Standard Version of 1901 about 40 percent is so printed.[33] Various translations have increasingly set poetry apart typographically, printing it as such, but as late as 1927 the well-known biblical scholar Edgar Goodspeed defended a new translation (by a collection of specialists) partially on the grounds of need for still "clearer recognition of poetic structures" as "clearly indicated by the parallelism of the structure."[34] An outstanding success was achieved in Proverbs (tr. Alex Gordon) where the oldest section (Chapters 10:1–22:16), as already noted, is comprised of a string of terse parallelistic couplets. They are printed as such, and even in translation the subordinate devices of rhythm, such as alliteration and chiasmus, help the memory, an indication of their ancient mnemonic role. Chapter 10 of the proverbs of Solomon begins:

A wise son (A) makes his father glad (B)
But a foolish son (a) is a grief to his mother (b) (10:1)

This is followed in the collection by such specimens as:

A wise man will take commands
But a prating fool will fall. (8)

As the whirlwind passes, so the wicked man vanishes
But the righteous is rooted forever. (25)

In both cases, in addition to exposing the basic parallelism, the translation exploits alliteration in the second verse.
Proverbs 10:23 reads:

To a fool (A) it is like sport (B) to do wrong
But it is hateful (b) to a man of sense (a).

Here analysis discovers the antithetical parallelism A/a::B/b where A is the opposite of a and "does" B which in turn is the opposite of b. The translation prints a chiastic structure: A-B-b-a.

Students of Hesiod may encounter moments approaching *déjà vu*:

A rich man's wealth is his fortress
The ruin of the poor is their poverty.

A slack hand brings poverty
But the hand of the diligent brings wealth.

A gracious woman wins respect
And diligent men win riches

Like a golden ring in the snout of a sow
Is a beautiful woman lacking in taste

He who tills the ground will have plenty of food
But he who follows empty pursuits is devoid of sense.

In the final example (Proverbs 12:11) it is even tempting to hear Hesiod nagging at his brother Perses, a reminder that such wisdom is universal.

The term "echo" has been stressed in this treatment, for the first verse in a parallelistic unit sets up an anticipation which is fulfilled in the second, so that the second part of the unit reiterates, or, more precisely, echoes, what was said in the first part in similar (or antithetical) words or thought. The following has become a well-known example from Ugaritic literature:

The heavens rain oil
The wadies run with honey.

Here the echo-principle should betray the roots of the device in mnemonics. However, this latter point is only slowly being recognized and accepted in Semitic scholarship and is not indispensable for grasping the basics of parallelistic construction. For example, the principle was accurately stated, but without the specific connection to mnemonics, by the biblical scholar T. H. Robinson when he observed that each rhythmical unit must contain two members, the second of which must more or less completely satisfy the expectation raised by the first.[35]

In detecting the echo-principle at work in the device of parallelism, identifying it as such and finding its origin in mnemonics, we are of course going considerably beyond the original discovery of Lowth, although we are not being unfaithful to the direction taken by later biblical scholars who have found the origins of parallelism in oral verse-making. It remains for oralists, however, to spell out the mnemonics, connect the device with the echo-principle, and delineate its place in the genus of the rhythmic utterance.

That all rhythm is based on the echo becomes more obvious in such rhythmic-mnemonic devices as alliteration, consonance, and assonance, devices which echo sound elements smaller than the word by ordering words in such a way as to repeat the sounds in close sequence. Or in chiasmus, which echoes elements by reversing or crisscrossing their order of first mention. At the mnemonic core of each device is the echo, the principle of anticipation and fulfillment, or simply "lead on" by association. The mind is led on or helped from *a* to *b* because it knows that something found in *a* will be echoed in *b*: the principle of acoustic response. Some recent results from Ugaritic research may make the case more persuasive.

Echo Devices at Work in Ugaritic Verse

Advances in understanding the Hebrew poetic unit both aided and was confirmed by the discoveries at Ras Shamra, a fact evident from the writings of an early decipherer, Cyrus Gordon, and other pioneering Ugaritic scholars. But it is to Frank Moore Cross and his students (in a series of mainly unpublished Harvard dissertations) that scholarship is especially in debt for insisting on the connection between parallelism and oral poetic composition. In an important article for *The Harvard Theological Review*, Cross writes: "The myths and epics of Ugarit are composed in poetic formulae and patterns which reveal original oral composition. Parallelistic structure derives, originally at least, from the techniques of orally composed poetry, and the use of traditional formulae including parallelistic pairs has been well established in Ugaritic and Hebrew poetry."[36]

Cross does not in the *HTR* article expand on this important discovery, but if the analysis offered in the above section of this paper is correct, parallelism emerges as a device for linking elements in memory by echoing them in sound or meaning. Such a device, extensively used, as in the case of the intricate systems of formulae analyzed by Parry, can only serve the needs of oral composers. Therefore, students of oral literatures might prefer to state the case this way: the extensive presence in a literature of parallelism—or the pervasive presence of any complex of devices based on the echo-principle—is an indication that composition was originally oral and had to meet the needs of preliterate memory.

Cross, in the article cited earlier, has made it possible to detect in some Ugaritic texts evidence of the echo at work in the related poetic mnemonic devices, even as Biebuyck did for the Nyanga examples above. Ugaritic examples are: symmetry of syllables (an "echo" or duplication related to parallelism), as in tri-cola of ten syllables each;[37] symmetry and euphony created by repetition of sound in one bicolon;[38] chiasmus;[39] sound links and euphony by repeating *hmk, hkm, hkmk* 6 times in a tricolon;[40] and, finally, what Cross happily designates an "impressionistic" parallelism, consisting of overlapping images which are formally contradictory.[41] All of course have direct analogues in Heraclitus' text with what I term "density," and the last-mentioned remarkably so.

Such composition is now acknowledged by experts to be oral in origin even though it was captured on clay at a point in time by the scribe's hand; indeed the name of master-singer and scribe are recorded on one tablet, an incident without analogue in Greece. It appears similar to what in Greek scholarship is sometimes called orally dictated texts, i.e., a singer who is illiterate dictating to an amanuensis, a common occurrence in a society which is craft-literate. A more developed example, revealing in important ways, is found in the Egyptian genre Instructions, which will be discussed below.

What the present analysis seeks to add to a series of important discoveries in Semitic scholarship is that in parallelistic construction the mind and ear employ the principle of echo in order to retain the verbal material, and so the echo emerges as the dominant principle of its composition. More sweeping, the echo in fact is the compositional principle at work in different ways in all the subordinate devices which create verbal rhythm, that is, in parallelism or alliteration or rhyme or assonance or whatever. The root mnemonic principle remains the same; the mind and ear must first be signaled to anticipate x' by hearing x, and know that its expectations of x' will be fulfilled. Parallelism thus emerges as fundamentally an ancient linguistic mnemonic device; its presence in a text with density should alert a reader to a prior tradition of oral composition.

The position being developed in this paper can be displayed sequentially as follows. What we have seen is a successive appreciation that (1) parallelism is a poetic device creating a rhythmic unit, in Hebrew poetry normally a couplet (Lowth) and that (2) parallelism, at least in origin, is a feature of oral poetry (Cross et al.). Oralists would add (3) that parallelism, like all other devices of verbal rhythm, originally was called into existence to serve the needs of memory and of "cultural storage" (Havelock et al.), a conclusion confirmed by (4) the fact that they all exploit an "echo" device which serves the needs of only oral composers. At root, (5) rhythm is an expression of the echo-principle at work in words at the level of either meaning or sound, parallelism being the outstanding example in the Semitic oral tradition. Finally, a point requiring further exploration in the next section of this paper, (6) such echo-devices linger in a people's literature with density (superficial literate imitation always being a problem) after the introduction of a script only if the cultural situation remains one of protoliteracy. That may mean a social and cultural situation in which a few can write, thus permitting the transcription of orally formulated material, or it may mean that composition involves a mix of oral and literate methods, as in an orally dictated text. In any case, the composition is still addressed mainly to ears and memories, a fact of which the composer must remain aware.

The reasons for a lingering protoliteracy may be that the script is inadequate for a people to achieve popular literacy, as in the case of Chinese (50,000 and more signs), the Egyptian syllabary, or the various Near Eastern unvocalized scripts, such as Old Phoenician; or the script may be adequate but popular literacy is being slowly achieved, as in Archaic Ephesus, modern rural Anatolia, and so forth. The reasons for such gradualism may of course be many—social, economic, religious—and require individual analysis for each case (here the research of Goody and his colleagues at Cambridge is especially valuable). Finally, a varied body of fluid literary prose (the prose tale is not a real exception) is a function of at least advanced craft literacy, and may indeed require a situation approaching popular literacy, defined roughly as that twenty percent, more or less, of the adult population can read fluently. But numbers are not important: what is at issue is that a composer anticipates that he will be widely read, and therefore he knows that his composition will require neither recitation nor memorization. With this anticipation, the oral or orational diction of his composition alters, a change which affects what an author will say and perhaps even what he can say.

Heraclitean scholars, especially editors of his text, are aware of how regularly what we have called the echo devices, notably parallelism, appear in the Heraclitean sayings. Is this casual literate imitation? A matter mainly of stylistic oddity and of no significance? In face of the evidence from such diverse cultures as those examined above, might the stylistic facts plausibly be directly related to the preliterate situation or expectations of his audience? Such questions are still premature and perhaps can never be answered with finality; deep differences of opinion are inevitable. But I suspect that any answer must continually return to the oldest and most haunting of Heraclitean questions: What manner of prose is this? Further help toward an answer is available from an unusual quarter for Greek studies, the wisdom literature of ancient Egypt, and specifically the attempt of a distinguished Egyptologist to define and properly to describe the special style of the genre Instructions.

The Saying in the Orational Style of the Egyptian Instructions

If the preceding analysis of poetized speech is correct, then what is characteristic of prose is that thought is moved forward in a series of sentences which are varied in structure and length; moreover, the words of these sentences and their component parts, syllables and phonemes, are not permitted to establish regular repetitions of number, position, stress, or pitch. Also, reiterations of thought are not systematically employed to create a series of shorter balanced compositional units. A regular rhythm is thus effectively precluded and, unless some other device is introduced, also excluded are predictability and easy recall. What has been eliminated, or, more precisely, not exploited, is the mnemonic device of the "echo," rhythmic or acoustic responsion.

It follows that, without the aid of writing, verbatim retention of a prose discourse of any length is, at least as a socially organized and dependable phenomenon, impossible; hence, unlike poetry, a body of literary prose can come into existence only in literate cultures, and then only gradually as its peculiar techniques are discovered and imitated. Popular verbatim retention for shorter self-contained utterances is hazardous without writing, but not impossible as long as the briefer utterance is poetized in some way. The latter is what the true saying does; it poetizes a shorter utterance and so makes it mnemonically seductive on its own merits.

Miriam Lichtheim, in "Literary Genres and Literary Styles," her informed and perceptive introduction to the first volume of her *Ancient Egyptian Literature*,[42] faced the problem of describing the style of the Instructions, which were not poetry in the more common (Western European) sense of a sequence of metered or rhymed verses, although neither were they prose as defined above. A subsidiary problem was the necessity to distinguish within the genre between the instructional content, the sayings, and the narrative material, which initially was a brief introduction, but which grew in length as the genre developed. The narrative sections were clearly in prose and initially of the simplest sort, but the prose became more complex as the centuries passed. On the other hand, the proverbs and sayings, the core of the genre, underwent no stylistic development; from first to last these were elegantly poetized.

Lichtheim solved the problem by determining that the Instructions, which date from the Old Kingdom onward, were composed in what she terms "orational style,"[43] a term chosen, as I interpret her, because it connects the style to *oratio*, something declaimed; the diction moreover reflects this fact by seeking to produce a certain effect. Thus, whether or not the collection was ever read privately, in part or as a whole, is strictly speaking not relevant, for the style of the core of the genre, the sayings or proverbs, remains that of something designed to be recited, and, it should be stressed, memorized. The orational style corresponds closely, as Lichtheim notes, to that of the Book of Proverbs; for what activates the orational style is, as in Hebrew poetry, the parallelism of members. Lichtheim, in the attempt to distinguish it from prose, also termed it a "third style." If, she observes, poetry is to prose as the dance is to the walk, then the third style is a kind of parade step. In the terminology of this paper it is simply a form of poetized speech, although an unusually uniform one, because it is rhythmed by exploiting the echo principle.

Direct evidence for an audience of hearers and memorizers must be internal to the texts—as indeed it is for Heraclitus, who knows only a world of hearers—since we do not have contemporary recordings. The Egyptian evidence is as unmistakable as it is neglected, and deserves further attention. The Instructions are pretended to be recited by father or sage or prince to auditors, sons or disciples, who, we note, hear them and memorize them, and are expected to live by them. Even in written narrative the oral situation is unfailingly preserved and, incidentally, an explanation is manufactured for the wide distribution of sayings in daily oral discourse, and apparently not only in aristocratic-scribal society. In the Epilogue of the Instruction of the Vizier Ptahhotep, which is preserved in the great Prisse Papyrus at the Bibliothèque Nationale, the thoughtful Vizier concludes his thirty-seven maxims with:

> If you listen to my sayings
> All your affairs go forward . . .
> Their memory goes on in the speech of men . . .
> It [this advice] is teaching a man to speak to posterity
> He who hears it becomes a master-hearer.[44]

At the outset, in the first maxim, Ptahhotep affirms that, while wisdom is as rare as jade anywhere, wise maxims have infiltrated every level of society, and so the ignorant can be consulted, for they too have sayings which deserve hearing.

> Good speech is more hidden than greenstone,
> Yet may be found among maids at the grindstones.[45]

In the Instruction to Kagemni, the opening is a caution about good speech itself spoken with an eloquence worthy of the Old Testament.

> The respectful man (A) prospers (B)
> Praised be (b) the modest one (a)
> The tent is open (C) to the silent (D)
> The seat of the quiet (d) is spacious (c).[46]

There follows the injunction: "Do not chatter!" The translation, in addition to the elegant parallelism, yields the chiastic structure A-B-b-a//C-D-d-c. The advice in maxims follows, and when it is concluded the Vizier's children are instructed by him not to go beyond his instruction. The manner of compliance is described. "They placed themselves on their bellies. They recited it as it was written. It seemed good to them beyond anything in the whole land. They stood and sat [that is, conducted their entire lives] accordingly."[47]

The Instructions are in fact the second literary genre (after so-called Autobiography) to emerge in the development of Egyptian literature, and the first to be severed from tomb texts. Perhaps it is more accurate to observe that instructional sayings became a literary genre, Instructions, when sayings were committed to writing by connecting a string of them together in the literary device of avuncular or sagacious or princely instruction. This innovation was, clearly, the work of priest-scribes. (The degree of literate contamination of older oral material, or of imitation/invention, is unmeasurable.) In the earliest surviving example of the genre (from the Old Kingdom) the narrative is brief, a single sentence. "Beginning the Instruction made by the Hereditary Prince, Count, King's Son, Hardjedef, for his son, his nursling, whose name is Au-ib-re. [He] says: . . . ."[48] The poetized sayings follow. But the instructional frame expands, as Lichtheim notes, until we reach the elaborate prologue and epilogue for the thirty-seven maxims of the Instruction of Ptahhotep. In the expansions, the style of the narrative in expository prose also slowly develops some grace.

The internal evidence of the texts confirms what the shape of the sayings indicated: the instructions, although preserved in writing, were primarily designed for recitation and memorization; the genius of their style is aural and mnemonic. Moreover, once again the importance of a literate society's culturally humble "saying" to a preliterate or protoliterate society emerges early in an ancient Near Eastern culture's surviving literature.

We have discovered that the Nyanga proverbs, the Hebrew proverbs, the Canaanite and Ugaritic collections, the sayings in the Egyptian Instructions, and the sayings of Heraclitus—for similar reasons—have been recognized by experts in the cultures which produced them to be poetized speech, and hence not to be ordinary prose. In my judgment, all are in fact "orational" in a sense close to the one in which Lichtheim uses the word. They came into existence in preliterate societies, or societies largely so, and even if subsequently written down (perhaps in some cases at the moment of original composition, likely enough for Heraclitus, although Heinrich Gomperz suspected that transcription was later) were intended for ears and memories. It is this fact, and the resulting effect on composition that it entails, which controlled their diction.

Specifically, in the Instructions, there is a total and even rigid dependence on parallelistic construction of members (enjambment is resisted absolutely), along with the use of other subordinate rhythmic devices, to generate the expectations and symmetries; this is also characteristic of the oldest sections of Proverbs, and of the Ugaritic material, the Hebrew material seeming to one untrained in the literature to have more freedom in sentence structure. The Nyanga proverbs demonstrate great dependence on parallelistic structure and, within individual sayings, high incidence of other subordinate devices. In Heraclitus there is partial (but in the longer sayings pervasive) dependence on parallelism, probably the greatest freedom and least monotony of sentence structure, and—perhaps not accidentally in light of the latter—also a high incidence of subordinate rhythmic-mnemonic devices.

In the Nyanga case, the style is unconscious, spontaneous, considered to be of divine inspiration, carries all moral truth worth knowing, and has retained the closest intimacy with music and dance, specifically imitation or *mimēsis*. This will not change until writing is introduced into tribal life and makes inroads; after that, since the script will be alphabetic and probably supported by externally developed educational materials, the erosion will be swift as the best brains in the tribe deploy their energies elsewhere. Predictably, within a generation the proverb dances will be a tourist attraction; and, as with the Yugoslav guslari whom thirty years ago Parry made world-renowned, the songs will be half-remembered but performed in increasingly exotic costumes. In the Egyptian case, the internal evidence of the texts themselves points unmistakably toward continued mnemonic and recitation requirements as explaining why the genre and style of the sayings resisted change for so long (several thousand years) after the introduction of partial literacy in the form of the Egyptian syllabic script. The script permitted recording but did not introduce popular literacy. The same was true, with suitable adaptation, for the Hebrews and for Ugarit, for at issue is the development of a body of private readers, which radically changes an author's expectations, not the introduction of minimal writing, which may change them little or not at all. In Heraclitus' case, the alphabetic script with full vowel notation had the potential of producing that body of readers, but in his day in Ephesus it had not as yet done so.

I conclude that Heraclitus composed and communicated under essentially the same conditions of protoliteracy which obtained in all cultures of the ancient Near East, one in which popular survival meant that an author had to anticipate and linguistically provide for the fact that his composition would be primarily heard and memorized. In doing this, Heraclitus consciously imitated what he heard around him in profusion, certainly Greek and probably a floating body of Semitic sayings and proverbs and poetized speech; what he borrowed was *form*, which easily transfers among peoples (as biblical scholarship has determined), and not, at least significantly, content, which is more resistant to cultural assimilation. This thesis offers the best explanation of the shape of his statements and his remarkable style—not, of course, the genius with which he employs it—and, above all, his pervasive, and otherwise highly puzzling, exploitation of the devices of the echo. Such a conclusion, one can anticipate, will be congenial to some and less so to others; differences in assessing the evidence are inevitable. In the end, the important clues must reside in his own text and not those of other cultures, and notoriously his sayings tell different accounts to different exegetical listeners.

When and how do preliterate and protoliterate cultures such as those discussed in this paper produce their eloquently protesting Heraclitus or relentlessly analytical Socrates? Egypt never did, nor, as far as the extant record reveals, did any of the great protoliterate societies of the ancient Near East. For the Nyagna, the whole story has not yet been told, but their culture, as presently preserved and communicated—a culture of, in Plato's sense, *mousikē*—is not a favorable or likely environment. For by any standards the distance between, let us say, the intricate structure of the argument of the *Republic*, or the thought of the *Critique of Practical Reason*, and Nyagna proverb dances is formidable; a literate's moment of nostalgia for the drums and night-fires, anklet bells and banana beer, cannot be permitted to blur that fact. But it is a distance swiftly traversed with an externally induced literacy and a scientific and intellectual vocabulary ready-made for adoption; it could, under favorable conditions, be accomplished in a few generations. Or, with persons directly introduced into the tradition of the European university (as Milman Parry once remarked, "no inglorious thing"), even in a single lifetime. In their task the Nyanga have a major advantage; unlike Presocratic Greece where the endeavor began, the language for logic and science has already been purchased for them to inherit, and when the time comes no doubt they will adopt it *en bloc*, whatever arbitrary sounds they add or alter in the process.

In Egypt, a culture as old and as formalized as any the earth has seen, a solitary Heraclitean note of protest was struck in a work which again reminds us of the control of traditional speech over even a revolutionary thinker if his society is protoliterate. He may seek to escape it, but he remains trapped by the manner in which his thought must be communicated to an audience. For a certain Khakheperre-Sonb (called Ankhu), a priest of high station in the rule of Sesostris II, the deposit of ancestral wisdom had become linguistically constrictive, and fortunately we have his *Complaints*. The work begins by dismissing the tiresome fiction of narrative instruction to his compliant son/-pupil/subject. Instead, he addresses his own heart and in his lament we seem to hear the voice of one who, like Heraclitus, had "sought himself." The author immediately reveals that he wishes to command new and unusual phrases and other than the traditional sayings; but even as he reaches for them he inescapably models himself on the speech of a past that he castigates, and in so doing admits to his bondage.

> Had I unknown phrases
> Sayings that are strange,
> Novel, untried words,
> Free of repetition
> Spoken by ancestors!
>
> I wring out of my body what it holds,
> In releasing all my words;
> For what was said is repetition,
> When what was said is said.
>
> Ancestors' words are nothing to boast of,
> They are found [useful] by those who come after . . .
> From the first generation to those who come after,
> They imitate that which is past . . . .[49]

Ex Oriente "form"?

M. I. West, in the work on Hesiod discussed above and in his other published writings, has reopened the tantalizing question of direct Eastern influence on Heraclitus, a thinker whose proximity to the Semitic sources was of course much closer than that of Hesiod. However, rather than reexamining the old question of the similarities of content between aspects of Persian culture and Heraclitean doctrine (older treatments often centered around Zarathustrian fire worship), I propose a more probable candidate for transference from the East, the "form" of the saying, and especially the use of parallelism in order to poetize speech and make it memorable. Parallelism was of course not unknown in Greek literature, but with the greater dependence on meter in the Greek tradition the parallelisms generally ranged over larger portions of composition, for example, ring composition and the like; that is, large scale echoing was utilized as an aid to oral recall and recitation as well as composition. What is distinctive about the Semitic tradition is the pervasive use of parallelism to create a rhythmic unit on a much smaller scale, a couplet or a few sentences—that is, a linguistic unit roughly (or at least not exceeding) the length of the Heraclitean saying. What we shall discover is that all the sayings longer than a single sentence utilize some form of parallelistic construction, a point noted (but using a different nomenclature) by Kirk in referring to the "architectonic" of Heraclitus' expository method, what Kirk calls the a-b-a-b structure of B1, 2, 114 and other sayings which contain more than a single sentence.

In scholarly discussions of direct influence between cultures, two issues dominate the debate when no linguistic "hard" evidence (such as word borrowing) is available: proximity or opportunity for the borrowing, and striking similarities of a sort not likely to be coincidence. In terms of proximity, Heraclitus, of course, lived in a great and cosmopolitan city which, for his entire lifetime, was occupied by an Eastern empire, Persia, but (and this is neglected in Heraclitean studies) that empire's normal language of administration was not Persian. Rather, from the late seventh century onward the normal administrative language used in the Achaemenid chancellories was a Semitic dialect—and this even in areas in which other than Semitic languages were spoken. The dialect was the so-called Imperial Aramaic (Reichsaramäisch), a decendent of Old Aramaic, and whereas it was primarily an administrative tool, it also served as a literary language.[50] Evidence of literary use has survived (in addition to inscriptions) in the form of biblical Aramaic, notably in the Aramaic portions of Daniel and Ezra. This Aramaic dialect is a not too distant ancestor of the dialect spoken by Christ. So, the main language of Persian administration had close affinities to Canaanite dialects and to Old Hebrew. Trilingualism (at least) must have been a common feature of Ephesian life: Greek, Persian, and Aramaic.

There are, however, additional linguistic possibilities. Ephesus was prominently situated on trade routes of land and sea shared by Greek and Phoenician; moreover, the trade with Egypt—where there was a large Greek entrepôt, Naucratis—must have been extensive. The great harbor of the old city, now under water and marsh, must have been teeming with foreign people, ideas, and languages; to the list of the latter we should perhaps add Phoenician (sometimes perhaps less than welcome) and Egyptian. It is unlikely that a thinker as curious and boldly original as Heraclitus, who advocated the necessity for "philosophic men"[51] to know many things and who exhorted them to practice Ionic *historiē*, personal investigation, would have isolated himself from such influences.

Consideration should next be given to how tenacious Near Eastern wisdom literature is, and how readily in its original separate and oral pieces it seems to have passed from one people to another. This was made easier because of close affinities among the Semitic languages, a fact which has been of great importance to modern biblical scholarship. Ugaritic (and now potentially Eblaite) texts have permitted new readings for many puzzling passages. For example, in Proverbs 26:33 the dubiously meaningful "silver of dross" has been corrected through Ugaritic to "glaze," which makes excellent sense. And at Proverbs 18:1 we find:

A gossip's whispers are like savory morsels
And they go down into the innermost belly.

The phrase translated "innermost belly" means literally "rooms of the belly" and requires an archaic reading of the Hebrew word *heder*, "room, chamber," a usage related to Sumerian and now to Eblaite, a fact which, in the late M. Dahood's judgment, "bespeaks the antiquity of the proverbs which the biblical redactor may have culled from Canaanite collections of proverbs."[52]

Less suspect, perhaps, of special pleading, is the verse from Genesis "from the dew of heavens/and from the fat of earth" and its close counterpart in the Ugaritic literature, "Dew of Heavens/Fat of Earth," with the same consonantal roots for the four key words in the parallel clauses. Examples proliferated as more Ugaritic texts were deciphered, leading Cyrus Gordon and other pioneer Ugaritic scholars to champion the view, now widely accepted, that it was not the form but some of the doctrinal content of the Old Testament which was the unique Hebrew contribution. The language and the literary forms reflected in literary genres were inherited from an older

Caananite population; moreover, these literary forms had long and widespread oral life reaching back into man's preliterate ages and down into Hellenistic times. Not least in the catalogue of these ancient and tenacious forms must be placed the saying, memorable human wisdom forged into poetized speech by the rhythms of parallelistic construction.

The conclusion of Albright and those who have followed his lead, notably Cross at Harvard, is becoming increasingly probable: it is necessary to postulate a kind of "floating body" of poetry in the related Semitic languages of the Near East, a body of poetic wisdom which is ancient and tenacious and which finds its way with remarkably little alteration into speech and thus into the written literatures of many Semitic peoples over millenia. I would add that the style of this floating body of poetry was initially oral but under scribal influence may have blended into orational. Its ultimate origins, like those of ritual incantation and of epic, are in the preliterate ages of man, and so timeless.

Albright and others, notably Dahood and Cross, in postulating a pan-Canaanite floating body of such poetry, have also argued that, contrary to previous supposition, the Phoenicians did indeed have a rich literature, but poetic and oral, which survives to be read in distilled and adapted form in the Bible. Such a suggestion again revives the question of a direct borrowing by Heraclitus, not by reading (although such is not an impossibility: he was an intelligent and curious man) but mainly by listening to speech around him, and from conversation with bilinguals. The degree to which Heraclitus, like the biblical authors—certainly the redactor of Proverbs—was heir to this floating body of oral literature will of course remain unknown, but some exposure to it in commercial Ephesus at the turn of the fifth century is highly probable. In addition, some kind of discussion (given his station and family connections) with Persian administrators of Ephesus who seem to have used a Canaanite dialect closely allied to Old Hebrew, is at least likely. His seeking out and questioning intelligent bilinguals—even an intelligent *magos*—would not be out of character. Much more than this we cannot say. But the internal evidence of his sayings affords additional confirmation for the supposition of a direct Semitic influence at least in the form of the Heraclitean saying. Heraclitus and the Semitic wisdom literatures exploit the same ancient devices—above all the echoes created by parallelistic construction—in the process of forging that compressed and memorable form of poetized speech, the saying. The content of course varies, but the form is remarkably persistent.

Heraclitus' Orational Style

The essential ingredients of Heraclitus' prose style are: terseness, rooted in minimum strain on memory, and rhythm, rooted in maximum aid to memory. In combination they produced a highly impressive form of speech to the orally trained ear of sixth century Ephesus, a fact to which Heraclitus, who surely labored over his lapidary sentences no less than did the priest Ankhu, was hardly indifferent. The result is a style I have termed "orational" because, although for the most part the sentences are not metered, neither are they ordinary prose. Rather, it is a special form of poetized speech which has been rhythmed in ways which will be seductive to the ear and memory, a fact which has determined its peculiar diction. An orational style may also be oral in the sense of composition without the aid of a script, but need not be. In Heraclitus' case my subjective opinion is that the sayings were forged with the aid of writing, probably over many years, and collected by the author in some sort of manuscript form, a collection which of course now escapes us; from it he or others may have read to groups in forums similar to those often described in Plato's dialogues,—for example, the opening scene of the *Parmenides*, whose dramatic date is about forty years after Heraclitus' life ended.

Terseness as a feature of Heraclitean style ("terrific compression" is the designation of a noted expert) is well known, evident even in translation, although most translations tend to print upwards of one and a half words for each of his, and in what follows I will not be at pains to observe it. Rhythm, as argued above, should be considered the genus of which the echo/mnemonic devices enumerated below are species. The most important of these for an analysis of Heraclitus' style is the most neglected by traditional Heraclitean scholarship, parallelism.

Space forbids detailed analysis of these devices in all of the transmitted sayings, and prudence forbids an economical but subjective selection. My procedure will, I hope, be economical, prudent, and fair. Diels, as is well known, stated in the Preface (1903) to what became the standard source book, that he was convinced that the Heraclitean fragments were in their original form sayings or aphorisms and that he despaired of finding any coherence among them and so refused to print them in any order other than one which resulted in random or chance arrangement: alphabetic, by the first letter of the name of the primary source in which the statement occurs.

I propose to examine the first fifteen fragments in the Diels collection from the standpoint of this question: What is the density in them of the seven elements or subordinate devices of rhythm/echo which emerged in the earlier sections of this study as being universal devices of either oral or orational composition in preliterate and protoliterate societies? Thus, I am not proposing to select the fifteen sayings which best suit my thesis, although such would be defensible and tempting. I propose instead to examine sayings essentially taken at random, that is, the first fifteen sayings in Diels-Kranz, with the following caveats. B1, the famous *Logos* statement, the first in the collection and the longest Heraclitean statement, has been so exhaustively analyzed (for example, by Deichgräber, Kirk, Marcovich, Havelock, and Kahn)[53] that I will, in the interest of space, deal with it cursorily and be content simply to note its complicated parallelisms, word plays, and so on, as explored by others. I will, however, in dealing with B2, also consider B114 since they may have been one saying, as many editors have concluded. For a few entries in Diels on which there is scholarly consensus that a complete or genuine saying has not been transmitted, I substitute sayings which serve to illustrate some aspect of a preceding or succeeding saying.

The internal oral devices of rhythm and recall exploited by Heraclitus are seven in number. They are (1) meter (which I discount as an important feature of Heraclitus' composition), (2) alliteration and similar but internal "sound-links" such as (3) assonance, consonance, and "consonant chime." These are exploited for acoustic effect or mnemonic utility, as are (4) parallelism and (5) chiasmus, related to parallelism, and (6) word plays, including plays on popular sayings and (7) onomatopoeia. The term parallelism, more familiar in biblical scholarship than in Hellenic, is preferred to mathematical and other designations ("continuing geometrical proportions," and so forth) sometimes employed by Heraclitean scholars because the root of the device is in the echo, not in mathematics; item B responds in some way to item A and helps or leads the mind onto it.

Word play is used broadly to include exploitation of such orally favored (and mnemonically useful) items as riddles, acoustic or etymological similarity, or deliberate play on the polysemous character of certain words (*moros* and the *dok*-words were among Heraclitus' Greek favorites). Thus word play would include, but not be restricted to, such famous examples as B48, where a change of accent (*biós/bios*, not noted in the script of the fifth century) changes the meaning of the word from an old word for "bow" to "life," a pun doubtless noted earlier than Heraclitus. However, the combination of word play with the antithetical parallelisms word (name)/deed (work), life/death is pure Heraclitus. Also the terseness; ten words translates seven.

Of the bow the name is life
the work death.

Heraclitus' intense interest in and exploitation of familiar popular sayings (and hence the orally preserved wisdom of ancestors) deserves special notice. When he picks up a popular saying he normally exploits the familiar words (often an entire saying, but sometimes a phrase familiar from epic) by distortion (twisting their meaning), or extension (applying them to new, often epistemological areas), or flat exasperated contradiction (the canonical poets come in for a drubbing here: see Kahn's excellent discussion of B17 where sayings of Homer, Hesiod, and Archilochus are turned upside down; p.

102ff.). This prominent Heraclitean feature can now be only partially recognized by us since we have no record of daily popular speech from his Ephesus and hence can discover these popular oral sayings only as they happen to survive in other authors, or when denominated as such (*phatis*, *rhēma*, and so forth), or reveal themselves by their form. The incidence of Heraclitean exploitation would doubtless be much higher (it is impressive as it stands) were we to have the evidence required for complete assessment, and perhaps, too, some of the more (to us) obscure Heraclitean statements might sharpen in meaning and thrust.

An example of his exploitation of a popular saying is B34, and it deserves somewhat extensive notice because it is typical and because the term "saying" (*phatis*) is introduced.

B34. Popular saying, riddle?

> Noncomprehending even after hearing
> they are like the deaf
> to them witnesses the saying
> absent yet present.

The *polloi*, even after they have heard, are likened to the deaf in what must have been a saying every Ephesian knew: present (in body); absent (in comprehension, mind). The "non-comprehending" here, the referent for "they" in v.2, and the vilified object of the polemic, is, as in many Heraclitean sayings, *anthrōpoi*, most Greeks, his contemporary Hellenes. We have no alternative but to conclude that his regular audience of hearers knew and fully appreciated and perhaps even relished the taunt—each listener being like the member of a congregation who assumes that the damning sermon is addressed to his neighbor. The philosopher's confinement of his philosophical activity to one city afforded him this slight suspension of the fundamental rule of the self-contained aphorism, that it stand radically on its own.

Heraclitus is giving a popular saying an epistemic edge which the original surely lacked: most Greeks are like the deaf in the *phatis*: passive (mentally: as Kahn suggests, "off on their own trip") and not comprehending, not thinkers. Elsewhere, Heraclitus suggests that a cause of this Greek mental deficiency is their addiction to listening to bards (B104) and their "loving to soar" (B87) on what perhaps could be designated an *idian phronēsin*. This situation was unforgettably captured in the description of the hysterical epical audience in Plato's *Ion*.[54] Since they do not know how to listen with intelligence—keen listeners in a physical sense they certainly were—neither, concludes the philosopher, can they speak with it (B19).

We note, incidentally, the importance of oral witness (v.3 in the verbal form): the image evoked is of oral swearing. Also, buried in the popular saying there is probably a riddle. Question: Who is absent while present? Answer: A deaf person. The daily speech of Heraclitus' Ephesus, in this respect similar to preliterate societies the world over, was filled with such familiar sayings and riddles; most, unlike these, escape the notice of readers twenty-five centuries later. We can catch him in the act in this case because of the designation *phatis*, and because of independent verification of the saying in Aristophanes (*Knights* 119).

What the non-comprehending oral audience has finished listening to is not specified. If we confine ourselves to what is specified in other sayings, the possibilities are: the *Logos*, Heraclitus, itinerant country singers, rhapsodes who specialized in the hexameter (also normally itinerants) or the *logoi* of unnamed persons to which Heraclitus himself has also listened. The latter I would suppose to be treatises, prose or poetry, of the sort being read at the opening of the *Parmenides*, that is, something of common interest to a smaller group. What the taunt in this saying suggests is that the philosopher lives in a society of auditors, not readers, that the philosopher himself wants to command the ears and mental attention of his fellow Hellenes, and that he has met with competition and frustration.

> Stupid men! They love to soar
> at every logos they hear! (B87)[55]
>
> What wit or intelligence is in them?
> they follow the poets of the peoples . . . (B104)
>
> Homer deserves to be thrown out of the contests and beaten with his
> own rhabdos, and Archilochus too. (B42)[56]
>
> Not knowing how to listen, neither can they speak. (B19)

But the philosopher is a strong competitor, as we see below. In the following section the text discussed is that of Marcovich unless otherwise noted; in translation, I generally follow his divisions into cola, since orational style begs for such arrangement and for Heraclitus the cola are determined by the rhythm of the saying with little room for serious disagreement.

Catalogue-making is dull work and makes for duller reading. The exercise, deliberately reduced as far as possible to a "listing-type" of treatment, is in a sense an appendix to the argument of this paper, since all Heraclitean scholars and translators are aware of these devices and require no catalogue of them. The question is rather one of what conclusion must be drawn from the facts once they are admitted. But the exercise may serve a purpose even for those familiar with Heraclitus' text, for even when the devices are noted in one or another critical edition, it is generally in passing, no attempt being made to explore their density or to connect them with common features of the saying in preliterate societies. Deichgräber's pioneering

German monograph is a partial exception, but only partial, for he stresses
meter as a systematically deliberate device, as I do not; and he ignores much
that I include, as reviewed in the earlier sections of this paper. Thus it remains the case that no one has sought to isolate these orational elements as
being both rhythmic and mnemonic elements in Heraclitus' style and to connect them with the philosopher's place in the progress of Greek literacy.

Catalogue of the Orational Elements in the Style of Heraclitus

B1. Parallelism, word plays, alliteration, sound links.

> Of this Logos which exists forever
> men ever prove non-comprehending
> both before they have heard it and once they have heard it.
> For of all things happening according to this account (*logos*)
> men act as if without experience
> when they experiment with such words and works
> as I myself expound
> taking each apart according to its nature
> and showing how it is.
>
> As for the rest of men,
> they remain unaware of what they do when awake
> even as they are unmindful of what they do when asleep.
>
> *tous de allous anthrōpous*
> *lanthanei hokosa egerthentes poiousin*
> *hokosper hokosa heudontes epilanthanontai*

The final three lines contain sound links and balances evident even to the eye
in reading the transliterated text but which become unmistakable when the
lines are recited.

A complicated antithetical parallelism (*Logos/anthrōpoi*, truth/non-
comprehension, awake/asleep) of structure and sense, evident as thought
moves from colon to colon, runs through this, the longest of the sayings, and
is displayed graphically by Marcovich's useful table (p. 7).

Word plays: The word play in *apeiroisin eoikasi peirōmenoi* (v.5) is captured in several translations and by Havelock (this volume). Kahn has
defended deliberate multiple use of *aiei* (which I translate in vv. 1 and 2) as a
Heraclitean feature (see B5 below). The last word of the saying (*epilanthanon-
tai*) is unnecessary; it was added for the word play on *lanthani* which begins
the concluding two lines, and for the sake of parallelism, a neat balancing.
The sound repetition and word play at the beginning and end of the two concluding lines, each line made up of four words, constitute an elegant and in-
tricately balanced couplet. This in turn is reinforced acoustically by internal
sound repetitions of *-ous* in introducing the couplet and of *eontes, hok—*
within the couplet, aided by the repetition of *hokosa* in the same place in each

line, an additional balance of position. These are, as we have seen above in the Ugaritic and other examples, standard features of an orational style, although the complexity suggests written composition for oral delivery.

The final couplet sums up the deficient mental state of *anthrōpoi*, just as concluding aphorisms (the gnome) sum up or generalize the point of the moral of the narrative in epic recital.

Alliteration in v.2: a- a- g- a-, so Marcovich, p. 9: "intentional." Finally, although this is the longest saying in the collection, and in my judgment was composed in writing (although on orational rules, that is, clearly designed for declamation), a terseness and compression are observed which no translation could match. In Marcovich 100 English words translate 55 Greek words.

B2, 114. Parallelism, word plays, chiasmus.

> Those who speak with intelligence
> must put firm confidence (*ischurizesthai*) in what is common
> even as a city in its laws
> and even more confidence (*ischuroterōs*).
> For all human laws are nourished
> by one law, the divine
> for it has the power as far as it will
> and is enough for all
> and still is not exhausted.

> Therefore one ought to follow what is common
> but although the Logos is common
> the many (*polloi*) live as though they enjoyed a private mental
> vision (*idian phronēsin*).

Many Heraclitean scholars (Bywater, Heinrich Gomperz, and Marcovich with his references) have concluded that B2 depends on B114, and print them as one saying. Despite unusual length for Heraclitus this is probably correct because (1) verbal terseness is retained relative to the complexity of thought and (2) awareness of the possibility of written, in addition to mnemonic, preservation creates a boldness for length in orational style, as in the Egyptian Instructions and (3) B2 reads as though it could be an aphoristic summary and generalization of the thought of B114. If so, then it is an imitation of the aphoristic "triumphs" or gnomic generalizations which so often conclude narrative parables and examples in epic.

There is some question about the meaning *idian phronēsin* in the final line, which Marcovich interprets as "religious wisdom." But that is an unusual rendering unsupported by context. I suggest that the term refers to the interior dream world so loved by *anthrōpoi* and so often denounced by Heraclitus (B1, *passim*). *Idios* can be pejorative in Greek, as referring to one who puts himself outside the city's life, "peculiar"; here it gives a pejorative tinge to what otherwise is a Heraclitean approval word, *phronēsis* (see Kirk, p. 61 and his references); a private or subjective *phronēsis* seems to be a term of contempt, the opposite of the term of approval in this and other sayings, "what is common."

Parallelistic structure v. 1–3 of: a:b::c:d. Here: a = "those who speak with sense"; b = rely on what is common; c = *polis*; d = relies on its *nomos*, law. Marcovich (p. 94) also detects the chiastic structure: *legontas:xunōi:-:nomōi:polis* = a-b::b-a, *kata chiasmon*.

Word play in sound in v.1 between *xun noōi* (with sense) and *xunoi* (what is common)—a word play noted by most editors—the two then equated in meaning: those who rely on what is common (= what is accessible to the observation and investigation of all) act with superior intelligence. But *anthrōpoi*, the many, follow the bards, imagine to themselves (*dokousi*: deliberately polysemous in B17?), hence dream-thinking (B1), non-comprehending. Word play: *ischurizesthai* in v.2 and *ischuroterōs* in v.4.

Nomos in this saying probably refers to a written law code, perhaps set up in stone as the recently discovered Draco's Law of Homicide had been set up across from the porch of the *Archon Basileus* in Athens, the setting for Plato's *Euthyphro*. Add B100: It is necessary for the people to fight for their law (*nomos*) even as for their walls. Given Heraclitus' disdain for popular custom and the habits of the *polloi*, I doubt that *nomos* in these sayings means oral custom and precedent, taking the mob or *polloi* as a teacher and guide, condemned in B104. If this supposition (shared by a number of scholars) is correct, then Heraclitus is the first Western thinker of record to appreciate the superiority of written law, and indeed to place supreme political value on a society's law achieving written (hence fixed) form. It is equal to the protection of walls, the loss of which in antiquity often meant slavery or death.

B3. Meter. Not a genuine saying?

Three words (in effect: wide as a human foot—the context in Aetius indicates that they refer to the sun) in Greek are in epic meter and fill out the second half of the hexameter after the caesura in the third foot, a feature found in three other sayings in the collection. The required rhythm is: $\overline{\cup\cup}/\underline{\ \ }\overline{\cup\cup}/\underline{\ \ }\overline{\cup\cup}/\underline{\ \ }\underline{\ \ }$. Clearly this is not a complete saying, and may in fact be from a Hellenistic version of the collection in hexameters. However, this is also the common rhythm for proverbs, being the part hexameter after the male caesura. An example is the proverb alluded to by Alcibiades in the *Symposium*, *oinos kai paides alētheis*, truth is found in wine and children. A shortened form was simply *oinos kai alētheia*, in effect, *in vino veritas*. See further on B5 below, in which this rhythm completes a line and is likely from Heraclitus.

B4. Not a genuine saying. No Greek text; a Latin paraphrase in Albertus Magnus.

B5. Parallelism, chiasmus, word play, meter, (?) popular saying.

They vainly try to purify themselves with blood
being polluted by blood
as if one who had stepped into mud
could be cleansed with mud.
He would seem mad
if any sane man were to observe him doing such a thing.
Yet they pray to these images
as if to converse with their houses
knowing nothing of gods or even heroes, what they are.

Chiasmus: the chiastic structure (a:b::b:a) favored by Heraclitus has been detected in vv. 1–4, combined with parallelism, a standard feature of orational style. Meter: the concluding four words (*oud' hērōas hoitines eisi*) of the saying complete the second half of the hexameter.

Parallelism: in this case complex and ingenious. The first parallelism is: *anthrōpoi* in their temples (a) purify with blood, that is, a sacrifice involving pig's blood, and are (b) defiled by blood, that is, they murder fellow human beings, the *miasma* of homicide. As if: (c) to plunge into mud (d) expecting to be washed by mud. Thus: a:b::c:d. Heraclitus then adds that to the intelligent bystander the mud ritual would seem utter madness, as should the equally worthless and hence "mad" sacrificing of pig's blood each time one incurs a blood guilt (retaining *allōs* in v.1 and assuming iteration). Note that the paradox is intensified by deliberate dual construction, a single word doing double duty, in this case *haimati*, "with blood" (human and pig) constructed with a preceding verb and following participle; by blood both purified and polluted. This form of word play is common in orational style (there are examples in many of the literatures discussed in earlier sections of this paper), but it irritated Aristotle, who did not understand it in B1 (assuming that *aei* goes with both *eontos* and *axunetoi*). Most commentators, including Kirk and Marcovich, feel with Aristotle that a choice is necessary, but (1) all admit that either construction gives a meaning which was sound Heraclitean doctrine; (2) moreover, the construction is attested elsewhere in the sayings; and (3) it is a feature of orational style, a kind of word play for added impressiveness. Kahn gives other examples from Heraclitus and makes a strong case for the intentional use of the device, relating it to the deliberate use of polysemy, which is word play employed to similar purpose. Both are distant cousins to name/word magic, a device which is more impressive to oral societies than to literate.

Further, in their temples *anthrōpoi* pray (a) to statues (b) as if to converse (c) with a house (d). Again: a:b::c:d, a condemnatory epistemic summary concluding the second parallelism as also one concluded the first: "not knowing what gods and heroes really are," a piece of knowledge which even *anthrōpoi* apparently recognize as the final stupidity.

Popular saying (?): I suspect that Heraclitus' partially metrical (the last four words in v.9) conclusion was already in use as the conclusion of a proverb, a circumstance which may help explain *ginōskon*, the singular, where the plural is the grammatical expectation (or *ginōskontes*). Proverbs were commonly part hexameters' filling out a line in dactyllic verse from a standard caesura in the hexameter, as in this case; but they could be complete hexameters, or they could have non-metrical beginnings or lead-in. Or, because they are so familiar, they could be quoted in partial form, but with the syntax slightly manipulated. An example is Alcibiades' remark that, as the saying goes, *oinos aneu te paidōn kai meta paidōn en alēthēs* (*Sym.* 217E). In v.9 virtually the whole line may have already been proverbial (possibly with *anthrōpous* for *theous*?) and so is quoted by Heraclitus in the familiar form, even though this involves a slight violation of grammar, something we also do with familiar sayings. Thus to the effect: Critobolus is so stupid that he does not know a person worthy of respect when he sees one, not only ordinary men but even an Achilles! Typically, Heraclitus would be playing on the familiar as he exploits it for a new purpose, to condemn religious stupidity, but the original which was familiar to his hearers has not survived. Or, the complete hexameter was familiar and Heraclitus retains the meter only for the part normally retained in proverbs; then *ou ti theous eidōs*, or some such metrical introduction, may well have begun the line. (See the discussion of Marcovich, pp. 462–463.) Less likely, *ginōskōn* is singular by archaic attraction to the preceding *tis*.

Word play (acoustic): between the participle *miainomenoi* ("defiled" "polluted") and the later verb *mainesthai* ("mad"). This is evident to the eye of the reader, but the acoustic echo would be emphasized in declamation.

B6. Not a complete saying. Perhaps six words embedded in a sentence in Aristotle's *Meterologica* belong to Heraclitus; they are to the effect that the sun is new every day.

B7. Not a complete saying. Seven Greek words mixed into a sentence of the pseudo-Aristotle (*De sensu*).

B8. Not a saying as transmitted. "There is now general agreement that (as Bywater had already supposed) this text is a reminiscence rather than a direct quotation." (Kahn, p. 193. See Kirk, p. 220ff.)

B9. Parallelism, popular saying.

Asses prefer chaff to gold.

B9 either is or evokes an existing popular saying. The comparison
between golden chaff (thrown away) and real gold (precious, hoarded) seems
common to many folk literatures. (See Marcovich's reference |p. 187| to S.
Thompson, *Motif Index of Folk Literature*. The common proverb *onos eis-
achura* supports "chaff" and locates the provenance of the saying among
vernacular proverbs, although among those in use in Ephesus *ca.* 500 B.C.
which now escape us. As in B5, we can be reasonably sure that the familiar is
being manipulated in some way, and since the original was already embedded
in popular memory, the association helped Heraclitus' saying to attain the
same status. The mnemonic potential of such plays on the familiar—saying,
verse, whatever—should not be underestimated, even as we should not underestimate how handicapped we are in our ability to recover such plays.

An understood parallelism saves the saying from barnyard banality and
makes it worthy of Heraclitus. As asses (*anthrōpoi*) are to the enlightened, so
chaff (popular custom/decorative poetic statement of no real worth?) is to
gold (knowledge of the Logos, which is worth preserving, and Reality, versus
a dream world?) In any case, there is a note of complaint; the preferences of
the beast in question are proverbial and the prophet knows he will be without
kleos.

Also, as Kirk rightly argued, the saying is an instance of the *coincidentia
oppositorum*. Perhaps it should be noted here that the fact that this idea plays
a prominent role in the Heraclitean philosophy is no argument that in a given
saying Heraclitus is exploiting another example of *coincidentia* and not the
echo device of parallelism. The philosophical position made the device all the
more attractive to him; if in any philosopher content and style are wedded it
is in Heraclitus. Thus, extensive perception of opposites and pervasive exploitation of the echo device of parallelism should not be seen as alternative
explanations of a given saying, but as complementary. Also, arguing from
Semitic examples, the parallelism may be created by familiar association (as
in the cities Sodom and Gomorrah, of standard opposites, gods and men, and
so forth). Great popular familiarity—and preliterate memories were
remarkable—permits both the echo to be exploited and the implied parallelism to be elliptical, as often in the Hebrew examples. (See note 29.)

B10. Parallelism, chiasmus, assonance, alliteration, word play.

Comprehendings
wholes and not wholes
things convergent/things divergent
consonant/dissonant
out of all one
and from one all.

The parallelisms and echo advantages for impressive recital of a list of opposed items whose names have acoustic echoes perhaps require no comment. Meaning presumably prevails over sound in this saying, but the advantages of the sound links in *sumpheromenon/diapheromenon, sunaidon/- diaidon* are powerful in Greek recital and poorly portrayed in printed translation. Assuming, as seems to be the case, that *diaidon* is a Heraclitean neologism (literally "singing apart," coined for assonance and antithetical parallelism, a balance in meaning and sound, with *sunaidon*, "singing together"), then the point was not lost on him, as we would expect.

A similarity in sound, specifically acoustic echo, is being exploited to render persuasive a similarity or identity between items more normally thought of as opposed. This as a form of persuasion or "logic" is not uncommon in oral societies—the Old Testament affords many parallels—and again may not be too distant a cousin to name/word magic. Sound links are here exploited to accomplish what word play (puns and etymological invention) are elsewhere in Heraclitus used to accomplish: "to reveal a connexion between apparently different things which bear similar (but not necessarily identical) names" (Kirk, p. 68).

Chiasmus: vv.5–6; perceptively Kahn, "this final chiastic paring of antithetical terms . . ." (p. 285). Terseness: no translation can match it; in Marcovich 51 English words are required for 16 Greek words.

B11. Alliteration, antithetical parallelism (of meaning: paradox).

Every beast with blows is pastured.

Alliteration in the first three words, p-p-p; so Marcovich, p. 148. The visual image being evoked is that of a boy bringing cows home to green pastures. The paradox/antithesis is set up by "with blows" the boy does this. Moreover, the word evokes epic associations with the thunderbolt of Zeus, in turn the opposite of a humble shepherd boy. B64: "Thunderbolt steers all." The destructive weapon is that by which Zeus guides and governs, brings good order and well-being, to the cosmos and to human society. The word translated "beast" (*herpeton*, something that creeps on the ground) also has Homeric associations, used in epic by gods, who fly about, to refer to men, the earth-creepers. The familiar (to an Ephesian audience) associations emphasize the antithetical parallelism. In the *Theogony*, after a ten-year battle among the immortals, Zeus finally leaps from the parapet of Olympus with thunderbolts flying, and the final consequence of his action is that the cosmos settles down to a situation of physical order and reasonable calm, and the social proprieties and dispensations are established.

In B11 the antithetical paradox (we shrink from blows but welcome the green pastures to which they guide us), rivets in memory an unforgettable association. In the Greek text the mnemonics are aided by the alliteration and extreme compression into four words. In these features this saying bears comparison with two others, B54 and B30.

B54. Assonance, antithetical parallelism (paradox), word play (polysemy).
Harmony visible over invisible prevailing.

Again four Greek words, a noun followed by three adjectives, the final adjective (*kreittōn*) in the genitive, with the opening noun understood by ellipsis. Word play: *kreittōn* is polysemous, intended by Heraclitus: the invisible *harmoniē* is both more powerful and preferable. The other two adjectives imply association by assonance, *aphanēs* / *phanerēs*, the privative and positive epithets respectively for *harmoniē*, creating an antithetical parallelism. The visual image is also an antithetical paradox: a visible force, perhaps a massive army in daylight displayed proudly on the plain; but an invisible force, like a hidden enemy in the night, overwhelms it (I owe this suggestion to Eric Havelock). The hidden *harmoniē* is something not visual, yet both preferable and more powerful: The *logos*? What happens according to it? What the mind can with hard thinking (not dream-thinking) grasp?

These orational devices are displayed in one of the most impressive and memorable (even in translation) of the sayings, B.30.

B30. Parallelism, alliteration, word play, word repetitions, sound links, exploitation of familiar formulas and epithets.
The cosmos, the same for all
no one of gods or men has made
but is and was and ever shall be
fire everliving
kindling in measures and quenching in measures.

The opening words exploit the "o" sound six times; the word *cosmos* here for the first time enters the vocabulary of science and philosophy as a description of the ordered universe, a permanent contribution; v.2, antithetical parallelism involving a standard opposition familiar from epic—a so-called polar expression; v.3 exploits the hieratic formula with the normal *aei ēn* reversed for the sake of enhanced alliteration (so Marcovich, p. 271); v.4, a divine epithet; v.5 exploits the ending in -*ōn* three times combined with the solemn repetition of *metra . . . metra*. The antithetical parallelisms and echoes in thought from colon to colon have been well analyzed by Havelock in an earlier paper (see note 2, above).

All three of these sayings are highly compressed in language and thought, even the complicated B30, and have unmistakable markings of orational style: terse, utterly self-contained, exploiting one or more echo devices, impressive and unforgettable in delivery.

B12. Alliteration, word play, assonance, parallelism (syllable balance), onomatopoeia.

Upon those who step into the same rivers
other and still other waters flow.

Potamoisi toisin autoisin embainousin
hetera kai hetera hydata epirrei.

As Marcovich notes, this obviously is a "rhythmical and balanced Heraclitean saying, consisting of 2 x 13 syllables." In the first colon there are sound links in the endings of all four words: *-oisi*, *-oisin*, *-oisin*, *-ousin*. This approaches nursery rhyme. In the second verse onomatopoeic sound links in *hetera kai hetera* (regularity of passage in moving waters, rightly Kirk p. 378, and others) have been recognized. But further analysis is possible on the assumption that the style is orational and designed for declamation. *Hydata* (waters) is the next word and in recitation would likely be sounded with what preceded in what approximates Gerard Manley Hopkins's "consonant chime": *te- te- da- ta-*, *hetera kai hetera hydata*; the whole phrase is a unit linked by sound and meaning. Under the suggestion of the nursery-rhyme effect of v.1, the phrase may have been followed, after a decisive pause, by an artificially elongated *epirrei*, *"epi-r-r-ei"* drawing out or trilling the "r" sound. This is highly conjectural, of course, but as early as Plato's *Cratylus*, the potential for onomatopoeia in the *"rho"* or *"r-r-r-"* sound, suggesting "flow," was correctly detected. Socrates suggests that the name-giver cleverly detected that the letter "rho" was an admirable instrument (*kalon organon*) for conveying in sound the sense of motion, especially when the rapidity of motion was at stake, and so in such words as *rhein* (flow) and *rhōē* (current) he imitates rapidity in the *rh-* sound. The point is made with varying degrees of seriousness at many places in the dialogue: *eros* flows into us from without through the eyes; could it be mere accident that Kronos and Rhea were also the names of rivers? The *nomothetes* above all else knew how to embody in sounds and syllables the name which by nature was right.

The usefulness of onomatopoeia as an echo device for fixing in memory an association between sound and meaning needs little elaboration. The discussions in Ronald Englefield's remarkable (and neglected, perhaps because he held no academic post) book, *Language: Its Origin and Relation to Thought*, are especially perceptive. "Where memory is concerned associations are essential . . . . This is, no doubt, why there are many onomatopoeic words in all languages . . . . Such words are not invented because they sound like what they mean, they merely survive because they are easy to remember."[57]

B13. Popular saying, sound links, parallelisms.

Pigs delight in muck rather than in clear water.

Another of Heraclitus' barnyard sayings which plays on an existing popular saying the exact form of which has not survived. If, as Marcovich
plausibly reconstructs (p. 182, see his references) it was *hus en borboroi
kulindetai*, then the Heraclitean *mallon ē katharoi hudati* added weak sound
links in *-oroi, -aroi* and antithetical parallelism in "dirty mud" echoed by
"pure water." The banal now becomes philosophically useful since,
presumably, *anthrōpoi* are again being vilified, adding elliptical parallelism:
anthrōpoi/pigs:muck/poetry, wine?:clear water/statement of *logos*?

B14. The saying as transmitted (DK prints 3 sentences) is corrupt, very likely
a mixture of sayings, perhaps two complete genuine sentences or lines from
separate sayings. The first line is a list of night-wandering mystery-mongers,
the list blended with St. Clement's (the source) own syntax to the degree that
much controversy has centered around what belongs to him and what (if any)
to Heraclitus. The other sentence which may be genuine cannot stand alone
(so Kahn: "it calls out for some context") but I suspect that the sentence
which preceded it has not survived. The list, as Kahn persuasively argues,
looks genuine enough, but it too requires some context, which in my judgment has not survived. Therefore these words, even if Heraclitean, are not
relevant to the thesis of this paper. To Kahn's reasons for accepting the list,
one might give slight consideration to the very Heraclitean sound links in the
five words taken as genuine. *-oi(s), -oi(s), -ai(s), -ai(s)*. Occupied (*magoi*),
cosmopolitan (*Lenai/Bacchoi*) Ephesus seems to have had its nights filled
with the sounds of strange rites; in declamation, the list in nursery rhyme
tones could become a derisive mocking chant: *nuktipoloi, magoi, Bacchoi,
Lēnai, Mustai* [they are everywhere]. Since standard Persian custom required that a *magos* be present at all rites even though merely as a silent
observer, the *magoi* must have done a lot of nocturnal scurrying about.

B15. Chiasmus, word plays, parallelism, sound links.

If it were not to Dionysius that they make the procession
and sing the hymn to the phallus
the things they are doing would be utterly shameless.
Hades and Dionysius are the same,
for him [only: Dionysius] they go mad and celebrate Lenaia.

Chiasmus: vv. 1–2, the Greek word order has the chiastic structure
a,b,c:c,b,a; so Lesky, as early as 1936, cited with approval by Marcovich (p.
253). Also: "The balance requires that Dionysius and *phalli* are equipollent
(both implying 'life' (Marcovich, p. 253). The antithetical parallelisms
between Hades (death) and Dionysius (life), rational/irrational, run through

the saying. Stupid *anthrōpoi* celebrate only life (Dionysius, not Hades; they are the same), and so are doubly irrational (by honoring only one of the identical gods) in behaving so irrationally (going mad at his rites: Lenaia, a festival for Dionysius).

Word play: the unexpected *anaidestata* in v.3 (for *asebestata*; most impiously) is for the sake of word play; so Marcovich, p. 253, and others. The complex word plays of this saying involve *aidoia* (genitals), *aidōs* (reverence, shame, the inner feeling not to go beyond proper bounds, as Achilles did in mistreating the body of Hector) and *anaidestata* (utterly shameless), and perhaps *Aidēs* (Hades; remembering that the Ionic dialect of Heraclitus did not have the initial aspirate, a fact which I have ignored where sound links would occur in either case but which would to the Ionic ear support the etymology of the god's name from *a-idēs*, not visible, an etymology reported as already common in the *Cratylus* (406A). Apparently it is inviting to conjure up the "invisible" god of death, the grim reaper. The etymology, if common in Attica, must have been a commonplace in Ionia, not something likely to escape exploitation by Heraclitus, even if he remained as skeptical as Plato seems to have been. For an exploration of the complex word plays, see Kahn and his reference to the always perceptive work of Bollack and Wismann. In declamation, the ear would be likely to catch the repeated *ai*-sound (*ais-*, *aid-*, *anaid-*) linking the words played upon, since word play invites a sound emphasis. Terseness: forty-eight words are required in Marcovich to bring out what is compressed into 20 Greek words by Heraclitus.

This completes an examination of a group of Heraclitean sayings, chosen essentially at random, that is, of B1–15 from DK restricting the analysis to statements which have a claim to both completeness and authenticity, and supplying appropriate substitutions in three cases where such a claim could not be sustained. The proposal was to investigate the density of the traditional orational elements and echo/mnemonic devices which were discovered and analyzed in the earlier parts of this paper. In the figures which follow I set aside the fact that often the same device (for example, word play or assonance) appears several times in a saying, a fact which, if considered, would inflate these figures dramatically. The question now is simply: In how many of the sayings is a device exploited at least once? Also, for the purpose of computing the percentages below, the nine genuine and complete sayings from DK 1–15, plus the three substitutions, are the basis for the calculations.

Parallelism emerges as the dominant orational device, a feature of eleven of the twelve sayings, or 91.6 percent. Even if a few cases of (especially) elliptical parallelism were denied or discounted, the figure would remain remarkable. This finding confirms a point first stressed adequately by Deichgräber, who discovered a fundamental parallelistic construction in a number of the sayings also analyzed above (see his index). Word play(s) have been detected in nine sayings, or 75 percent. Deliberate alliteration is found in five sayings and related sound links (assonance, consonance, and so forth) in six, or 50 percent. The two latter features taken together result in sound— namely, how the word(s) is heard by the ear—being exploited in at least eleven sayings, or 91.6 percent, and again often more than once in a saying. (A degree of coincidence in any highly inflected language is probable, but Heraclitus had a sensitive ear). Popular sayings, along with familiar epithets and riddles, are exploited in at least five sayings, or, again, 41.6 percent.[58] Chiasmus is found in four sayings (26.6 percent) and the hexameter meter in either one or two sayings, depending on whether B3 is included, which in this analysis it was not. In all of the sayings the terseness and compression remain extreme; indeed, a breach of it (here as in all orational literature the connecting particles are the usual culprits) is the first signal of a garbling in transmission. There is a final comment, which cannot be defended here: these figures are not aberrant for the corpus of the surviving complete and authentic sayings, but typical of it.

What conclusions can be drawn from these facts? At the very least, I suggest that one must concede that this is not ordinary prose and that Heraclitus exploits with density features which are standard oral/orational devices known from many literatures the world over. In addition I would conclude—as have Diels, Kirk, Eric Havelock, and others—that the philosopher's thought, or at least that part of it which he gave to the public, was distilled into the form of the traditional saying or aphorism, a form which Heraclitus exploits with an ingenuity no other Greek author would match or, it would seem, would feel the impulse to attempt to match. Could the reason be that Heraclitus was poised at a unique point in the progress of Greek literacy—one never again to be repeated in that culture—at the very inception of literary prose composition? He may subtract (Eric Havelock's terminology) from the epic deposit the generalizing gnome, the memorable aphorism; but in shaping his statements does he not refurbish them with a contribution *ex oriente* as well? The shape of the orational aphorism will be detectable in later authors (one thinks especially of "Democritus") but, as the emphasis on ear and memory decrease with the spread of literacy, the potentiality for sustained prose, and with it for sustained argument, rapidly increases.

Conclusion

The term "oracular" as a designation for the celebrated Heraclitean style has proved to be imprecise and misleading because it says too little and some of what it does say is mistaken. But the designation "oral" recently adopted by some also lacks precision because it can imply too much. If the evidence of this paper has been persuasive, then such terms should be replaced by "orational," a designation borrowed from discoveries in Egyptology. The term aptly reflects what the Heraclitean statements are, utterances which are in poetized speech the diction of which has been shaped by the needs of ear and memory: they will be declaimed, recited over and again, and held in the memories of those who recite them. The term is strictly neutral—and non-provocative, as "oral" may not be—to questions of whether the statements were composed with aid of the pen or only recorded with it, or whether the original collection and its order were due to the author or to another, and so on.

The Heraclitean diction has been found to be a traditional one; similarly, the shape of the Heraclitean statements has emerged as being that of the traditional saying: a self-contained utterance of deserving wisdom which has been linguistically framed so as to be repeatable as uttered. The density in Heraclitus' text of the standard echo/mnemonic (that is, orational) devices— parallelism emerging as the most important even as in traditional scholarship it is the most neglected—has been explained by consideration of several overlapping causes. (1) *Imitation and familiarity*: Ephesus was close to its preliterate ages and hence the sounds of its daily speech (and nightly, given the complaint in *nuktipoloi*, B14) was filled with them. (2) *Mnemonic utility*: his sayings even if read by a few were, he knew, destined to be heard and memorized by far more—that is, his major audience was of preliterates in an advanced culture, and hence, to borrow a term from Marcel Jousse (also borrowed by Parry), superb "mnemono-technicians," but with their mnemonic habits already formed by poetry. (3) *Persuasive euphony*: the sayings are designed not only to be remembered and repeated as heard, but also in the hearing to be mightily impressive, as indeed they are.

The inclusion of persuasive euphony as a great philosopher's conscious motive, and the goad to no small part of his professional labor, will be distasteful to some because today it is remote from professional philosophers' training and goals. Truth and clarity are thought to be better served when uncluttered by attention to prose style, and mathematical notation is the purest truth of all. But the philosopher's own complaint is unambiguous; he was forced to compete for an audience with street singers and rhapsodes, masters of aural appeal—no less than the poets of Greece in the persons of their contemporary reciters and performers, master artists—and to that competitive end he forged a rare verbal artistry. As we have seen, he castigates even as he shrewdly imitates, for he knows the power of the familiar to evoke a persuasive nostalgia. And so he weaves great verses from the ancient poets—and even, like fading echoes, fragments of their meters—into his composition; he plays on notable familiar sayings even as he creates astonishing ones of his own.

The lesson of his stylistic decisions (and they were as deliberate as they were shrewd) may once again be that of Thompson's Irish sojourn. Total literacy has never been achieved in any society, just as the genius of orality has never been quashed. What Heraclitus could not have known were the fundamental reasons why his oral and orational devices were so effective, and why literacy meets such a formidable opponent in oral habit. Total non-literacy was for tens of thousands of years the human condition because the human brain has been organized for speech, which is a matter of managing sounds, not scratches; skill in the matter of transferring sounds onto clay or paper or leather by encoding them in visible signs is a late intruder into the bag of useful human tricks. For this exercise our evolutionary past has not prepared us; the acquisition of socialized literacy, unlike the acquisition of speech, depends on all sorts of conditions which are not genetically encoded or biologically transferred—from the adequacy of a script, to motive, to economics. Unlike speech, socialized literacy need not be acquired by human beings at all, but if it is it will be by degrees. The result is that pockets of residual oralism are apt to flourish in even advanced literate societies, as in ours today when some of the best poetry—words heard, remembered, savored, and repeated in times of joy or grief, but words virtually never read by those who live with and by them—are to be found in words wedded to the music a people loves.

I conclude with an example, or at least a harmless test, consisting of a surviving text transmitted with reasonable faithfulness from a traditional culture. To my eye and ear this text bears internal evidence of an orational style precisely because the original words were composed to be heard, memorized, and recited. The synoptic gospels were composed in a society more advanced in literacy than Heraclitus' Ephesus; but New Testament experts agree that, in part, they were compiled from original accounts and versions orally composed and orally disseminated in the Christian communities before they were, in anything like their final form, committed to writing. A gospel was something spoken or preached, that is, declaimed, long before anyone thought of writing one. The famous remark of Papias (ca. 137 B.C.?) reminds us that oral versions of the sayings of Jesus were preferred well into the second century even in the most literate Hellenistic cities. As a noted biblical scholar recently observed, analysis of the gospels reveals that they were composed out of units of traditional oral material, such as " 'saying-stories' which contain an important piece of the teaching of Jesus, 'miracle stories,' parables, and so on . . . the tradition about Jesus took its shape from the way Christians handed it on by word of mouth . . . ".[59]

The operative phrase in this description may be unobtrusive: namely, the verbal "shape" of the preserved and transmitted utterance. If the argument of this paper has been correct, then the orational style should be in evidence at places in the shape of the utterances found in the gospels even if there has been literate reworking; that is, the parallelisms, repetitions, and balances, the evocation of familiar phrases, the echoes and the aphoristic triumphs, and the rest should all be there. Are they? That question systematically explored is appropriately abandoned to those trained to answer it. Instead, I translate a single example from the gospel of Matthew (11:16–19) chosen almost at random and rendered without elegance but as close to the Greek syntax and diction as intelligible English permits. In this case, proof will be not in the eyes of the beholders but in their ears, for the proof requires one concession, that Matthew be read aloud, as the sayings of Heraclitus deserve to be.

> He who has ears let him hear.
> To whom shall I liken (*homioso*) this generation?
> Like (*homoia*) it is young children sitting in the market place
> who sounding toward the others they are saying (*legousin*),
> We played the flute for you and you danced not
> We wailed for you and you beat your breasts not.
> Came then John neither eating nor drinking and they are saying (*legousin*),
> A Demon he has!
> Came the Son of Man eating and drinking and they are saying (*legousin*),
> Behold a man gluttonous and a wine drinker
> of tax collectors a friend and of sinners.
> So again: wisdom was proved from the works thereof.

Kevin Robb

University of Southern California

NOTES

1. See Wallace McLeod, "Oral Bards at Delphi," *Transactions of the American Philological Association* 92 (1961), pp. 317–52.

2. See E. A. Havelock, "Pre-Literacy and the Pre-Socratics," in *Bulletin of the Institute of Classical Studies*, University of London, 13 (1966), pp. 44–67.

3. Miriam Lichtheim, *Ancient Egyptian Literature, Volume I: The Old and Middle Kingdoms* (Berkeley and Los Angeles: University of California Press, 1975), pp. 5–12.

4. G. S. Kirk, *Heraclitus: The Cosmic Fragments* (Cambridge: Cambridge University Press, 1954), p. 7ff.

5. Hom. *H*.3. 146ff.

6. B42.

7. B104: *dēmōn aoidoisi*.

8. *Ion*, 535D.

9. The earliest surviving written law code (from Crete) is assigned to the seventh century, but, as Athenian practice makes clear, Greek cities did not rush to follow Cretan precedent. The use of *nomos* to designate written law in Athens is discussed in M. Ostwald, *Nomos and the Beginnings of Athenian Democracy* (Oxford: Oxford University Press, 1969), p. 55ff. A clue may be found in the fact that *paranomos* and its derivitives (as in *paranomon ti*, "doing something unlawful" to another person) make their first appearance in the extant literature only in the later fifth century, but then in many Athenian authors. Michael Gargarin writes that "it is a plausible conclusion that the word was coined only after *nomos* came to be used of written laws" ("The Athenian Law Against Hybris," in Bowersock, Burkert, Putnam, eds., *Arktouros: Hellenic Studies Presented to Bernard M. W. Knox* [Berlin and New York: Walter deGruyter, 1979] p. 234). Heraclitus is a linguistic innovator (as in the use of *kosmos* in a new sense) and may well have been the Ephesian innovator for the use of *nomos* to refer to written law. For *kosmos* it has been overlooked that a hereditary priestess of the Artemisium was the *kosmēteira* (*SIG*. 1228; *CIG*. 2823) although her function and how early this office was established remain obscure. The name probably implies investiture of some sort (image or celebrant); if the office is early then part of the thrust of the opening of B30 "This *kosmos*, none of gods or men has made" becomes: "unlike some person or image requiring adornment, this universe required no god or person, no *kosmēteira*, to bestow upon it order or beauty, for it was and is and ever shall be. . . ." At least the thought and linguistic manipulation would be Heraclitean.

10. George Grote, *History of Greece*, vol. 2, (London: John Murray, 1849), pp. 182–84.

11. The motive for Greek adoption and adaptation, and the period of the transfer, are discussed in Kevin Robb, "Poetic Sources of the Greek Alphabet: Rhythm and Abecedarium from Phoenician to Greek," in E. A. Havelock and J. Hershbel, eds., *Communication Arts in the Ancient World* (New York: Hastings House, 1978), pp. 22–36. The argument of this article has gained support from Havelock in his *The Literate Revolution and Its Consequences* (Princeton: Princeton University Press, 1982). Also cf. Kevin Robb, "The Dipylon Prize Graffito," in *Coranto* 7 (1971). There is now general agreement that the alphabet was adopted in the eighth century, and that the earliest inscription, the Dipylon, should be dated to ca. 730 B.C. The *terminus ad quem*, when popular literacy was achieved, has for Athens seen the debate narrowed to the fifth century, either earlier in that century (Turner and Harvey), or near its close (the late J. A. Davison, Havelock). A recent contribution which reviews the literature on the debate (and argues for the former position) is A. Burns, "Athenian Literacy in the Fifth Century B.C.," *JHI* 42 (1981), pp. 371–87. Interestingly, Burns concedes to Havelock the primary impetus of literacy in the Greek movement toward greater abstraction (that word as usual remaining vague), but he believes that its work was done by the end of the fifth century, which would argue for the importance of literacy/orality to the analysis of Presocratic thinkers covered in the present volume, but not for Plato. Havelock, of course, in *Preface to Plato* (Cambridge, MA: Harvard University Press, 1962; reprinted 1982) extends the influence of orality down to the argument of Plato's *Republic*. A neglected nuance supporting Havelock is to count the usages of *akouein* (to hear) and its cognates (along with "sing") in the description of the revised primary education for guardians in *Republic* II–III. Plato assumes without exception (perhaps unconsciously from contemporary practice?) that even the "edited" material, mostly poetic, will be heard and sung, *never* read—at least

not by the pupils. On the vexed question of silent reading in antiquity see the (as ever) sensible and enjoyably written remarks of Bernard Knox, "Silent Reading in Antiquity," *Greek Roman and Byzantine Studies* 9 (Winter, 1968), pp. 421–35.

12. See now the very persuasive argument of Kahn, "Philosophy and the Written Word," in this volume.

13. See Barnett on the traveling masons in the Archaic period in *Journal of Hellenic Studies* 68 (1948), p. 1. The inscription of King Darius at Susa mentions Ionian stone cutters; for the text see W. Hinz in *Journal of Near Eastern Studies* 9 (1950), pp. 1–7. In general, see Boardman, *The Greeks Overseas* (London: Thames and Hudson, rev. ed., 1980) and his useful notes for additional references.

14. See Boardman, *Greeks*, p. 72 and his references. The temple, never finished, was being constructed in the late sixth century and was over 180 feet long.

15. See Jacoby, *Atthis: The Local Chronicles of Ancient Athens* (Oxford: The Clarendon Press, 1949), p. 11. His comment should be noted before assuming too much about literacy at the Artemisium: " . . . there is no evidence of early chronicles kept by priests at Samos or at Didyma or at Ephesos" (p. 359). Of course this says nothing against more informal lists. On the civic side, the Local Chronicle or Local History was, as Jacoby rightly insists, a genus of literature—not even a species or subspecies—invented in Ionia, in the spirit of Ionic *historiē*, in the *second half of the fifth century*. Moreover, in the closing years of that century the genre was transferred from the East to Athens and elsewhere (p. 68). The fourth century then becomes the great era of the Local Chronicle, virtually an explosion of them, and as the century proceeds they are written in dialect and by locals. Had it been early in the fifth century that literacy was achieved, in Athens or anywhere else, then over a century delay (and the use of imported chroniclers from Ionia) for the development of Local Chronicles seems peculiar and indeed inexplicable, a point neglected in the "when in the fifth century popular literacy?" debate.

16. In what follows this general point is developed, although the rather obvious fact that alliteration is an echo device with its origins in mnemonics goes somewhat neglected. For an entertaining correction borrowed from a non-Hellenic and non-Semitic culture, see three sections ("Laws for illiterates" "The law gets rhythm" and "Anglo-Saxon Old English") in David Mellinkoff, *The Language of the Law* (Boston: Little, Brown & Co., 1963) pp. 42–49. The use of rhythm as a mnemonic device, especially alliteration and rhyme—features borrowed from old English oral poetry—in an age of illiterates begins with the first Anglo-Saxon invaders (p. 39). For the earlier Celts (invaded as illiterate as invader, as Mellinkoff notes) the same may have been true; but we have less direct evidence for it because the early Gaelic tradition was oral and poetic. As described in the ancient Irish book of the law, *Senchus Mor*, the law was " . . . the joint memory of the ancients, the transmission from one ear to another, the chanting of the poets" (quoted in Mellinkoff, p. 37).

17. George Thompson, *Studies in Ancient Greek Society* (New York: Citadel Press, 1965), p. 540.

18. Thompson, *Studies* p. 540.

19. Ibid.

20. George Biebuyck and Kahombo C. Mateene, *The Mwindo Epic* (Berkeley and Los Angeles: University of California Press, 1971). The introduction is by Biebuyck and contains references to his substantial publication on the Nyagna.

21. Biebuyck, in *Mwindo*, p. v, 7–10, Also cf. p. 72 n123; p. 141 n277.

22. Ibid., p. 7.

23. Ibid., p. 8.

24. Ibid., p. 13.

25. Ibid., p. 7, 10, 14.

26. The use of riddles for oral mnemonic purposes has been somewhat neglected by oralists. But see the excellent article in *Pauly-Wissowa*, s.v. Rätsel. Perceptively, Thompson: "The riddle, which is as universal as it is ancient, was in origin a vehicle for catechism. . . . In Greece the riddle preserved its metrical form, which means that it was sung, or had been (*Studies*, p. 499). Also see note 58 below.

27. Biebuyck, in *Mwindo*, p. 8.

28. B31: "In Priene lived Bias son of Teutames, who is of more account (*logos*) than the others." The play on the word *logos*—one of whose meanings was "tally" or "account" (and so "worth")—is the reference to the famous *logos* or saying of Bias, quoted without naming Bias, as the concluding words of B104, *ho polloi kakoi, oligoi de agathoi.* (For Heraclitus, those of *intellectual* worth are few.) Heraclitus can assume that his preliterate listeners will appreciate the allusion. A saying from Bias is referred to by Socrates as among those from the Seven which are on everyone's lips in the famous *Protagoras* (343 A—B) passage. A late source, the scoliast on Lucian (*on Phalar,* I, 7) connects a saying to each of the Seven. There is a peculiar and anonymous MS. in the Laurentian Library which compiles no less than ninety-two sayings and which is entitled: "Maxims of the Seven Sages Which Were Found Carved on the Pillar at Delphi." In general, see Eliza Wilkins' Chicago dissertation (privately printed by the University of Chicago Libraries, 1917) *"Know Thyself" In Greek and Latin Literature.*

29. The great pioneer work on the vast number of word plays in the biblical material was I. Casanowicz, *Paranomasia in the Old Testament* (Baltimore: Johns Hopkins University Press, 1892). See now especially Stanley Gervitz, "Of Puns and Patriarchs . . ." in *Hebrew Union College Annual* (Cincinnati, 1973), pp. 33—54, and his many references both to biblical examples and to other literature. Gervitz recommends for the Mesopotamian material E. A. Speiser, "Word Plays in the Creation Epic's Version of the Founding of Babylon," *Orientalia* 25 (1956), pp. 317—23. Also (pp. 40—41) Gervitz has a discussion of the use of ellipsis in parallelism, with references to other works for both Hebrew and Ugaritic.

30. M. I. West, *Hesiod's Works and Days* (Oxford: The Clarendon Press, 1978). West assumes that the Sumerian proverbs (text dated 2500 B.C.) are the oldest examples of the genre, but they may now have a rival from Ebla. Among the tablets, mostly economic and accidentally fired ca. 2500 B.C., there are literary texts. Most are not yet available to the layman but the excavator reports, as we could anticipate, 20 myths, epic narratives, hymns and incantations, and "collections of proverbs" (G. Pettinato, *The Archives of Ebla* [Garden City, NY: Doubleday, 1981], p. 238).

31. I am grateful for this observation to Thomas Rybar, a member of a small orthodox Ashkenazic community in Guatemala City, who had been asked by the congregation to take over a required weekly recitation in the absence of a cantor. He remarked to me that in some texts (much to his comfort) marks in addition to the diacritics have been added to help in chanting. This comment led me to inquire how far back we could trace the musical accents in written form, which would seem to be back to *De accentibus linguae hebraicae* (Hagenau, 1518), which in turn was based on an Ashkenazic local oral tradition. The Sephardic cantillation followed, at least in published form, in 1699. The term "trop" in Jewish literature seems to have originated with the great Rashi, but of course as a term with a non-Hebrew linguistic tradition. Some evidence for an earlier (at least in Europe earlier than Lowth) ap-

preciation of parallelism as a poetic form was collected by Gray, in his *The Forms of Hebrew Poetry* (London: John Murray, 1915), but Gray placed emphasis on sense rather than sound parallelism. The oral/musical transmission, as it relates to the recognition of parallelistic construction, and as the tradition seems to have been passed down orally among Ashkenazic Jews, may deserve further examination from those qualified to undertake the research, as I am not. The oral tradition in Rashi's time, even if not fixed, existed and reached back how far? One instructed another, in an oral tradition that was or was not broken? For some references in this matter cf. Eric Werner, "Trop and Tropus," *Hebrew Union College Annual* 46 (Cincinnati, 1975), pp. 289–96.

32. An English translation appeared in 1847. A good discussion of the types of parallelism now recognized by biblical scholars is found in C. A. and E. G. Briggs, *A Critical and Exegetical Commentary on the Psalms* (New York: Scribner's, 1912), Introduction. The forefront of scholarship in this area seems now to be in a series of Harvard dissertations, mainly under the direction of Frank Moore Cross, dealing with the poetic structure and orality of both early Hebrew and Ugaritic poetry. Scandinavian scholars have devoted considerable research to the oral background of the Old Testament, notably Engell, Hyberg, Pedersen, and E. Nielsen. A group of Nielsen's valuable papers which were first published in *Dansk Teologisk Tidsskrift* have been translated into English and published under the title: *Oral Tradition* (London: SCM Press, 1954).

33. The figures given by James Muilenburg in *An Introduction to the Revised Standard Version of the Old Testament* (Toronto and Edinburgh: Thomas Nelson & Sons, 1952), pp. 62ff.

34. Edgar Goodspeed, *The Complete Bible: An American Translation* (Chicago: University of Chicago Press, 1923), pp. xiii–xiv.

35. In T. Robinson, *The Poetry of the Old Testament* (London: Peter Duckworth, 1947), p. 21.

36. F. M. Cross, "Prose and Poetry in the Mythic and Epic Texts from Ugarit," *Harvard Theological Review* 67 (1974), pp. 1–17. The references below are from this article.

37. *CTA* 2.1.7–8.

38. Ibid. 2.4.7–10.

39. Ibid. 3.5.38; 4.4.41. Cross (p. 3) notes an analogous chiastic structure with word repetitions in Isaiah 55:1.

40. In the same text mentioned above, n38; also chiasmus in *CTA* 15.3.17–19.

41. P.7. Cross reconstructs an example from garbled transmission in the *KRT* epic and *CTA* 14.3.159–61, and then compares it with an impressive example in Judges 5:25.

42. Lichtheim, *Ancient Egyptian Literature* (hereafter *AEL*,) pp. 3–12. See n3 above.

43. Lichtheim, *AEL*, p. 11.

44. In Lichtheim, *AEL*, p. 73. *P. Prisse* is from the Middle Kingdom. In Lichtheim's opinion only the Instruction of Hardjedef is composed in a language archaic enough to have been transmitted from the Old Kingdom without major literary reworking. Cf. Lichtheim *AEL*, pp. 6ff.

45. Lichtheim, *AEL*, p. 63.

46. Ibid., p. 59. The elegant parallelism is: A/a:B/b:C/d:D:d.

47. Ibid., p. 60.

48. Ibid., p. 58.

49. Ibid., p. 146.

50. See the discussion by Matthew Black in Ackroyd and Evans, eds., *The Cambridge History of the Bible*, vol. I (Cambridge: Cambridge University Press, 1970), pp. 5–6.

51. B35, retaining *philosophoi andres*, which probably belongs to Clement. Perhaps the saint is substituting a familiar phrase for one (to his audience) less familiar. But something does seem to be required or at least probable and Clement is right; this sort of person came to be called a *philosophos*, but seemingly not before Socrates' time. (See n30, above.)

52. M. Dahood, "Ebla, Ugarit and the Bible," in Pettinato, *The Archives of Ebla* (New York, 1981), p. 182.

53. In what follows references, unless otherwise specified, are to the following works: G. S. Kirk, *Heraclitus: The Cosmic Fragments* (Cambridge: Cambridge University Press, 1954); M. Marcovich, *Heraclitus* (Merida, Venezuela: Los Andes University Press, 1967); Charles Kahn, *The Art and Thought of Heraclitus* (Cambridge: Cambridge University Press, 1979); K. Deichgräber, *Rhythmische Elemente im Logos des Heraklit* (Mainz: Academie der Wissenschaften und der Literatur, 1962). My general analysis of the shape of the Heraclitean saying, and the interpretation of B11 and B54 specifically, owe debts to an earlier paper by Eric Havelock, "Preliteracy and the Presocratics" (see n2, above) which has been reprinted in E. A. Havelock, *The Literate Revolution in Greece and Its Cultural Consequences* (Princeton: Princeton University Press, 1982). It is no longer possible for me to document precisely my debts to the many Heraclitean scholars not mentioned below, or entirely to separate my own thinking from their reflections on Heraclitus' text. But I mention especially my debt to the work of Heinrich Gomperz, a most perceptive reader of Heraclitus (and his boldest punctuator). I have deliberately not cited the work of four scholars—Hölscher, Fränkel, Snell and Gigon—whose analysis of Heraclitean style is in places sympathetic to the analysis attempted in this paper only because much of what they say is in a different nomenclature from mine and written from a different orientation.

54. *Ion* 534–37. In the famous image of the magnetic rings, the "inspiration"— which before long Socrates is calling a mania and describing as hysteria—passes from the god (Muse or Apollo) to the epic composer (Homer) to the epic singer (Ion) who works (*ergazesthe*) the same effects—and here Plato's hostility seems strongest—on the listening audience. They weep, terror leaps up in their hearts, hair stands on end, and all the rest.

55. Punctuating after *anthrōpos* and changing to the plural in translation.

56. There is an untranslatable reference to the rhapsode's staff, the *rhabdos*, in a verb normally translated "to beat." If we had the English verb "to crosier," meaning to beat someone, then the equivalent would be to drive a bishop out of his diocese and crosier him (with his own crosier).

57. Robert Englefield, *Language: Its Origin and Relation to Thought* (New York: Scribner's, 1973).

58. The role of riddles in the sayings has often been noted, but not their mnemonic utility. For the most famous of the riddles in the Heraclitean text, see Kirk, "The Michigan Alcidamas-Papyrus; Heraclitus Fr. 56D; The Riddle of the Lice," *CQ* 44 (1950), and his reference to epic riddles (in the *Agon*) and the literature on Greek riddles.

59. E. J. Tinseley, in *The Cambridge Bible Commentary: The Gospel According to Luke* (Cambridge: Cambridge University Press, 1965), pp. 19–20.

ORALITY AND PHILOSOPHY

For many years Eric Havelock has laid great emphasis in his scholarly writings on the complete orality, or non-literacy, of Dark Age Greece, and the only partial literacy of the centuries that followed. Many scholars would agree with Havelock thus far. His distinctive contribution is to argue that literacy, once acquired, is the cause of a wide variety of phenomena in Classical Greece. Even if Havelock's arguments prove ultimately untenable, his works have served a valuable purpose: they direct our attention to one of the most easily overlooked differences between early Greek civilization and our own. It is *prima facie* likely that so striking a difference had important consequences, even if not the consequences claimed by Havelock; and if there were in fact no consequences, or no important ones, this state of affairs would be sufficiently remarkable to merit our attention.

Havelock evidently believes that, in his account of the effects of the development of literacy in a previously non-literate culture, he has a hypothesis of great explanatory power. His belief may be correct, even if the particular effects claimed in his works prove to be not demonstrable; but it is essential to state the hypothesis as precisely as possible, to indicate any problems of interpretation there may be, and to test it. The first part of my paper will attempt this task; the second will briefly suggest what remains to be done.

It will be useful to state which of Havelock's claims are not in dispute here:

(1) Dark Age Greece (at least to about 750 B.C.) was non-literate. (The exact date is unimportant for my purposes.)

(2) Non-literacy does not preclude great sophistication in many aspects of culture. (Indeed, Havelock may underestimate the possibilities.)

(3) There is a difference between the language of Homer and the language of Aristotle sufficiently great to prevent the expression of Aristotelian philosophy in Homeric language. (The nature of the difference may not be that claimed by Havelock.)

(4) When literacy appeared (or reappeared) in Greece, it was possessed by only part of the population.

(5) Even those Greeks who were literate did not make the same use of books as is customary in the modern world. (This consideration in fact leads me to have some doubts about Havelock's general claim

concerning the importance of literacy as cause in early Greece. See my discussion of (15) through (18) below.)

Havelock apparently makes at least the following additional claims in his writings:

(6) The Homeric poems preserve a type of language which is characteristic of non-literate societies.

(7) Non-literate societies necessarily store cultural and other data in the memories of their members.

(8) In non-literate societies and, apparently, in general, nothing that is not rhythmic or metrical is memorizable.

(9) In non-literate societies and, apparently, in general, nothing that is not expressed as the narrative of actions is memorizable.

Accordingly,

(10) A non-literate society "must prefer mythos to logos." (p. 13, "The Linguistic Task of the Presocratics"—see my note 1).

From (6) through (10) Havelock derives certain claims about the language of the Homeric poems, including

(11) It is impossible to make timeless statements using the verb "to be" (*einai*).

A fortiori,

(12) It is impossible to make timeless statements with abstract subjects, using the verb "to be" (*einai*). From (11) and (12) follows

(13) It is impossible to produce definitions of the form "Justice is ϕ," or express such propositions as "the angles of a triangle are equal to two right angles."

Havelock also maintains that in the non-literate language of Homer

(14) The idea of a system is impossible.

However, after literacy, in the restricted sense appropriate to ancient Greece, (re-)appears, the following changes gradually occur:

(15) The technology of the written word attracts the attention of (some) literate Greeks.

(16) The word (sentence? paragraph? written work?) becomes an object clearly distinguished from the writer or reader.

(17) Since the written sentence, paragraph, or written word has structure, (some) literate Greeks are drawn to inquire whether what is denoted by the written words also has structure.

(18) The existence of written words now for the first time renders abstraction possible.

At this point of the development in Greece,

(19) The Presocratics turn to their task of remedying the deficiencies of oral language.

(20) The syntax of the new, improved language is different from that of the old.

(21) Statements can be made in the new language which cannot be made in the old.

(22) The new language is the language of logos (10), worded "so as to replace agents by impersonal forces and the acts of agents performed upon other agents by statements of relationships between impersonal entities."

Havelock nowhere sets out his theory in precisely this form; but his discussions of the Greek concept of justice and of abstraction in the Presocratics seem to commit him to at least the foregoing.[1] It may be that I am misrepresenting his argument in some respects; in which case future discussions will serve to clarify the position. I shall argue here that Havelock's readers need a more precise statement of the hypothesis than has yet been offered: the processes postulated in (15) through (18) are particularly obscure.

I shall discuss Havelock's claims in the order in which they appear above. Havelock seems committed to (6) in a very strong sense. The Homeric poems furnish the data on which his theory of the nature of oral speech is based. He cannot exclude particular linguistic usages found in the poems on the grounds that they result from the subsequent recording of the poems in writing, since such an argument would be circular. (He might exclude passages which Homeric scholars on other grounds regard as later interpolations by literate poets; but scholarly agreement on such matters is rare.)

If we interpret (7) as meaning merely "any data transmitted from generation to generation in a non-literate culture must be stored in the memories of its members," (7) is evidently true, unless we posit convenient literate neighbors or visiting anthropologists to perform the task of recording. But to accept (7) does not commit us to accepting Havelock's theory of the conscious purpose of epic, which I have discussed elsewhere.[2] However, even if that theory be rejected, Havelock evidently insists in his discussion of the Presocratics[3] that both (8) and (9) be taken with (7), with the consequence that any information to be transmitted by memory from generation to generation must be cast in the form of metrical or rhythmic narrative of actions.

Even if one granted that a memorizable work of epic length must take this form, geometrical proofs and philosophical arguments are characteristically somewhat more brief; and if we survey societies known to us from late sixth-century Greece onward, it is simply untrue that all mnemonics are metrical or rhythmic narratives of action. Mnemonists at least from the Greek Simonides in the late sixth and early fifth centuries B.C., through the orators and teachers of oratory in the ancient world, to the mnemonist studied by A. R. Luria[4] and beyond, have used a method of remembering lists of unrelated facts which rely not on meter or rhythm, but on locating imagined objects, with each of which one item is associated, in three-dimensional space in an imagined landscape. Nor need metrical mnemonics contain narrative. Those acquainted with Kennedy's *Shorter Latin Primer* will recall a mnemonic beginning "A, ab, absque, coram, de,/ Palam, clam, cum, ex, and e," a mere list of prepositions; and innumerable British school children learn, or once learned, "Willie, Willie, Harry, Steve, . . ." a metrical mnemonic recording the list of Kings and Queens of England. Narrative occurs without meter, and with a subject-matter entirely unrelated to what is thereby memorized: for example, the musician's "*Father Charles Goes Down And Ends Battle*." Meter occurs without narrative, and with a subject-matter entirely unrelated to what is thereby memorized: "*Barbara Celarent*. . . ." Mnemonics may contain no "real" words at all: VIBGYOR (the order of colors in the spectrum). The number of methods available to stimulate the human memory is large. One might reply on Havelock's behalf that at least some of these would be unlikely to occur to the non-literate. The particular examples given may warrant the reply in some cases; but I am concerned not with the particular examples but with the associative memory processes which they illustrate. The Simonidean method and the metrical name-list are evidently available to the non-literate; and it is not clear how the acquisition of literacy could endow one with new powers of memory. It seems necessary to replace (8) and (9) with "So far as modern scholars are aware, non-literate early Greeks regarded only the rhythmical or metrical narrative of actions as being memorable (or memorizable)." This claim is much weaker, since there is no evidence for or against the use of other mnemonic methods in early non-literate Greece; and it offers no warrant for making any claims about the use of mnemonic devices in non-literate societies in general. Since the ingenuity and sophistication of non-literate societies is not in dispute, it would be strange if Havelock wished to claim that some mnemonic devices—methods of association of ideas in the mind— could in principle be discovered only by the literate.

If the Homeric poems employ only narrative, the reason is not that only narrative could be memorized. If we imagine—as Havelock's language sometimes suggests—very early Greeks discussing the need for memory-stored data in their non-literate culture, mentally surveying all possible kinds of language, and deciding that only narrative would serve their purpose, we must conclude that they were mistaken; and we shall not be tempted to treat the mistake as necessarily characteristic of all non-literate cultures. If on the other hand we suppose—as Havelock himself seems sometimes to suppose— that the ordinary unmemorized speech of early Greece, like most of the speech (and writing) of most cultures, was narrative in form, we shall surely conclude that the Homeric bards composed and memorized narrative because they wanted to tell a story, and that their contemporaries enjoyed such stories. There is no reason—or at all events Havelock has shown no reason—to suppose that the bards, or some other Greeks, could not have memorized other types of material, had such been available; and even if the non-literate Greeks in fact knew of no other mnemonic methods, it would be difficult to argue that *no* non-literate thinker could discover any of them. Unless non-literate cultures are prevented in some other way not yet discussed from developing, for example, proofs in geometry, the wide variety of mnemonics available would facilitate the preservation of such proofs, once discovered. If a non-literate culture "must prefer mythos to logos," the reason is not evidently linked with the powers of the human memory. I shall accordingly not discuss Havelock's mnemonic claim further, but rather discuss the language of non-literate societies as such. I shall discuss later whether the visible existence of written words and sentences supplies some other aid to the abstractive powers of the human mind, as Havelock claims in (15)-(18).

It is worthwhile to explore further the consequences of (10). It seems evident that Havelock intends his claim in a very strong sense: not that a non-literate culture must choose mythos over logos fifty-one percent of the time, but that it must prefer mythos over logos one hundred percent of the time. Indeed, since the members of a non-literate culture, on Havelock's argument, do not know what a logos would be like, it would be more precise to maintain that they are constrained by the circumstances of living in a non-literate culture to express themselves in mythos, not logos.

But the situation remains unclear: Does Havelock claim that 'he members of an oral culture *in isolation from any literate influences* cannot achieve logos, or that *in no circumstances* could non-literate persons arrive at logos, by which Havelock means language which contains at least some propositions of the kind deemed impossible in Homer in (11) through (14)? (The second claim imposes much greater restrictions on the powers of the human mind.) Suppose that in about 360 B.C. the literate philosopher Plato, en route to or from Sicily, had been carried away by a storm to the island of Barataria, whose inhabitants were intelligent but non-literate; and suppose that at least one Baratarian had known the Homeric poems in the original language, and hence had possessed a knowledge of non-literate Greek. Would it have been possible for Plato to engender any capability for philosophy or abstraction in the Baratarians, unless he had also taught them to read and write?

If it would not have been impossible, then the literacy of the population is not a necessary condition of philosophizing; and if an intelligent Baratarian could learn thus from Plato, he might surely philosophize on his own account thereafter, if he had appropriate mental attributes, and stimulate others to do likewise after Plato's departure. Further, it is clear that literacy is not a sufficient condition for the production of philosophy: many literate cultures have made no significant contribution to philosophy, and most literate persons are not philosophers. But if literacy is neither a necessary nor a sufficient condition for the production of philosophy, it is difficult to discover what Plato could do for the Baratarians that a Baratarian with suitable intellectual endowments could not do.

I now turn to claims (11) through (13). I have discussed them elsewhere;[5] but a brief résumé is necessary here, since they are implicit in much of Havelock's paper.

Havelock argues (11) that the verb *einai* ("to be") cannot be used in Homeric Greek in general, universal, or timeless propositions:[6] "That precisely is why *einai* is not there [in these propositions], for if it were, it would intrude the notion of a presence limited to particular circumstances, valid (now) or 'sometimes,' 'somewhere,' or somehow.' " As Havelock's examples indicate, timeless propositions need not be general or universal: Havelock cites *Iliad* 1, 589, as an example without *einai*; and there Zeus is the subject. But, to take one counter-example, Zeus says of himself, *Iliad* 8, 17, "I am (*einai*) the most powerful god of all." Zeus evidently intends no restriction of time or place.

Despite claim (12), such predication occurs in Homer also without a personal subject. In *Iliad* 17, 446–47 we find "of all the creatures that breathe and move on the face of the earth, nothing is (*einai*) more miserable than a man." It seems difficult to assert that a language capable of expressing "Nothing *einai* φ " could not express (13) "Some abstract quality *einai* φ ," the *einai* in both cases being a timeless 'is'. *Einai* cannot be equivalent to "stands there": language users sophisticated enough to produce the "No-one" trick of *Odyssey* 9—which is discussed below—would not utter "nothing stands there more miserable" without noticing the quaintness of the expression; and if they did utter it, it constitutes precisely the kind of expression which might be expected to engender philosophical thought in the nonliterate.

In thus querying claim (13), I am for the moment discussing the possibility of using words in combination in sentences. Words which a modern reader will interpret as abstract nouns occur in Homer; copulative *einai* occurs in Homer, with both personal and non-personal subjects; and adjectives occur in Homer. The necessary lexical items, grammar, and syntax are present: if Havelock is correct to claim that "[some abstract quality] *einai* φ" cannot be expressed by Homeric man (in some yet to be determined sense of "cannot"), the reason seems not to be linguistic in any obvious sense.

But even if one granted Havelock claims (11) through (13) with respect to *einai*, Havelock himself points out that a verbless locution, in which subject and predicate are juxtaposed without a verb, is available for use in general, universal, or timeless expressions.[7] (I shall render the verbless locution by "[is].") The verbless locution would suffice if copulative *einai* were absent. In *Iliad* 9, 256, Odysseus says "*Philophrosune ameinon*," "cooperation [is] better than [hostility]." The sense is clear, and the sentence is general or universal in scope. Such sentences could be used to express definitions. The early elegiac poet Tyrtaeus[8] wished to change the current view of *arete* (human excellence). After nine lines of verse in which he rejected other qualities as criteria for possession of *arete* he wrote "This [is] *arete*" of steadfast fighting in the hoplite phalanx. Tyrtaeus used no verb; but he offered a definition of *arete*, even if it was not a type of definition of which Havelock or Socrates would approve.[9]

Tyrtaeus might have been asked for a definition of *arete* in a similar verbless manner: "What [is] *arete*?" No such question, and no such precisely expressed definition, occur in the Homeric poems; and Tyrtaeus is assigned a *floruit* about a century after the currently accepted date for the composition of the Homeric poems in their present form; but it is the difference in genre, not any linguistic difference, which accounts for the absence of a definition of *arete*, or of anything else, from the Homeric poems. When, in *Odyssey* 8, 244, Alcinous wishes Odysseus to "remember our [the Phaeacians'] *arete*," and continues "for we are not excellent boxers or wrestlers; rather we are swift-footed and best with ships . . ." the subject of his discourse is Odysseus' *arte* (mentioned in 8.237), the Phaeacians' *arete*, and the difference between them. Had Odysseus asked Alcinous "What [is] your *arete*?" Alcinous would have understood.

I turn now to claim (14), which is concerned with the possibility of expressing the idea of a system in the language of the Homeric poems. Havelock writes (p. 13) that "as long as preserved communication remained oral, the environment could be described or explained only in the guise of stories which represent it as the work of agents, that is, gods." Abstract terms such as space, void, matter, body, element, motion, immobility, change, permanence, substratum, etc., were lacking. "Aside altogether from the coinage of abstract nouns, the conceptual task also requires the elimination of verbs of doing and acting and happening, one may say, of living and dying, in favor of a syntax which states permanent relationships between conceptual terms systematically." The required linguistic mechanism was furnished by the timeless present of the verb to be—the copula of analytic statement. "The angles *are* equal to two right angles. They are not born that way or become or are made so."

"Systematically" here evidently does not mean "methodically," "diligently": it must mean "in such a manner as to express a (philosophical or scientific) system." I have already disputed the claim that the grammar and syntax of Homer are thus deficient. I do not dispute the absence from Homeric vocabulary of the terms, or rather their Greek equivalents, listed by Havelock; the significance of their absence I shall discuss later. Here I confine myself to a single question: Even if one were to grant claims (12) and (13) to Havelock, would claim (14) be substantiated?

Consider *Iliad* 15, 187–93. The god Poseidon has made his way down to the battlefield of Troy, in defiance of the commands of Zeus. Zeus now demands that he leave the field; and Poseidon angrily refuses, saying to Zeus' messenger:

"For we are three brothers . . . Zeus and I and Hades. . . . All things are divided into three, and each has a share of possessions and status. When the lots were cast, I drew the lot to dwell always in the grey sea, and Hades drew the dark gloom, while Zeus drew the broad heaven among the aether and the clouds. The earth [is] still common to all, as is mighty Olympus."

No one would suppose himself to be reading Aristotle's *Physics*, or even Parmenides. The speech is made by an angry anthropomorphic deity who, using the customary values of Homeric mortal and Homeric god, expresses his claim to fight for the Greeks against the Trojans in defiance of Zeus' wishes. But the claim rests on a systematic apportionment of different parts of the universe; and though the apportionment resulted from the actions of deities, it is now conceived as existing over against those deities, as a permanent state of affairs: and that state of affairs ("are divided," "has a share") is expressed by the perfect aspect (an Indo-European phenomenon)[10] of the Greek verb, whose function is to express states of affairs as states of affairs. The perfect aspect is undeniably a phenomenon of non-literate Greek; and its existence indicates that non-literate Greeks (and indeed Indo-Europeans) had from earliest times experienced the need to express states of affairs as states of affairs, and to distinguish them sharply from momentary or continuous *actions*. That the state of affairs is the result of an action seems to render the system no less a system: the verb-form emphasizes the state of affairs, and the expression is comprehensible without the preceding narrative. On hearing it, one need not have the agents in mind: the perfect passive of *teuchein*, "to make," is routinely used in Homer as a virtual synonym for "is," in contexts where an action of making or an existent maker are not in question.[11] In earlier non-literate Greek the usage may have been confined to contexts in which there was an expressed maker and occasion of making. Havelock points to analogous developments over time in the Presocratic philosophers. But this development is complete in the Homeric poems, and so routine a usage gives no indication of being a recent innovation. Havelock presumably must concede that it is a long-standing usage of oral speech since it is frequent in the Homeric poems; so that not merely is the perfect aspect available to express states of affairs—the function which it indeed was developed to perform—but it is already used to express states of affairs without reference to any agent or action which brought the states into being. Even without the copulative *einai*, and without the verbless usage, Homeric man possesses the linguistic resources to express a system as an abiding state of affairs.

With claim (15) we reach Havelock's causal hypothesis: that the differences between the language of Homer and the language of Aristotle's *Physics* are the result of "the changing technology of the written word."[12] Even a Hesiodic description of the environment "rendered the logos in which it was written an artifact, an object separate from the describer's own consciousness. As this happened, the opportunity arose, and the desire with it, to render the object more explicit, to tie it down as a system or structure instead of a series of events issuing from the mouth of the poet or his muse."

Thus far we have been concerned with claims to which empirical evidence is relevant and for which such evidence is available. I have already argued that the facts are not altogether what Havelock claims; but on the assumption that it would be possible to arrive at an agreed version of the facts, the acceptability of the hypothesis depends to a considerable extent on its explanatory power compared with other competing hypotheses. It is a possible hypothesis, for the Greeks did pass from non-literacy to literacy during the relevant period. Our estimation of its explanatory power will rest in part on the precision with which it can be stated. Havelock's statement above is very general; and in an effort to render it less general, it will be necessary to raise some questions to which empirical evidence is relevant.

If we suppose that the Greeks assigned crucial importance to the technology of the written word, to the book—or rather papyrus roll—as object, we might reasonably infer that in the hands of a people as energetic and gifted as the Greeks, the papyrus roll would become not merely an object endowed with technical efficiency, rendered as easy to read as possible, but also an object of considerable beauty. (Compare the history of the Greek vase.) We might expect that legible handwriting, clear word-divisions, an adequate system of punctuation, and careful division of paragraphs would be the norm. Our earliest extant papyrus fragments postdate the invention of the papyrus roll by several centuries; and none of them, nor any Greek written text produced for a long time thereafter, have any of these characteristics. We know that it was customary in the ancient world for one person to read to a group; and the person was frequently a slave. In the circumstances, the book as object before the eyes seems less characteristic of the culture than the book as a source of those streams of auditory sensations familiar from Havelock's account of non-literate cultures; and the absence of any technical effort to increase the readability of the book seems to point in the same direction.

Furthermore, Havelock's hypothesis, though not precisely stated, seems to require that an interest in the structure of the cosmos, and in the development of a language to express the structure of the cosmos, be derived from a perception of the structure of the written account on the papyrus roll. The structure of the written account must be either the aesthetically pleasing pattern of the words on the page, or the grammatico-syntactical structure of sentence, clause, and phrase. The former is absent from our earliest extant papyri, and nothing suggests that earlier papyri were more visually patterned; and on Havelock's own—in this case very reasonable—principles, we should not postulate a perception of grammatico-syntactical patterns unless vocabulary indicates that the concepts were in fact in use. But it is well known that even in Platonic Greek clearly defined and distinguished terms for "word" "phrase," "sentence" are lacking; that Plato can distinguish between noun and verb, or noun and predicate, but little more; and that even Aristotle's grammatical vocabulary lags far behind his logical vocabulary.

Havelock's hypothesis here is quite different from the hypothesis that the ability to write down a poem produces a consciousness of individuality in the poet, and the development of personal styles, and a feeling that the poem is a (not necessarily economically valuable) possession of the poet. Such effects postulate merely the existence of the poem as an object distinct from the poet. By the same argument, the ability to write will produce philosophers, historians, and tragedians with similar heightened consciousness of individuality and awareness of personal achievement; but Havelock's hypothesis requires more of the writing as artifact than that it merely exist independently of its author. We need to know precisely what kind of perceived structure on the written page produces the conviction that the world about us itself has structure; and we need positive evidence that the early Presocratics were able to perceive the structure in question on the written page.

In the absence of greater precision, it is impossible to grant explanatory power to Havelock's hypothesis; and I have given reasons for doubting whether the facts to be explained are those which Havelock claims. I now wish to consider the relationship of geometry to literacy, and the possibility that a member of a non-literate culture might have both the skill and the interests to raise philosophical questions.

Havelock's views on geometry are difficult to ascertain precisely. "The triangle stood firmly, its two legs astride the ground, stoutly defending its two right angles against the attack of the enemy" is one of his favorite examples of oral narrative utterance. Considered as an epigram, the sentence is vivid; but considered as a claim about linguistic and conceptual possibilities, it is confusing. The empirical triangular object has three corners which it might defend; and these it does not require geometry to perceive. Knowledge of the two right angles depends on geometrical reasoning of a kind which Havelock denies to non-literate cultures, so that the sentence could not appear in the narrative of such cultures. Geometric reasoning is a prerequisite, and such reasoning requires copulative *einai* and the kind of abstract concept formation which, in Havelock's view, depends on the ability to write down "angle" (or rather "corner"), "line," and similar words. Despite the apparent implications of this epigram, I shall assume that Havelock wishes to deny the possibility of enunciating any geometrical propositions, or "doing geometry," in a non-literate culture.

The Greek word *"geometria"* transparently means "land measurement," which suggests that the early Greeks, like the Egyptians,[13] were acquainted with at least one of the right-angled triangles whose sides are commensurable. Anyone who has reached even this point presumably in some sense knows that all triangles whose sides are three, four, and five units in length have a right angle (or "square corner," if "right angle" is too abstract) opposite to the longest side; and it is not easy to see why only the literate could reach this point. Now one might scratch a triangle in the sand to explain some point in land measurement; and the scratched triangle represents the triangle of ropes which the Egyptians used in their surveying. Furthermore, the scratched triangle represents the *structure* of the rope triangle in a simple and obvious way. The scratched triangle seems much better suited than the word "triangle" to stimulate the human mind to abstract "line," "angle," "triangle," and similar concepts, and much better suited than are written words and sentences in general to stimulate the formation of abstract concepts in general. Whether or not the earliest geometers in Greece were in fact non-literate, on Havelock's own principles it seems necessary to conclude that a non-literate geometer is possible; and I have already argued that a non-narrative mnemonic could have been supplied.

Even if copulative *einai* were not available, *tetuktai* was available in pre-literate Greece, as was the verbless locution. The perfect aspect might appear particularly suitable for expressing the nature of the figure drawn in the sand and the ideal figure it represents; and Euclid regularly employs the perfect imperative passive ("let a line exist-as-drawn") for this purpose. The perfect aspect is less suitable for definitions; but copulative *einai* is in fact available, and the verbless locution is suitable here too. In Euclid's definitions, of the first ten occasions in which "is" in any sense would be required in translation, *einai* occurs in six, the verbless locution in four.

Could a member of a non-literate culture have both the skill and the interests to raise philosophical questions? I argued above that Havelock has not disproved the possibility, and now add some considerations in favor of it.

Consider Plato's *Phaedo*. There Socrates, in the course of his intellectual autobiography, says that he now gives to the question "What makes anything beautiful?" the answer (100d7) "All the beautiful things [become] beautiful because of the presence of the beautiful." He continues (100e5):

"And [are] the big things big and the bigger things bigger by reason of bigness, and the smaller things smaller by reason of smallness?"

Cebes agrees; whereupon Socrates continues (100e8):

"Then you would not agree if anyone were to say that one person was (*einai*) bigger than another by a head, and the smaller smaller by this same thing (that is, a head): you would protest that you say nothing else than that everything that is bigger than another thing is (*einai*) bigger by reason of nothing else than bigness, and [is] bigger on account of this, bigness, whereas the smaller [is] smaller by reason of nothing else than smallness, and [is] smaller on account of this, smallness; for you would be afraid, I suppose, that an opposing argument might come against you, if you say that someone is (*einai*) bigger or smaller than someone else by a head: first that the bigger was (*einai*) bigger and the smaller smaller by reason of (or "because of") the same thing (that is, the head), and secondly that the bigger was (*einai*) bigger by reason of the head which was (*einai*) small, and that this was something strange, that someone was (*einai*) bigger by reason of something small."

Juxtapose some lines from Homer. In *Iliad* 3, Helen, on the walls of Troy, is identifying some of the Greek heroes for Priam. Priam says of Agamemnon (168/9) that "others are (*einai*) bigger by a head," of Odysseus (193/4) that "he [is] smaller by a head than Agamemnon."

On the basis of these quotations from Homer and Plato, some observations seem justified:

(a) Plato possesses the fully developed use of copulative *einai*; but he still frequently uses the verbless locution to express the relationship. Havelock forbids us to speak of *einai* as "understood" in this relation,[14] as Platonic scholars frequently do; but whatever terminology is used, the situation in Plato and Homer, so far as concerns the use of *einai*, seems identical. The same sense can be expressed with or without *einai*. In *Iliad* 3, the relationship between "others" and "bigger," expressed by *einai*, is surely identical with that between "Odysseus" and "smaller," expressed verblessly.

(b) Whether or not the fragment of autobiography in *Phaedo* 100e7–101b2 is authentically Socratic, it is very plausible: the explanation in terms of "bigness" and "smallness," which in its complete enunciation is the Theory of Forms, might well have been evoked by the sophistic paradoxes at the end of the paragraph.

The material for these sophistic paradoxes lies to hand in the language of the *Iliad*, an oral poem. A Baratarian of average intelligence could surely understand the paradoxes if Plato expressed them orally. We are constrained to believe that no Baratarian, or non-literate Greek, could have discovered the paradox for himself only if we must believe that no non-literate person ever knowingly plays on words in a puzzling manner.

Consider now the encounter of Odysseus with the Cyclops in *Odyssey* 9. Trapped in the Cyclops' cave with his companions, Odysseus has told him that Odysseus' name is "No-one." When the Cyclops is blinded, he cries out in pain, and his neighbors ask (406) whether anyone is trying to kill him by means of cunning or strength. The Cyclops replies in a sentence which he intends to mean "No-one (the name of the assailant) is trying to kill me, by means of cunning (the wine), not by strength"; but the neighbors understand his words as "No-one is killing me either by cunning or by strength," and go away. The trick with the name is linguistically sophisticated; even more sophisticated is the manipulation of the Greek negative conjunction in the remainder of the sentence.

My argument is not that the bardic narrator of the "No-one" trick must have been, though non-literate, a philosopher of language or endowed with a philosophical interest in language, but that he was certainly consciously clever with words and possessed of a delight in his verbal dexterity—a delight which must have been shared by his audience. The word "No-one" is an object of his thought, a lexical item with which tricks can be played, a word which can deliver two messages and which, in combination with the negative conjunction, can produce a sentence which delivers two messages.[15] If the non-literate bard can thus focus his attention on a word and a sentence, it is difficult to understand why another non-literate Greek should not be drawn to inquire why words can behave in this manner, and thus arrive at questions of meaning and denotation, being and not-being, and certain logical problems. A similarly observant non-literate Greek might notice an apparent paradox in others being bigger than Agamemnon by a head while Agamemnon was smaller than Odysseus by a head, and might be led to a solution. Plato's (or Socrates') solution employs copulative *einai*, the instrumental dative, and the noun "bigness" (*megethos*), all of which are available in the Homeric poems, Havelock's source of non-literate data.

The conclusion seems warranted that:

(a) Not only the literate may be consciously concerned with words as words, and with the puzzles that they may generate.

(b) Not only the literate might attempt to solve such puzzles.

(c) Language used in everyday contexts ("bigger by a head") can generate major philosophical problems, and lead to the development of abstract terminology, just as readily as the need adequately to express cosmological ideas.

One might perhaps add:

(d) Developments in abstract terminology, even with respect to terms such as "motion," "rest," "dimension," might be discernible in writers whose primary concerns are not philosophical.

I conclude that Havelock has not as yet demonstrated any *necessary* link between literacy and abstract thought; that he has not as yet demonstrated that *in fact* the stimulus to abstract thought in early Greece was the invention of writing; that some features denied by Havelock to be available in oral speech are found in the Homeric poems; and that other concerns than cosmology might lead to abstract thought.

In its present form, Havelock's hypothesis seems to have little explanatory power. But the hypothesis furnishes only the first stage of his paper on the Presocratics. He argues: a) the acquisition of literacy furnished the Presocratics with the capacity for developing a new syntax and new abstractive powers; b) endowed with this capacity, the Presocratics clearly perceived the deficiencies of the old "oral" syntax and vocabulary, and made it their principal task to produce improvements; c) it is possible to trace those improvements in extant Presocratic texts. (This is the substance of claims (19) through (22).)

Evidently the rejection of a) does not necessitate the rejection of b), merely its restatement and clarification. Even if he granted that the causal hypothesis is unproved, and that oral speech has some characteristics he has previously denied to it, Havelock seems still able to maintain that the Presocratics made it their principal task to make improvements in "oral" syntax and vocabulary in the interest of philosophy.

But further clarification is necessary. The classification of early Greek Literature into "oral" and "literary" is the work of twentieth-century scholars. If it is correct, there must have been a period in early Greece during which the Greeks themselves were aware of the distinction. But no extant Greek writer shows himself aware of it. This fact can be turned both to Havelock's advantage and to his disadvantage: to his advantage, in that when Heraclitus attacks in the same breath Homer and writers whom we distinguish as literate, Havelock can maintain that it is the "oral" syntax which these writers derive from Homer that is attacked; to his disadvantage, in that he cannot justify the claim that Heraclitus is attacking the "orality" of Homer *qua* orality; for there is no evidence that any Presocratic knew and distinguished oral literature as a separate category. Again, the restated b) could be treated as making a stronger or a weaker claim. The stronger portrays the Presocratics both as being aware that their language was deficient and as knowing what the deficiencies were; the weaker portrays them as being engaged in cosmological speculation, and as incidentally developing an abstract (or more abstract) vocabulary. Havelock makes the stronger claim, and writes of the Presocratic polemic "against language currently in use."[16]

But "language currently in use" is ambiguous. Havelock represents the Presocratic as complaining that the resources of the Greek language are inadequate to express what he wants to express; but the Presocratic might be complaining merely that the other Greeks use the available resources badly. (If one is ignorant about any subject, one will use language badly when discussing it; but the fault lies with the thinker, not with the vocabulary.) Now Xenophanes (B11, 12) complains that Homer and Hesiod portray the gods as immoral. His own deity is non-anthropomorphic (B23), and his complaint might have formed part of an argument for the inapplicability to deity of moral attributes as such (as in Aristotle, *EN* 1178b8–18). But Xenophanes' non-anthropomorphic deity sees, hears, and thinks, and seems to be concerned with the affairs of this world: Xenophanes does not write that it would be inappropriate to speak of his god as just or moral. Xenophanes is not claiming that both p and not-p are nonsense, but that p is true, not-p false.

Havelock does not distinguish between (i) misusing available vocabulary and (ii) having no suitable vocabulary. Xenophanes seems concerned exclusively with (i); as does Heraclitus. Certainly Parmenides (B8, 38–41) maintained that most Greek vocabulary is misused; but it is not evident that he supposes himself to be giving a new *meaning* to *einai*, rather than selecting it as the one satisfactory item in the available vocabulary. A philosopher who regarded his principal task as being to extend and improve philosophical vocabulary and syntax might be expected to devote time explicitly to the task. Neither Parmenides nor any other Presocratic does so.

Nor does Havelock furnish adequate evidence to prove that Homer in particular is the target of the Presocratics, or that he is attacked, when he is attacked, as the primary source of "the essentially fluid and mobile syntax in which the performative mythos of orally preserved speech seeks to describe the phenomenon of the environment."[17] Xenophanes attacks him as a purveyor of immoral and untrue stories about the gods. Heraclitus castigates Homer and Hesiod (B40, 42, 57, 106), apparently for their ignorance rather than their vocabulary; but he also castigates Xenophanes, Pythagoras, and the logographer Hecataeus, apparently on similar grounds. Havelock claims that Heraclitus' "Homer deserves to be expelled from the contests and clubbed: also Archilochus" (B42) demonstrates the philosopher's opposition to the competitive recitations and the culture which accompanies them; but Heraclitus does not argue that the contexts should be abolished, merely that Homer and Archilochus are unworthy to compete in them.

In the extant writings of the Presocratics there is little evidence for Havelock's strong version of b). The weaker version is uncontroversial, for it claims no more than that the practice of philosophy leads to linguistic refinements; and Havelock adduces evidence in his paper to show the development of one of the refinements—a capacity for increased abstraction—between the Homeric poems and the later Presocratics. The truth or falsity of c) is an empirical question; and there is clearly evidence in favor of c). It would be advisable, however, to work with a weak version of c) in the first instance. That language develops from sentences such as (i) "the horse moves beautifully" to "the motion of the horse is beautiful," and subsequently to (iii) "all motion is a kind of change" [Aristotle, *Metaphysics*, 1068a1] seems not implausible, at all events for languages of the Greek type, and Havelock has produced evidence for particular sequences of this kind. But to assert *ab initio* that all languages must develop in this manner, or that *no* usages of the degree of abstraction of (iii) occur, or could occur, in the Homeric poems is to propound a theory which will founder on one counter-example; whereas what is important is that the language of the Homeric poems contains very few abstract terms and expressions, while the language of Aristotle seems flexible enough to express any abstract thought which Aristotle is capable of thinking; and that we have probably an adequate amount of evidence—if not so much as we should wish—of linguistic development between the two periods. (In the light of what was said above,[18] it would be desirable to survey not only philosophical authors.)

I conclude my paper with a few suggestions—of many possible ones—for continuing the mode of inquiry suggested by c). They relate either to what is well known or to what is highly speculative; but the speculative could be confirmed or disproved by further empirical study.

Havelock's paper encourages us to look more closely at the manner in which the Greeks became capable of abstract thought, and acquired abstract terms for their vocabulary. The study has more than historical interest: the Greeks are our philosophical ancestors; their acquisition of abstract terms throws light on the relationship between thought and language; and some Aristotelian terminology in particular, by passing into the everyday speech of Western languages, now constitutes the metaphysics of ordinary language.

Havelock's own statements about the relationship between thought and language are not entirely clear. He writes:

> (i) The Presocratics not only had to invent a terminology suitable to describe an external world, they also had initially to realize that such a "world" or cosmos existed to be described[19]

and

> (ii) No supposition is commoner than that thought precedes language and is philosophically prior to it. Yet since thought is measurable only through words, the supposition violates a fundamental rule of empirical science.[20]

(i) seems to assert what (ii) denies, that the Presocratics could have formed a concept of something before they had a term for it; for the realization that the cosmos exists as a cosmos requires conceptualization of some kind, not merely the ability to see what everyone with normal vision has always been able to see. Havelock's statements sometimes suggest linguistic determinism; but he evidently grants that it is possible to invent a new term for a new concept, and the conceptualization must logically and temporally precede the invention of the term. Presumably Havelock means that the effective *communication* of any thought depends on its being expressed through the medium of some symbolic system, with such additions or modifications to the system as may be necessary; and this contention seems undeniable.

It is *prima facie* important to note whether a new word has been coined or the range of an old one extended. The coining of a new word as a technical term results from a deliberate decision: a new word was needed to express a new idea; and the new word possesses the meaning intended by its coiner. The extension of an old word may sometimes be gradual, the result of a thinker or thinkers groping for clarity; and the old word trails a cloud of connotative associations behind it, from which neither the thinker nor those with whom he is trying to communicate may be able to free themselves. (The distinction between new words and old is somewhat blurred in Greek by the fact that the Greeks have no dead languages from which to draw the roots of new coinages, and the familiar roots may transfer connotations from words in which they already familiarly occur; and in addition, the Presocratics rarely define their terms.)

But in any language one should not overemphasize the distinction: even when a new term is coined using roots from a dead language, though conceptualization precedes the coinage, and cannot be determined by the term not yet coined, the thought-processes which reveal the need for a new term employ terms from the existing language, with their meanings and associations. One might think critically about any one or a group of these terms, but it is clearly impracticable to think critically about all of them; and insofar as one does not think critically about them, one's thought is molded by them without one's realizing the fact; so that when one comes to realize the need for a new term to express a new concept, the realization occurs in a context of already existing concepts and terms, many of which have not been subjected to critical analysis. In these circumstances it is unnecessary to use the term "linguistic determinism," but "linguistic inertia" seems quite appropriate.

Havelock's paper throws some light on this situation, and should stimulate further study. Language constrains thought and communication, but it also makes them possible; and the manner in which early Greek constrains and facilitates is well worth our attention.

Linguistic inertia is always and everywhere inevitably at work; but the Presocratics and other early Greek writers particularly merit our study, since the transition to the abstract and philosophical, and the particular conceptualization of the abstract arrived at in the works of Aristotle, is of great importance for Western thought and philosophy. If we direct our attention not to what we post-Aristotelians suppose that the Presocratics were trying to express philosophically, but to what at his own particular stage in the development of Greek thought and language each Presocratic was able to express philosophically, the communication which he was in fact able to make to his contemporaries, we may well make significant discoveries about the relationship between thought and language.

Language constrains by furnishing one set of semantic and syntactical options rather than others. Some sets may favor the development of philosophical thought; and the history of Greek thought suggests that prephilosophical Greek was potentially an excellent medium or tool for the philosopher. The Presocratics developed a philosophical language quickly: not, so far as extant fragments suggest, by thinking directly about the deficiencies of existing language for their purposes,[21] but by engaging in philosophical thought. Their contemporaries in other cultures neither engaged in similar thought nor developed a similar language. (The early Presocratics owed much to other cultures,[22] but made their borrowings distinctively their own; and the distinctive quality is the quality we term philosophical.) The ancient Greeks would have been in no doubt as to the reason: they were simply cleverer than the barbarians. We need not be so chauvinistic on their behalf; but with Havelock's encouragement we might begin to study prephilosophical and early philosophical Greek thought and language more systematically than has been attempted till now, in an effort to discover what characteristics favored the development of philosophy, or of the kinds of philosophy which in fact developed in Greece.

In such an inquiry, it is important to survey not merely the manner in which individual words are coined or adapted for use in philosophic contexts, but also the total linguistic and semantic resources of the language at a particular time, for knowledge of these resources will make clearer what constrains or encourages the kind of philosophical developments which occur. To simplify my exposition, I take an extreme case. A modern philosopher might say that Empedocles' cosmos is in a condition of entropy when passing from *neikos* (strife) to *philotes* (love), of negative entropy when in the other phase of the cycle. Yet it would be very misleading to use such a term: Empedocles could not have developed the concept of entropy, nor enunciated the Second

Law of Thermodynamics, not because—or not directly because—he was too close to a non-literate state of culture, but because the concept and the law were developed in the context of a world-view with a very different stock of words, symbols, and concepts, including some mathematical ones, a stock which no one thinker could develop for himself. (A study of Empedocles' terminology in its historical context would throw light on the concepts which he was able to develop.) To read Aristotle back into the Presocratics is less strikingly anachronistic, but no less misleading.

When considering the manner in which early Greek facilitates philosophical thought, and the kind of philosophical thought that it facilitates and encourages, one might consider, among others, these well-known and/or speculative suggestions:

(i) Greek can readily combine the definite article with adjectives, participles, and infinitives to produce different kinds of abstract terms. This linguistic capability facilitates certain types of conceptualization, and doubtless favors certain kinds of philosophy over others.

(ii) New words can be much more readily coined in Greek than in many other languages. Consequently Greek has a much larger vocabulary than, for example, Latin, to perform essentially the same range of tasks. In these circumstances it seems likely that each word is called upon to perform a smaller range of tasks, and so acquires a lighter load of connotative associations: a fact which favors philosophical thought, or certain types of philosophical thought.

(iii) The word-stock of the prephilosophical language may encourage some philosophical preferences. For example,

(a) The fact that *eidenai*, an important word for "know," is etymologically derived from a root meaning "see" may favor certain models for knowledge. (*Eidos* and *idea*, two of Plato's words for "Form," are derived from the same root.) On the other hand, it may be that prevalence of "visualizers" among the Greeks favored both the development of *eidenai* for "know" and of the models of knowledge.[23]

(b) The words and concepts which have importance in prephilosophical paterns and systems of thought may encourage the development of one philosophical system rather than another. I have recently argued[24] that in early Greek belief the concept of divine law is of much less importance than the concept of due shares which give rise to claims which, when they conflict, have to be adjudicated. Even had "law" been of greater importance in Greek religion, the concept of law—in a rather different, but derivable sense—might not have been important in Greek cosmology and philosophy of nature; but such importance seems much less likely in the actual circumstances.

Philosophical development—or the development of a particular kind of philosophy—does not depend merely on a capacity for abstraction, but on the terms and concepts which attract the attention of the philosopher.

Although such topics as these are relevant to all philosophical discussion, they do not usually engage the attention of students of Presocratic philosophy. However, the devotion of this volume in the Monist Library of Philosophy to the discussion of Havelock's paper suggests an interest in the topics, of which much more discussion is needed. There are studies of individual terms and concepts to draw on; but there is need of much more discussion which, like Havelock's, combines philological and philosophical concerns. The goal is to relate the linguistic and conceptual development of early—and later—Greek philosophers to the lexical, conceptual, grammatical, and syntactical resources of the Greek languages at the earliest point at which we are able to study it, while making every effort to discern what constrains, what facilitates, and what inclines the thinker in this direction rather than that. From such studies much might be discovered; and it might be possible also then to estimate the contribution made by literacy to the whole development.

Arthur W. H. Adkins

University of Chicago

NOTES

1. My version of Havelock's theory is constructed from material supplied by his *The Greek Concept of Justice*, (Cambridge: Harvard University Press, 1978), hereafter referred to as *GCJ*; and "The Linguistic Task of the Presocratics" (hereafter referred to as "Linguistic Task") published in this volume of The Monist Library of Philosophy.

2. See my review article in *CP* 75 (1980), pp. 256–68.

3. Havelock, "Linguistic Task," p. 14.

4. A. R. Luria, *The Mind of a Mnemonist* (New York: Basic Books, 1968). See Havelock, *GCJ* p. 44, and my comments in *CP* 75 (1980), pp. 264–65.

5. *CP* 75 (1980), pp. 265–67.

6. Havelock, *GCJ*, p. 244.

7. Havelock, *GCJ*, pp. 243–45.

8. Fragment 12 in M. L. West, *Iambi et Elego Graeci* (Oxford: Oxford University Press, 1971).

9. See my discussion, *CP* 75 (1980), pp. 266–67.

10. See, for example, C. D. Buck, *Comparative Grammar of Greek and Latin* (Chicago: University of Chicago Press, 1933), pp. 238–39.

11. See the examples in *LSJ*, s.v. *teuchō*, III, especially *Iliad* 4.84 and 14.246, where the subjects are gods, who were not "made" by anyone. In 14.246, the god Oceanos "*tetuktai* [is] the origin of all things."

12. Havelock, "Linguistic Task," p. 15.

13. As Herodotus informs us, 2.109.

14. Havelock, *GCJ*, p. 244.

15. Though the words differ in accent, there seems also to be a play on *mētis* "no-one" a few lines later, 9, 414 (and cf. 405, 406, 410).

16. Havelock, "Linguistic Task," p. 15.

17. Havelock, "Linguistic Task," p. 18.

18. Ibid., p. 20.

19. Havelock, "Linguistic Task," p. 20, *passim*.

20. Havelock, "Linguistic Task," p. 41.

21. Contrast the wording of Lucretius' complaint about the resources of Latin, *De Rerum Natura* I, 136–39.

22. See M. L. West, *Early Greek Philosophy and the Orient* (Oxford: Clarendon Press, 1971).

23. On this topic, see C. J. Classen, *Sprachliche Deutung als Triebkraft platonischen und sokratischen Philosophierens* (Munich: Beck, 1959), and my review in *JHS* 81 (1961), pp. 187–88.

24. In "Laws Versus Claims in Early Greek Religious Ethics," *History of Religions* 21 (1982), pp. 222–39.

THE EMERGENCE OF PHILOSOPHY

Speculation about the nature of language is at a remarkably primitive and tantalizing stage of development. It is also the most characteristic conceptual concern of our century. The pragmatists and positivists attempted without much success to formulate a theory of meaning and, to some extent, a theory of truth. The hermeneutic and deconstructivist thinkers concerned themselves with the relationship of and difference between oral and written language and the baffling problem of understanding texts and utterances in a methodologically rigorous way. Wittgenstein explored the inseparability of linguistic concepts and prevailing beliefs within the gradually shifting practices of a society; also, its bearing on understanding and misunderstanding the plural forms of life of distinct societies and the impossibility of capturing these in fixed and formulable rules. Chomsky and the new linguists have puzzled over the genetics of language and the prospect of reducing the immense variety of natural languages to phenotypic variations on some underlying set of genotypic codes interacting with local environments. Saussure despaired of construing the actual episodes of *parole* as the ordered relata of any single idealized and totalized structure of linguistic possibilities; or of construing any such system, justified for explanatory and predictive purposes, as psychologically internalized by the apt speakers of any natural language. He has been followed in this by the entire structuralist and semiotic tradition, which has so far failed to explain the legitimacy of its various synchronic systems that fall forever short of a self-imposed need for inclusiveness. The more semiotically minded have wavered between a strong sense of the provisional, historically shifting order of actual languages and a sense of having collected *ad hoc* codes of communication hardly more than informal reminders of the unanalyzed powers of the competent speakers they attempt to collect. Some, notably those who have followed the speech-act model developed by John Austin—though somewhat contrary to Austin's own immensely scrupulous caution—have either found it impossible to reach an end to a reasoned catalogue of distinct speech acts or to defend an essentialist view of any of them; or have found that they were (after the fact, so to say) forever translating into their own idiom vacuous, obvious, or unsystematizable rules governing supposed conversational implicatures or their analogues in literary contexts. Some, like the Marxists, never quite resolved the significance of the intelligibility of language across class lines or extended over remarkably long intervals of time; or, like the Russian and Czech formalists, never quite provided for both the apparent autonomy of the linguistic and the literary and the historically effective intrusion into that "world" of the real engagements of languaged men. And those who have sought to formalize language in severe extensional ways—say, in accord with Carnap's or Quine's or Tarski's programs—have been forced to admit either that natural languages do not fit the constraints favored (without thereby incurring any loss of significance) or that it is not in the least clear that they can be made to fit them fully. This is not, of course, to say that language is "a chaos that is not worth studying,"[1] only that we must beware of quick pronouncements.

I

Now to this very large brew comes Eric Havelock with a most intriguing technological theory of the stylistic and substantive development of language.[2] Havelock's theory is technological in the same sense in which Louis Morgan's *Ancient Society*[3] and Franz Boas' *Primitive Art*[4] are technologically motivated accounts of historical change. It is disarmingly persuasive and straightforward. But it must be said that it is a theory on a very grand scale. It proposes to explain, through the unique historical achievement of ancient Greece, the (probably) invariant processes of conceptual development from the stage of oral or non-literate culture to fully literate culture. In Greece, the structure of this movement is made legible (Havelock claims) by the unusually rich accomplishments of its oral phase (in literature, particularly the work of Homer and Hesiod); the remarkable invention of a true alphabetic notation (perhaps as late as the end of the eighth century), not to be confused with the pre-Greek syllabic systems of the Mediterranean world—in particular, the "unvocalized syllabary" of the Phoenicians[5]; and the extremely late development of democratized literacy (certainly at least as late as 650 B. C., possibly as late as 500, and even for "the full effect . . . of the alphabetic revolution" so late as to be traced down into the fourth century). There is no dearth, of course, of objections to Havelock's estimate.[6] This part of Havelock's thesis is neatly summarized in the warning that "In considering the Greeks, we had better come to terms at once with the fact that their civilization began in non-literacy."[7] The thesis, therefore, and the problem it addresses are not at all unreasonably drawn into the company of the largest speculations about the nature of language and the possibilities of human thought.

The critical term "civilization" is intended technically: "I suggest [says Havelock] that the operative meaning [of 'civilization'] appears at that theoretical point when a linguistic group ceases to be satisfied with the en-coding of its folkways at the unconscious level, and instead seeks to devise a special statement of what these are in order to identify them." Havelock goes on to explain that such an effort requires resources "outside the casual usage of the vernacular, for at the conversational level language is ephemeral." Language must then be organized to make "the resources of memory" effec-tive, to facilitate the documentation of the oral; and this he thinks is peculiar-ly aided by the devices of rhythm—which, for various reasons, lead to favor-ing the poetized forms of epic narrative.[8] Such transcription, making possible for the first time accuracy in a people's conscious recollection and use of its own oral and "corporate tradition . . . would be made in the first instance for the benefit of the composers themselves rather than their public, [so that] the products of the Greek poets who followed Homer would be devised for memorization by listening audiences, not for readership by literates."[9] Havelock then traces the sequence of cultural phases from (what we might call) the unconscious or conversational oral to the preliterate but (literately) documented oral ("scribal" for the most part in the Mediterranean world, but potentially democratic in Greece, because of the transcriptional accuracy that the alphabet made possible) to the dawning literary (where composition mixes devices addressed to the eye with those addressed to the ear, still favor-ing the latter) to the fully literary. These somewhat fanciful labels are not Havelock's; but they are, I think, in full sympathy with his story and make explicit the sense in which his own account belongs to the genre of nineteenth-century theories of social and cultural evolution—a distinction hardly in-tended pejoratively.

A second, somewhat specialized, part of Havelock's theory concerns the development, in ancient Greece, within this larger movement, of an abstract vocabulary suitable for philosophy. Havelock claims to have identified a cer-tain essential antagonism between the conceptual—even the "documentary"—requirements of philosophy and the interests of a fully oral tradition; hence, the late flowering of literacy in Greece helps us both to date the onset of genuine philosophy and to appreciate its revolutionary character. It is hard to give a fair impression of the explicitness of the antagonism Havelock means to press, but perhaps the following brief passage will serve to fix his intention:

> The syntax of memorized rhythmic speech is . . . not friendly to that type of state-ment which says "The angles of a triangle are equal to two right angles" or "Courage consists in a rational understanding of what is to be feared or not feared." It is not friendly precisely to that kind of statement which the Socratic dialectic was later to demand, a statement which prefers its subject to be a con-cept rather than a person, and its verb to be an "is" verb rather than a "doing" verb. Neither principles nor laws nor formulas are amenable to a syntax which is orally memorizable.[10]

Here, the division between epic narrative, lyric poetry, drama, proverbs and "sayings," on the one side, and Euclid's geometry, Archimedes' mathematics, Plato's dialogues, Aristotle's treatises, Herodotus' and Thucydides' histories, and (with some uncertainty) substantial parts of the work of the Presocratics, on the other, draw up the principal lines of contrast. Havelock's thesis, then, maintains: (1) that the achievement of civilization, possible among pre-literate peoples, requires devices like those of rhythm and epic narrative to sustain the necessary powers of memory; and (2) that the achievement of philosophy within civilization, possible only with the facilities of a script (perhaps only with the facilities of an alphabetic script) requires intermediate stages of abstractive conception that gradually provide for the attenuation of an epic and conversational idiom so that a genuinely philosophical one may be grounded in the conceptual abilities thus enlarged. It is in this sense that Havelock advances a technological theory.

The briefest review of early Greek philosophy (always bearing in mind the fragmentary and indirect evidence on which our account depends) suggests the possibility of constructively resisting Havelock's special view of the conceptual powers of philosophy. For example, Parmenides wrote in verse, but he is the author of a peculiarly pure philosophical doctrine—distinctly modern, even professional, by contemporary standards. He appears to draw on the resources of the oral tradition; but he has managed to mix an agonistic style with the statement of what are possibly the most abstracted doctrines conceivable, an achievement quite obvious in the *Epicheirêmata* of his disciple Zeno. It is difficult to suppose—rather in the spirit of Havelock's own reasonable style of speculation—that doctrines as magisterial as Parmenides' are likely not to have had a considerable history of development. Rohde, in fact, characterizes Parmenides' work as a "doctrinal poem,"[11] which, given his own strong interest in recovering the oldest strata of the Greek oral tradition, intimates an implicit confidence about the compatibility of the philosophical and the strongest features of the oral tradition and its documentation. It is, precisely, part of Rohde's thesis that the late work of classical Greece, including that of the philosophers, is both continuous with and already incipient in the Homeric poems.[12] Xenophanes of course had already been both a severe critic of the corrupting influence of Homer and Hesiod and a poetic speculator in the kind of natural philosophy that Parmenides considers in the latter part of his own poem. But to admit this continuity, linking (say) the Ionians to Heraclitus on down to Parmenides, is to extend the philosophical tradition back to about the beginning of the sixth century—which is to say, to recover the conventional picture. The point at stake is not the mere dating of the philosophical tradition (or of the other currents which Havelock arrays against the core of the purely oral tradition): it is rather the dating of this tradition *vis-à-vis* the dating of the literary tradition due to the influence of the newly invented alphabet. For, *if* the philosophical tradition is actually *older* than the invention of the alphabet or at least older than the development of widespread literacy in Greece, then it is both the case that Havelock's linkage of the philosophical with the literate is mistaken *and* that the conceptual character of philosophy and the oral tradition cannot be as inimical or as opposed to one another as he holds. There seem to be good reasons for favoring these judgments against Havelock's thesis, and the reasons that may be brought forward prove to be of exactly the same generous gauge as those that Havelock himself advances. In particular, they are reasons largely of a technological sort. The upshot is that, if they are sustained, we may well support Havelock's instructive account of the role of the alphabet and democratized literacy in the classical and post-classical phases of Greek life, while at the same time disagreeing with him about the conceptual capacity of the oral tradition itself and its relationship to a fully literate tradition. To put the challenge in an absolutely frontal way, Havelock appears to have conflated the flowering and loss of certain *values* characteristic of the oral tradition prior to and during contact with the literate and the relative *conceptual powers* that distinguish the oral and the literate. He favors the values of the first very highly, but he somehow concludes that their eventual displacement during the ascendent phase of the latter entails a severely restricted conceptual capacity within the former that, in effect, precludes the special abstractive work of philosophy and science and history that eventually flourished during the latter. This, in another commentator, would be a *non sequitur* pure and simple; in Havelock, it is rather the conclusion of a sizable but unconvincing argument. What remains to be supplied are details.

The single most important counterconsideration may, by an unintended irony, be drawn from Havelock's own careful discussion of the distinction between the Greek alphabet and the syllabic systems (particularly the vowelless systems) of the pre-Greek world. For, if he is right about its uniqueness, then the very nature of the notational systems that preceded the Greek alphabet (the vowelless syllabic or the ideographic) either specifically fostered a philosophical or proto-philosophical profession or tradition or else was at least entirely hospitable (in a conceptual sense) to such practices. And, so far as this argument is concerned, what holds true for philosophy holds equally true for mathematics and science. Havelock's own argument in this regard quite reasonably maintains that if Rhys Carpenter's dating of the invention of the Greek alphabet stands,[13] then "the presupposition that Greek literature presented the full flowering of a *literate* culture which had already been incubating for some centuries [must be] put in jeopardy."[14] But saying this much does not at all entail that "the presupposition that Greek literature presented the full flowering of a culture [including philosophical work] which had already been incubating for some centuries was put in jeopardy." The error at stake clearly concerns only the antiquity of a "literate culture"; it does not yet entail anything about the strength of the claim that the Greek literature of the last half of the eighth century—and of even more recent times—must, in being oral in nature, have precluded the philosophical. If, then, the oral was sufficiently rich to encompass the abstractive work of philosophy and science, the (adjusted) presupposition could well be true. (This, of course, is not to concede Havelock's dating of literacy.)

Now, the force of the irony remarked is simply this. What Havelock shows is: (a) "that pre-Greek systems of writing in their application [to reading and interpreting texts] could not be democratized"; and (b) that their inherent imprecision (in comparison with the Greek) entails the skill of somewhat professionalized scribes, since "to read . . . a script [transcribed according to the earlier syllabaries] required a series of decisions basically acoustic in their nature."[15] Substantive choices regarding the meaning of key syllables were inescapable, the management of which "called for a degree of professional skill restricted to a class of specialists who had the ability and leisure to master it."[16] And the work of this class was peculiarly focused on regularizing and collecting the conceptual distinctions that acoustically grounded interpretive decisions made possible. It seems very reasonable to suppose that, *here*, rather than in the democratized possibilities of the Greek alphabet, the prospect of, and interest in, developing and controlling a ramified abstractive idiom were already in place. Why not? What Havelock shows is that the peculiarly democratic flowering of Greek civilization could not have occurred if syllabic notation had not been replaced by the genuinely alphabetic; but he does not show that what was conceptually distinctive of the Greek—in the direction of philosophy, science, and mathematics—depended on what facilitated the *democratic* pattern. And indeed, it is counterintuitive that it should. It may well be puzzling that the Hebrew tradition veered off in the direction of articulating its supernatural monotheism and the import of that extraordinary conception on the development of the moral law—without producing a body of work similar to Greek philosophy; and it may well be puzzling that the Mesopotamian tradition veered off in the direction of computing most carefully (even obsessively) the changes in the tides and the position of the heavenly bodies—without producing a body of work similar to Greek science. But the reasons may well have to do with the peculiarly focused genius of these different peoples (perhaps accountable in technological terms) and not with their having failed to produce an alphabet before the Greeks did. It looks very much as if, by an accident of history, the scribes (or at least the literates) of these three cultures effectively assigned to themselves alternative—but equally abstractive—functions. (There seems to be no evidence of scribes among the Greeks.)

The argument, of course, is both provisional and conditional; but I respectfully submit that, thus far considered, it is more reasonable than Havelock's thesis and fits all the facts he would adduce. The important double point is: that the pre-alphabetic world, not the alphabetic, required and naturally generated a class of scribes whose essential function centered on the professional collection, ordering, management, application, and refinement of a ramified abstractive system of categories; *and* that this professional function must have been fully compatible with the effort to document and preserve the approved interpretation of an oral culture's own perceived tradition. In short, *an oral tradition lacking an alphabet is bound to produce either a philosophical practice or an alternative but equally abstractive practice.* This is a direct consequence of the technological features of non-alphabetic notation within an oral culture concerned with the accuracy and approved standing of interpretations of its own record. Among the Mayans, for instance, it produced a mad numerology together with a considerable body of precise astronomy. It is the very imprecision of the non-alphabetic, then, not the precision of the alphabetic, that probably accounts for the brilliance of the theological (among the Hebrews), the astronomical (among the Mesopotamians), and the philosophical and mathematical (among the Greeks). This is not to deny that the impact of the alphabetic on the development of a literate culture was bound to be manifested in conceptually distinctive ways; it is only to say that there is very little reason to suppose that that impact bore on the origination and early flowering of either philosophy or science. All its absence means is that, whatever form that flowering might take, it would not be democratically distributed through an entire population.

II

Turn now to the conditional aspect of the argument. Havelock wavers between two rather different theories about the Presocratic—and later—philosophers. Sometimes he introduces the one by holding that "the Presocratic poets" (notably, Xenophanes, Heraclitus, Parmenides, and Empedocles) apparently "expected to be heard rather than read"; and sometimes he introduces the other by holding that the prose writers (notably, Zeno, Melissus, Anaxagoras, and Diogenes) compose in a style "still derived from oral forms of communication,"[17] though with distinct literate accretions. The difference in the two doctrines is obscured by Havelock's apparently believing that another difference—that between a text's being addressed to the ear or the eye—substantially captures the first. But it does not. Havelock remarks that, as late as the Periclean age, Athenian authors worked with a notion of "audience control" suitable to listeners rather than readers, which directly affected both "the style and substance of what they said."[18] This may be so, but it is either ambiguous or irrelevant to the essential issue. It may mean that the stylistic requirements of audiences within an oral tradition account for the topics and manner of presentation of *the orally developed philosophical tradition*, or it may mean that *the philosophical tradition that is itself distinctly literate* is quite different in its conceptual orientation from the oral tradition from which it gradually emerged, by way of (intermediary) Presocratics. That the second reading is false is clear (provisionally) at least from the example of Parmenides. That the first is true may be readily admitted, but it has as yet absolutely no bearing on the conceptual limitations of the philosophy of the oral tradition. That issue is the pivotal issue. Furthermore, *if* the philosophers among the Greeks of the oral tradition performed scribal or interpretive functions for various reasons, not necessarily restricted to those that belonged chiefly to the scribes of syllabic notation or to those needed to democratize the oral tradition—for instance, like Protagoras and Gorgias, rather late in the story, who seem to have pursued visiting lectureships, or like Pythagoras, rather early in the story, who seems to have organized a brotherhood of some sort, or like Parmenides, who had explicit disciples in Zeno and Melissus, or like the Ionians, who may have been distinguished as the leading thinkers of a loose network of talented discussion groups in touch with one another, or like Heraclitus and Empedocles, who seem to have been concerned to focus a particularly pointed, somewhat "elitist" criticism of Homer and Hesiod and of a popular and widespread point of view—then it may well be beside the point *what devices were available for the acoustic receptiveness of the people at large*, so long as there were manageable ways for insuring accuracy and understanding with regard to the central texts. Havelock concludes his first summary of the Presocratics by saying that "competition between mythos and logos has begun."[19] But what does he mean?

There is a crucial and curious leap in Havelock's argument, relating to the appearance of the alphabet. Havelock takes the alphabet to have first come into use around 700 B.C., and he takes the Greeks themselves to have been largely non-literate until at least 650 B.C., possibly until much later.[20] But he then hurries on to insist that, for an oral culture, the "storehouse" of its experience and information can be preserved "only in the individual memories of persons, and to achieve this the language employed—what I may call the storage language—must meet two basic requirements, both of which are mnemonic. It must be rhythmic, to allow the cadence of the words to assist the task of memorization; and it must tell stories rather than relate facts: it must prefer mythos to logos." Its devices are "unfriendly to abstracted and conceptual speech."[21] Here, two difficulties arise. For one thing, Havelock cannot be speaking of a society that has access to any syllabic or alphabetic notational devices for "storing" its literature, since he considers only the most severe constraints on the unaided "individual memories of persons." But the philosophical tradition could easily have had the benefit of even alphabetic notation, as far as chronology is concerned: the non-literacy of *the general populace* would then be irrelevant—particularly if the authors belonged to suitably privileged groups with scribal-like or at least literate abilities, or if written notation was primarily designed to insure reasonably accurate texts for a listening audience. The same might well have been true of the bards that recited Homer and Hesiod. Secondly, there is absolutely no reason to suppose that the materials of the philosophical tradition were ever offered to the Greeks in a generally democratized way. Herodotus may well have read his history to people gathered in a public place; and the tragedies were obviously performed in a public theatre. But there is nothing in the Presocratic materials that suggests that they were ever intended for democratized public consumption. If they were not, as indeed what we have of Parmenides, Heraclitus, Xenophanes, and Empedocles strongly indicate, then there is no reason to suppose that, within the gradually democratized space of Greek culture, there was no room for the privileged work of small, literate groups increasingly aware of the novelty of philosophical reflection and of the related speculations of other groups. Once these concessions are made, then there remain no reasons for supposing that philosophy during the period of oral culture (which, though pre-literate in its democratized practices, need not have been completely deprived of literate aids to memory) must have been composed in ways that exclusively favored those patterns exhibited by unaided collective and conversational memory. The upshot is that, even with regard to whatever conceptual orientation the alphabet might have facilitated, *there is no reason to suppose that the philosophical impulse had to wait until well into the sixth century*—say, for the Ionians. Effectively, this is to postpone an essential part of the argument.

When he treats the Presocratics as condemning the poets and the conceptual thrust of what was "stored" in the popular language, when he admits that they "could begin to dispense with some of the pressures to memorize" because they had the incipient advantage of the new notation, Havelock says that they could now word what they said "so as to replace personal agents by impersonal forces and replace the acts of agents performed upon other agents by statements of relationships between impersonal entities."[22] Here, presumably, is the point of the contest between mythos and logos. But even with respect to written language, there is, as we have already argued, good reason to think that the imprecisions of syllabic (vowelless) notation were probably even more hospitable to philosophical and scientific abstraction than the alphabetic. If so, then there might well have been a body of pre-Greek philosophy that the Greeks could have examined—unless the genius of earlier peoples inclined them in the direction of other kinds of abstraction. There seems to be no special linkage between philosophizing and the alphabet as distinct from that between philosophizing and some manageably accurate notation. At least, Havelock offers none.

This suggests a nice concession in Havelock's favor, though one still opposed to his own explicit claim. It is certainly possible that philosophical abstraction would not flourish without some form of suitable written notation. The question whether philosophy would *flourish* or could even *be practiced* without notation is not an issue that Havelock directly examines. His convictions are clear, but he offers no convincing evidence. Furthermore, it is certainly not clear that the composition of the high poetry of the Greeks "between 1100 and 650 [was] achieved . . . without the help of *any* script whatever."[23] It is one thing to say this; it is quite another to say that "Greece must have remained *largely* non-literate till at least 650 B.C."[24] To put the best face on the matter, we may say that Havelock has raised a crucial but unanswered question about the technology of language: Can, and to what extent can, a completely oral culture pursue philosophy, science, mathematics, theology, poetry, and history? The fact remains that there is not one of the great civilizations of the ancient world that is entirely non-literate. We simply don't know the answer.

But Havelock sometimes argues that the *memory* of oral cultures lacking alphabetic notation could not support the democratized processing of complex philosophical abstractions; and sometimes he argues that the *conceptual powers* of essentially oral cultures even possessing scribal or privileged notation could not produce and sustain significant philosophical abstractions. Both are technological claims, and both may well be false; but, at the very least, the truth of the first entails nothing about the second. The most Havelock has shown is that the orientation and interest of an oral culture would probably favor mythos over logos—unless, of course, there were in place actual societies or special infrasocietal arrangements that encouraged the reverse pattern. Imagine, for instance, that the astronomers of Uxmal and Chichén Itzá played such an intimate instructional role in the daily life of the Mayans that the people became completely absorbed in a peculiarly abstract number magic degenerately drawn from a precise system of calendrical calculation that, being still pre-literate, they could not themselves have understood. Or imagine that the public management of complex calculations was, under priestly direction, incipiently democratized among the Mayans. Is this impossible or merely unlikely? And is the pattern different for mathematics and science and philosophy?

III

Here, we must finally consider what may be meant in speaking of philosophical abstraction. This is the most troubling part of Havelock's account. There are, surely, many different notions of linguistic abstraction—in particular, of that sort of abstraction that is genuinely philosophical. Two preliminary constraints seem incontestable. For one thing, *all* predicates are abstract—equally abstract— in the sense Quine marks as that of "the divided reference of general terms,"[25] that is, of the ability of general terms to be predicatively applied to indefinitely many different things at the same time that they are applicable to any one. Consequently, language must be hospitable to philosophy; for, noting that fact is itself philosophically most important. Secondly, the very achievement of the Greek alphabet is notably "abstract" in the benign sense that the set of consonants it posits cannot be voiced atomically—that is, without uttering them in the company of uttering vowels. Consequently, the very genius of Greek literacy, even in the period of largely oral culture, must have been hospitable to "logos" as distinct from "mythos"—in a sense precisely opposed to the moral that Havelock draws. In fact, the unvowelled Phoenician script may actually have preserved a more explicit sense of act and agency than the Greek alphabet, since it could never have been supposed that what it stored was unpronounceable.

The issue becomes more speculative from this point on. But there is very good reason to believe that Havelock is committed either to a remarkably naive notion of philosophical abstraction or else to a distinctly prejudiced view: that the special systems composed by Plato, Aristotle, and the atomists constitute the *first* genuine philosophy. There is a great deal in Havelock's discussion of the Presocratics that supports both alternatives. On the first, philosophical abstractions are *terms (or concepts) that make no reference to the physical but are (probably) invented by being detached or abstracted from their original moorings in mythic or oral contexts.* (Call this Thesis A.) On the second, philosophical abstractions are *terms (or concepts) that strongly resemble the terms (or concepts) of Thesis A, even if they are brought to bear on the physical or at least the changing and contingent world, provided that they are coherently integrated in a single conceptual system, of which Plato's, Aristotle's, and the atomists' are the paradigms.* (Call this Thesis B.) On Thesis A, Havelock simply dismisses *as philosophy* (or as more than the barest philosophical incipiency) *any* Presocratic utterance that still shows a strong linkage with Homeric originals or with usage regarding the homely physical distinctions and human behavior of the oral tradition. Thus, for instance, commenting on Xenophanes' use of the term *theos*, Havelock remarks that "The simple assertion of the existence of a total one, comprehending and including all things, what I have called the act of integration, was an essential first step to take in the task of *escaping from and superseding* the narrative flux of previous language."²⁶ And, most notably, reviewing Parmenides' accomplishment regarding the concept of "that which is," Havelock actually states:

> ... I do not think there is any metaphysics in Parmenides, properly speaking; any more than there is in any other Presocratic. What the philosopher does is to clothe the abstract noun with a physical or at least spatial dimension . . . the frame of reference is surely physical or spatial, not metaphysical. . . . Taking the law of integration first partially expressed by Xenophanes and applying it rigidly to the external world, Parmenides proposes in modern terms a conception of space-matter.²⁷

It is difficult, in fact, to separate the bearing of these passages on the two theses taken together. What Havelock means, apparently, is, first, that both Xenophanes and Parmenides do not free their notion of the One from the physical order and, second, that the One, integrated over the flux of the physical world, has genuinely novel abstracted properties like that of being indivisible, timeless, self-identical, full, and the like, that constitute an important preparatory (but only a preparatory) step for the invention of a genuine philosophical system. This also explains that other invention of the Presocratics—notably, Parmenides', again—the use of *esti* ("is") as the verb of the timeless present, "the copula of analytic statement," prefigured perhaps in Heraclitus.²⁸ Construing Parmenides' accomplishment regarding abstract categories as he does, Havelock is also bound to construe his use of the verb as he does. These then become the necessary precursors (as indeed they are) of the full achievement of the classical philosophers. But the question remains, Why are they not significant philosophical achievements in their own right?

Consider, now, Thesis C, a doctrine more or less in accord with contemporary views of the nature of philosophy: philosophical abstractions are *terms (or concepts), particularly terms (or concepts) fundamental to theorizing about knowledge and reality, that are employed in a metalinguistic or second-order sense.* Hence, insofar as they are concerned to theorize about the proper way in which to understand the *use* of critical terms in speaking of human knowledge and the world, the Presocratics—and Homer and Hesiod, and the Phoenicians, and the Hebrews, and the Mesopotamians, and the Egyptians, and the Hindus, and the Mayans, and the Chinese, and the Easter Islanders—were all capable of philosophy. There is, in short, a seamless continuum of reflection from bare assertion (oral or written) to grammar, science, and philosophy; and the differences, profound as they may be, from the oral to the literate have absolutely nothing to do with the *onset* of philosophical capacity, though they have very much to do with forming the special theories favored in one society or another. In any case, it is *not* a mark of the genuinely philosophical—as opposed to being a mark of the genuinely Parmenidean or Platonic or Plotinean—that terms central to Thesis C exhibit the peculiar features of terms proper to Thesis A or favored by the paradigms of Thesis B. There is every reason to think that Havelock is right about the relevance of "the prompting mechanism" of "the changing technology of the written word." But he is simply wrong or arbitrary or naive in holding that, say, the Milesians could not have initiated philosophy, as is generally supposed, for "close as they were to the oral culture of Greece, it is not likely that they anticipated a level of conceptual abstraction which only begins to become visible in Anaxagoras and the Atomists."[29] Havelock is simply looking for the wrong abstractions—or looking at abstractions in the wrong way. Not philosophy but the impulse to pursue philosophy as pointedly as the Greeks did needs to be brought into accord with their technology—not only their impulse but their special prejudices and visions as well. The world of Forms, for example, is by no means either philosophically irresistible or essential to the flowering of a competent philosophical tradition. The question of the causal role of the alphabet, of literacy, of the democratization of literacy is a fair question; but what we are to understand by philosophical abstraction is simply not a causal question, though it is bound to set limits on the pertinence of the first. What were the technological constraints on language and literacy that both slowed and made possible the conceptual marvel of the Platonic dialogues? Surely, at least whatever slowed and made possible the marvel of Parmenides' poem.

There is no more natural way in which to show how the oral, pre-literate tradition can be made to harbor philosophical reflection, congruently with its own conversational and mythic patterns but also consistently with a variety of philosophical choices, than to recall Socrates' eliciting elements of Pythagorean geometry from the boy Meno and reflecting on the import of that achievement. There is nothing in this episode or its elaboration that appears inaccessible in principle to the Presocratics, except perhaps the technical use of particular terms that have a later history; but then, the Presocratics could have invented alternative technical terms for pursuing such an inquiry—and, on the evidence of the fragments we have, they did just that. There are, for instance, no syllogisms in the Dialogues; but there is a clear sense of an order of formal argument that Socrates guards that is on its way to syllogistic form, that is entirely accessible to a largely pre-literate but intelligent audience. It is a form of argument that schematizes and regularizes the very form of conversational argument, without disturbing its spontaneity at all. And there is no such formal argument in Parmenides, but there is a set of very memorable, very cleverly chosen pronouncements about "what there is" that, though admittedly very, very subtle, appears not at all inaccessible to a pre-literate audience:

> Come, I will tell you—and you must accept my word when you have heard it— the ways of inquiry which alone are to be thought: the one that IT IS, and it is not possible for IT NOT TO BE, in the way of credibility, for it follows Truth; the other, that IT IS NOT, and that IT is bound NOT TO BE: this I tell you is a path that cannot be explored; for you could neither recognize that which is NOT, nor express it.
> For it is the same thing to think and to be.[30]

It is an essential teaching, boiled down to a mnemonic form that is at once formulaic and argumentative. It is not so much a theory about the world and knowledge as an utterly simple, unqualified, unrestricted second-order insight about the conceptual limits of any particular theory. It is unforgettable and has an hypnotic ring of truth. It does not so much explain the logical properties of first-order claims and truths as it obliges those who attend to consider the bearing of this would-be second-order constraint on any and all first-order utterances. It makes the dialectical advance to second-order reflections on *esti* entirely natural and instant, by preparing a trap of conceptual consistency no more complicated than any that could arise in a conversational setting. Even Havelock pretty well admits this, in discounting its philosophical standing. Hence, since (on Thesis C) he is mistaken in treating the Presocratics as not fully philosophical, he must also (on the Thesis) be wrong in opposing the philosophical and abstractive capacities of the (largely) oral, pre-literate phases of Greek culture.

The characteristic features of Presocratic philosophy bear this out, because they actually trade on the strongest features of the Homeric tradition itself. For example, they fix on cosmic unity and order, on changes involving paired opposites, on cyclic patterns of change, on the capacity of an unchanging order to comprehend apparent change, on the opinions of the many and the pronouncements of the initiate, on the doctrines attributed to Homer and Hesiod that may be contested, on the essential patterns of conversational dispute. It would be a shame if the issue of Havelock's theory merely depended on a verbal choice among the three Theses offered (or of another of the same sort). But it looks as if much of that interesting theory could be effectively recast in terms of the development of a changing vocabulary, aids to memory, shifting motivation within a culture that is a civilization, and the flowering of particular doctrinal insights, that would recover the "prompting mechanism" of the technological without the inadequately justified linkage between philosophical abstraction and the particular abstractions Havelock is interested in accounting for. There may well be a technologically instructive approach to philosophy as such: obviously, it is impossible without a developed language. But it is much more likely that a comparative study of the flourishing of different philosophies—or, at any rate, of different philosophically informed speculations of any sort—would be more rewarding than the attempt to identify the very onset of the philosophical impulse at the extremely late stage of cultural reflection that Havelock associates with the democratization of literacy. That connection just looks like a mistake.

Joseph Margolis

Temple University

NOTES

1. This is Chomsky's worry, should it turn out that his own theory of language was mistaken—should it turn out, that is, that, on empirical grounds, non-linguistic factors (beliefs, attitudes, historical practices) would have to be incorporated in a distinctly productive sense into the theory of grammatical structure. See Noam Chomsky, *Language and Responsibility*, tr. John Viertel (New York: Pantheon, 1977), pp. 152–53.

2. Eric A. Havelock, "Prologue to Greek Literacy," *Lectures in Memory of Louise Taft Semple*, Second Series (Cincinnati: The University of Cincinnati, 1971), hereafter cited as "Prologue"; and "The Linguistic Task of the Presocratics," *The Monist*, in this issue, hereafter cited as "Linguistic Task."

3. Lewis Henry Morgan, *Ancient Society* (New York: Holt, 1877).

4. Franz Boas, *Primitive Art* (Cambridge: Harvard University Press, 1929).

5. "Prologue", pp. 6–7, 11.

6. "Prologue," pp. 15–16, 59–60. Perhaps the most recent review of the matter, reasonably balanced and compendious but opposed to Havelock's view, appears in Alfred Burns, "Athenian Literacy in the Fifth Century B.C.," *Journal of the History of Ideas*, 42 (1981). A large part of the principal literature is collected and cited by Burns.

7. "Prologue," p.18.

8. "Prologue," pp. 27–28, 31.

9. "Prologue," pp. 31–32.

10. "Prologue," p. 51.

11. Erwin Rohde, *Psyche*, tr. W. B. Hillis, 8th ed. (London: Routledge and Kegan Paul, 1925), p. 372.

12. Cf. ibid., ch. 11.

13. Rhys Carpenter, "The Antiquity of the Greek Alphabet," *American Journal of Archaeology*, 37 (1933), pp. 8–29; and "The Greek Alphabet Again," *American Journal of Archaeology*, 42 (1938), pp. 58–69, cited by Havelock.

14. "Prologue," p. 4. Italics added.

15. "Prologue," p. 7.

16. *Loc. cit.*

17. "Linguistic Task," 2.

18. "Linguistic Task," 1.

19. "Linguistic Task," 2.

20. "Prologue," pp. 14, 15.

21. "Linguistic Task," 3.

22. "Linguistic Task," 5.

23. "Prologue," p. 16. Italics added.

24. "Prologue," p. 15. Italics added.

25. W. V. Quine, *Word and Object* (Cambridge: MIT Press, 1960), p. 94; cf. §19.

26. "Linguistic Task," 5. Italics added.

27. "Linguistic Task," 5.

28. "Linguistic Task," 3, 4. The complexity of the issue of the copula and of the philosophically pertinent force of distinctions of being, whether explicitly captured (verbally, or not) is focused at least in Emile Benveniste, "Categories of Thought and Language," in Mary E. Meek, ed. *Problems in General Linguistics* (Coral Gables: University of Miami Press, 1971). Cf. also, Jacques Derrida, "The Supplement of Copula: Philosophy *before* Linguistics," in Josué V. Harari, ed, *Textual Strategies* (Ithaca: Cornell University Press, 1979). Havelock does not address these matters at all.

29. "Linguistic Task," 3.

30. Kathleen Freeman, *Ancilla to The Pre-Socratic Philosophers* (Oxford: Basil Blackwell, 1952), p. 42.

CONCERNING THE "KNOWLEDGE"
OF THE PRE-PLATONIC GREEKS

Eric Havelock is well-known and widely appreciated among classical scholars and students of the earliest Greek literature and philosophy for a series of studies in which he has contested, with great plausibility, certain traditional views of the development of Greek thought and culture, especially in its relationships with the emergence of written language and general literacy among the Greeks. His more significant claims can be usefully viewed as falling into two main classes.

There are, first, claims about the order of events in the cultural history of the Greek peoples, along with explanations of the special qualities for which the earliest writings of those peoples—such as those attributed to Homer, Hesiod, and the Pre-Socratic philosophers—are notable. In this first class there fall, for example, his theses about the point in time at which the alphabetization of the Greek language occurred, about the function of "poeticized language" being primarily the transmission of culture, and about the "formulaic" features of the earliest writings being a reflection of the requirements for language that could be more easily memorized. Perhaps we should also locate in this first class the main points in his interpretations of the Pre-Socratic philosophers and of Plato.

Then, secondly, there are his claims about the nature of the consciousness which was possible for the Greeks, or about the nature of the "Greek mind" in its various phases. And these claims are accompanied, or even based upon, a set of assumptions about the nature of mental acts and processes in the human mind in general. These assumptions are never, so far as I can tell, argued for or even explained in general philosophical terms by Havelock. But they certainly do seem to play some important role in his thinking, and therefore require some consideration for any adequate appreciation and evaluation of his contributions. My aim here is to isolate the assumption about the process of cognition which seems to me most important to his overall outlook, to say why it does not seem to me to be a defensible assumption, and, finally, to explain how a great deal of what he has said in interpreting Greek thought and culture really need not be made to rest upon any such assumption.

In order to provide a precise focus for my remarks, I shall concentrate upon a single thesis of Havelock's, but one that pulls together all of the various issues which need to be considered here. I have in mind his claim that, in an "oral" culture such as that of pre-Homeric Greece, what we *today* would call knowledge *cannot* exist. In his words: "All 'knowledge' in an oral culture is temporally conditioned, which is another way of saying that in such a culture 'knowledge' in our sense cannot exist."[1] A few pages before this statement (p. 180) he introduced the convention of putting the English term 'knowledge' into scare-quotes precisely to indicate that whenever he uses that term to apply to the pre-Homeric mind it is intended to have a sense that radically varies from the one it normally has today, or, perhaps, has had for all more or less educated persons who have lived since, roughly, the time of Socrates.

But we must not suppose that the issue here concerns the word 'knowledge' alone. The point which Havelock is making is not, it seems, that certain beliefs present in classical Greece are now held in such a way—with such increased understanding, possibly, or upon such adequate grounds—that *we* can call them knowledge, whereas they were not so held in pre-Homeric Greece. Rather, he is saying that *thoughts* of the type which go into what we today call our knowledge could not then be thought *at all*. If I understand him rightly, not only 'knowledge,' but also 'belief,' 'doubt,' 'fear (or hope) that . . . ,' and all other terms expressing propositional attitudes must go under the scare-quotes. In relation to the pre-Homeric Greeks we could, then, equally well speak of "belief" and "doubt," rather than belief and doubt, as we must, if the account is correct, speak of 'knowledge' rather than knowledge.

The sorts of thoughts which, according to Havelock, could not be present in the consciousness of pre-Homeric Greeks are today expressed, to take his own examples (p. 182), by the sentence, "Human beings are responsible for the consequences of their own acts," and even more so by, "The angles of a triangle are equivalent to two right angles." In general terms, "Kantian imperatives and mathematical relationships and analytic statements of any kind are inexpressible and also unthinkable" (ibid.).

The *reason* for this impossibility is, the account goes, that pre-Homeric language is incapable of a ". . . true generalization couched in the language of universals" (p. 181). This amounts to the same thing as saying that pre-Homeric talk and consciousness does not involve *concepts* (cf. p. 188), which in turn means much the same as that such consciousness dealt only with concrete images of particular persons, things, or events immersed in a flow of actions or events. The consciousness supposedly corresponding to the opening lines of the *Iliad* is described by Havelock as follows:

> . . . the image of the powerful wrath of Achilles leads at once into an image of activity which by habit men are prone to associate with such wrath—that of killing people; the killing is then filled out by adding the image of the ghosts despatched to Hades and the bodies lying on the battle-field. . . . The images evoked in the

verbs and in the nouns succeed each other paratactically; each unit of meaning is self-subsistent; the linkage is essentially that which is rendered possible by adding fresh words which exploit or vary associations already present in previous words.[2]

With this we have before us the essential nature of the pre-Homeric mind; according to Havelock. It is a flow of *images* of persons, or of person-like agencies, engaged in actions or sequences thereof. In the last chapters of *Preface to Plato* we learn that this kind of consciousness does not permit the thought of an ordered world existing independently of the one who is conscious, nor the thought of the one who is conscious as a distinct entity thinking and acting on its own. Indeed, with all of this, it is not clear to me why Havelock refrains from putting the very term 'conscious' under the scare-quotes along with 'knowledge,' 'belief,' etc. But more on this later.

We now turn to the question of what reason Havelock might have for thinking that the pre-Homeric mind has the character we have just described. His grounds turn out to consist of two interrelated points: one having to do with the kind of syntax present in Homeric Greek as written down, and the other having to do with the relationship alleged to hold between consciousness and language. The earliest Greek language of which we have record does not contain a timeless 'is' such as could express consciousness of abstract entities corresponding to concepts. That is the first point. It is then assumed that the writings which we have are an adequate indication of the syntactical character of the total language actually in use by the Greeks.[3]

But granting that the syntax of pre-Homeric Greek generally is totally as Havelock claims, what further is needed to support his view of the Greek *consciousness* of that period? Obviously there must be some very close connection between what can be uttered and what can be thought. Precisely what he takes that connection to be is, however, a matter of considerable obscurity, due to the fact that he never systematically discusses the topic for its own sake. It may be useful, therefore, to distinguish several different views on the relationship between thought and language, and to consider Havelock's statements with those views as a background. We shall distinguish an ontological, a causal, and an epistemic position.

On the ontological position the act of thinking, say, that the angles of a triangle are equal to the sum of two right angles is—is exactly the same thing as—the act of utilizing (in some fashion standing in need of clarification) an appropriate sentence. This view is, of course, much stronger than any view according to which language only *assists* us in thinking. John Stuart Mill, for example, held it very important for the logician and philosopher to study language, for it was, he said, ". . . one of the principal instruments or helps of thought."[4] Indeed, ". . . reasoning or inference, the principal subject of logic, · is an operation which usually takes place by means of words, and in complicated cases can take place in no other way. . . ." (ibid.). But elsewhere Mill insists that language is truly essential to communication only, not to thinking as such, and hence not to logic. What logic studies, in studying inference, has in its own inherent nature nothing to do with language. (See the end of the third subsection of the Introduction to the *Logic*.) It is clear, therefore, that Mill did not hold the position here in question. And that is also true of most, if not all, major philosophers prior to the twentieth century. Perhaps, by contrast, Wittgenstein did hold that thinking and linguistic activity are identical. He at least seriously considers the view that ". . . thinking *essentially consists in operating with signs.*"[5]

A weaker thesis about the relation of thought and language holds some sort of causal relation between the act of thought and linguistic acts and items. Here we have distinctness (non-identity) but, possibly, not separability—at least no separability of thought from language. The act of thinking that the angles of a triangle together equal two right angles can occur only in one who simultaneously (or slightly earlier?) engages in some more or less fully executed linguistic act, even if it be only the twitching of lips or fingers or the imaging of words. Any claim to a thoroughly rigorous correlation might be weakened in various ways. Mill's words, quoted above, suggest some such weakened version. We might hold that only especially difficult or refined thought processes absolutely require accompanying linguistic processes, and perhaps exempt especially brilliant people from even this requirement. Or we might simply hold that thinking is easier and in general more successful when accompanied by linguistic moves. Or we might only hold that a certain type of language is a social condition of a certain level of intellectual performance, without directly connecting the intellectual and linguistic acts in their particular occurrence in the particular individual. I do not wish to suggest that these are the only possible ways in which the general thesis of dependence (not identity) of thought upon linguistic activities might be specified, but they are some of the more interesting ways, and possibly Havelock's view is among them.

Finally, and apparently placing still more distance between language and thought, we might suppose that not thought itself, but only our knowledge *of* thought depends upon (our knowledge of) language. On this view, whatever we claim to know about the nature of thought can only be derived from something we know about words or language in the fairly straightforward sense commonly understood. And, conversely, we can be quite sure about conscious processes if we know certain things about language. It will be readily apparent that this epistemic position on the relationship of language to thought will depend for its justification upon the details of the actual relationship between them, whatever they may be, and that it will become more attractive the more likely it becomes that identity or strong resemblance or strong dependence holds between thought and linguistic activities. This position also becomes more attractive (quite erroneously, I think) the more one feels obliged to support empiricism generally, and hence with regard to our knowledge of thought also. Language, it is frequently presumed, is subject to empirical knowledge in some interesting fashion not true of thought itself, and thus—given its supposedly intimate relationship with thought—it is regarded as providing a firm (empirical) foundation for our claims about thought itself.

Now Havelock's statements seem to commit him beyond all doubt to the epistemic position just outlined. In *Preface to Plato* he states that "Direct evidence for mental phenomena can lie only in linguistic usage" (p. vii). The word "direct" here is somewhat puzzling, unless he takes the mental phenomena to be a directly inspectable *part* of linguistic usage. Other things he says discourage such an interpretation, however. In the second paragraph on page 41 of his paper in this present volume he remarks:

> How do you know a concept or category exists except as the name for it tells you it exists? No supposition is commoner than that thought precedes language and is philosophically prior to it. Yet since thought is measuable only through words, the supposition violates a fundamental rule of empirical science.

This statement seems to indicate that "words" alone are empirically accessible, and that thought is *not* directly present, but only to be arrived at through the words. In any case, the clear intent is that a concept or category can only be known to exist through language—whatever 'through' means.

But beyond this epistemic position, Havelock is committed to some fairly strong *causal* claim. True, some of his wordings may suggest otherwise. On page 13 of "The Linguistic Task of the Presocratics," for example, he speaks of ". . . the precise linguistic forms in which the Greek experience of the environment has previously [to the pre-Socratic philosophers] been clothed." And we know, of course, that clothes maketh not the man, while the entire tenor of Havelock's work surely is that, in some important sense, language does make the thought. Returning to *Preface to Plato* we read in the Foreword: "It is a fair presumption that until the fit word is present, you do not have the idea, and the word to become fit requires a suitable context of usage." The closer fit than clothes can still, however, be taken in (at least) two senses.

According to one interpretation (our "causal position" outlined above), the idea and the fit word are distinct, and the idea just happens as a matter of fact to depend for its occurrence upon the occurrence of the word. If this is the view intended, however, it is not clear why anyone would want to hold it, beyond the fact that it is in our day such a widely accepted view. On such a view, induction or confirmation of the view as an empirical hypothesis would seem to be the only way in which it could be supported. Yet such support has never, so far as I can tell, been actually offered by anyone. There are occasional vague suggestions that it *could* be offered, but no carry-through into a definite program of research. Possibly this is because there is such a profound degree of conceptual unclarity about the terms of the alleged dependence that no coherent research program could be proposed. I think that this is in fact the case.

It therefore seems quite possible that Havelock takes the above statement in the sense of an "ontological" relationship between thought and language, or between idea and "fit word." That is to say, he holds that you cannot have the idea until the fit word is present, just because having the idea *is* essentially the same thing as a linguistic activity (or disposition), which of course would demand just the right sort of linguistic component. If this is his view, then one can also understand his insistence that we know thought through knowledge of language, for in that case the language is essentially part—though possibly not the whole—of the thought to be known. I think, therefore, that the most reasonable construction to put upon Havelock's statements is that consciousness is, in general, a linguistic activity. It would not be necessary, I believe, for him to hold such a strong view in order to advance the views he does about the oral and literary phases of Greek culture, but if he does hold such strong views about the relation of thought to language, then it would be reasonable for him to say what he does about developments in that culture. And I do not clearly see what weaker view he might be holding that would make it reasonable to say what he does.

Now of course it must be admitted that such a strong view is not unique to Havelock in the contemporary world. It is, one could fairly say, *the* modern dogma on the relationship of thought to language, although it was not shared in its completely general form by any of the great philosophers prior to this century. Nominalists, such as Hume, have indeed held all *conceptual* thought (disregarding the question of whether there is any other kind) to be essentially linguistic. For on their view, as Hume says, ". . . all general ideas are nothing but particular ones, annexed to a certain term, which gives them a more extensive signification, and makes them recall upon occasion other individuals, which are similar to them."[6] Combining Nominalism with the general anti-mentalist tendencies of contemporary Anglo-American thought, and buoyed upon the "empiricism" of a culture dominated by science and technology, we easily arrive at a view which is almost universally accepted today among English-speaking philosophers, but is best expressed, to my knowledge, by Wilfrid Sellars:

> . . . *All* awareness of *sorts, resemblances, facts* etc., in short, all awareness of abstract entities—indeed, all awareness even of particulars—is a linguistic affair.[7]

This, then, is the one philosophical assumption which seems to me to be at the heart of Havelock's scholarly enterprise: namely, that cognitive consciousness is essentially a linguistic activity. It seems to me that *he* takes this assumption to be central to his interpretation of the Greek mind and its development. I cannot help thinking, however, that this assumption is false; and it further seems to me that Havelock's interpretations of the Greek mind are, in fact, not logically dependent upon the assumption here in question— nor, indeed, upon whether or not the pre-Homeric Greeks had, in general, knowledge (belief, doubt, etc.) in the sense that we do. I shall conclude by briefly discussing these two points.

I have elsewhere offered a detailed critique of the very idea of "thinking in language."[8] The two points most important to consider, for anyone who takes thinking to be an essentially linguistic activity, are the following:

(i) *Most* of our thinking does in fact occur without any actual deployment of the sorts of items (sounds, marks, etc.) that make up words and their complications. This point can be evaded only by counting as words what could never function in communication as words, even with oneself. It is, of course, precisely in the public, social arena that the rules which govern *linguistic* use come into play; and nothing which is not governed by those rules should be allowed to count as language. (Sometimes in the literature one finds the mere thought *of* or "image" *of* a word treated as itself a word. One who has accepted such an equation will probably not be open to further reasoning on this topic.) But then (ii) words and their complications being what they *must* be, if the remarks just made are correct, they are not the sorts of things *with* or *to* which mere thought or mere mental "effort" of any kind could do anything. This is, of course, not to deny that the *literal* use of literal words and other actual symbols does have great effects upon our thinking, or that much careful work needs to be done in describing *how* language really does interact with thought and, more generally, consciousness. Nor is it to deny that thought as we now know it in ourselves in our world might never have come to be without a long process of linguistic development preceeding it. (Think only, for example, of the transition from Roman to Arabic numerals, or of the introduction of the zero into our symbolisms.) But we can never, I believe, come to the serious business of investigating the ways in which thought does depend upon language until we have freed ourselves from the idea that thinking just *is* doing something to and with language.

But let us proceed to consider the conclusion which Havelock apparently derives from the assumption that thought is a linguistic activity: namely, that the pre-Homeric Greeks did not have knowledge in the sense that we today do. If the assumption is false, then—even given the further assumption that the time-bound 'is,' found in the earliest writings, is the only copula in pre-Homeric Greek generally—we have no good reason to think that persons at that time could not think conceptually, for it then is not clear that the forms of human thinking must find expression in the forms of human speaking. One way of reading the old slogan that the grammatical form of a proposition is not always its real form is that the form of the sentence in question is not an adequate representation of the form of the thought expressed in it. There is surely no reason why the forms of written sentences during a certain period in the development of a language could not systematically fail to represent the forms of thought in that period—especially once we surrender the identity of thinking with linguistic activity. Efforts at linguistic reform, such as Havelock points to, could then be understood as attempts by the more cultured elements of the society to bring the forms of the current language into line with the forms of thought to accomodate, precisely, the advance of knowledge—which need not be the same thing as advancing from "knowledge" to knowledge.

But everything which we know about what the Greeks (and other ancient peoples) *did* surely indicates that they had beliefs, both founded (knowledge, therefore) and unfounded, in exactly the same sense that we do. Any country maiden of pre-Platonic times *knew* quite as well as any in the Greece of the third century B.C. or today that milk left in the summer sun would sour faster than milk placed where it would be cooler. This is conceptual knowledge just as truly as claims about the angles of triangles. The only difference is that the classes of things unified under the concepts used in the two cases are different types of classes: of particular events or things in the former case and of abstract entities in the latter. But this only goes to show that not all conceptualized consciousness is *about* abstract entities (concepts or universals), not that there is concept-free consciousness. And here I return to my earlier question as to whether Havelock should not, after all, put the term 'consciousness' itself within scare-quotes. If the pre-Homeric person did not know, believe, doubt, fear, hope, or merely think that . . . as we do, in what sense did he *act*. Plato's description of non-philosophical persons as sleep-walking[9] would have to be taken in a certain grim literalness which surely all—and perhaps Havelock most of all—would wish to disassociate from that bright era of human history into which Keats peered through Chapman's Homer. We should consider well whether, given such restrictions on the early Greek "consciousness" as Havelock envisages, there could be a *history* of such creatures. In what sense were the pre-Homeric Greeks men?

It may be that such consequences need not be drawn, as Havelock considers the matter, because of the power he attributes to image "thinking." He understands the early Greek mind to be organized in terms of images of persons involved in actions and sequences thereof. But expressions of action in stories are not *alternatives* to conceptualized thought and language. They presuppose it. No *statement* of any kind is an expression of a mere sequence of images. At best we could have a *list*. And as F. H. Bradley pointed out long ago, in his critique of Mill and others who would derive thought from the association of images, the very association of images itself occurs only through conceptual mediation.[10] We have a fine illustration of this from Havelock himself, in a passage already referred to. His discussion of the experience which, supposedly, occurred upon the recitation of the opening lines of the *Iliad*[11] refers to the shift from the wrath of Achilles to the mind of Zeus in relation to the Achaeans. Havelock remarks: "There is an associative linkage even here; Achilles is the most powerful of men, Zeus the most powerful of Gods; the two are paired in common action."

But *in concreto* the action is not common. The associative linkage in question is precisely a common abstract feature, that of being most powerful within one's proper domain. Indeed, Havelock makes the general point here and elsewhere that the unity of the associative sequence is "variation within the same." He does not seem to notice that "the same" which provides the unity of the sequence is, as Bradley pointed out, not an image or concrete particular, but precisely an abstract conceptual content of the kind which, supposedly, the pre-Homeric mind could not deploy. It is this oversight, I surmise, which allows Havelock to proceed as if the early Greeks had minds but not "knowledge."

Now if all that I have said to this point were true, it would be very fortunate indeed if the substance or substantial parts of Havelock's interpretations of the early Greek writings did not depend upon or entail his general views of pre-Homeric consciousness or his view (if it is his view) that thought is a linguistic activity. And it does seem to me that we could concede almost everything which he says about the nature of the experience of the poetic performance and about its role in transmitting culture—even concede his interpretations of what the pre-Socratics, Socrates, and Plato were (mainly) about in relation to the educational system of the Greeks—without concluding that the early Greeks did not know (believe, etc.) in the sense that we do. Moreover, we could argue for much of his interpretation without invoking as an essential premise any claim that those Greeks did not know as we know or have the cognitive type of consciousness which we do. It would seem quite enough for Havelock's purposes that *the language and experience involved in the transmission of culture* be as he understands it. And it seems to me quite reasonable to suppose that *that* experience *did* substantially take the form of a flow of rationally unchastised images under "poetic" control. Indeed, I imagine that something very little different from that takes place today among the generality of our population.[12] But this is to make quite a different point from one concerning what forms of consciousness in general are possible—then, or now.

Dallas Willard

University of Southern California

NOTES

1. *Preface to Plato* (New York: Grosset and Dunlap, 1967), p. 182; and see n45 on p. 232.

2. *Preface to Plato*, pp. 183–84. Cf. p. 190; also "The Linguistic Task of the Presocratics" in this volume, pp. 32–33.

3. I am not sure how one could know that the restricted syntax was not simply a peculiarity of the earliest *written* Greek, or a peculiarity associated with the obviously very special class of people (with their special purposes) who wrote it. Do we have independent evidence that Greek generally, at the time, used only the temporalized 'is'?

4. *Logic*, Bk. I, ch. 1, first paragraph.

5. *Blue Book* (Oxford: Basil Blackwell, 1960), p. 15. In reading those who hold that thought or consciousness *is* a linguistic activity, one has to be prepared for generous extensions of the term 'language' (or 'sentence' or 'word'). R. B. Braithwaite, for example, retreats from *explicit* words—but is there any other kind?— to " . . . some symbolism, visual, auditory, kinaesthetic or laryngeal, which is synonymous with the word 'cat' . . . ." (p. 23 of "The Relevance of Psychology to Logic," *Proceedings of the Aristotelian Soceity*, supplementary volume XVII, 1939). More recently, writers such as Wilfrid Sellars and Gilbert Harman, along with most of those who speak of a "language of thought," are prepared to treat entities or events which could never be used in communication as "words" or "sentences," provided only that they have a *role* or function in certain human processes or behaviors which is relevantly like the role of, say, an English word in the process of an English conversation.

But surely one must draw the line somewhere, and for me it falls at the point where the "word" is no longer the sort of thing that is publically observable in the context of communicative discourse. If we are not allowed private referents, we surely are not allowed private words or sentences. Such"words" *could not* have a role relevantly like the role of an English word in an English conversation.

6. *Treatise*, Bk. I, sec. vii.

7. *Science, Perception and Reality* (New York: The Humanities Press, 1963), p. 160.

8. See "The Absurdity of 'Thinking in Language,' " *The Southwestern Journal of Philosophy* 4, no. 1 (Spring 1973), pp. 125–32. My own views concerning the nature of thought largely coincide with those of Edmund Husserl, and are further explained in chapter IV of my *Logic and the Objectivity of Knowledge*, forthcoming from Ohio University Press.

9. *Preface to Plato*, p. 190.

10. *The Principles of Logic* (London: Oxford University Press, 1922), Bk. II, Pt. II, chap. I.

11. *Preface to Plato*, pp. 183f.

12. See Neil Postman's, "The Las Vegasizing of America" (*National Forum*, April 1982, pp. 6–9), for an informative discussion of how this actually occurs today.

FROM WATER TO ATOMS:
THE TRIUMPH OF METAPHYSICS

Some current Greek coins and paper money bear a purported portrait of Democritus and juxtaposed thereto the interlaced ellipses symbolic of nuclear energy. Coming from Berkeley, one's first reaction on seeing them may be that everybody wants to get in the act. But no. It is sober and literal truth to credit Democritus with the fundamental theoretical work on the project.

He did it scarcely a century and a half after the eclipse of 585 B.C. that Thales is said to have foretold—a stretch of time roughly the same as that from Dalton (1808) to Fermi (1940). And Thales started science from scratch!

Two striking features of the (lamentably and absurdly so-called) pre-Socratic tradition are the thoroughness of its break with the past and the rapidity of development culminating in the right kind of answer to the question of how things are. In this paper I shall try to give an account of the salient features of the revolution and of the internal logic of its progress. I shall make no attempt to explain what circumstances beyond individual genius made it possible.

I

In Miletus occurred a mutation of thought such as never happened independently anywhere else in the world: an intellectual Olympic leap compared to which every subsequent "paradigm shift" is but a hop and a skip. How absolute the discontiunity is between *mythos* and *logos* may be brought home by detailing a few aspects of their opposition.

Both myth and science tell us why things are as they are, but myth ascribes their constitution to their having been made for some purpose. The viewpoint is that of the ruler or administrator issuing commands to implement a policy. It is personal and subjective. Its principal categories are person, society, purpose, will, good, and evil. It demands acceptance as a whole and simply because it is traditional or else because it is put forth by authoritative persons acknowledged to have special sources of insight. It can be rejected but not argued with or amended.

Contrast Milesian and post-Milesian cosmogonies: the world is as it is because it inexorably developed that way from a (relatively) simple starting condition. The viewpoint, as Farrington has stressed [5], is that of the mechanic or artisan, the executant who must physically manipulate his sometimes refractory materials. It is impersonal and objective. Its categories are unit, configuration, growth, force, motion, stuff, regularity. Its claim to status as knowledge is from observation, inference, and analogy; it tries to persuade by compelling argument, as in a court of law; and it is liable to piecemeal improvement.

Though Thales wrote nothing and at most two sentences remain from the books of his fellow citizens, later testimonies[1] enable us to discern at least the following scientific elements in the thinking of the Milesians:

First, all of them operated with a notion of natural causality—the "leaving Marduk out" that Farrington celebrated as Thales's great achievement. Anaximander produced the present world out of the Boundless by an explicitly natural evolutionary process, and then land animals, including human beings, from the sea; even social institutions seem to have been described as developing from the necessities of human nature [4, 12A10]. And Anaximenes, though less daring in his speculations, continued the naturalistic tradition.

Second, according to Eudemus [4, 11A20], Thales proved some theorems of geometry. The testimony seems credible if only because the propositions cited are so simple and obvious; merely to have asserted them would have been nothing noteworthy. Thales must then have had the conception of a rational proof exhibiting the necessary truth of an assertion; we know of no one earlier who did. It marks the beginning of mathematics as a science rather than an art.

Third, the Fragment of Anaximander exhibits grasp of the idea of a law of nature: things regularly return into that from which they take their origins "as is fitting; for they make reparation and pay penalty to one another for their injustice according to the ordering of time." [4, 12B1] No divine decree requires them to do it, they just do it.

Fourth, all these thinkers have an ideal of unified explanation and the connectedness of things. They tell of how the present complicated state of affairs arose out of a primordial simplicity. But they go farther than that: they use their sweeping cosmogonic hypotheses to account for diverse and not obviously connected phenomena. Thus Thales explains earthquakes on the model of flotsam on agitated water [4, 11A15];[2] while in Anaximander's system the mist-and-fire hoops not only explain the heavenly revolutions and the nature of eclipses but by making the cosmos symmetrical show why, by the "principle of sufficient reason," the earth though unsupported does not fall. [4, 12A26; cf. 7] Furthermore, these hoops are the ancestors of electrons, genes, and phlogiston as postulated explanatory entities.[3]

Fifth, in Anaximander's assertions that the earth is a drum three times as broad as thick, and that the diameters of the celestial hoops are in multiples of nine earth radii, we have the earliest instances of quantification of natural phenomena. His connection with the gnomon is additional evidence for his interest in applying mathematics to the study of nature, even though we have no information as to how he arrived at these neat numbers.[4] Dynamic symmetry, "feedback," one might even say Newton's Third Law are prefigured in the "paying penalty and making reparation" of the Fragment.

Sixth, and perhaps most important, Milesian thought is progressive; and this is true even though in retrospect the system of Anaximenes is seen as inferior to Anaximander's. Anaximander was an "associate" of Thales, not his disciple. But neither did he reject the system and start all over again; he selectively modified it, stating his reason for doing so [4, 12A16]; and the tradition of "conjecture and refutation" thus established was carried on by Anaximenes and through the lifetime of Greek science.[5]

II

The men of Miletus through whom this mutation of thought came to pass were not the first to address the questions of what the world is made of and how it came to be as it is. Nor was their first answer—that it emerged from watery chaos—so novel. Many religions of the region had said so. And the religions too aimed at unified cosmic explanation. But these are the only points of contact. Religions had no notion of development through natural causality. They never dreamed of proving theorems. While the ideas of a more or less impersonal Fate ordaining what is to be, and of Furies who restore balances that have got out of whack, may lie behind the conception of law of nature, Anaximander's significant insistence that the wrongdoers pay penalty and make reparation *to one another* (not to judges and overseers) shows the break with myth. Religions are not at all concerned with numbers and measures. And of course the very idea of criticism is the primary anathema for all institutional religion, including Greek.[6]

What the Milesians did, then, was not religion and not continuous with it. But was it science? Or was it (merely) philosophy?

Surely Anaximander *redivivus* would be welcomed as a colleague in the Cavendish Laboratory and on Mount Palomar, as he would be shunned in the Vatican and Arkansas. Or would he? Is seeking to account for things in terms of necessity, causality, natural law, and quantities enough for admittance to the club? Some would say no, that the Milesian nature-philosophy lacks two essentials of science: it never developed any method of experiential testing; and in any case its hypotheses were untestable.

Remarks of this sort about the pre-Socratics are less common and taken less seriously than they were a generation ago when the Verifiability Principle was in flower. It may still be instructive, however, to consider why and to what extent they are misplaced.

The assumption behind them is that there is something worthy of being called The Scientific Method that is the same for all times and places; that it includes controlled experimental testing of hypotheses; and that inquiries not using such means are to that extent not fully scientific, in the sense that they would have been more efficiently and fruitfully conducted had they done so. Thus Farrington argued [5] that Greek science got off to a great start because Thales and his associates were men of the people personally skilled in the technologies of the time, from which they took their ideas of how nature operated; but that the enterprise petered out when it was taken over by aristocrats like Plato who would not deign to get their hands dirty. Cornford [3], unimpressed by the scanty evidence for experimentation or even detailed observation by the early thinkers, saw the same people as shamans and mystagogues.

But it is ludicrous to try to imagine experimental procedures for deciding whether everything comes from water, or the Boundless, or fog; and their absence is no proof of "shamanism." The Milesians certainly did not close their eyes and wait for inspiration. The reasons Aristotle assigned for Thales's choice of water as the fundamental element, though conjectural, comport well with what we know of his style, and are based on observation; while Anaximander's repertoire of data encompassed everything from the parturition of sharks to (probably) the presence of marine fossils on hilltops. But observation and experiment are futile and misleading if not based on and related to an articulated conceptual scheme. And we are talking about the very beginning of science, when there were as yet no theories; nor were there, as Professor Havelock reminds us [6], even the elementary concepts in terms of which theories might be expressed.[7] At this first stage what needed to be done was to make the questions more precise and explicit and to try out various types of answers to see whether they made sense and were consistent with the obvious facts—whether they could "save the appearances." These things the Milesians and their successors accomplished with maximum directness.

III

As Professor Havelock shows [6], the Milesians lacked the abstract vocabulary for phrasing the question, What is the basic stuff of the world, and by what processes did the present constitution of things evolve from it? But the very first sentence that has been preserved from their writings, speaking of the "return of things into that from which they take their origins," shows well enough that they were capable of thinking of cosmic stuffs and processes. The question presupposes that there *is* (at least) one basic stuff, and that there *was* an initial condition of (at least relative) homogeneity. Why make such assumptions?

As to the first, to deny it would be to admit the possibility of something just popping up, something coming from nothing; and though the absurdity of such an occurrence is first stated explicitly by Parmenides, it is clear that no Greek before or after him ever thought otherwise. Philosophy began in leisure, but not in so much leisure that the possibility of getting something for nothing could yet be seriously envisaged. On the other hand, the second assumption could be denied without absurdity; Aristotle did so, and before him Heraclitus.[8] The belief seems to be taken over from the myths; but perhaps it would be better, following Havelock's account, to ascribe this feature of both religion and early science to the oral pattern of thought which demands narratives rather than stated descriptions.

Another way to put the Milesian question is: What is it to which conservation laws apply? That again is not the way they did formulate it, or could have; but they understood that what all other things come from cannot itself come from anything prior. Therefore, it must be "ageless," as Anaximander said; and, however transformed, it cannot disappear or "give out": its essential nature persists, it is "deathless."

Naive inspection of the world shows it to be composed of four kinds of stuffs: solid (earth), liquid (water), foggy (air), and bright (fire). So the simplest kind of answer to the Milesian question, predestined to be tried out first, was that one of these four was basic. What reason might there be to grant priority to a particular one? Thales perhaps noted the pervasiveness of water even where at first it may not seem to be lurking, its necessity for sustaining life (thought to be coextensive with being, or nearly so), and above all its capacity to appear, disguised, as it were, in solid and foggy states. And so Thales had his reasonable answer.

Then the questioning began. Just exactly what *is* water? Is it nothing but wetness? Then dust and fire can hardly *be* water. "If one were infinite, it would have swallowed up all the rest." So it can't be water in this palpable and obvious sense. It must rather be something underlying wetness, capable of bringing forth wetness—and by the same token capable of bringing forth all the special qualities, the heat, cold, wetness, dryness, of all the rest: the Boundless of Anaximander. What would it be like to get hold of a pure specimen? Neither hot nor cold, neither wet nor dry—so a neutral mixture of all of them, damp and tepid? Or an unperceivable potentiality?

But if it lacks all character, Anaximenes pointed out, it is a mere X. And so he returns to the thought of Thales, only shifting the neutral point on the scale, so to speak, from water over to fog—a maneuver that is logically indifferent but no doubt had the psychological advantage of focusing attention on a more manifestly agile stuff: fog congeals out of bright (fiery) sky and further thickens into rain right before our eyes all the time. So the same stuff is always there, now thickened under the action of cold, now thinned by heat. What about the heat and the cold? Where do they come from? Are they conserved? We are not told.[9]

IV

Heraclitus and Pythagoras had much in common, as we might expect from the denunciations of the latter by the former. In choosing fire as the basic stuff, the Ephesian was not merely ringing another change on a theme by Thales; for although all things are exchange for fire, that fire is "ever-living, kindling in measures and going out in measures." That is to say, the structure of things, their *logos*,[10] is emphasized over their stuff, and is the eternal basis. It is discovered not with the eye alone but by the mind, the interpretive, pattern-recognizing, sizing-up faculty. The Samian came to much the same conclusions, evidently by meditating on the power of the disciplined mind to contemplate the truth of how things must be, and on how the raw data of eyes and ears—planetary paths, pleasing and displeasing combinations of sounds—submit to being marshaled by numbers. And so "things are numbers"; geometrical properties, quantitatively expressible patterns turn out to be their eternal structures, revealed to mind when purified by contemplation. There is no distinct stuff that *is* patterned—it drops out, becomes only "the void" that the unit "inhales" in the beginning. So much for the fog of Anaximenes.

But mathematics (the science of patterns) was not destined to inhale and absorb physics (the science of nature) quite so directly and easily. Parmenides would not allow it.

The Eleatic, in making explicit the conditions that must be laid on our conception of anything basic, ruled out all the stuffs of common experience. It must be eternal, that is, ungenerated, indestructible, and changeless. And the truth about it must be likewise eternal. Fog and water and fire and what we think we know about them utterly fail to fill the bill. What does, then? Parmenides answers: whatever certain knowledge—that is, mathematics—is about. He did not have the word "continuum" to label it, or even "space"; but that did not prevent him from having the conception, which he described as "one, holding together, . . . stretching out equally in all ways from the middle, with no more here than there." [4, 28B8]

Parmenides cannot be overpraised for having delineated the nature of *a priori* knowledge and its object. Unfortunately he did so in such a way that he interpreted himself as having shown that the quest begun by the Milesians was futile. So-called knowledge not *a priori* but derived from the "unseeing eye and ringing ear and tongue" could be no more than "mortal guesswork," its objects sharply cut off from the eternal Reality. In short, physics could not be a science. [8]

Empedocles sought to rescue physics by declaring that there are eternal and unchanging "roots," which happily turned out to be just the four elementary bodies. Each is identifiable by one pair from the two opposites hot/cold and wet/dry. Being eternal, they are proper objects of proper knowledge. Other things, with their diverse qualities, are mixtures of the elementary bodies, just as all the colors of the spectrum can be produced by mixing only three primaries. This ingenious theory, accepted in principle by Aristotle, has a long history. However, it is hard to see how, strictly considered, it can account for any qualities of things other than degrees of temperature and dampness.

Anaxagoras noted this drawback. "How can hair come from what is not hair," he asked rhetorically, "or flesh from what is not flesh?" [4, 59B10] And so he declared all qualities equal and compresent in everything. If bread does not look, feel, taste, or smell hairy, that is because the hair is masked by the wheaten and yeasty components; but the stomach can concentrate what is needed for our nourishment and reject the rest.

Thus, in a way, Anaxagoras returns to Anaximander. There is not a stuff, identifiable by perceptible characteristics other than hairiness, that *becomes* hair by some process somehow generating the hair-character; there just *is* (all the time) hair, which *is* neither more nor less than the assemblage of perceptible hair-characters. From time to time it surfaces.

In Anaxagoras's theory pre-Socratic thought simultaneously achieves consistency and bankruptcy. Consistency, for the principle "nothing from nothing" is in no way fudged: what a thing is, it always has been, though perhaps scattered and hidden. Bankruptcy, because the theory can explain nothing. When we ask after the generation of hair, we *do* want to be told how, in some sense, hair comes from what is not hair. We want an explanation to provide a unified account of the thing explained. We feel with Xenophanes that all things are one at least in some sense; at any rate, nothing is gained if the explicans is every bit as diverse and complex as the explicandum.

Yet Anaxagoras came within a hair's breadth of enunciating a satisfactory conceptual scheme. We can see this if we note that, after all, there are some perceptible characters that his theory leaves out: sounds, for instance. Brooks are not only cool and clear and wet; they are babbling. "But how can a babble come from what is not a babble?" Anaxagoras would not ask so silly a question, for he knew that the babble is not something the brook *is*, it is something the brook *does*; it does not *exist*, it *happens*. And there is no temptation to ask about the conservation of happenings.

If only it had occurred to Anaxagoras that being red or sour is more like being noisy than like being solid, he might have come up with a theory that both rigorously excluded something-from-nothing and had explanatory power.

V

The Atomists took this final step, which was both inevitable and only to be made by genius. Color, sweet, bitter—all the characters by which things are identified save only size, shape, solidity, and weight were declared to be "by custom," that is, not out there on their own, but phenomena arising from the interaction of the things that are out there with the sense organs of the perceiver. Generated and perishing macro-objects were to be understood as temporary combinations of eternal micro-objects not even in principle perceptible by any sense save touch. Knowledge of them was possible—they satisfied the Parmenidean requirements—by the Mind that could also know the eternal truths of mathematics. In a way, indeed, the atoms *were* Pythagorean "numbers," as Aristotle pointed out [1, 303a9].

Later atomists provided many "empirical" arguments for the proposition that the constituent parts of things must be very tiny: the wearing away of metal rings, the seepage of water through seemingly solid rock, and so on. But what is really distinctive about atomism, and what makes it the right model of things, is the insistence that what later came to be known as "secondary qualities" do not inhere as perceived in external bodies but arise through interaction with the perceiver. This made possible the reduction of the temporary characters of things to their permanent bases, thereby vindicating physics as a science. Things, essentially separable at last from colors, smells, and all the other ephemera, partook of the eternal. And "nothing happens at random, but everything from reason and under necessity." [4, 67B2]

VI

Put even more briefly, this unique sesquicentennium saw first, all at once and suddenly, the birth of science and philosophy, the mutation in thought that afforded an alternative world-view to the anthropomorphism so natural to the human species. The main problem of the new discipline was the explanation of the world as we know it, changeable in its every aspect, in terms of something permanent, conserved. Inevitably the first essays in this direction would take as basic some stuff, identified by and with its perceptible characteristics. That was the route of Thales and Anaximenes. But it could not be satisfactory because the selection of one stuff out of all the possibilities was bound to be arbitrary. The alternative, proposed by Anaximander, was to suppose the basic stuff to be identifiable not by any definite characters, but to be, so to speak, actually neutral or characterless, while potentially capable of manifesting itself in all ways. That did not work either; in the absence of some plausible account of the process of actualization, it afforded only a verbal solution.

Three developments of special importance can be singled out from the subsequent history. First, the establishment of the method of mathematical proof. Second, the drawing out of the implications of mathematics by Parmenides: the existence of certain knowledge, taking precedence over sense perception and inference based on it, and with a special eternal object accessible only to the intellect. Third, the coming to awareness (mainly in Empedocles and Anaxagoras, though there had been adumbrations of it in Heraclitus) that sense perception is not a direct grasping of the perceived object but an interaction, an event.

Parmenides, with his sharp distinction between real knowledge and mere sense perception, concluded that there can be no science of anything but the entities revealed to the mind. Empedocles and Anaxagoras attempted to save physical science through the discernment of eternal basic constituents of physical objects. But as these elementary things were identified by and with perceptual characteristics, their systems were ultimately not exempt from the shortcomings of their Milesian predecessors: artibrariness or lack of explanatory power, or both.

The solution, the satisfactory answer to Parmenides, consisted in ceasing to identify stuffs with their perceptual characters, or at any rate with all of them. It became possible to do this once attention was paid to perception as a process. The bothersome temporary qualities of things could be reduced by analysis to changing combinations of eternal elements, and the thing as it was in itself could be described in objective terms. This is not to say, of course, that there were not plenty of loose ends left hanging around—particularly those associated with Democritus' unfortunate propensity to regard the reduced secondary qualities as unreal, and sense perception as untrustworthy. But none of this should obscure the radiant fact that the true picture of the world and of man's place in it had been sketched in its main outlines.

VII

Now: Was this science? Or was it philosophy?

If the preceding outline is not altogether off the mark, we have seen that the process of "conjecture and refutation" eventuated in the establishment of a conceptual scheme. That, presumably, is metaphysics. In Aristotle's terms, it is certainly First Philosophy, the inquiry into the nature of Being as Such. And it is thus that I would justify the title of this essay.

Nevertheless, it was at the same time an inquiry into the nature of things by the only rational methods available, appropriate and relevant. Such an enterprise deserves the name of science if anything does.

So, metaphysics is science after all. At least sometimes.

Wallace I. Matson

University of California,
Berkeley

NOTES

1. It seems absurdly self-denying to eschew the testimonia altogether in studying the pre-Socratics, as Havelock recommends [6]. Doxographies must be used with caution—but so must fragments. And it is misleading to suggest that the pre-Socratics were engaged primarily in a "linguistic task," and excessively dramatic to say that their "target" was "the Greek language as such." In giving new senses to "*sol oriens*" and "field," Copernicus and Faraday were hardly making war on Latin and English.

This is not to imply, of course, that Havelock's substantive results are not valid, enlightening, and of the first importance.

2. Admittedly, this is not very far from Poseidon shaking the earth with his trident. But Thales "left Poseidon out."

3. But they are not the first postulated entities; gods are.

4. If, as historians unanimously allow, Anaximenes held that the four elements are transmutable into one another by "rarefaction and condensation" (quantitative notions), then this otherwise comparatively inconsequential thinker is the originator of reduction of quality to quantity. However, *pyknosis* and *manosis* (or *araiosis*), the words of the doxographies [4, 13A5], are almost certainly not those employed by Anaximenes himself; and he may have meant no more than that water is *thickened* air, and so forth. Thick/thin, unlike condensed/rarefied, are not (necessarily) quantitative terms: adding cornstarch to a sauce does not condense it.

5. This is not of course to deny the existence of "schools"; but even Pythagoreanism is only a partial exception to the no-discipleship generalization. It is clear that individual Pythagoreans altered the doctrines of Himself, in some cases drastically, however they may have tried to conceal the fact.

6. Theological arguments all boil down to the contention that the opposing party has misinterpreted the sacred tradition. Apologetics and "natural theology" are religious mimicry of scientific procedures and thus do not afford counterexamples.

7. Both Milesian acuteness of observation and its pitfalls are illustrated by Anaximenes' "experiment" of blowing on the hand first gently through the wide-open mouth and then sharply through pursed lips [4, 13B1]: the warmer feeling experienced in the first trial was supposed to confirm his theory according to which the thinner things are, the hotter. Modern physical theory draws an exactly opposite conclusion from the data; but the explanation can be given only in terms of the dynamic notion of expansion, as opposed to the static ideas of rareness (or even merely the qualitative concept of thinness; see note 4 above), which was all the conceptual apparatus Anaximenes had available. Moreover, the modern explanation brings in considerations derived from evaporation of sweat on the palm, which, if Anaximenes noted, he could hardly have deemed relevant.

8. As well as Empedocles, to the extent that his homogeneity condition, the Reign of Love, is only a point in the eternally recurring cycle and not an absolute beginning.

9. And probably never were. It is unlikely that Anaximenes felt any difficulty at this point.

The view of Anaximenes as essentially "back to Thales" depends on the interpretation of Anaximenean *pyknosis* as congelation (see note 4 above). In its favor is the circumstance that "felting" (*piloumenon*: 4, 13A6), held to have been his model of the cosmic process, requires heat and pressure, neither of which is associated with fog becoming rain or water freezing to a solid. If *pyknosis* were true condensation, the problem of finding a cosmic force to effect it would be at once obvious and insoluble.

10. Havelock, like Burnet [2, 132f.], wants to translate *logos* here as "statement." But this is evidently impossible. Fragment 50 begins, "Listening not to me but to the *logos*. . . ." "Don't listen to me, listen to my statement" provides no significant antithesis. The *logos* is out there, though of course Heraclitus is the one who by his enunciation apprises us of it.

REFERENCES

[1] Aristotle. *On the Heavens*.

[2] Burnet, John. *Early Greek Philosophy*, 4th ed. (New York: Barnes & Noble, 1930).

[3] Cornford, Francis M. *Principium Sapientae* (Cambridge: Cambridge University Press, 1952.)

[4] Diels-Kranz. *Die Fragmente der Vorsokratiker*, 10te Aufl. (Berlin, 1961).

[5] Farrington, Benjamin. *Greek Science* (Harmondsworth: Penguin Books, 1944).

[6] Havelock, Eric A. "The Linguistic Task of the Presocratics," in the present volume.

[7] Matson, Wallace I. "The Naturalism of Anaximander," *Review of Metaphysics* 6, no. 3 (March, 1953), pp. 387–95.

[8] ————. "Parmenides Unbound," *Philosophical Inquiry* 2, no. 1 (Winter, 1980), pp. 345–60.

DICTION AND DIALECTIC: THE LANGUAGE
OF PLATO'S STRANGER FROM ELEA

Having Eric Havelock as a colleague has a stimulating and salutary effect on anyone interested, as I am, in Greek philosophy. His method sets an example for looking at language closely; and reminds even a metaphysician concerned with what early thinkers were *trying* to say that he must pay close heed to the language at hand, in which a given thinker could, could not, or most of the time could *almost* say it.

A second interesting effect has been Eric Havelock's discussion, and constant reminder, of the location of Plato at a crisis point between a dominant oral tradition and a newer "literate" mentality. Without his recreation of the spell of the oral tradition, without which there might be the temptation to take Platonic dialogue as a discontinuous leap into literacy, a modern reader is likely to misread the texts. For example, we easily assume—because we have not thought about it—that reading was done silently in Plato's time; that there were equivalents of our copyrights and publishers; even—in some cases—an axiom that "mature" thought must be expressed in clear, monochrome treatise. All of this helps misunderstand the dialogue form.

As Plato writes, we are *overhearing* conversation—between people with different personalities, professions, and life styles. Their creator may not agree with his characters—in fact, he often seems to agree partially with each of a set, rather than having one as his spokesman against the rest. In the *Republic*, as a case in point, Glaucon and Adeimantus constantly contribute needed reminders that the human self as we know it, existing in space and time, is composite, not pure reason alone.

The purpose of my present comments is to relate this framework to the interpretation of Plato's *Sophist*, with a passing glance at the *Statesman*. In particular, I want to follow up a suggestion I made earlier, that the principal speaker, the Eleatic Stranger, is an imported bounty-hunter, brought in to shoot the Sophist down (or, more exactly in the absence of the rifle, to catch him in a net). The "weapons" are, perhaps, new (or old) techniques of method and language. (For this simile, compare Socrates' remark in the *Philebus* that he will now require "weapons of a different kind" to resolve a shifted point under debate.)[2]

This is a rather difficult point to establish, and I can only suggest it in outline for the present. The style and dramatic structure of the *Sophist* are a terrain that literary critics and connoisseurs of style have left unexplored.

This dialogue, and its companion piece, the *Statesman*, have never been described as particularly poetic or romantic—indeed, for almost a century, many scholars doubted whether anything so pedestrian could be authentic.[3] Once their title to authenticity was recognized, however, the general tendency was not only to regard them as the work of Plato, but to identify the audience with a group of students in the Academy, with the preliminary training required to follow this intricate pair of analytic lectures, centering on semantics. (This is a particularly congenial notion to some of our contemporary analytic philosophers who, given the chance, would have delivered just such presidential addresses to the graduate scholars of ancient Athens. Of course, this congeniality does not prove that the interpretation is wrong.)

Two recent studies, an article by V. Tejera and a book by Mitchell Miller, find more drama and character in the *Statesman* than had been previously recognized.[4] And an article by Frederick Oscanyan actually develops the notion that the first set of definitions-by-division in the *Sophist* displays a sense of humor on the Stranger's part.[5] If he is right, perhaps even here, in what the nineteenth century found arid treatises, we are more in the spirit of the genuine dialogue and the oral tradition than one at first believes.

The Stranger is certainly a guest professor with an odd, pedantic sense of humor. (Noted by Jacob Klein in his asides to the effect that the Stranger is "smiling, perhaps," in his *Plato's Trilogy*.)[6] For example, he thinks it a "good joke" when he points out that quadrupeds walk as the power of human diagonals—this has provided later readers with only slight laughter.[7] (Even if they avail themselves of the relevant picture, sketched by a scholiast in the margins of Vienna W.)[8] Actually he is more amusing as he insults various well-known Sophists by his first set of "definitions," which take the form of discreditable genealogies.[9] Professor Oscanyan shows how these "definitions" match Plato's sardonic characterizations of Sophists in the earlier dialogues: manufacturers, exporters, and retailers of food for the soul; debaters with a likeness to a wolf; paid hunters of rich young men. To put this in the form of genealogies locates them in a standard classical and modern Near Eastern genre of literary insult, the fictitious ancestry. (Note also that this theme of genealogy was apparently much more of a living metaphor in Plato than it seems to us today.)

The Stranger is also a logician, and brings with him what he represents as a relatively unfamiliar logic. He is addicted to his "great method of division," a method that, just from the name, sounds as though it might be the "art of division" praised by Plato's Socrates at the end of the *Phaedrus*.[10] But the fondness is not uncritical: the method left to itself can go astray. In the *Statesman*, a first try at definition locates man as a featherless biped; a rerun finds him a two-footed pig. To explain this misfiring, there are variations on a theme first proposed by Lewis Campbell: we are shown how to use the method correctly by successive corrections of defective use, commented on as such. A. E. Taylor follows this line of interpretation: so does Mitchell Miller; so, I think, does Jacob Klein as he points out that some of the apparatus of division is not to be taken too seriously. It certainly is the case that points that we, as readers of the *Phaedrus*, had thought obvious, emerge only with much elaboration. In fact, if we did not have the *Statesman* with its continuation of the lessons on method from the *Sophist*, most of the needed qualifications would not emerge at all. For example, the stress on dichotomous division in the *Sophist*—which is certainly a rule of safety when one is hunting with a net—is finally modified late in the *Statesman* to the alternative rule that divisions should match the number of different coordinate kinds there are in the large class being divided. Perhaps in part to emphasize the break with the earlier technique that this involves, the example chosen divides into an arithmetically unlikely set of *seven* as the total of coordinate "kinds."[11]

Although there has been a tendency to identify this visitor with Plato himself, there have been some other suggestions. We might make him a Sophist (Tejera); a formal logician (A. E. Taylor, Mitchell Miller); a surrogate Socrates (Diès, if I understand him); or something of a traveling pedant (Hamilton and Cairns suggest this, without actually saying it; some of my undergraduates at Yale say it).[12] Whatever we decide about character, I want to suggest a closer look at the Stranger's *diction*. He brings his own philosophic dialect with him, I think. This seems to be a language not yet sharpened and made technical by the Megarians, by Socrates, even by Prodicus. This may be the point underscored by the fact that while the narrator of this conversation, Euclides, and his auditor, Terpsion, are Megarians, the Stranger shares with them only a more distant ancestry; he is from Elea. (One is reminded of Cephalus, narrator of the *Parmenides*, who also invokes a more remote philosophic past by his opening statement that he and his philosophic companions are from Clazomenae.)[13]

The Stranger uses the terms "form" (*eidos*) and "being" (*to on*), with a sort of pre-technical and simple signification, something he would not have done if he had come from, and represented, contemporary Athens or Megara. The equation of being with "power" is variously regarded by later metaphysicians; in context, it is at least a sort of neutral device to get the opposing gods and giants to communicate with one another.[14] And the adventures of *eidos*, which includes such "forms" as gluttony and impiety on the same level as the rest, has a similar wide extension and at best only semitechnical sense.[15] (The shops of Athens today amaze the passing Platonist by their continuation of this ordinary use of *eidos*, as they seem to advertise

ELECTRIC FORMS, ELASTIC FORMS, even ALL OF THE FORMS.)
While the Stranger would be understood in the Academy, it would be by an
audience that believed they had a technical language that was philosophically
better. As early as the *Phaedo*, when Socrates talks about *eidē* "that
everybody recognizes," it is Platonic forms with Pythagorean affinities, not
nondescript natural abstractions, that he is discussing.[16]

A similar thing seems to me to hold for the Stranger's use of *nomos* in
the *Statesman*. The true statesman, he insists, is "beyond the law."[17] But the
remark holds because here "law" is used in one ordinary sense, that of "written statute." The true statesman, having an art, is not merely the custodian
and enforcer of rules engraved on stone. We may safely assume, I think, that
some of Plato's intended readers would have thought of the "statesman" as
bound by established statute, and not have had the conception of a "Political
art," the norms of which would of course be binding. (In this connection,
there is an interesting stylistic point: when the Stranger mentions "law," the
immediate context usually also contains the expressions "writing" or "written law." Later, Aristotle uses a similar device to keep clear one technical
sense of *eidos* by associating it, in context, with the term *schēma*.) But for the
present, I will return to the Stranger in his role as Sophist-hunter.

If this visitor were really speaking for Plato, there would have been a
critical change in the doctrines of Platonism from the middle dialogues to this
later stage in the Academy. Interestingly enough, it seems to be a weakening
of the earlier metaphysical position in two directions. The sharp break
between being and becoming is moderated by the new equation of being with
power. This is a metaphysical qualification that A. N. Whitehead admired,
and saw as a change in Plato's thought toward process philosophy. The identification of the forms with meanings seems to be a new development: as early
as *Republic V*, it was clear that all meanings can be forms but the conversion
by which all forms count as meanings is a modification in the direction of
language analysis and analytical philsosphy. The method of collection and
division that is praised in the *Phaedrus* is projected into a mechanical logic of
descriptive dichotomous classification, a long way, apparently, from any
theory of recollection as an account of our recognition of form. The
Statesman, however, if we take the idea of the ruler as "beyond all law" in the
sense which that phrase would have had in the *Republic* or the *Laws*, marks
the sharpest break with the middle dialogues. The ideal ruler of the *Republic*
is the maker of statutes, but he makes them as imitations of the objective
form of political excellence—sketching and painting as he *imitates*. Far from
being beyond law, he is bound by his vision to contormity with an ideal, and
so are the legislators of the *Laws*.[18]

But if Plato is *not* here speaking for himself, why should he reach back into an ancestral past and create this personage with high intelligence but pre-technical diction? There are two considerations that may offer an answer.

The first is a philosophic reason for the modifications Plato has the Stranger make in Plato's own theory. Some pairs of philosophic positions can't communicate with each other directly; they seem to be mutually unintelligible.[19] Platonism stands in this relation to the various types of atomic theories, with whatever kinds of atom. And the Sophist who figures in the present dialogue has developed an atomism of isolated appearances as his philosophic view.[20]

Atomism *can* be argued with (and the arguer can claim it has been refuted) from either an Aristotelian or an Anaxagorean philosophic orientation. Both of these can communicate with Platonism: the former because it shares a formalist explanatory direction, the latter because it shares a synthetic "dialectical" method.[21] Since Plato's overall intention is to defend the theory of forms, he turns over the critique of the Sophist to an expert who is much more of an Aristotelian than Plato (rather than to an Anaxagorean).

The Stranger is able to mediate the two positions involved. Thus he introduces notions of "being" which include the views of both the "gods" and the "giants." He uses a barely disguised lecture method: only two or three moments of genuine dialogue brighten his conversations. He is able, as Aristotle was later, to disconnect problems of semantics and syntax from questions of ethics, or physics, or metaphysics. His gradual refinement of a technique of definition or division moves in the direction of Aristotelian genus and species classification. And he is able to argue, on the basis of premises the Sophist will admit, the thesis that some sort of formalism must be presupposed even by Sophistry.

The second consideration is the overall strategy that structures the dialogues later than the *Republic* and the *Phaedrus*. Plato treats three themes, having to do with three extensions and applications of the vision of the middle dialogues: the three can be roughly characterizec as logic, physics, and ethics. The logical extension, with which we are most immediately concerned, may have been designed as the set *Parmenides-Theaetetus-Sophist-Statesman-Philosopher*, though the last of these was never written.[22] The theme seems to be a defense of the theory of forms by showing that it is presupposed by scientific deduction, by arts and crafts, and even by meaningful use of language. It is not the theory in its full metaphysical development that is shown presupposed in each case, but only the partial version adequate to the immediate point. (The arts, for example, presuppose craftsmen's *criteria*; the relation of these to a larger architectonic need not be developed to make this point.)[23]

The second set of later dialogues deals with the relation of Plato's vision to the findings of empirical science and the relation of value to history. The program for this called for a tetralogy: the *Republic-Timaeus-Critias-Hermocrates*; of this set, the *Hermocrates* was never written, and the *Critias* was left incomplete. Plato's *first* point here, made by the *Timaeus*, was to show that the theoretical structure of the *Republic* actually matched detailed models and measurements in the world of scientific fact.[24] Since Timaeus is a Pythagorean, *his* way of thinking and talking about *forms*, about *being* and *becoming*, about *classifying formulae*, is like that of the *Phaedo*, where the two main respondents also are Pythagorean.[25] The discrepancy between Timaeus and the Stranger from Elea can in this way be explained by the difference in Plato's purpose in the dialogues in question. And this relation holds regardless of the relative chronological dating of the *Timaeus* and the *Sophist*.[26]

The third direction of application and extension in the post-middle dialogues, in the direction of ethics and politics, is presented by the *Philebus* (the latest Socratic dialogue) and the *Laws* and *Epinomis*. The grand philosophic vision is applied to practical ends in these latest writings: to outlining—for an audience not expert in technical philosophy—"the good for human life," and to writing out a model legal code, in as full detail as if it were about to be adopted for actual implementation.

Guest experts take the conversational lead in parts of each of these three enterprises. Timaeus is, as we have seen, a Pythagorean scientist from South Italy. An Athenian Stranger is the main speaker in the *Laws* and its appendix, the *Epinomis*. Parmenides, the great logician from Elea, is the historical figure who introduces the "logical" sequence. And the *Sophist* and *Statesman*, later in that series, have as the leader of their conversations the Stranger from Elea.

We will turn now to the strategy of the *Parmenides-Theatetus-Sophist-Statesman* series. The first three of these occupy successively lower levels of the schematism of the divided line in the *Republic*. In the *Parmenides*, it seems that the "method of hypothesis," while necessary mental training, cannot decide between alternative "hypotheses" without appeal to forms of a normative kind. In the *Theaetetus*, the attempt to define knowledge on the level of physical process, of *technē*, with models of the mind as tablet and aviary, fails to account for the certainty and universality that mark knowledge of forms—as opposed to particular sensibles. This looks like the beginning of a *reductio* proof that the theory, in its full four-level *Republic* version, is indispensable. (It is worth noting that later systems of Western philosophy do in fact advocate schemes that are like Plato's, but with less apparatus in the form of levels of reality. Pragmatism, for example, operates at the level of the *Theaetetus*; logical positivism, with its relegation of "framework" questions to pragmatic concerns, admits three levels but not the top, fourth. Existentialism in some guises, beginning with Sartre's order of precedence for existence over essence, looks like an attempted reduction to a supremely individual one-level order.) The objection to the reduction of the line to three levels, in the *Parmenides*, is that then we can have no philosophy; the objection to the reduction to two levels in the *Theaetetus* is that then we can have no mathematics (an ironic result since Theaetetus himself is a mathematician), and no dialectic of a Socratic sort, either. What is the comparable objection to a reduction of knowledge to a single level of words and semblances? It seems to me the point must be that unless we introduce something like a distinction of levels between kinds of symbol and referent, meaningful communication can't be shown to be possible. This need not require the full theory of forms: the *Theaetetus* inquiry would have worked as well in the absence of the third level of the line, without invoking the fourth. But what must be shown is that the domain of meanings is objective and immune to the challenges of neo-Eleatic notions of lack of meaning for terms supposedly without any reference. *If* the Sophist admits selective "combinations" of forms as meaningful and not meaningful, the presuppositions of that admission are capable of being shown inconsistent with his nihilistic division of statements into truth and nonsense. Since the Sophist depends on communication for his livelihood, he cannot afford to hold a view that implies that meaningful discourse is impossible. But there is a problem here: the Sophist keeps moving to questions of metaphysics (questions with an Eleatic ancestry) to evade issues of semantics.[27] Socrates and Plato have developed a technical, or semi-technical language of thier own. (Or at the very least, have selected certain types of use from the rather diffuse ordinary language that is discussed in the *Cratylus*.)[28] It presupposes certain possibilitess for discourse: there is a theory of reference which involves meanings; these in turn relate to forms in an abstract, descriptive domain; while the latter are given relevance and order through their relation to forms of systematic scope and normative type.[29] It is important to distinguish designation from denotation in this theory: a meaningful term or statement must designate some combination of meanings, but it need not denote any sensibly existenct facts or instances.[30] The Sophists, by doing two things, can obscure the issues. They can insist on an identity of designating and denoting; and they can then appeal to Eleatic metaphysics to argue that negative and false terms and expressions have nothing to denote. Thus when Socrates, discussing virtue with Euthydemus and his brother, tries to show them that their view is false, they rejoin that falsehood is impossible. Plato's final word on the matter, in *Letter VII*, is that when someone tries to explain the forms themselves, anyone who wants to can upset his argument, because of the weaknesses inherent in language.[31] In that case, it would not be good strategy to introduce considerations of the forms themselves into a debate with the Sophist in the dialogue named for him. One topic after another, from sense to reference, could be rejected by way of a critique of the language used.[32] Thus the appropriate character for the confrontation with the Sophist is not Socrates himself—his interest is primarily ethical; nor would it be Plato himself, for his interest remains primarily metaphysical; but some guest expert whose orientation is logical, and who can't be accused, even by the Sophist, of smuggling in Platonic logic or vocabulary. That is why the Stranger uses a logic of classification which is a simple descriptive net: no invidious value judgments are built into it. He uses a vocabulary which is deliberately "neutral" in its definitions of key terms—neutral as between gods and giants in the notion of "being," neutral as between Platonic, ordinary, and Sophistic uses of "form."

Thus I see the Stranger as carrying on the major project of a defense of Platonism in an "ordinary" language, non-Platonic enough so that even the Sophist can't object that he doesn't accept or understand its technicalities. When the Sophist wants to appeal to Eleatic metaphysics, the Stranger overrules him: Parmenides is not to be invoked as authority in this cause.[33] (It is not as rude a criticism as Aristotle's exasperated remark that a true denier of the possibility of contradiction would be "no better than a vegetable," but I think it makes the same point.) As the programmed series of later dialogues goes on, we expect that the theory of forms will emerge, level by level, each as presupposed by the one below it.[34] But for the present level, we need an expert semanticist, introducing, for the sake of this argument, a weaker theory than Plato or his Socrates would like to defend. Socrates would want to *improve* the Sophist ethically; Plato, if he put himself onstage, would want to educate him metaphysically; but the Stranger from Elea is content to entangle him in a net semantically. It is indeed interesting that the Stranger's analysis can be detached from the background of the Socratic-Platonic theory, even though, if I have understood Plato's strategy, it will be shown to presuppose that theory as we move beyond meaning to being. It is a remarkable view of Plato's skill as an analyst to see him work out this position.[35] But this need not be, and in fact is not, a new doctrinal version of Platonism.

I like this guest professor, with his professorial sense of humor. I am even glad that he came from the ancient, but now provincial, intellectual center of Elea, rather than the more flashy recent sites of Athens, or Megara, or Cyrene. He can do things that Plato's Socrates, his younger namesake, Young Socrates, and his image, Theaetetus, cannot. The reason is that while he sympathizes with their metaphysics, he does not wholly share their language, their logic, nor even Socrates' ironic sense of humor.

At any rate, I prefer my notion to the alternative idea that Plato himself has suddenly changed his philosophical position. He can't carry on a dialogue with the Sophist in his own proper person and vocabulary; but he can invent a guest logician able to refute the Sophist from a position mediate between Sophistry and the Academy. That Plato himself sees his forms functioning as "meanings" on occasion is clear from such dialogues as the *Cratylus*, and from Book V of the *Republic*. But to assume that meanings and forms are identical is quite a different thing.[36] In the research of the Academy, and the philosophy of Plato, the forms are objective entities studied by set theory, logic, mathematics, and normative ethics; and the distinction holds firm betwen being and becoming.

To explore my conjecture in more detail we too will need experts—visiting strangers or resident academicians—with the sensitivity and subtle technique for the hearing and tracing of classical language—vocabulary and style—in its relation to thought, which Eric Havelock's work has instantiated and applied.

Robert S. Brumbaugh

Yale University

NOTES

1. R. S. Brumbaugh, "Plato's Relation to the Arts and Crafts," in *Facets of Plato's Philosophy* ed. W. H. Werkmeister (Assen: Van Gorcum, 1976), p. 47. "In fact, the Stranger from Elea who is brought in to 'track the wily monster down,' reminds me of the team of bounty-hunters hired, in another time and context, to gun down Butch Cassidy and the Sun Dance Kid." See also n. 31, p. 51.

2. *Philebus* 23B5.

3. See W. Windelband, *History of Philosophy*, tr. J. H. Tufts (Norwood, MA: 1893), p. 103. "Among the doubtful writings the most important are the *Sophist*, *Politicus*, and *Parmenides*. These probably did not originate with Plato, but with men of his school who were closely related with the Eleatic dialectic and eristic. The first two are by the same author." See also W. W. Waddell, ed., *The Parmenides of Plato* (Glasgow: 1894), pp. i–xix.

4. V. Tejera, "Plato's Politicus, an Eleatic Sophist on Politics," *Philosophy and Social Criticism* 5 (1978), pp. 85–104; 107–25. See also Mitchell H. Miller, Jr., *The Philosopher in Plato's Statesman* (The Hague: Martinus Nijhoff, 1980).

5. Frederick S. Oscanyan, "On Six Definitions of the Sophist: *Sophist* 221C-231E," *Philosophical Forum* 4 (1972–73), pp. 241–255.

6. Jacob Klein, *Plato's Trilogy* (Chicago: University of Chicago Press, 1977). For example, p. 27: " . . . the Stranger says to Theaetetus, similingly, we suppose . . . "

7. *Statesman* 266A, referred back to at 266C.

8. For the W. Scholion, see R. S. Brumbaugh, "Logical and Mathematical Symbolism in the Plato Scholia," *Journal of the Warburg and Courtauld Institutes* 24 (1961), fig. 1h.

9. Ibid., pp. 49–50.

10. *Phaedrus* 265D–266E.

11. *Statesman* 287C–289B. See the comments of J. B. Skemp, ed., on this division in *Plato's Statesman* (New Haven: Yale University Press, 1954).

12. Tejera, "Plato's Politicus"; Miller, *Philosopher in Plato's Statesman*; A. E. Taylor, tr., *Plato, the Sophist and the Statesman*, ed. Raymond Klibansky and Elizabeth Anscombe (London: T. Nelson, 1961), pp. 3–91; Skemp, *Plato's Statesman*; Gilbert Ryle, *Plato's Progress* (Cambridge: Cambridge University Press, 1966); A. Diès, ed. and tr., Platon, Le Sophiste, Budé edn. (Paris, 1925); Edith Hamilton and Huntington Cairns, eds., Plato, *Complete Works*, tr. Lane Cooper et al. (New York: Pantheon Books, 1961), pp. 1018–19; et al.

13. For the importance of this detail of arrival *from Clazomenae*, see R. S. Brumbaugh, *Plato on the One* (New Haven: Yale University Press, 1961).

14. *Sophist* 247E; gods and giants, 246ff.; A. N. Whitehead, *Adventures of Ideas* (New York: Macmillan, 1933), p. 165; see also F. M. Cornford's comment on Whitehead's reading, *Plato's Theory of Knowledge* (New York: Liberal Arts Press, 1957), n. 1, p. 5.

15. Sophist 257D ff. An interesting triad here, the members of which are asserted to be real: the Ugly, the Short, and the Unjust.

16. *Phaedo* 76E, " . . . these absolute realities . . . which we are always talking about. . . ." (Tredenick's translation).

17. *Statesman* 299 D–1.

18. *Republic* V 501B.

19. N. P. Stallknecht and R. S. Brumbaugh, *The Compass of Philosophy* (New York: Longmans, Green 1954); R. S. Brumbaugh, "Cosmography," *Review of Metaphysics* 26 (1972), pp. 333–47.

20. Plato could propose alternatives to the atomic theory, but there is no record of a *direct* confrontation with it; perhaps *Laws X* comes closest. What the Sophist in the present dialogue has done is to set up an atomism of sharply insulated phenomena, all on the same footing; thus he believes he has prevented questions of appearance and reality from arising.

21. Unlike Plato, Aristotle has a good deal to discuss with the atomic theorists; it is Heracliteans that *he* fails to communicate with.

22. Regarding the philosopher, see my paper "Doctrine and Dramatic Dates of Plato's Dialogues," SAGP meeting, New York, December, 1979.

23. *Statesman* 284E, with what seems the promise of a future detailed discussion of "normative measure" at 284D1.

24. Note the claims implicit in the Myth of the True Earth and the Myth of Er: if these are true in principle, what follows on the level of observation? (The *Statesman* myth makes a rather different point.) Aristotle (*Meteorology* II.1 355b32–356b2) takes the geology of the True Earth myth seriously.

25. Simmias and Cebes, the main respondents, are Pythagoreans from Thebes.

26. There has been considerable discussion of the relative date of the *Timaeus* and the *Sophist*. Stylistically, the *Timaeus* falls into the "later" group; but the version of the theory of forms seems rather to match an "earlier" set of statements. I don't think

enough attention has been paid to the fact that an extensive encyclopedia of this sort may not have *a* date, but rather may have been developed over a considerable period of time.

27. The *Euthydemus* is the clearest case study.

28. In the *Cratylus*, ordinary language turns out not to embody a single, consistent metaphysical view. This is not surprising when we review the list of different "givers of names" who have contributed to it. The list includes scientists and mathematicians, Heracliteans, gods, primitive astronomers, and women.

29. As the theory develops its full scope—for example, as one moves through the educational curriculum of the *Republic*—the forms first appear as *meanings*, but then refer beyond these to objective *structures* ("hypotheses"), which also serve, at least in some cases, as *criteria* and which are held together in an ontological *system*.

30. Charles Morris, *Foundations of the Theory of Signs* (Chicago: University of Chicago Press, 1938), introduces this distinction of "designation," which relates a term to the abstract form it refers to, and "denotation," which relates it to the particular individuals it indicates. This suggests an interpretation of Plato's *Seventh Letter*, with its "name, image and formula." The image is rather like the denotation, the formula like the designation, the name like the term in Morris's scheme.

31. *Letter VII*: No one will try to discuss the thing itself in writing, "because of the weakness of language."

32. I am not sure which of the Sophistic devices that he recognizes matches Plato's notion of "upsetting the [Platonist's] argument" in *Letter VII*. Certainly taking all metaphors literally can be damaging—in the *Euthydemus*, the brothers make fun of Socrates' doctrine of "participation" in that way. Falling back on a supposed Parmenidean argument that rules out the possibility of negation, privation, falsehood, and semblance can neutralize an attempt to establish degrees of reality. Trying to reject arguments by analogy, by appeal to the thesis that "everything is like and unlike every other" (*Protagoras*) would be a third attack.

33. The Stranger's dissent from Parmenides, *Sophist* 258C–E.

34. For the projected "emergence" of the forms from criteria of arts to postulates of science and mathematics to ideals, cf. my SAGP paper, cited above, n. 22.

35. Here Ryle (*Plato's Progress*) is very perceptive in seeing a development in Plato's thought, as it becomes clear to him that questions of meaning and semantics are more complex than the simpler models that seemed adequate for the middle dialogues. But it is clear, even from the indication at the end of the *Theaetetus* that the *Phaedo* is to be read *after* the *Sophist* and *Statesman*, that Plato did not intend to identify metaphysics with this sort of analysis, nor to give up the former as unnecessary.

36. An illicit conversion of "all meanings are forms" to "all forms are meanings" turns Plato's theory into something quite different. Plato himself seems insufficiently cautious in failing to stress the non-identity of meanings and forms in the middle dialogues, particularly *Republic V* and the *Phaedrus*.

SELECT BIBLIOGRAPHY ON ORALITY AND LITERACY

The following is only a partial bibliography of mostly English language scholarship which treats of the oral poetic tradition in early Greece, the introduction of the Greek alphabet or the growth of Greek literacy. Included also are some works in areas such as cognitive psychology and cognitive anthropology which discuss the effects of literacy on linguistic and cognitive behavior. I have also listed some studies in Greek literature and philosophy the authors of which either anticipated or took note of recent scholarship demonstrating the oral character of archaic Greek composition. A study of their references should lead the reader to most of the major works in this increasingly important field of philosophical scholarship. My intent is to provide the interested reader with a list of some of the recent studies which have prompted scholars to change the ways in which they approach Greek literature and philosophy, and in view of which, as Walter Ong remarked on the occasion of his Terry lectures at Yale, "our entire understanding of Classical culture stands in need of revision."

Adkins, A. W. H. "Homeric Values and Homeric Society," *Journal of Hellenic Studies* 91 (1971), pp. 1–14.

————. *Merit and Responsibility: A Study in Greek Values*. Oxford: Oxford University Press, 1962.

Beye, Charles Rowan. *Ancient Greek Literature and Society*. Garden City, New York: Anchor-Doubleday, 1975.

————. *The Iliad, the Odyssey and the Epic Tradition*. Garden City, New York: Anchor-Doubleday, 1966.

————. "The Rhythm of Hesiod's *Works and Days*," *Harvard Studies in Classical Philology* 76 (1972), pp. 23–43.

Bruner, Jerome. *Beyond the Information Given*. Jeremy Anglin, ed. New York: W. W. Norton and Company, 1973.

————. "Language as an Instrument of Thought," *Problems of Language and Learning*, Alan Davies, ed. London: Heinemann, 1975.

Bowra, Maurice. *Homer*. London: Duckworth, 1972.

Carpenter, Rhys. "The Antiquity of the Greek Alphabet," *American Journal of Archaeology* 37 (1933), pp. 8–29.

————. "The Greek Alphabet Again," *American Journal of Archaeology* 42 (1938) pp. 58–69.

Chadwick, John. *The Decipherment of Linear B*. Cambridge: Cambridge University Press, 1970.

Cherniss, Harold. *Aristotle's Criticism of Presocratic Philosophy.* New York: Octagon, 1964.

————. *The Riddle of the Early Academy.* Berkeley, California: University of California Press, 1945.

Claus, D. B. "Defining Moral Terms in *Works and Days*," *Transactions of the American Philological Association* 107 (1977).

Cole, Michael and Peg Griffin. "Cultural Amplifiers Reconsidered," *The Social Foundations of Language and Thought,* David R. Olson, ed. New York: W. W. Norton, 1980, pp. 343–64.

Cole, M., J. Gay, J. Glick and D. Sharp. *The Cultural Context of Learning and Thinking.* New York: Basic Books, 1968.

Cole, Michael and Sylvia Scribner. *The Psychology of Literacy.* Cambridge, MA: Harvard University Press, 1981.

Davison, J. A. "The Homeric Question," *A Companion to Homer,* Alan J. B. Wace and Frank H. Stubbings, eds. London: Macmillan, 1962.

Deichgräber, Karl. *Der letze Gesang der Ilias.* Mainz: Akademie der Wissenschaften und die Literatur. Wiesbaden, 1972.

Dow, Sterling. "The Linear Scripts and the Tablets as Historical Documents: (a) Literacy in Minoan And Mycenaean Lands," *Cambridge Ancient History,* I. E. S. Edwards, C. J. Gadd, N. G. L. Hammond, and E. Sollberger, eds. Cambridge, Cambridge University Press, 1973, pp. 582–608.

————. "The Linear Scripts and the Tablets as Historical Documents: (b) The Linear B Tablets as Historical Documents," *Cambridge Ancient History,* I. E. S. Edwards, C. J. Gadd, N. G. L. Hammond, and E. Sollberger, eds. Cambridge: Cambridge University Press, 1973, pp. 609–626.

Edwards, G. Patrick. *The Language of Hesiod in Its Traditional Context.* Oxford: Blackwell, 1971.

Furley, David J. "Notes on Parmenides," *Exegesis and Argument: Studies in Greek Philosophy Presented to Gregory Vlastos.* E. N. Lee, A. P. D. Mourelatos, and Richard Rorty, eds. *Phronesis,* Supplementary Volume I (Assen: Van Gorcum, 1973), pp. 1–15.

Gagarin, Michael. "*Dikē* in Archaic Greek Thought," *Classical Philology* 69 (1974), pp. 186–97.

————. "Dike in the Works and Days," *Classical Philology* 68 (1973), pp. 81–94.

Gelb, Ignace. *A Study of Writing.* Chicago: University of Chicago Press, 1963.

Goody, Jack. *The Domestication of the Savage Mind.* Cambridge: Cambridge University Press, 1977.

Goody, Jack and Ian Watt. "The Consequences of Literacy," *Literacy in Traditional Societies.* Jack Goody, ed. Cambridge: Cambridge University Press, 1968.

Greenfield, Patricia M. "Oral or Written Language: The Consequences for Cognitive Development in Africa, the United States and England," *Language and Speech* 15 pp. 169–77.

Grube, G. M. A. *How Did the Greeks Look at Literature?* Cincinnati: University of Cincinnati Press, 1967.

Guthrie, W. K. C. *The PreSocratic Tradition from Parmenides to Democritus.* Volume II of *A History of Greek Philosophy.* Cambridge: Cambridge University Press, 1965.

Hainsworth, J. B. *The Flexibility of the Homeric Formula.* Oxford: Clarendon Press, 1968.

Havelock, Eric. "The Ancient Art of Oral Poetry," *Philosophy and Rhetoric* 12, no. 3 (Summer, 1979).

————. *The Greek Concept of Justice: From Its Shadow in Homer to Its Substance in Plato.* Cambridge, MA: Harvard University Press, 1978.

————. *The Literate Revolution and Its Consequences.* Princeton: Princeton University Press, 1981.

————. *Origins of Western Literacy.* Toronto: Ontario Institute for Studies in Education, 1976.

————. "Parmenides and Odysseus," *Harvard Studies in Classical Philology* 63 (1958), pp. 133–143.

————. *Preface to Plato.* New York: Grosset and Dunlap by arrangement with the Harvard University Press, 1967.

————. "Pre-Literacy and the Presocratics," *BICS* (Bulletin of the Institute of Classical Studies) University of London, 13 (1966), pp. 44–67.

————. "The Pre-Literacy of the Greeks," *New Literary History* 8 (1977), pp. 369–91.

————. *Prologue to Greek Literacy.* Cincinnati: University of Cincinnati Press, 1971.

Havelock, Eric and Jackson Hershbell. *Communication Arts in the Ancient World.* New York: Hastings House, 1978.

Marcovich, M. *Heraclitus: Greek Text with a Short Commentary.* Merida, Venezuela: Los Andes University Press, 1967.

Hoekstra, A. *Homeric Modifications of Formulaic Prototypes: Studies in the Development of Greek Epic Diction.* Amsterdam: North Holland Publishing Company, 1969.

Jeffery, L. H. *The Local Scripts of Archaic Greece: A Study of the Origin of the Greek Alphabet and Its Development from the Eighth Century to the Fifth Centuries B. C.* Oxford: Clarendon Press, 1961.

————. "Writing," *A Companion to Homer*, A. J. B. Wace and F. H. Stubbings, eds. London: Macmillan, 1962.

Jevons, F. B. *A History of Greek Literature from the Earliest Period to the Death of Demosthenes.* New York: Scribner, 1900.

Johnson-Laird, P. N. and P. C. Wason, eds. *Thinking: Readings in Cognitive Science.* Cambridge, Cambridge University Press, 1977.

Jousse, M. *Le Style oral rhythmique et mnemotechnique chez les Verbomoteurs.* Paris, 1925.

Kahn, Charles. *The Art and Thought of Heraclitus.* Cambridge: Cambridge University Press, 1951.

Kirk, G. S. *Homer and the Epic.* Cambridge: Cambridge University Press, 1951.

————, ed. *The Language and Background of Homer.* Cambridge: W. Heffer, 1964.

Knox, Bernard. "Silent Reading in Antiquity," *Greek, Roman and Byzantine Studies* 94.

Lord, A. B. "Homer's Originality: Oral Dictated Texts," *Transactions of the American Philological Association* 84 (1953), 124–34.

————. *The Singer of Tales. Harvard Studies in Classical Philology* 72 (1967), pp. 1–46.

McCarter, P. Kyle. *The Antiquity of the Greek Alphabet and the Early Semitic Scripts.* Harvard Semitic Museum, Harvard Semitic Monographs, F. M. Cross, ed., no. 9 (1975). Missoula, Montana: Scholars Press, 1975.

McDiarmid, J. B. "Theophrastus on the Presocratic Causes," *Harvard Studies in Classical Philology* 61 (1953), pp. 85–156.

Meillet, A. *Les Origines indo-europeenes des metres grecs.* Paris, 1923.

Mourelatos, Alexander P. D. "Determinacy and Indeterminacy, Being and non-Being in the Fragments of Parmenides," *New Essays on Plato and the Presocratics,* Roger Shiner and John King-Farlow, eds. *Canadian Journal of Philosophy,* Supplementary Volume II (1976), pp. 45–60.

_____. *The Route of Parmenides: A Study of Word, Image and Arguments in the Fragments.* New Haven: Yale University Press, 1970.

Murko, Mathias. *La Poésie populaire épique en Yugoslavie au début du XXe siècle.* Paris, 1929.

Notopoulos, James A. "Homer, Hesiod and the Achaean Heritage of Oral Poetry," *Hesperia* 29 (1968), pp. 177–97.

_____. "The Homeric Hymns as Oral Poetry: A Study of the Post-Homeric Oral Tradition," *American Journal of Philology* 83 (1962), pp. 337–68.

Olson, David R. "Culture, Technology and Intellect," *The Nature of Intelligence,* Lauren B. Resnick, ed. Hillsdale, New Jersey: Halstead Press, 1976, pp. 189–202.

_____. *The Social Foundations of Language and Thought.* New York: W. W. Norton, 1980.

Ostwald, Martin. *Nomos and the Beginnings of the Athenian Democracy.* Oxford: Clarendon Press, 1969.

Oxenham, John. *Literacy: Writing, Reading and Social Organization.* London: Routledge and Kegan Paul, 1980.

Page, Denys. "Archilochus and the Oral Tradition," *Foundation Hart Entretiens X Vandooeuvres-Genève,* 1963, pp. 119–63.

_____. *History and the Homeric Iliad.* Berkeley: University of California Press, 1966.

Parry, Adam. "Have We Homer's Iliad?" *Yale Classical Studies* 20 (1966), pp. 177–216.

Parry, Milman. *The Making of Homeric Verse: The Collected Papers of Milman Parry,* Adam Parry, ed. Oxford: Clarendon Press, 1971.

Perry, B. E. "The Early Greek Capacity for Viewing Things Separately," *Transactions of the American Philological Association* 68 (1937), pp. 403–27.

Pope, M. W. M. "The Parry-Lord Theory of Homeric Composition," *ACTA, Proceedings of the Classical Association of South Africa* 6 (1964), pp. 1–21.

Richardson, N. J. "Homeric Professors in the Age of the Sophists," *Cambridge Philosophical Society Proceedings* 201 (n.s. 21) (1975), pp. 65–81.

Robb, Kevin. "Greek Oral Memory and the Origins of Philosophy," *The Personalist* 51, (1970), 5–45.

_____. *The Progress of Literacy in Ancient Greece.* Los Angeles: Printed for the University of Southern California, 1970.

_____. "Oral Bards at Mycenae," *Coranto* 9 (1974), pp. 8–16.

_____. "Poetic Sources of the Greek Alphabet; Rhythm and Abecedarium from Phoenician to Greek," *Communication Arts in the Ancient World,* Eric Havelock and Jackson Hershbell, eds. New York: Hastings House, 1978.

Rosch, Eleanor. "Linguistic Relativity," *Thinking: Readings in Cognitive Science,* P. N. Johnson-Laird and P. C. Wason, eds. Cambridge: Cambridge University Press, 1977, pp. 501–19.

Russo, Joseph. "Homer Against His Tradition," *Arion* 7 (1968), pp. 275–95.
————. "How and What Does Homer Communicate?" *Classical Journal* 71 (1976), pp. 289–99.
————. "The Structural Formula in Homeric Verse," *Yale Classical Studies* 20 (1966), pp. 219–40.
Russo, Joseph and Bennett Simon. "Homeric Psychology and the Oral Epic Tradition," *Journal of the History of Ideas*, 29 (1968), pp. 483–98.
Scribner, Sylvia. "Modes of Thinking and Ways of Speaking: Culture and Logic Reconsidered," *Thinking: Readings in Cognitive Science*, P. N. Johnson-Laird and P. C. Wasson, eds. Cambridge: Cambridge University Press, 1977.
Stubbs, Michael. *Language and Literacy: The Sociolinguistics of Reading and Writing*. London: Routledge and Kegan Paul, 1980.
Van Groningen, B. A. "Eléments inorganique dans le composition de L'Iliade et L'Odyssée." *Revue des Etudes Homériques* 5 (1935), pp. 3–24.
Ventris, Michael and John Chadwick. *Documents in Mycenaean Greek*. Cambridge: Cambridge University Press, 1970.
Webster, T. B. L. *From Mycenae to Homer*. New York: Praeger, 1964.
West, M. L. *Early Greek Philosophy and the Orient*. Oxford: Clarendon Press, 1971.

Joanne Beil

University of South Florida

Contributors

A. W. H. Adkins

Arthur Adkins is Professor of Classics and Chairman of the Department at the University of Chicago. Previously Professor Adkins was professor of classics at Reading, and (1979–1980) Senior Visiting Fellow, Society of the Humanities at Cornell. Among his books are *Merit and Responsibility: A Study in Greek Values* (Oxford University Press, 1960), *From the Many To The One*, and *Moral Values and Political Behavior in Ancient Greece* published in the Norton Library "Ancient Culture and Society" series. Professor Adkins is noted as the author of a series of influential articles on early Greek values and political attitudes which have appeared in *such journals as Classical Quarterly*, and *Bulletin of the Institute of Classical Studies* of London University.

Joanne Beil

Professor Joanne Beil is a graduate of Manhattanville College and did her graduate work in Greek philosophy at the University of Southern California. At present she is Assistant Professor at the University of South Florida, and is at work on a book on the origins of logic and on changes in types of reasoning and argument as a culture such as that of Archaic Greece advances from orality to literacy.

Jonathan Barnes

Jonathan Barnes is Fellow of Balliol College and Professor of Philosophy at Oxford. Professor Barnes's two-volume study on the Presocratics (*The Presocratic Philosophers*) published in the Routledge and Kegan Paul series "The Arguments of Philosophers" has made a major impact on Presocratic studies, especially by opening bridges to contemporary philosophical argument. He has edited a noted collection of articles on Aristotle, and is himself the author of numerous learned articles in philosophy. Recently he was appointed editor of *Phronesis: A Journal for Ancient Philosophy*.

Robert Brumbaugh

Robert Brumbaugh has been Professor of Philosophy at Yale University since 1952. Previously he taught at Bowdoin College and at Indiana University, and has been a Visiting Fulbright Professor at Hebrew University in Jerusalem (1967) and Fellow of the American School of Classical Studies in Athens. His many books include *Plato's Mathematical Imagination*, *The Spirit of Western Philosophy*, *Philosophers of Education*, *Plato On The One*, *The Plato Manuscripts* (the latter two with Yale Press), and over fifty learned articles.

Eric Alfred Havelock

Professor Havelock is Sterling Professor Emeritus of Classics at Yale University and, at the time of his retirement from Yale, was serving as chairman of the Department of Classics. His previous appointment was at Harvard, where he also served for many years as chairman of Classics. Retirement from Yale was followed by two years as Raymond Professor at the State University of New York at Buffalo.

Among Professor Havelock's books are: *Preface to Plato* (Harvard), *The Liberal Temper of Greek Politics* (Yale), *The Lyric Genius of Catullus*, Prometheus (a study and modern translation of Aeschylus' tragedy), and in 1979 published by Harvard University Press, *The Greek Concept of Justice*. In 1983 Princeton University Press published a collection of Professor Havelock's papers, most of which relate directly to the theme of the present volume: *The Literate Revolution in Greece and Its Cultural Consequences*. Two monographs are devoted to that theme: *Prologue to Greek Literacy* (Havelock's Semple Lectures at the University of Cincinnati, 1971) and *Origins of Western Literacy* (Ontario, 1976), as had been a previous pioneering article, "Pre-literacy and the Pre-Socratics."

Jackson Hershbell

Jackson Hershbell is Professor of Classics and Humanities and chairman of the Department of Classics at the University of Minnesota. Previously Professor Hershbell taught at Harvard, at the Universities of Wisconsin and North Dakota, has been a Fellow of the Insitute für Klassische Philologie, Universität München (1977 −78), and was Alexander von Humboldt Fellow at Munich. He is co-editor (with Eric Havelock) of *Communication Arts in the Ancient World* (1978) and has published widely in such journals as *Classical Journal, Phoenix: The Journal for the Classical Association of Canada; Phronesis, American Journal of Philology, Greek, Roman and Byzantine Studies*, etc. He is a noted authority on the sources for recovering the text of Empedocles. He is co-author (with Eric Havelock and Kevin Robb) of the forthcoming (with Oxford University Press) volume "The Pre-Platonic Philosophers of Greece."

Charles Kahn

Charles Kahn is Professor of Philosophy at the University of Pennsylvania. Previously Kahn taught at Columbia where he received his Ph.D. in 1958. He was for many years the American co-editor of *Archiv für Geschichte der Philosophie*.

His books include *Anaxamander and the Origins of Greek Cosmology*, which since its publication in 1960 has been widely considered the definitive work on the philosopher. Kahn's *The Verb "Be" in Ancient Greek* (a study of over 400 pages) made a major impact in modern linguistics as well as in philosophy. His most recent book, *The Art and Thought of Heraclitus*, published by Cambridge University Press in 1979, was widely hailed as a major modern contribution to the study of this philosopher.

Geoffrey Kirk

Professor Kirk is Fellow of Trinity College, Cambridge and Regius Professor of Greek in the University of Cambridge. His books, many published with Cambridge

University Press, include *The Presocratic Philosophers* (with J. E. Raven), *The Songs of Homer, Heraclitus: The Cosmic Fragments, The Bacchae of Euripides, Myth: Its Meaning and Function in Ancient and Other Cultures*, and in the Penguin series, *The Nature of Greek Myths*.

Joseph Margolis

Joseph Margolis is Professor of Philosophy at Temple University. He took his Ph. D. from Columbia, taught at the Universities of Toronto and of Western Ontario (where he chaired the Department) and among other institutions at Columbia and Minnesota. In addition to his numerous articles in several fields, Professor Margolis' books include *The Language of Art and Art Criticism, Psychotherapy and Morality, Contemporary Ethical Theory* (the latter two with Random House) and a widely used source book for classical and contemporary philosophy, *An Introduction to Philosophical Enquiry*.

Wallace I. Matson

Wallace I. Matson is Professor of Philosophy at Berkeley. An early book, *The Existence of God*, has remained an influential contribution to a perennial topic. More recently he is the author of *Sentience*, on the philosophy of mind, and of a widely appreciated criticism of Rawls's theory of justice. His many articles include a half dozen important contributions of the Presocratic philosophers.

Julius Moravcsik

Julius Moravcsik is Professor and Chairman of the Department of Philosophy, Stanford University. Professor Moravcsik was educated at Oxford and at Harvard where he worked with Eric Havelock and where he received his Ph.D. in 1959. He was Santayana Fellow at Harvard, was awarded a Guggenheim, and has been Visiting Professor at Göttingen. Professor Moravcsik is the author of an influential monograph on Plato's *Sophist*, and is editor of a distinguished volume of essays on Plato and another on Aristotle. In addition to numerous articles in Greek philosophy, he has written widely on contemporary philosophy of language and on the methodology of current linguistics.

Kevin Robb

Kevin Robb, the editor of the *Monist* volume, is Associate Professor of Philosophy at the University of Southern California. He did his graduate work as a Danforth Fellow at Yale, where he studied with Eric Havelock and Robert Brumbaugh. He has taught at the American College in Istanbul, and has been the recipient of a major research grant relating to Early Greek Philosophy from the National Endowment for the Humanities. He has published in journals of classics, archeology and philosophy, and is the author of several articles in the *Encyclopaedia Britannica*. A number of his publications relate to the theme of the *Monist* volume. He is co-author (with Eric Havelock and Jackson Hershbell) of a book forthcoming with Oxford University Press, "The Pre-Platonic Philosophers of Greece."

Dallas Willard

Dallas Willard is Associate Professor of Philosophy at the University of Southern California, and Director of the School of Philosophy. Professor Willard has published widely in such journals as *Mind*, the *Southern Journal of Philosophy*, *Analysis*, *Kant-Studien*, *Journal of Philosophy*, etc. Professor Willard has an interest in the relationship of thought to language and is the author of a provocative article on the subject. His book, *Logic and the Objectivity of Knowledge: Studies in Husserl's Early Philosophy*, is forthcoming from Ohio University.